HOW'S THAT UNDERLING THING WORKING OUT FOR YOU?

Other DILBERT® books from Andrews McMeel Publishing

Your Accomplishments Are Suspiciously Hard to Verify
ISBN: 978-1-4494-0102-3

Problem Identified and You're Probably Not Part of the Solution
ISBN: 978-0-7407-8534-4

I'm Tempted to Stop Acting Randomly
ISBN: 978-0-7407-7806-3

14 Years of Loyal Service in a Fabric-Covered Box
ISBN: 978-0-7407-7365-5

Freedom's Just Another Word for People Finding Out You're Useless
ISBN: 978-0-7407-7815-5

Dilbert 2.0: 20 Years of Dilbert
ISBN: 978-0-7407-7735-6

This Is the Part Where You Pretend to Add Value
ISBN: 978-0-7407-7227-6

Cubes and Punishment
ISBN: 978-0-7407-6837-8

Positive Attitude
ISBN: 978-0-7407-6379-3

Try Rebooting Yourself
ISBN: 978-0-7407-6190-4

What Would Wally Do?
ISBN: 978-0-7407-5769-3

Thriving on Vague Objectives
ISBN: 978-0-7407-5533-0

The Fluorescent Light Glistens Off Your Head
ISBN: 978-0-7407-5113-4

It's Not Funny If I Have to Explain It
ISBN: 978-0-7407-4658-1

Don't Stand Where the Comet Is Assumed to Strike Oil
ISBN: 978-0-7407-4539-3

Words You Don't Want to Hear During Your Annual Performance Review
ISBN: 978-0-7407-3805-0

When Body Language Goes Bad
ISBN: 978-0-7407-3298-0

What Do You Call a Sociopath in a Cubicle? Answer: A Coworker
ISBN: 978-0-7407-2663-7

Another Day in Cubicle Paradise
ISBN: 978-0-7407-2194-6

When Did Ignorance Become a Point of View?
ISBN: 978-0-7407-1839-7

Excuse Me While I Wag
ISBN: 978-0-7407-1390-3

Dilbert — A Treasury of Sunday Strips: Version 00
ISBN: 978-0-7407-0531-1

Random Acts of Management
ISBN: 978-0-7407-0453-6

Dilbert Gives You the Business
ISBN: 978-0-7407-0003-3

Don't Step in the Leadership
ISBN: 978-0-8362-7844-6

Journey to Cubeville
ISBN: 978-0-8362-6745-7

I'm Not Anti-Business, I'm Anti-Idiot
ISBN: 978-0-8362-5182-1

Seven Years of Highly Defective People
ISBN: 978-0-8362-3668-2

Casual Day Has Gone Too Far
ISBN: 978-0-8362-2899-1

Fugitive from the Cubicle Police
ISBN: 978-0-8362-2119-0

It's Obvious You Won't Survive by Your Wits Alone
ISBN: 978-0-8362-0415-5

Still Pumped from Using the Mouse
ISBN: 978-0-8362-1026-2

Bring Me the Head of Willy the Mailboy!
ISBN: 978-0-8362-1779-7

Shave the Whales
ISBN: 978-0-8362-1740-7

Dogbert's Clues for the Clueless
ISBN: 978-0-8362-1737-7

Always Postpone Meetings with Time-Wasting Morons
ISBN: 978-0-8362-1758-2

Build a Better Life by Stealing Office Supplies
ISBN: 978-0-8362-1757-5

For ordering information, call 1-800-223-2336.

HOW'S THAT UNDERLING THING WORKING OUT FOR YOU?

DILBERT

by **SCOTT ADAMS**

**Andrews McMeel
Publishing, LLC**

Kansas City • Sydney • London

Andrews McMeel Publishing, LLC
an Andrews McMeel Universal company
1130 Walnut Street, Kansas City, Missouri 64106
www.andrewsmcmeel.com

11 12 13 14 15 RR2 10 9 8 7 6 5 4 3 2 1

ISBN: 978-1-4494-0819-0
Library of Congress Control Number: 2011926178

www.dilbert.com

ATTENTION: SCHOOLS AND BUSINESSES

For Shelly

Introduction

You don't hear the word *underling* much these days. Corporations prefer more generous titles for their employees, such as Associate, Staff Member, Individual Contributor, or Teammate. That makes good economic sense, because anything that makes employees happy is a substitute for higher pay. And words are totally free!

Starbucks calls their store employees Baristas, which is brilliant because the average person would accept lower pay if it came with a cool job title such as that, compared with something along the lines of Java Monkey, Pusher, or Bean Slave. Starbucks definitely picked the right one. Words matter.

Corporations probably wish they had given their employees extra-bad titles years ago so there would be more room to grow. The gap between Underling and Associate isn't nearly as large as the gap between, for example, Meat Bag and Teammate. If corporations had started at Meat Bag, employees would be delighted with their eventual moneyless promotions to Underling. That's a lost opportunity.

Now that corporations have respectable titles for employees, where do they go from here? Will I someday have my groceries bagged by a fellow who was once an Associate but is now the Exalted High Priest of Celery? Will I call tech support and end up talking to the Sultan of Bits?

On the plus side, all of this title inflation for employees probably postpones the day that underlings rise up and crush their corporate overlords in a bloody revolution. I don't know exactly when that will happen, but if I hear one more story of a CEO becoming a billionaire just because he showed up for work on the same day an engineer invented something awesome, I'm going to start hoarding food.

I'd like to write more for this introduction, but the Empress of Tennis Ball Retrieval is growling at me to go play in the yard. Ever since we stopped calling her *the dog*, I've cut her treats by 20 percent, and she hasn't complained once.

S. Adams

Scott Adams
His Royal Drawness

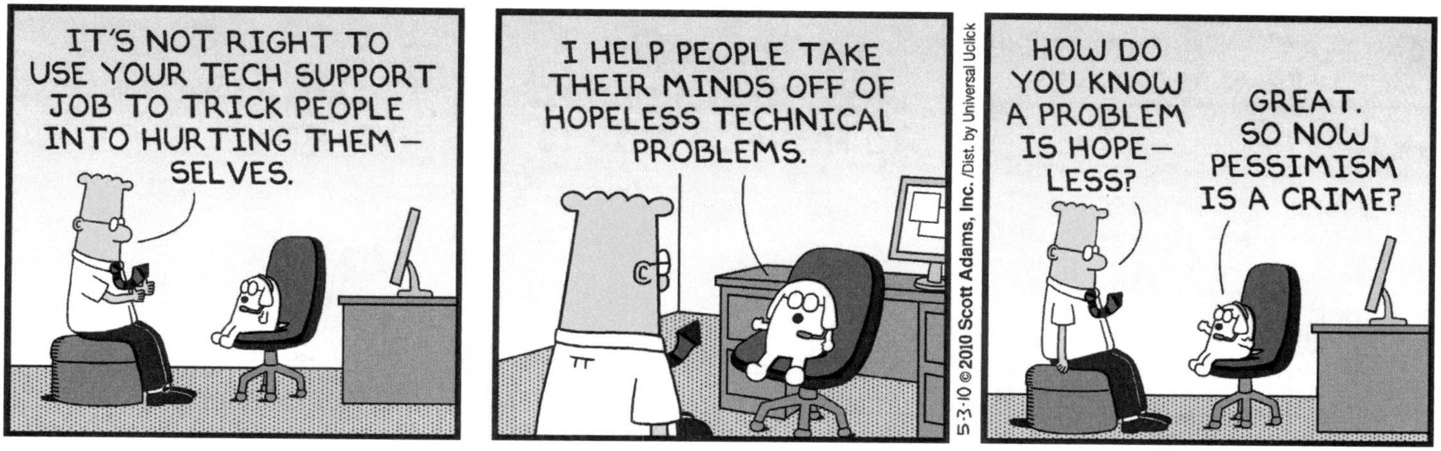
IT'S NOT RIGHT TO USE YOUR TECH SUPPORT JOB TO TRICK PEOPLE INTO HURTING THEM–SELVES.
I HELP PEOPLE TAKE THEIR MINDS OFF OF HOPELESS TECHNICAL PROBLEMS.
5·3·10 ©2010 Scott Adams, Inc. /Dist. by Universal Uclick
HOW DO YOU KNOW A PROBLEM IS HOPE–LESS?
GREAT. SO NOW PESSIMISM IS A CRIME?

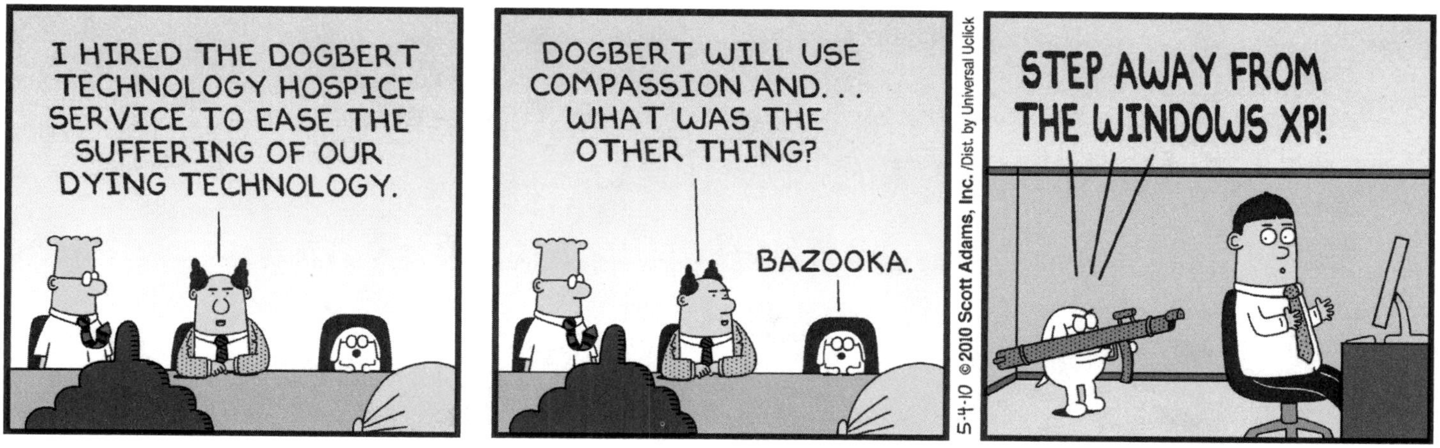
I HIRED THE DOGBERT TECHNOLOGY HOSPICE SERVICE TO EASE THE SUFFERING OF OUR DYING TECHNOLOGY.
DOGBERT WILL USE COMPASSION AND. . . WHAT WAS THE OTHER THING?
BAZOOKA.
5·4·10 ©2010 Scott Adams, Inc. /Dist. by Universal Uclick
STEP AWAY FROM THE WINDOWS XP!

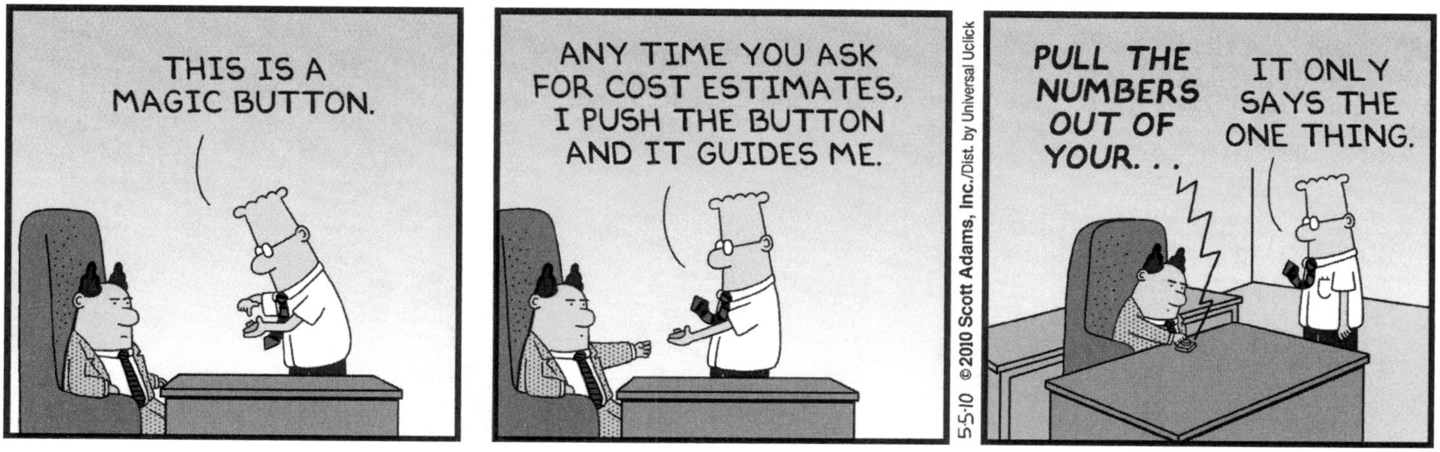
THIS IS A MAGIC BUTTON.
ANY TIME YOU ASK FOR COST ESTIMATES, I PUSH THE BUTTON AND IT GUIDES ME.
5·5·10 ©2010 Scott Adams, Inc./Dist. by Universal Uclick
PULL THE NUMBERS OUT OF YOUR. . .
IT ONLY SAYS THE ONE THING.

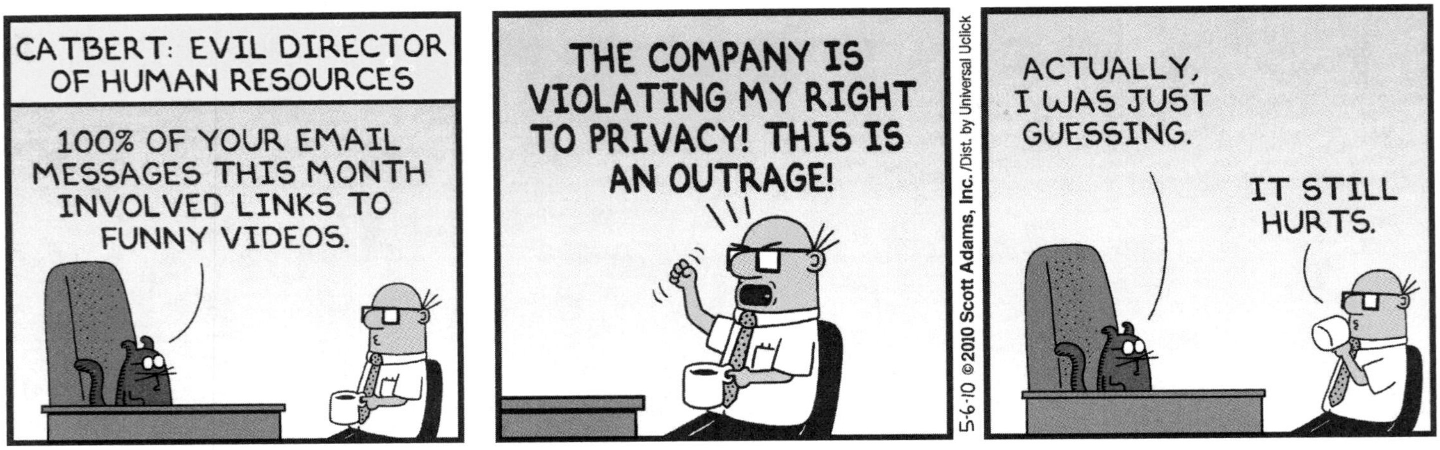
CATBERT: EVIL DIRECTOR OF HUMAN RESOURCES
100% OF YOUR EMAIL MESSAGES THIS MONTH INVOLVED LINKS TO FUNNY VIDEOS.
THE COMPANY IS VIOLATING MY RIGHT TO PRIVACY! THIS IS AN OUTRAGE!
5-6-10 © 2010 Scott Adams, Inc./Dist. by Universal Uclick
ACTUALLY, I WAS JUST GUESSING.
IT STILL HURTS.

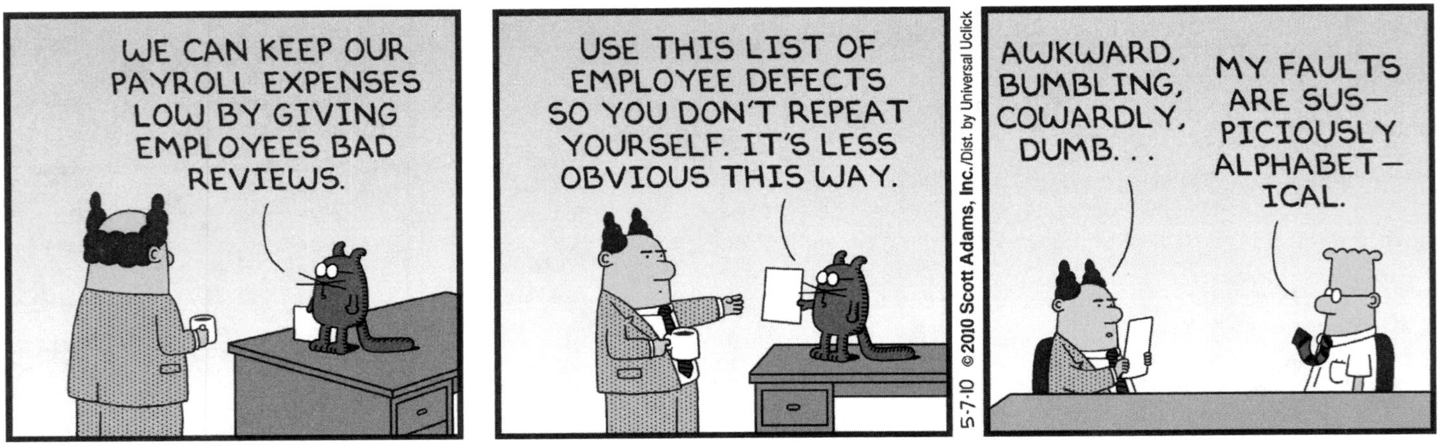
WE CAN KEEP OUR PAYROLL EXPENSES LOW BY GIVING EMPLOYEES BAD REVIEWS.
USE THIS LIST OF EMPLOYEE DEFECTS SO YOU DON'T REPEAT YOURSELF. IT'S LESS OBVIOUS THIS WAY.
5-7-10 © 2010 Scott Adams, Inc./Dist. by Universal Uclick
AWKWARD, BUMBLING, COWARDLY, DUMB. . .
MY FAULTS ARE SUS- PICIOUSLY ALPHABET- ICAL.

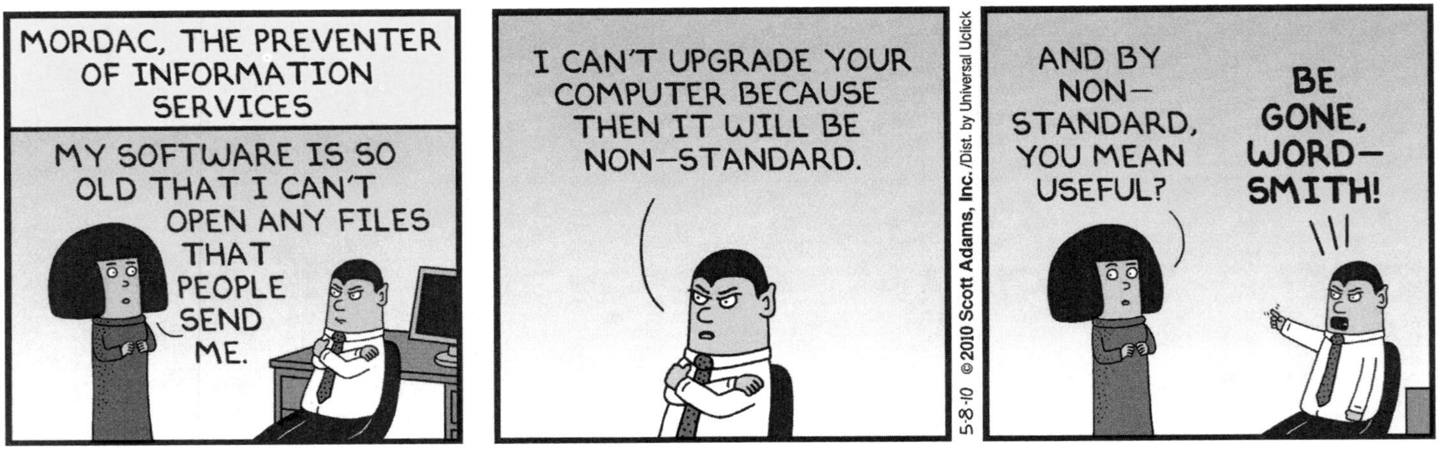
MORDAC, THE PREVENTER OF INFORMATION SERVICES
MY SOFTWARE IS SO OLD THAT I CAN'T OPEN ANY FILES THAT PEOPLE SEND ME.
I CAN'T UPGRADE YOUR COMPUTER BECAUSE THEN IT WILL BE NON-STANDARD.
5-8-10 © 2010 Scott Adams, Inc./Dist. by Universal Uclick
AND BY NON- STANDARD, YOU MEAN USEFUL?
BE GONE, WORD- SMITH!

AMBER, WOULD YOU LIKE TO GO TO LUNCH WITH ME?
SURE!
YES!!! I'M IN!
DO YOU MIND IF WE BRING BOB? I NEED TO TALK TO HIM ABOUT HIS PROJECT.
WELL, THAT WOULD BE. . .
HEY, BOB. MEET US IN THE LOBBY.
©2010 Scott Adams, Inc. /Dist. by Universal Uclick
LOOK AT US! WE'RE LIKE THE TWO MUSKETEERS, PLUS DILBERT.
THERE WERE THREE MUSKE-TEERS.
I'M PRETTY SURE THERE WERE TWO.
WAIT. . . I JUST REMEMBERED I HAVE A CONFERENCE CALL AT NOON. YOU TWO GO AHEAD WITHOUT ME.
5-9-10
WE'RE LIKE THE ONE MUSKE-TEER.
JUST EAT.

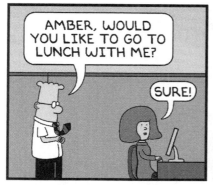

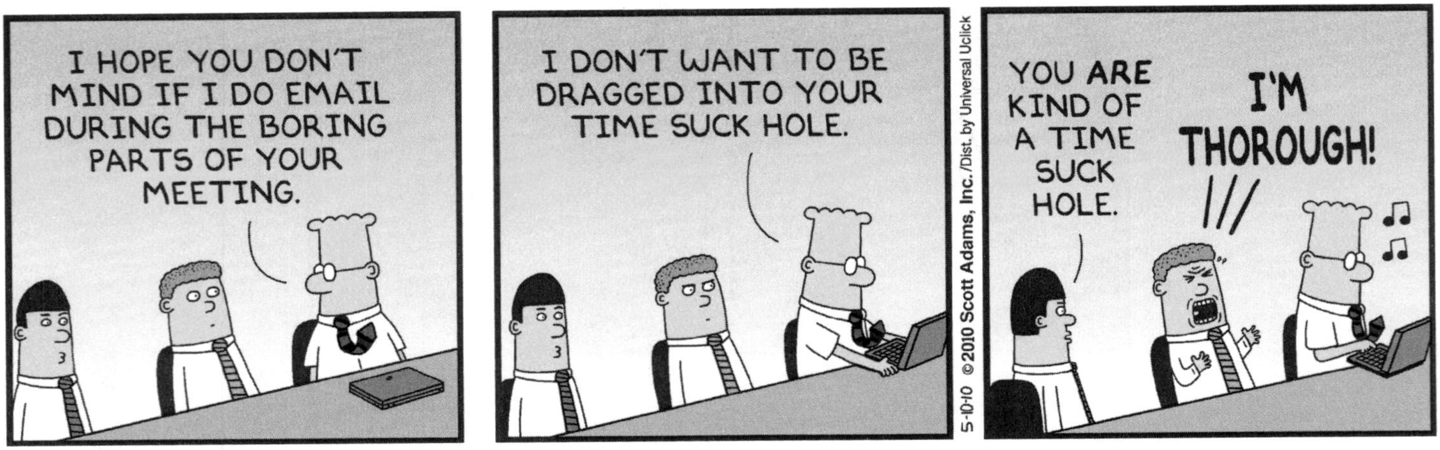
I HOPE YOU DON'T MIND IF I DO EMAIL DURING THE BORING PARTS OF YOUR MEETING.
I DON'T WANT TO BE DRAGGED INTO YOUR TIME SUCK HOLE.
YOU ARE KIND OF A TIME SUCK HOLE.
I'M THOROUGH!
5-10-10 © 2010 Scott Adams, Inc./Dist. by Universal Uclick

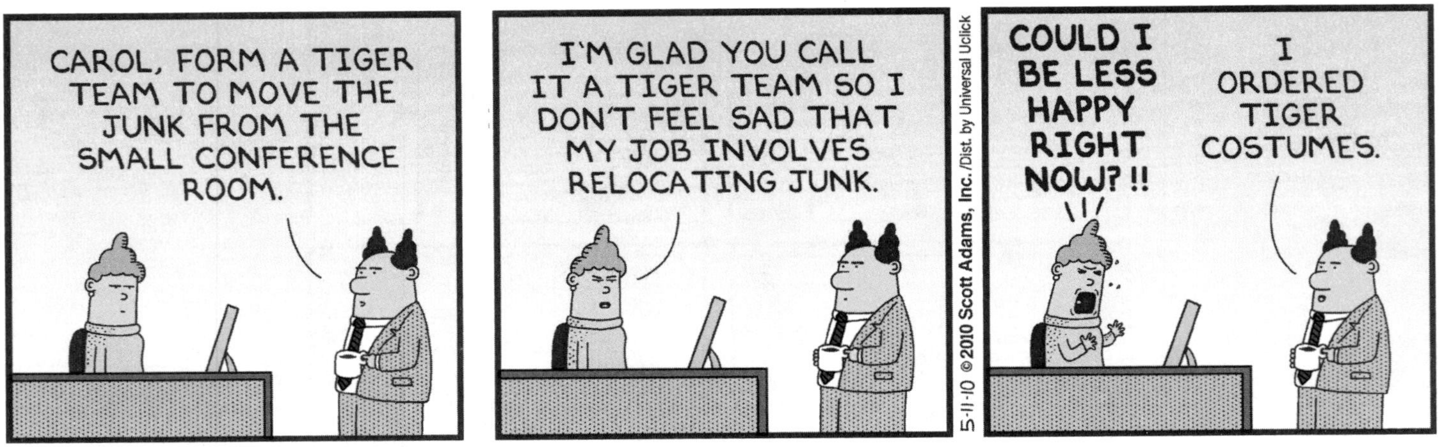
CAROL, FORM A TIGER TEAM TO MOVE THE JUNK FROM THE SMALL CONFERENCE ROOM.
I'M GLAD YOU CALL IT A TIGER TEAM SO I DON'T FEEL SAD THAT MY JOB INVOLVES RELOCATING JUNK.
COULD I BE LESS HAPPY RIGHT NOW? !!
I ORDERED TIGER COSTUMES.
5-11-10 © 2010 Scott Adams, Inc./Dist. by Universal Uclick

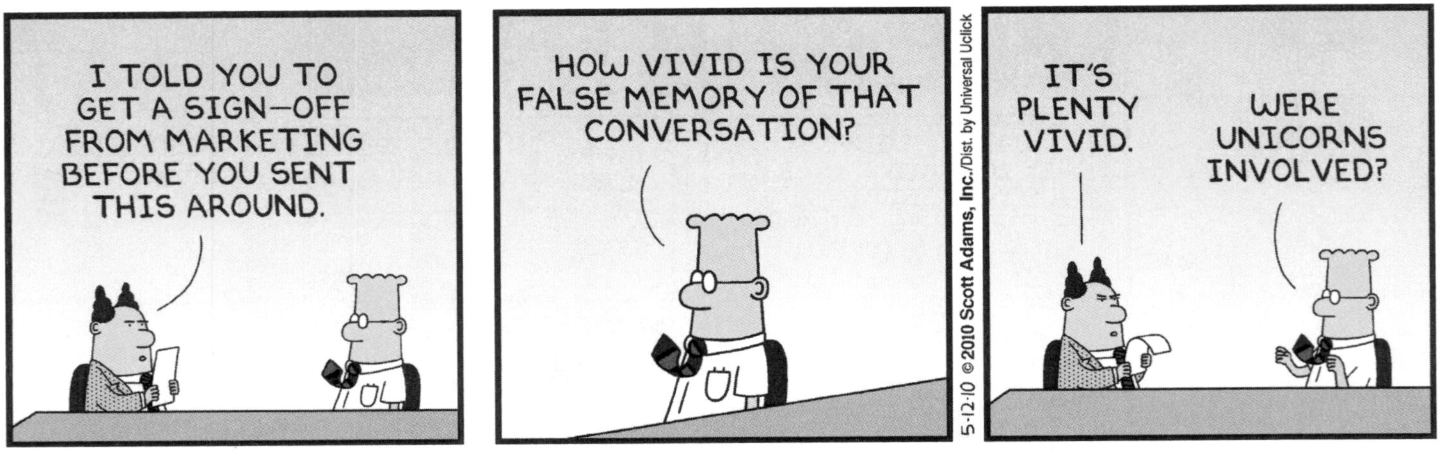
I TOLD YOU TO GET A SIGN-OFF FROM MARKETING BEFORE YOU SENT THIS AROUND.
HOW VIVID IS YOUR FALSE MEMORY OF THAT CONVERSATION?
IT'S PLENTY VIVID.
WERE UNICORNS INVOLVED?
5-12-10 © 2010 Scott Adams, Inc./Dist. by Universal Uclick

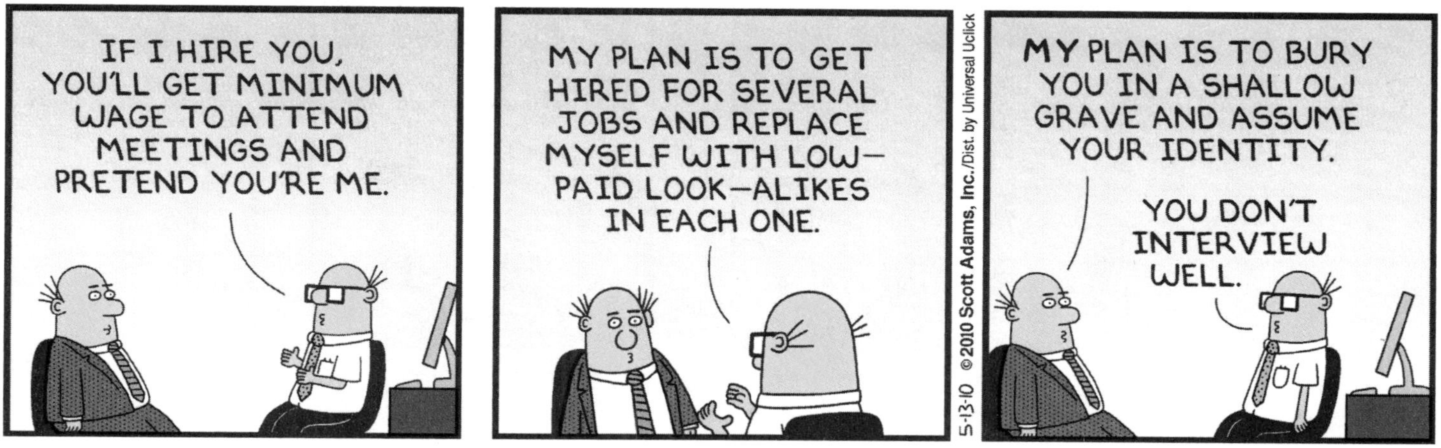
IF I HIRE YOU, YOU'LL GET MINIMUM WAGE TO ATTEND MEETINGS AND PRETEND YOU'RE ME.
MY PLAN IS TO GET HIRED FOR SEVERAL JOBS AND REPLACE MYSELF WITH LOW-PAID LOOK-ALIKES IN EACH ONE.
5-13-10 © 2010 Scott Adams, Inc./Dist. by Universal Uclick
MY PLAN IS TO BURY YOU IN A SHALLOW GRAVE AND ASSUME YOUR IDENTITY.
YOU DON'T INTERVIEW WELL.

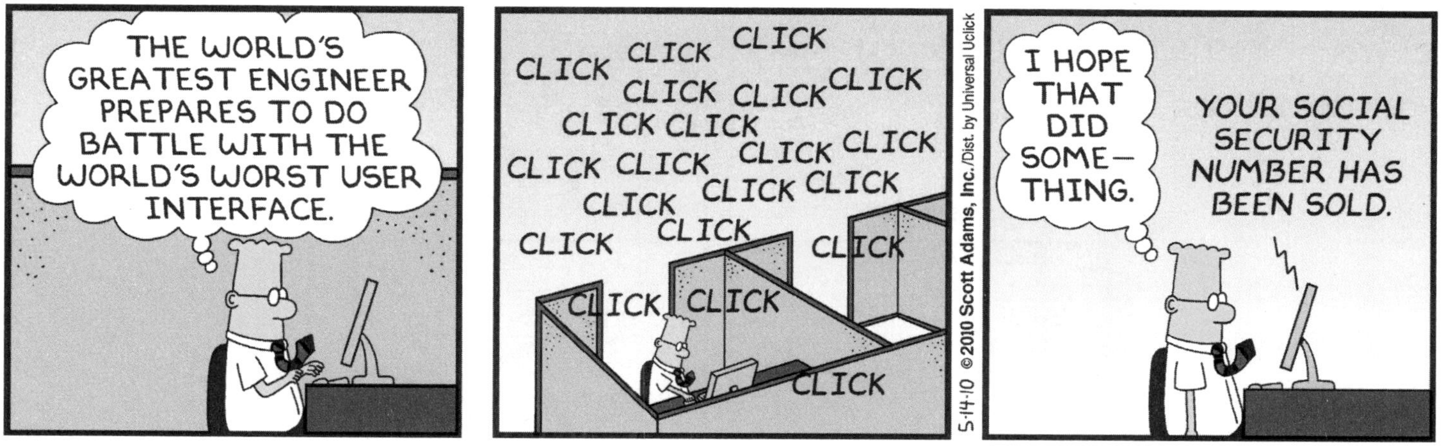
THE WORLD'S GREATEST ENGINEER PREPARES TO DO BATTLE WITH THE WORLD'S WORST USER INTERFACE.
CLICK CLICK
5-14-10 © 2010 Scott Adams, Inc./Dist. by Universal Uclick
I HOPE THAT DID SOME-THING.
YOUR SOCIAL SECURITY NUMBER HAS BEEN SOLD.

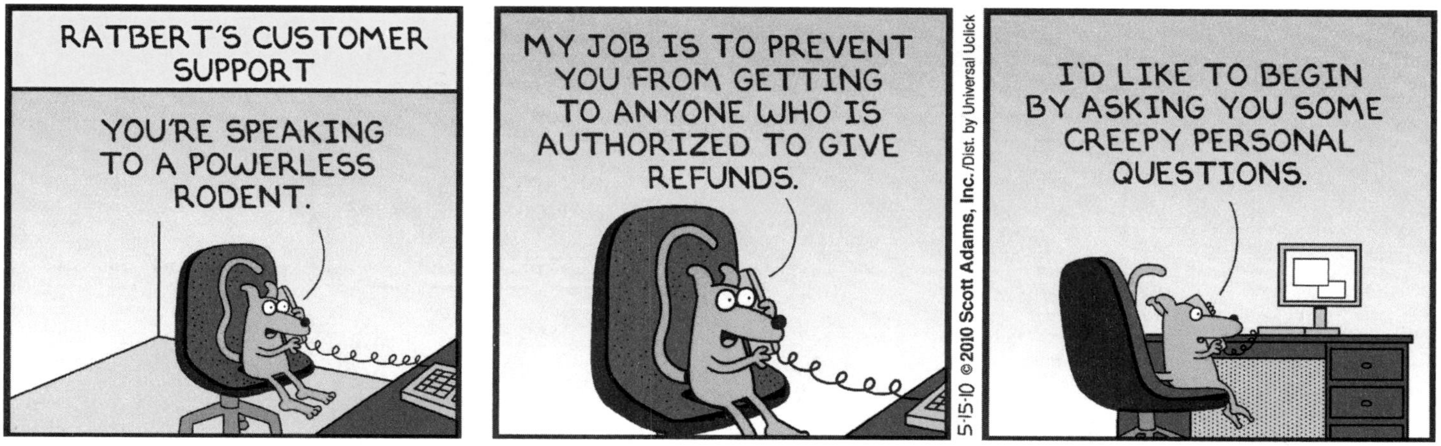
RATBERT'S CUSTOMER SUPPORT
YOU'RE SPEAKING TO A POWERLESS RODENT.
MY JOB IS TO PREVENT YOU FROM GETTING TO ANYONE WHO IS AUTHORIZED TO GIVE REFUNDS.
5-15-10 © 2010 Scott Adams, Inc./Dist. by Universal Uclick
I'D LIKE TO BEGIN BY ASKING YOU SOME CREEPY PERSONAL QUESTIONS.

I ASKED WOLFGANG TO JOIN US.
HE'S A SOFTWARE GENIUS, IF NOT A LEGEND.
HE KNOWS MORE THAN ALL OF YOU PUT TOGETHER.
PLUS HIS NAME IS WOLFGANG.
©2010 Scott Adams, Inc./Dist. by Universal Uclick
SOME SAY HIS TALENT IS A GENETIC MUTATION. OTHERS SAY THAT GOD SPEAKS TO HIM IN UNIX.
ALL WE KNOW FOR SURE IS THAT HE GLOWS, AND HE NEVER NEEDS TO EAT.
I FEEL A CHILL. IT MEANS HE'S APPROACHING.
PLEASE DON'T REPROGRAM MY DNA AND MAKE ME A MONKEY-MAN!!!
5-16-10
PEOPLE MAKE A LOT OF ASSUMPTIONS WHEN YOU CHANGE YOUR NAME TO WOLFGANG AND STOP SHAVING.

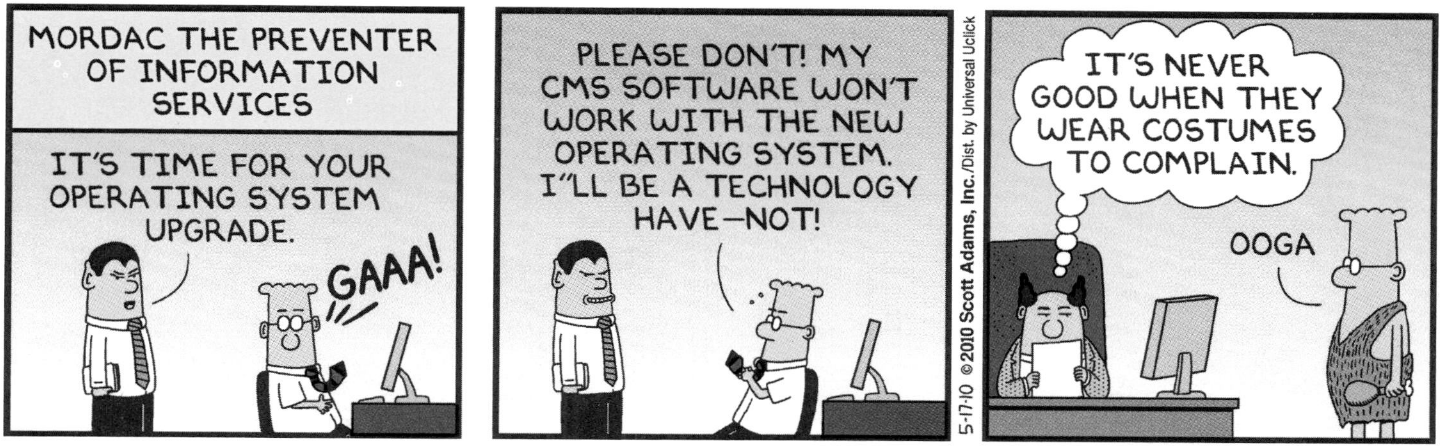
MORDAC THE PREVENTER OF INFORMATION SERVICES
IT'S TIME FOR YOUR OPERATING SYSTEM UPGRADE.
GAAA!
PLEASE DON'T! MY CMS SOFTWARE WON'T WORK WITH THE NEW OPERATING SYSTEM. I'LL BE A TECHNOLOGY HAVE—NOT!
5-17-10 © 2010 Scott Adams, Inc./Dist. by Universal Uclick
IT'S NEVER GOOD WHEN THEY WEAR COSTUMES TO COMPLAIN.
OOGA

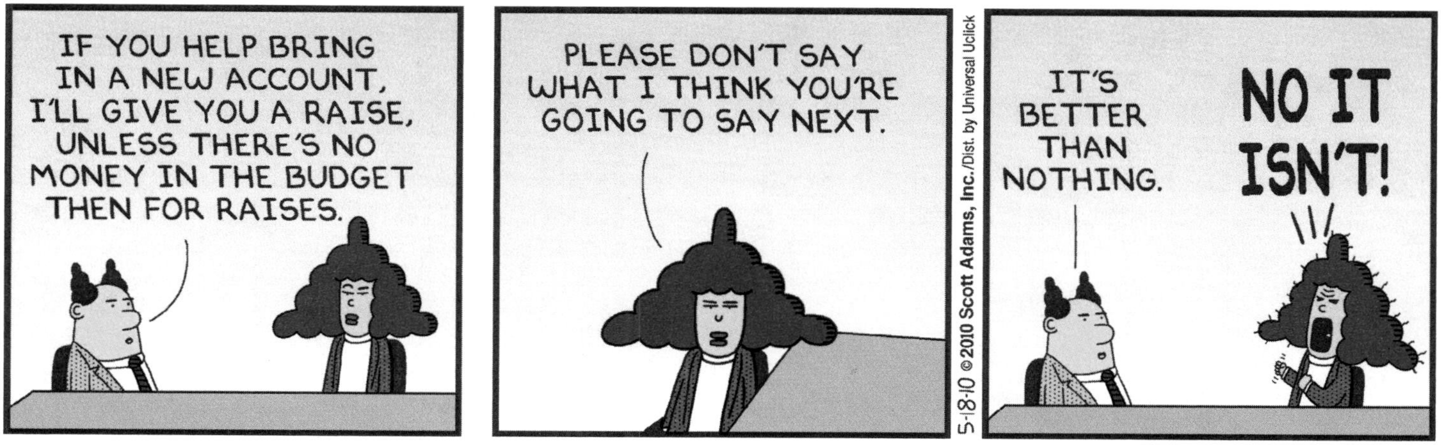
IF YOU HELP BRING IN A NEW ACCOUNT, I'LL GIVE YOU A RAISE, UNLESS THERE'S NO MONEY IN THE BUDGET THEN FOR RAISES.
PLEASE DON'T SAY WHAT I THINK YOU'RE GOING TO SAY NEXT.
5-18-10 © 2010 Scott Adams, Inc./Dist. by Universal Uclick
IT'S BETTER THAN NOTHING.
NO IT ISN'T!

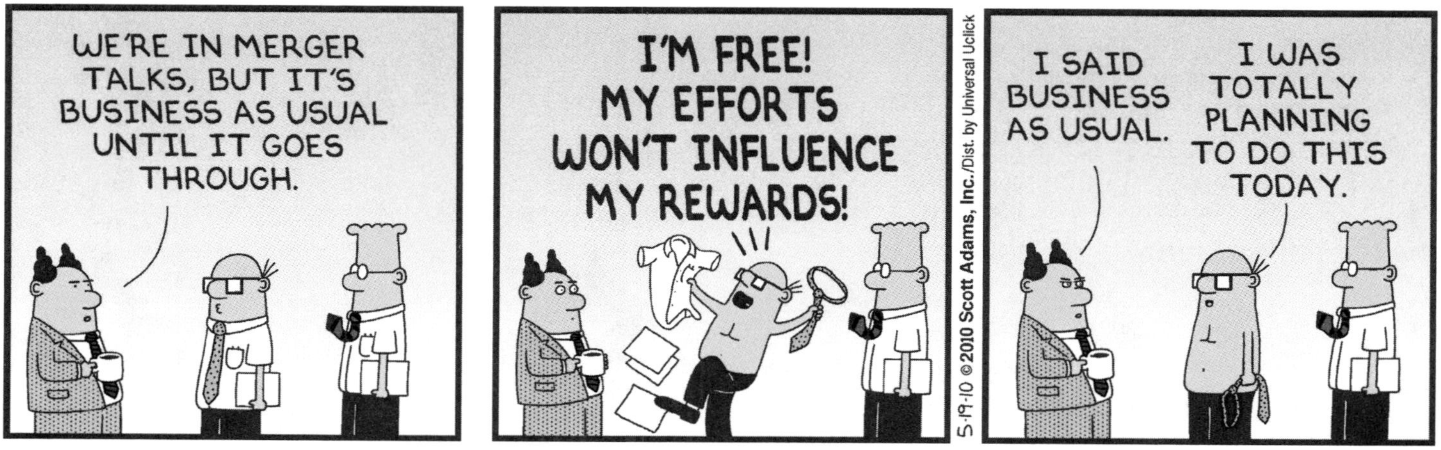
WE'RE IN MERGER TALKS, BUT IT'S BUSINESS AS USUAL UNTIL IT GOES THROUGH.
I'M FREE! MY EFFORTS WON'T INFLUENCE MY REWARDS!
5-19-10 © 2010 Scott Adams, Inc./Dist. by Universal Uclick
I SAID BUSINESS AS USUAL.
I WAS TOTALLY PLANNING TO DO THIS TODAY.

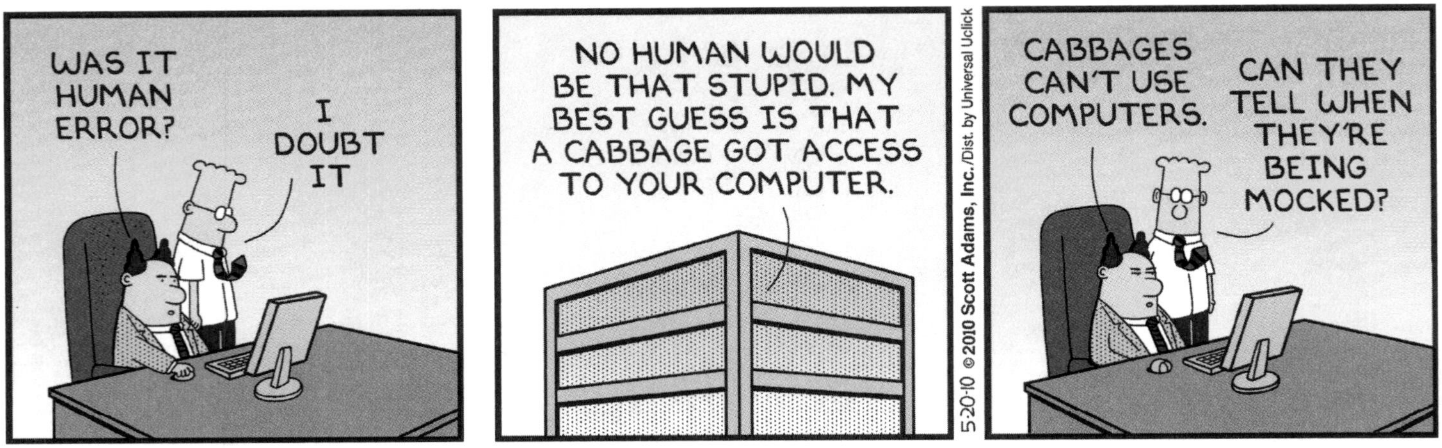
WAS IT HUMAN ERROR?
I DOUBT IT
NO HUMAN WOULD BE THAT STUPID. MY BEST GUESS IS THAT A CABBAGE GOT ACCESS TO YOUR COMPUTER.
CABBAGES CAN'T USE COMPUTERS.
CAN THEY TELL WHEN THEY'RE BEING MOCKED?
5·20·10 © 2010 Scott Adams, Inc./Dist. by Universal Uclick

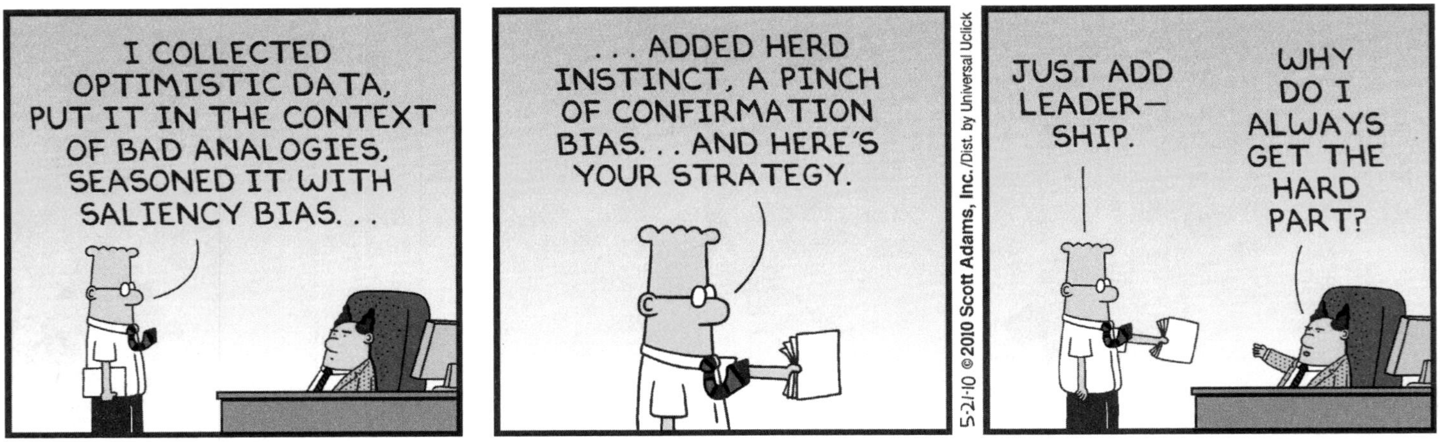
I COLLECTED OPTIMISTIC DATA, PUT IT IN THE CONTEXT OF BAD ANALOGIES, SEASONED IT WITH SALIENCY BIAS...
...ADDED HERD INSTINCT, A PINCH OF CONFIRMATION BIAS... AND HERE'S YOUR STRATEGY.
JUST ADD LEADER-SHIP.
WHY DO I ALWAYS GET THE HARD PART?
5·21·10 © 2010 Scott Adams, Inc./Dist. by Universal Uclick

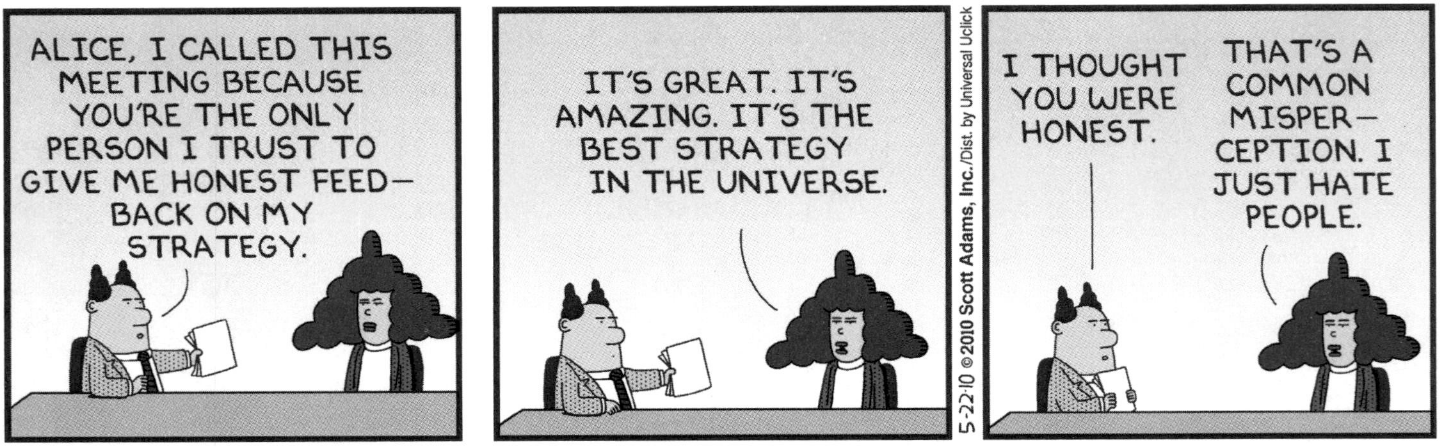
ALICE, I CALLED THIS MEETING BECAUSE YOU'RE THE ONLY PERSON I TRUST TO GIVE ME HONEST FEED-BACK ON MY STRATEGY.
IT'S GREAT. IT'S AMAZING. IT'S THE BEST STRATEGY IN THE UNIVERSE.
I THOUGHT YOU WERE HONEST.
THAT'S A COMMON MISPER-CEPTION. I JUST HATE PEOPLE.
5·22·10 © 2010 Scott Adams, Inc./Dist. by Universal Uclick

I FINISHED THE BUSINESS CASE.
YOU SAID YOU WOULD TRY TO GET FUNDING IF THE NUMBERS LOOK GOOD.
I NEVER SAID THAT.
I CLEARLY REMEMBER IT. I CAN DESCRIBE OUR CONVERSATION WORD FOR WORD.
I PROBABLY SAID SOMETHING THAT SOUNDED LIKE "I WILL GET FUNDING" AND YOU HEARD IT WRONG.
WHAT EXACTLY SOUNDS LIKE "I WILL GET FUNDING"?
LANDFILL WET HUNTING.
THAT'S NOT EVEN A GOOD TRY!!!
SHAKE IT OFF.
©2010 Scott Adams, Inc. /Dist. by Universal Uclick
5-23-10

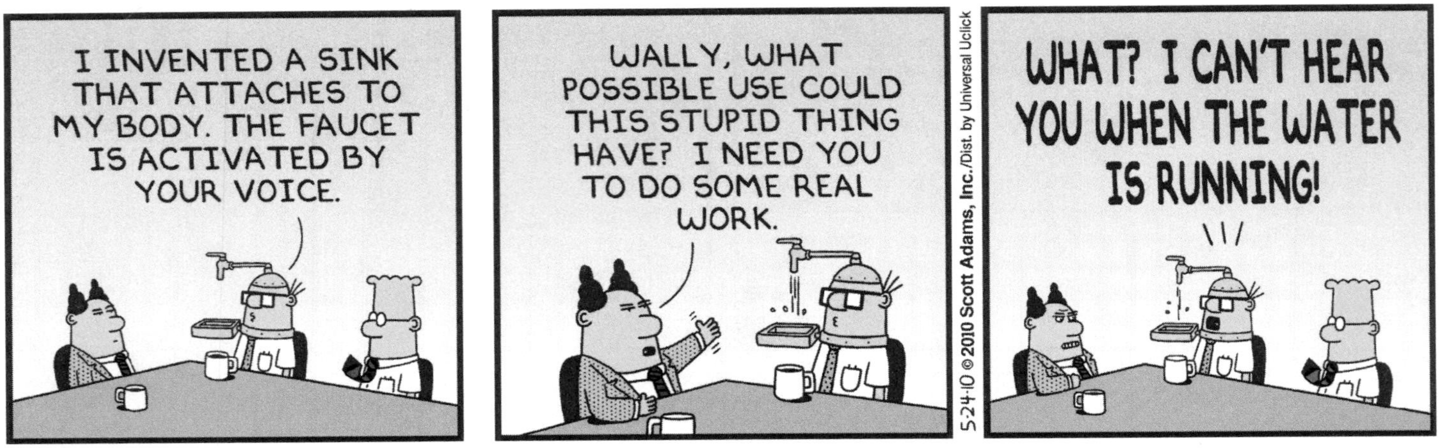
I INVENTED A SINK THAT ATTACHES TO MY BODY. THE FAUCET IS ACTIVATED BY YOUR VOICE.
WALLY, WHAT POSSIBLE USE COULD THIS STUPID THING HAVE? I NEED YOU TO DO SOME REAL WORK.
5·24·10 © 2010 Scott Adams, Inc./Dist. by Universal Uclick
WHAT? I CAN'T HEAR YOU WHEN THE WATER IS RUNNING!

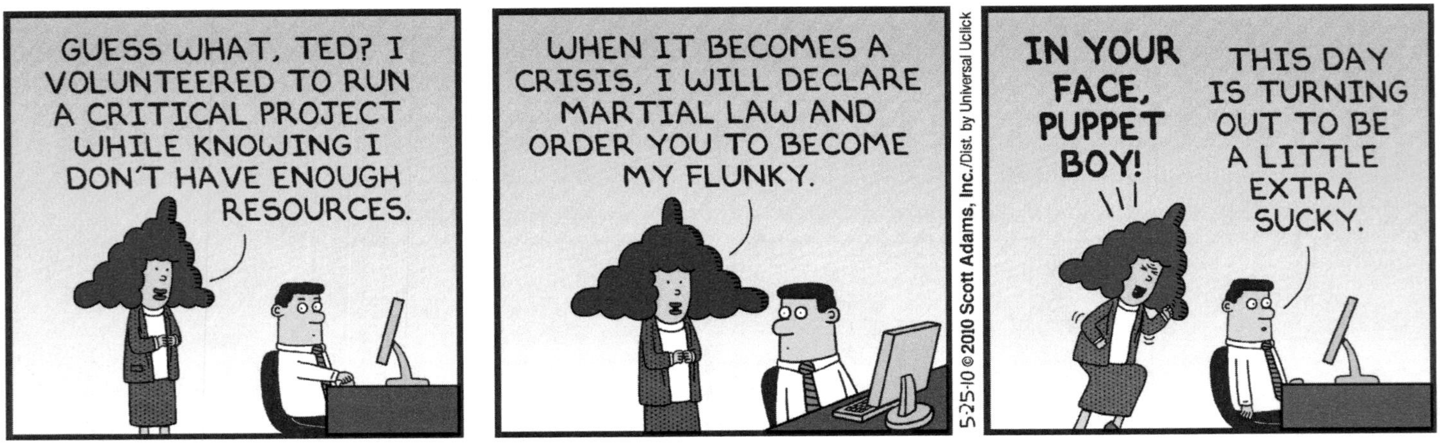
GUESS WHAT, TED? I VOLUNTEERED TO RUN A CRITICAL PROJECT WHILE KNOWING I DON'T HAVE ENOUGH RESOURCES.
WHEN IT BECOMES A CRISIS, I WILL DECLARE MARTIAL LAW AND ORDER YOU TO BECOME MY FLUNKY.
5·25·10 © 2010 Scott Adams, Inc./Dist. by Universal Uclick
IN YOUR FACE, PUPPET BOY!
THIS DAY IS TURNING OUT TO BE A LITTLE EXTRA SUCKY.

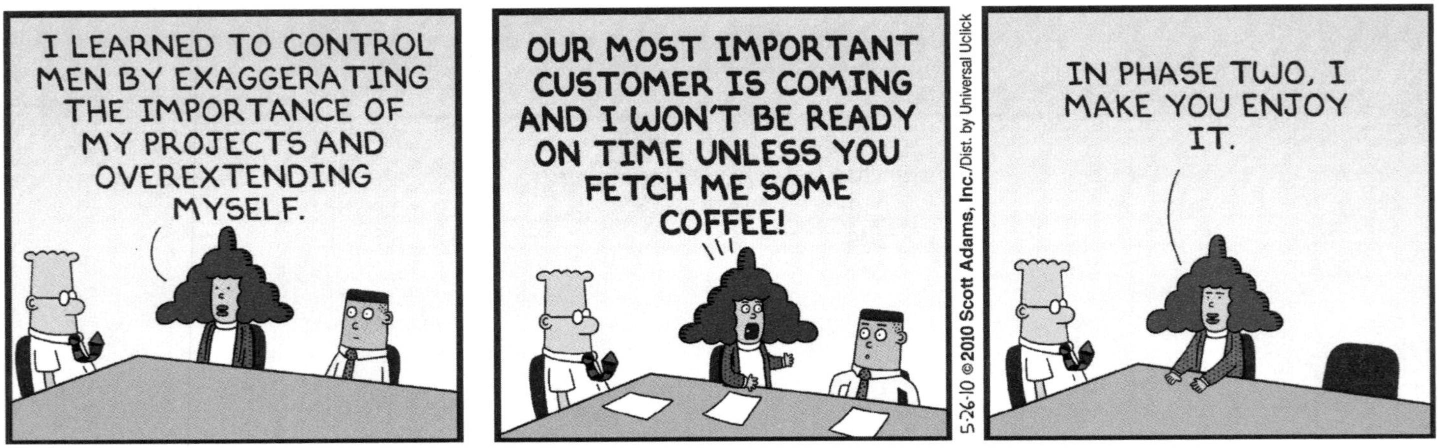
I LEARNED TO CONTROL MEN BY EXAGGERATING THE IMPORTANCE OF MY PROJECTS AND OVEREXTENDING MYSELF.
OUR MOST IMPORTANT CUSTOMER IS COMING AND I WON'T BE READY ON TIME UNLESS YOU FETCH ME SOME COFFEE!
5·26·10 © 2010 Scott Adams, Inc./Dist. by Universal Uclick
IN PHASE TWO, I MAKE YOU ENJOY IT.

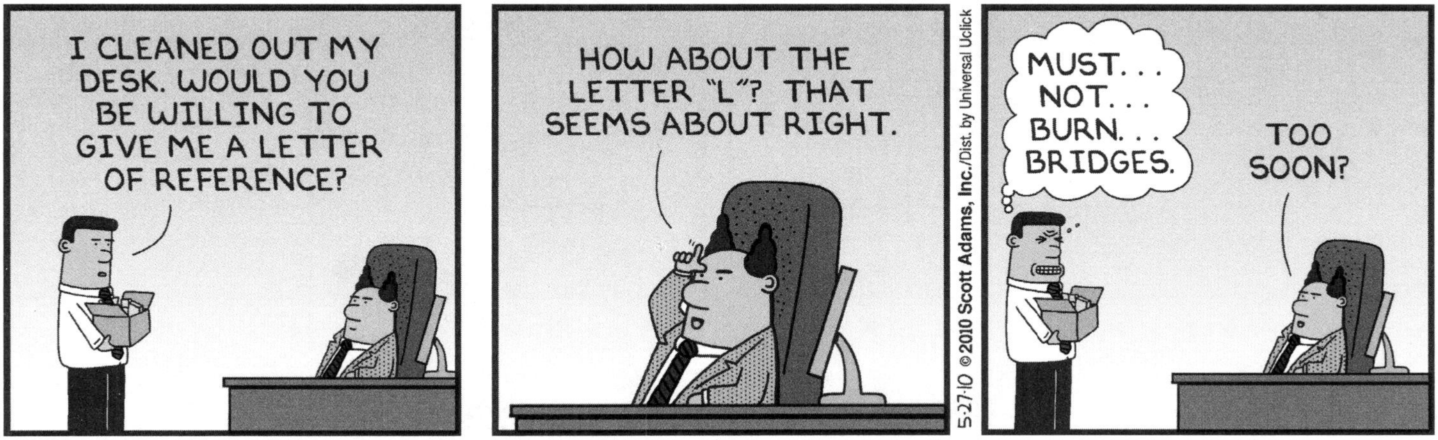
I CLEANED OUT MY DESK. WOULD YOU BE WILLING TO GIVE ME A LETTER OF REFERENCE?
HOW ABOUT THE LETTER "L"? THAT SEEMS ABOUT RIGHT.
5·27·10 © 2010 Scott Adams, Inc./Dist. by Universal Uclick
MUST... NOT... BURN... BRIDGES.
TOO SOON?

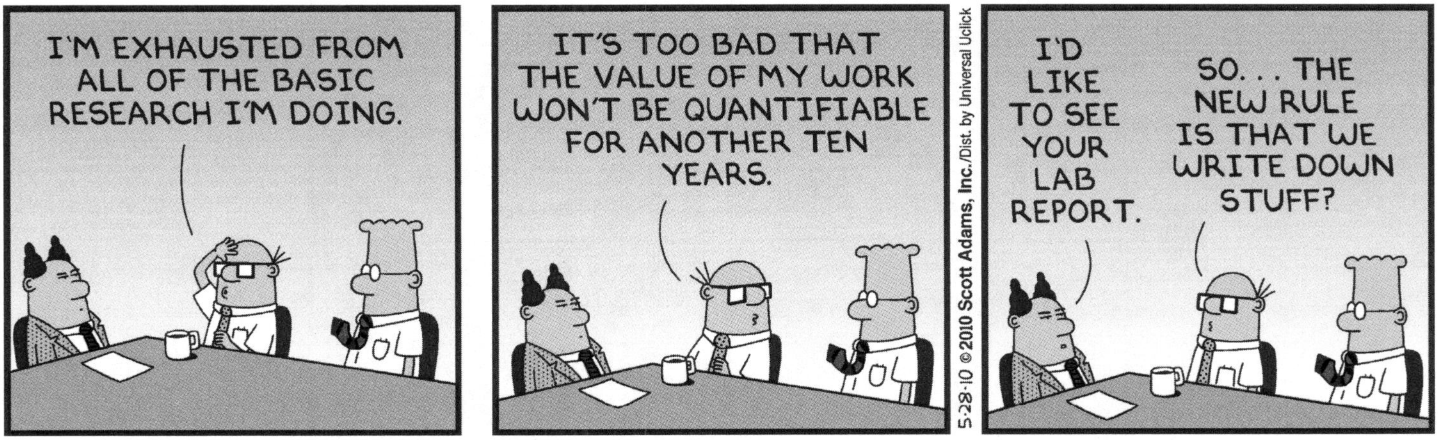
I'M EXHAUSTED FROM ALL OF THE BASIC RESEARCH I'M DOING.
IT'S TOO BAD THAT THE VALUE OF MY WORK WON'T BE QUANTIFIABLE FOR ANOTHER TEN YEARS.
5·28·10 © 2010 Scott Adams, Inc./Dist. by Universal Uclick
I'D LIKE TO SEE YOUR LAB REPORT.
SO... THE NEW RULE IS THAT WE WRITE DOWN STUFF?

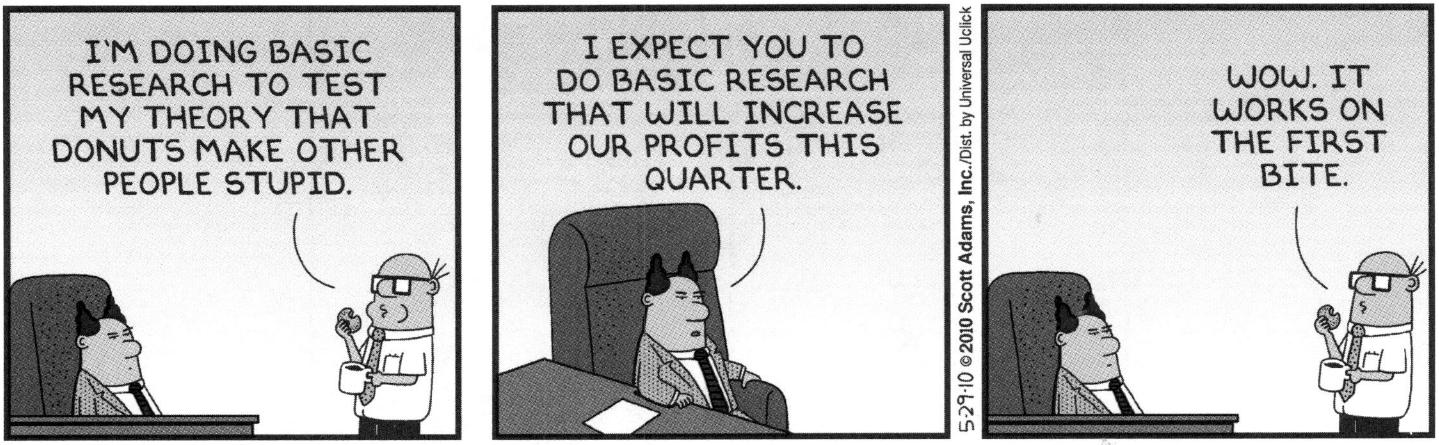
I'M DOING BASIC RESEARCH TO TEST MY THEORY THAT DONUTS MAKE OTHER PEOPLE STUPID.
I EXPECT YOU TO DO BASIC RESEARCH THAT WILL INCREASE OUR PROFITS THIS QUARTER.
5·29·10 © 2010 Scott Adams, Inc./Dist. by Universal Uclick
WOW. IT WORKS ON THE FIRST BITE.

I ACCOMPLISHED NOTHING THIS WEEK BECAUSE I WAS GOING THROUGH CERTIFICATION.
DON'T ASK. DON'T ASK. DON'T ASK.
CERTIFICATION FOR. . . WHAT?
PLAN B: MOUNT A PASSIONATE DEFENSE AGAINST AN ARGUMENT THAT NO ONE MADE.
HOW CAN YOU SAY THAT CERTIFICATION IS A WASTE OF TIME?!
WITHOUT CERTIFI-CATION, MANAGEMENT WOULD BE REDUCED TO RANDOMNESS!
DO YOU THINK YOU'D BE HAPPIER JUST *GUESSING* WHO IS QUALIFIED TO DO WHAT? DO YOU? DO YOU?
THERE'S SOME-THING WRONG WITH YOU.
APOLOGY ACCEPTED.
NEXT.
5-30-10

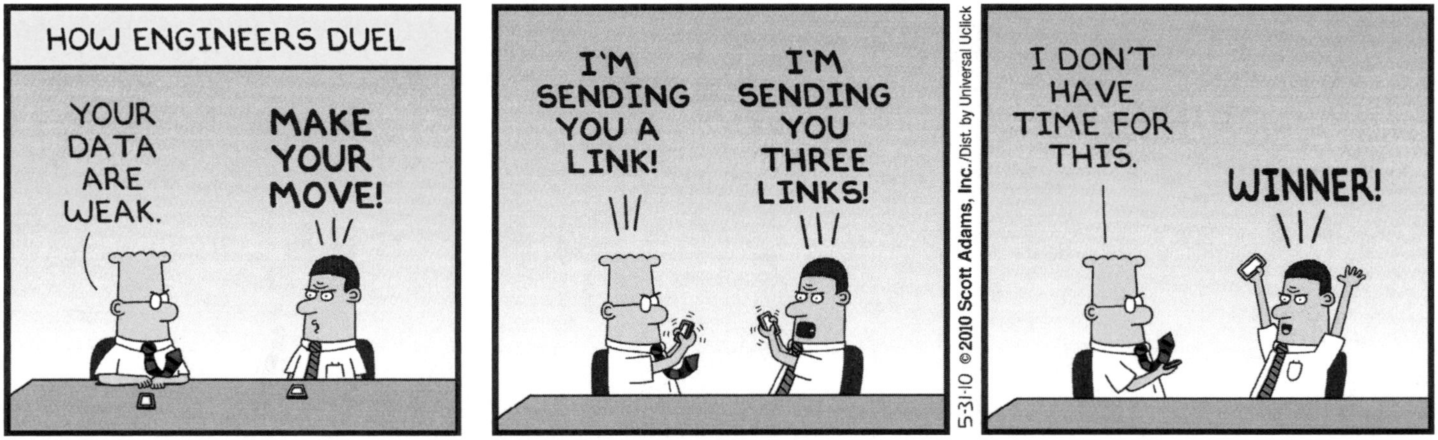
HOW ENGINEERS DUEL
YOUR DATA ARE WEAK.
MAKE YOUR MOVE!
I'M SENDING YOU A LINK!
I'M SENDING YOU THREE LINKS!
5-31-10 © 2010 Scott Adams, Inc./Dist. by Universal Uclick
I DON'T HAVE TIME FOR THIS.
WINNER!

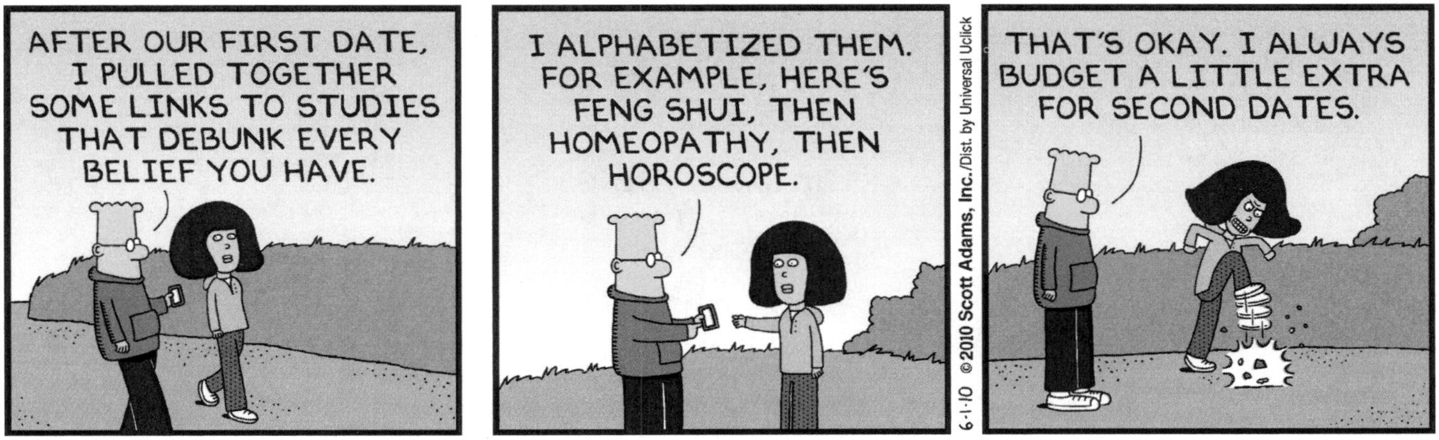
AFTER OUR FIRST DATE, I PULLED TOGETHER SOME LINKS TO STUDIES THAT DEBUNK EVERY BELIEF YOU HAVE.
I ALPHABETIZED THEM. FOR EXAMPLE, HERE'S FENG SHUI, THEN HOMEOPATHY, THEN HOROSCOPE.
6-1-10 © 2010 Scott Adams, Inc./Dist. by Universal Uclick
THAT'S OKAY. I ALWAYS BUDGET A LITTLE EXTRA FOR SECOND DATES.

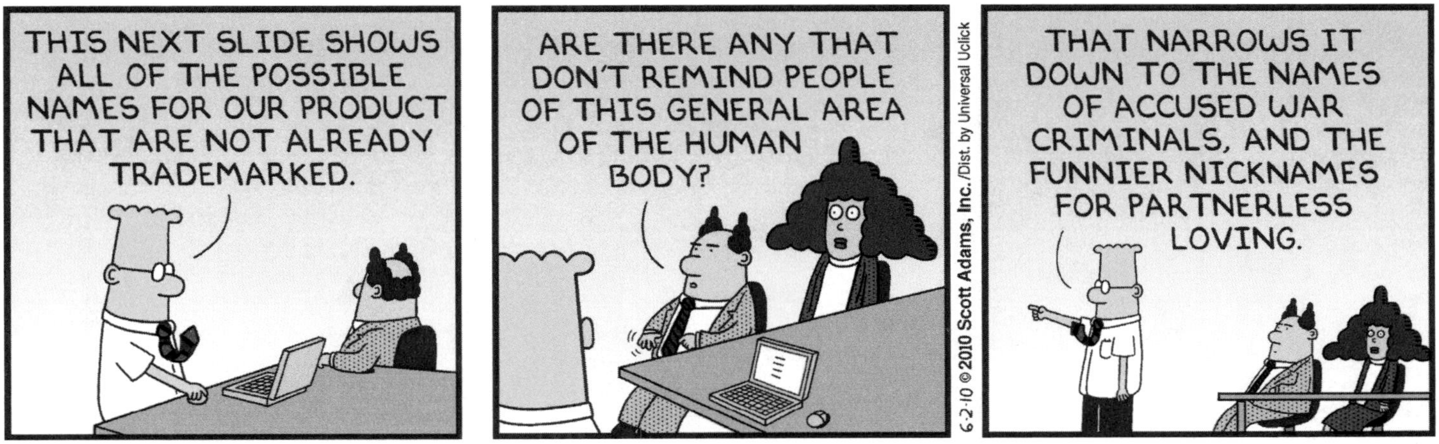
THIS NEXT SLIDE SHOWS ALL OF THE POSSIBLE NAMES FOR OUR PRODUCT THAT ARE NOT ALREADY TRADEMARKED.
ARE THERE ANY THAT DON'T REMIND PEOPLE OF THIS GENERAL AREA OF THE HUMAN BODY?
6-2-10 © 2010 Scott Adams, Inc./Dist. by Universal Uclick
THAT NARROWS IT DOWN TO THE NAMES OF ACCUSED WAR CRIMINALS, AND THE FUNNIER NICKNAMES FOR PARTNERLESS LOVING.

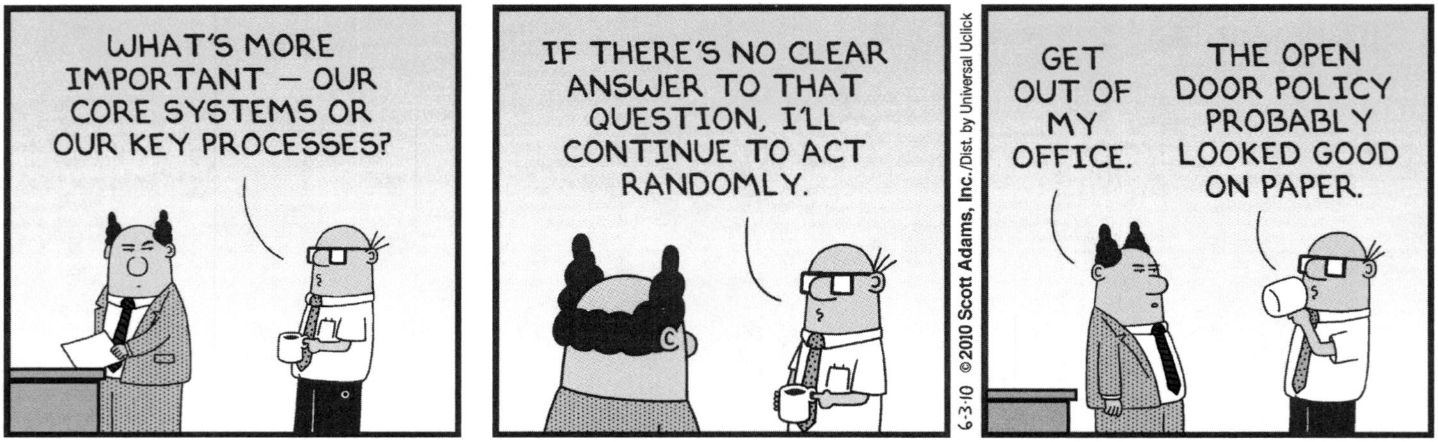
WHAT'S MORE IMPORTANT — OUR CORE SYSTEMS OR OUR KEY PROCESSES?
IF THERE'S NO CLEAR ANSWER TO THAT QUESTION, I'LL CONTINUE TO ACT RANDOMLY.
6-3-10 ©2010 Scott Adams, Inc./Dist. by Universal Uclick
GET OUT OF MY OFFICE.
THE OPEN DOOR POLICY PROBABLY LOOKED GOOD ON PAPER.

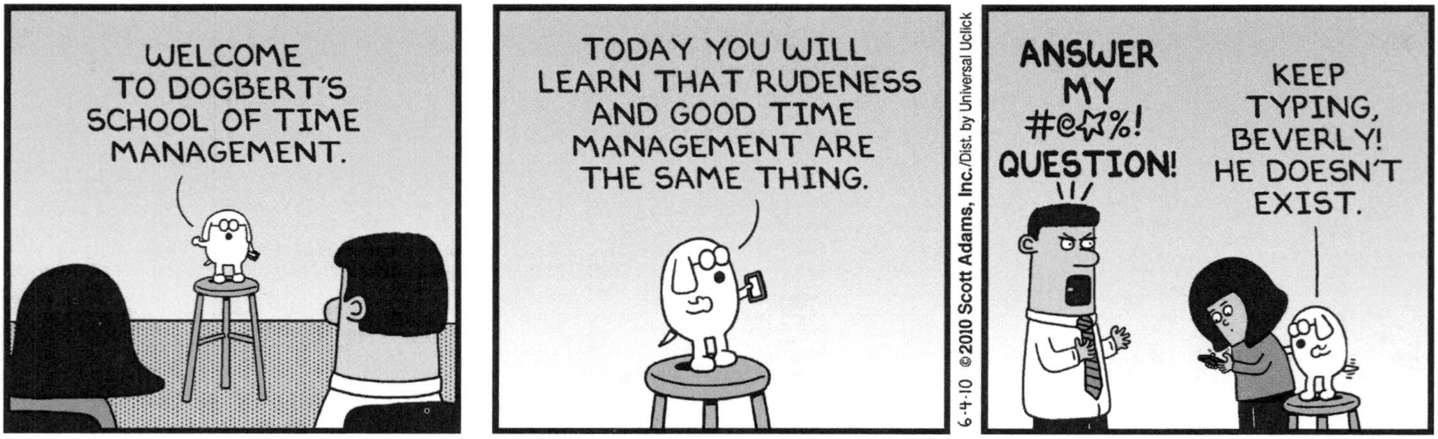
WELCOME TO DOGBERT'S SCHOOL OF TIME MANAGEMENT.
TODAY YOU WILL LEARN THAT RUDENESS AND GOOD TIME MANAGEMENT ARE THE SAME THING.
6-4-10 ©2010 Scott Adams, Inc./Dist. by Universal Uclick
ANSWER MY #@☆%! QUESTION!
KEEP TYPING, BEVERLY! HE DOESN'T EXIST.

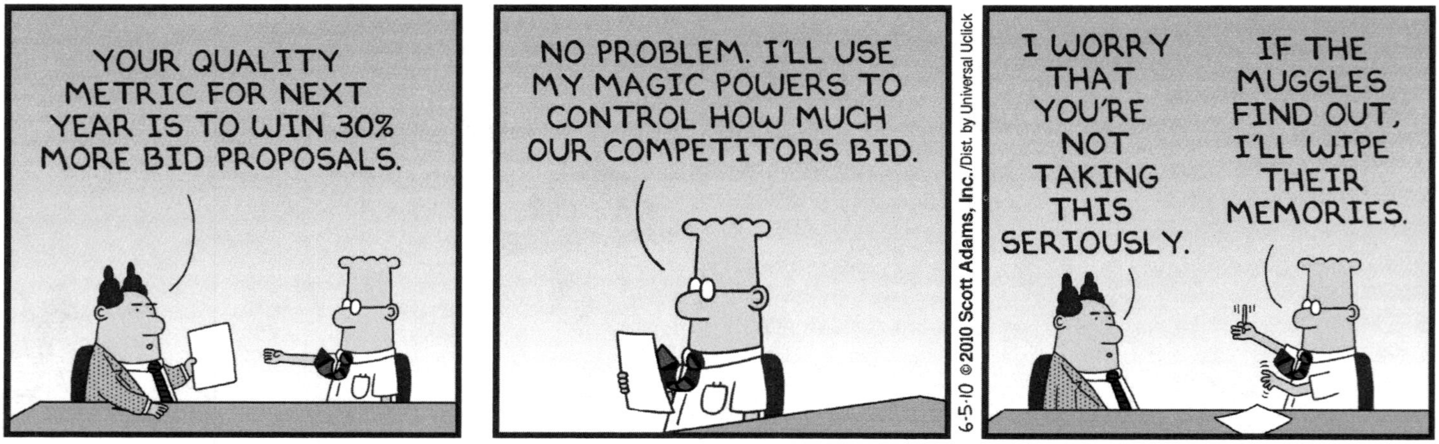
YOUR QUALITY METRIC FOR NEXT YEAR IS TO WIN 30% MORE BID PROPOSALS.
NO PROBLEM. I'LL USE MY MAGIC POWERS TO CONTROL HOW MUCH OUR COMPETITORS BID.
6-5-10 ©2010 Scott Adams, Inc./Dist. by Universal Uclick
I WORRY THAT YOU'RE NOT TAKING THIS SERIOUSLY.
IF THE MUGGLES FIND OUT, I'LL WIPE THEIR MEMORIES.

I'M COLLECTING MONEY FOR TED'S BIRTHDAY.
PASS.
I CAN'T STAND THAT IDIOT.
HIS FACE LOOKS LIKE A FERRET EATING A LEMON.
© 2010 Scott Adams, Inc./Dist. by Universal Uclick
HE MAKES MY SKIN CRAWL.
HE TELLS RACIST JOKES, AND I THINK HE'S EMBEZZLING.
I'VE BEEN DATING HIM FOR A MONTH.
6-6-10
I'D BE LYING IF I SAID THAT WASN'T WORTH A DOLLAR.

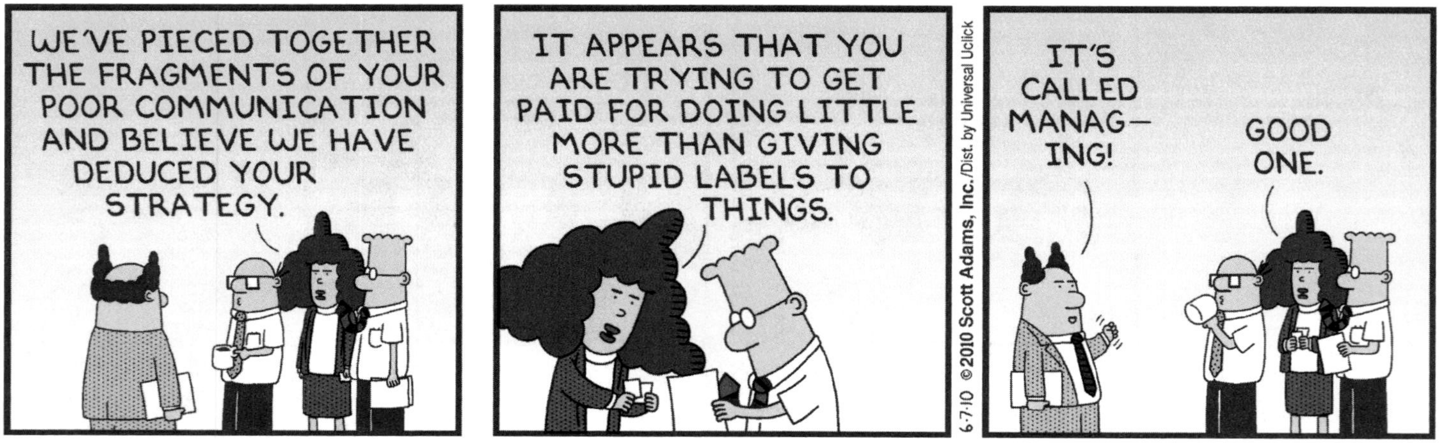
WE'VE PIECED TOGETHER THE FRAGMENTS OF YOUR POOR COMMUNICATION AND BELIEVE WE HAVE DEDUCED YOUR STRATEGY.
IT APPEARS THAT YOU ARE TRYING TO GET PAID FOR DOING LITTLE MORE THAN GIVING STUPID LABELS TO THINGS.
IT'S CALLED MANAG-ING!
GOOD ONE.
6-7-10 © 2010 Scott Adams, Inc./Dist. by Universal Uclick

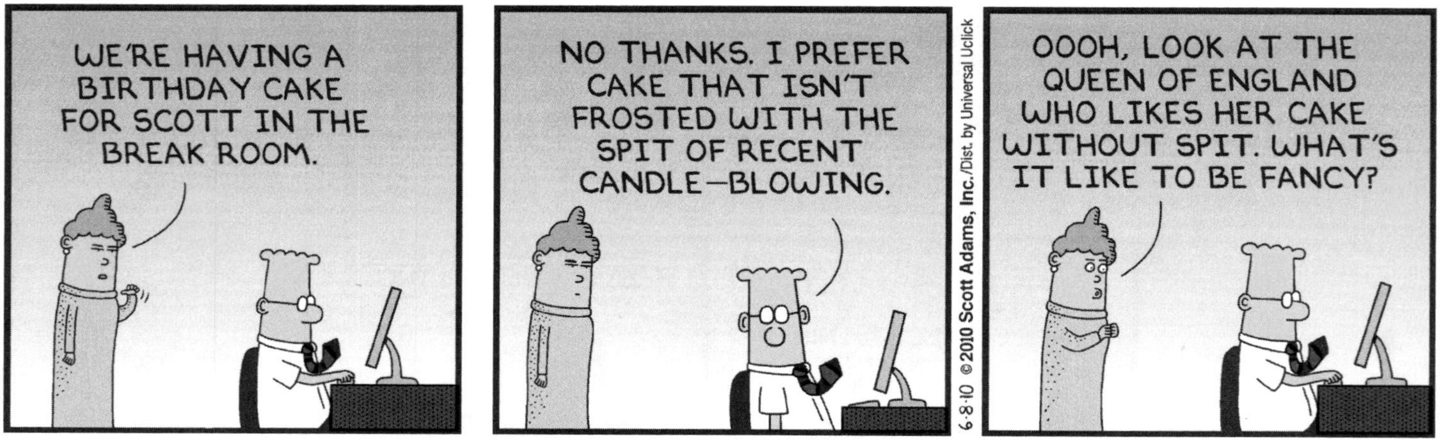
WE'RE HAVING A BIRTHDAY CAKE FOR SCOTT IN THE BREAK ROOM.
NO THANKS. I PREFER CAKE THAT ISN'T FROSTED WITH THE SPIT OF RECENT CANDLE-BLOWING.
OOOH, LOOK AT THE QUEEN OF ENGLAND WHO LIKES HER CAKE WITHOUT SPIT. WHAT'S IT LIKE TO BE FANCY?
6-8-10 © 2010 Scott Adams, Inc./Dist. by Universal Uclick

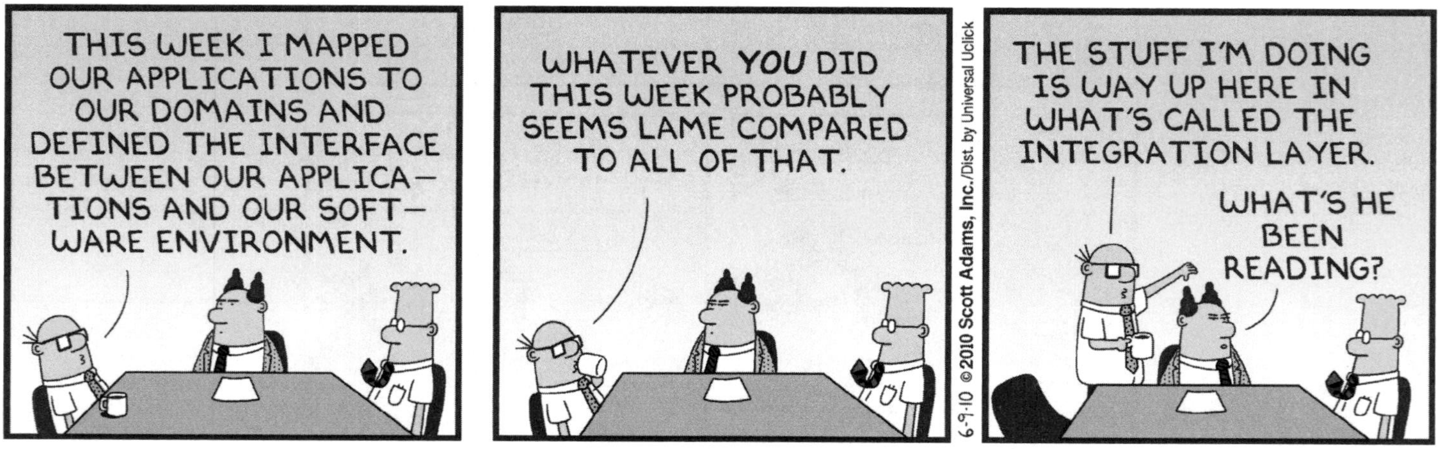
THIS WEEK I MAPPED OUR APPLICATIONS TO OUR DOMAINS AND DEFINED THE INTERFACE BETWEEN OUR APPLICA-TIONS AND OUR SOFT-WARE ENVIRONMENT.
WHATEVER *YOU* DID THIS WEEK PROBABLY SEEMS LAME COMPARED TO ALL OF THAT.
THE STUFF I'M DOING IS WAY UP HERE IN WHAT'S CALLED THE INTEGRATION LAYER.
WHAT'S HE BEEN READING?
6-9-10 © 2010 Scott Adams, Inc./Dist. by Universal Uclick

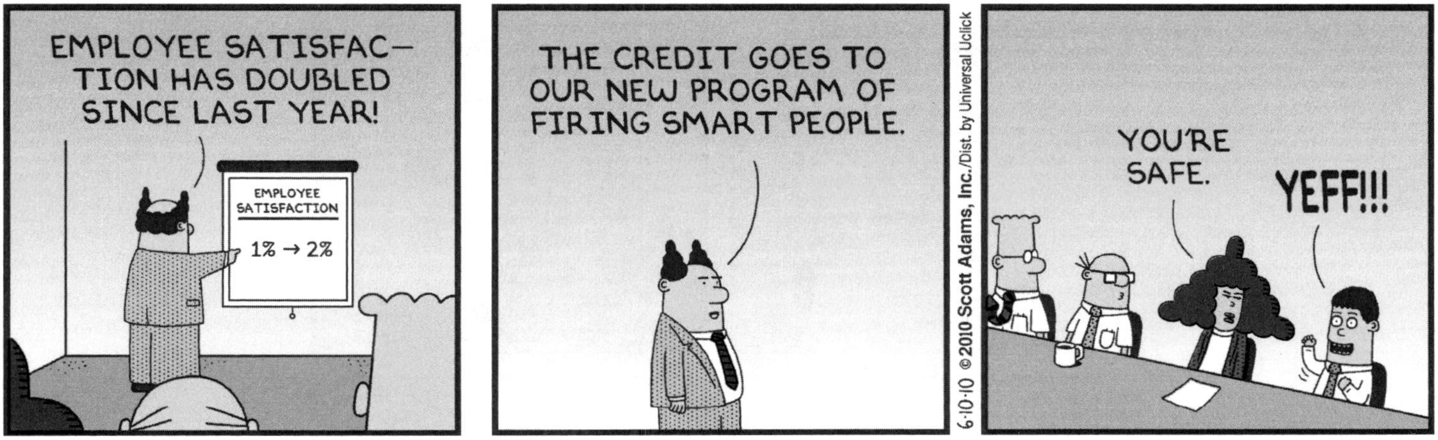
EMPLOYEE SATISFAC-TION HAS DOUBLED SINCE LAST YEAR!
EMPLOYEE SATISFACTION
1% → 2%
THE CREDIT GOES TO OUR NEW PROGRAM OF FIRING SMART PEOPLE.
6·10·10 ©2010 Scott Adams, Inc./Dist. by Universal Uclick
YOU'RE SAFE.
YEFF!!!

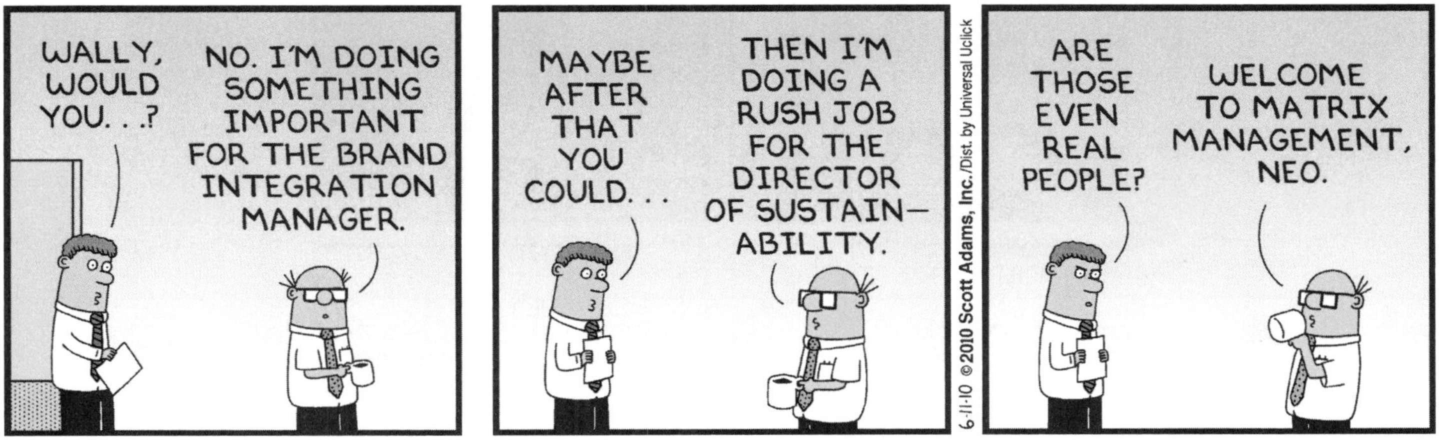
WALLY, WOULD YOU. . .?
NO. I'M DOING SOMETHING IMPORTANT FOR THE BRAND INTEGRATION MANAGER.
MAYBE AFTER THAT YOU COULD. . .
THEN I'M DOING A RUSH JOB FOR THE DIRECTOR OF SUSTAIN-ABILITY.
6·11·10 ©2010 Scott Adams, Inc./Dist. by Universal Uclick
ARE THOSE EVEN REAL PEOPLE?
WELCOME TO MATRIX MANAGEMENT, NEO.

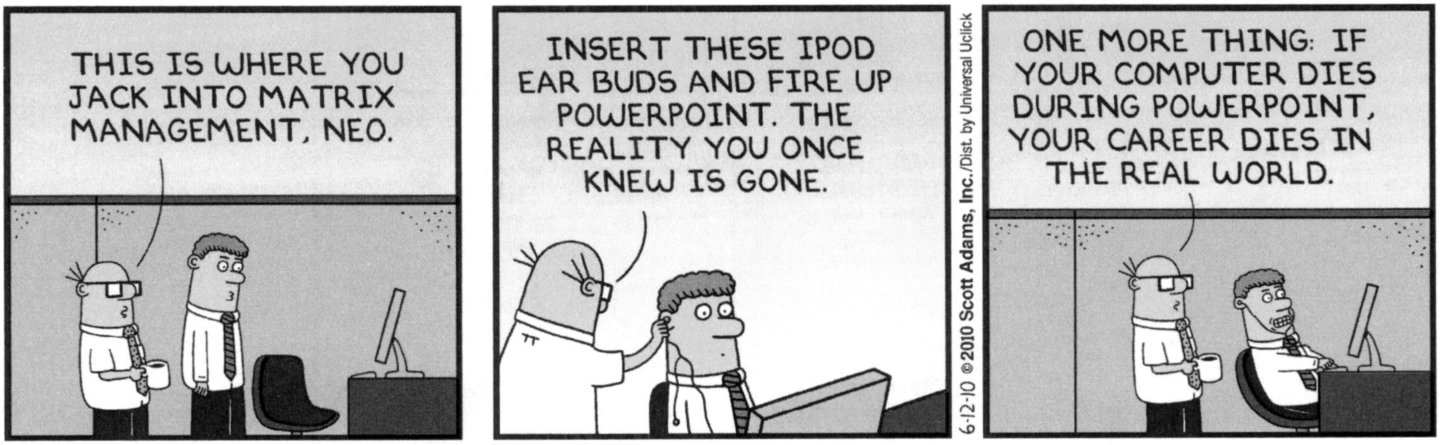
THIS IS WHERE YOU JACK INTO MATRIX MANAGEMENT, NEO.
INSERT THESE IPOD EAR BUDS AND FIRE UP POWERPOINT. THE REALITY YOU ONCE KNEW IS GONE.
6·12·10 ©2010 Scott Adams, Inc./Dist. by Universal Uclick
ONE MORE THING: IF YOUR COMPUTER DIES DURING POWERPOINT, YOUR CAREER DIES IN THE REAL WORLD.

DOGBERT CONSULTS

A GOOD LEADER CULTIVATES INTERNAL CRITICS SO ALL SIDES OF AN ARGUMENT ARE HEARD.

FOR EXAMPLE, I CULTIVATED DILBERT TO ARGUE THE POINT I JUST MADE.

YOUR PREMISE IS THAT A LEADER IS NOT QUALIFIED TO MAKE DECISIONS WITHOUT THE HELP OF CRITICS.

BUT SELECTING THE APPROPRIATE CRITIC IS *ITSELF* A DECISION.

©2010 Scott Adams, Inc. /Dist. by Universal Uclick

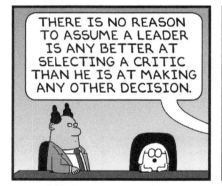

THERE IS NO REASON TO ASSUME A LEADER IS ANY BETTER AT SELECTING A CRITIC THAN HE IS AT MAKING ANY OTHER DECISION.

YOUR OVERPAID CONSULTANT IS RECOMMENDING THAT YOU ADD RANDOMNESS TO AN ALREADY FLAWED PROCESS.

IN SUMMARY, THIS MEETING IS A WASTE OF TIME, AND YOUR CONSULTANT IS RIPPING YOU OFF.

HOW GREAT WAS THAT?

YOU OWE ME $400 FOR MY TIME.

6-13-10

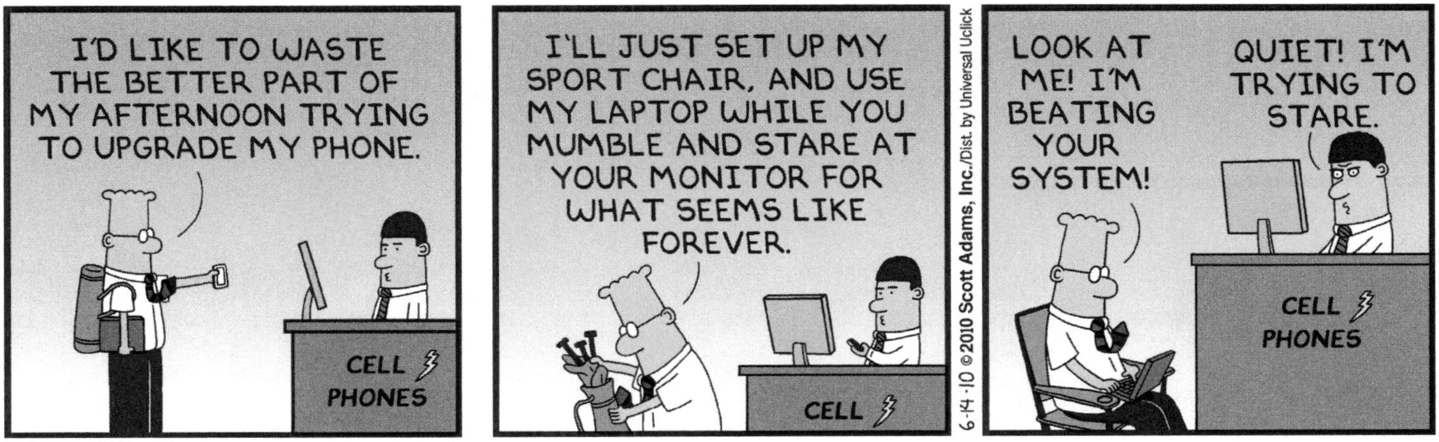
I'D LIKE TO WASTE THE BETTER PART OF MY AFTERNOON TRYING TO UPGRADE MY PHONE.
CELL PHONES
I'LL JUST SET UP MY SPORT CHAIR, AND USE MY LAPTOP WHILE YOU MUMBLE AND STARE AT YOUR MONITOR FOR WHAT SEEMS LIKE FOREVER.
CELL
6-14-10 © 2010 Scott Adams, Inc./Dist. by Universal Uclick
LOOK AT ME! I'M BEATING YOUR SYSTEM!
QUIET! I'M TRYING TO STARE.
CELL PHONES

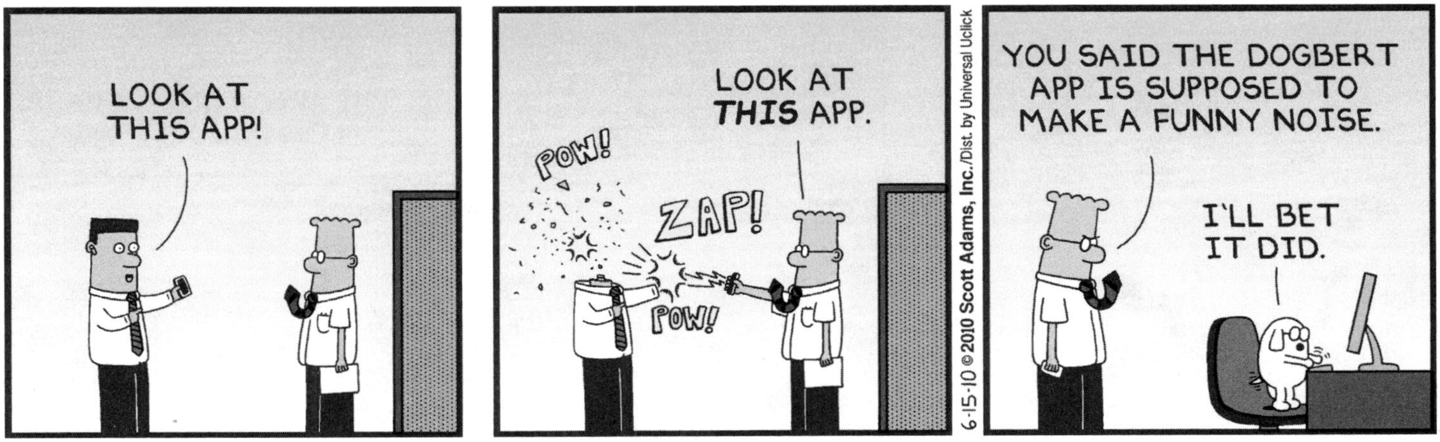
LOOK AT THIS APP!
POW!
ZAP!
POW!
LOOK AT **THIS** APP.
6-15-10 © 2010 Scott Adams, Inc./Dist. by Universal Uclick
YOU SAID THE DOGBERT APP IS SUPPOSED TO MAKE A FUNNY NOISE.
I'LL BET IT DID.

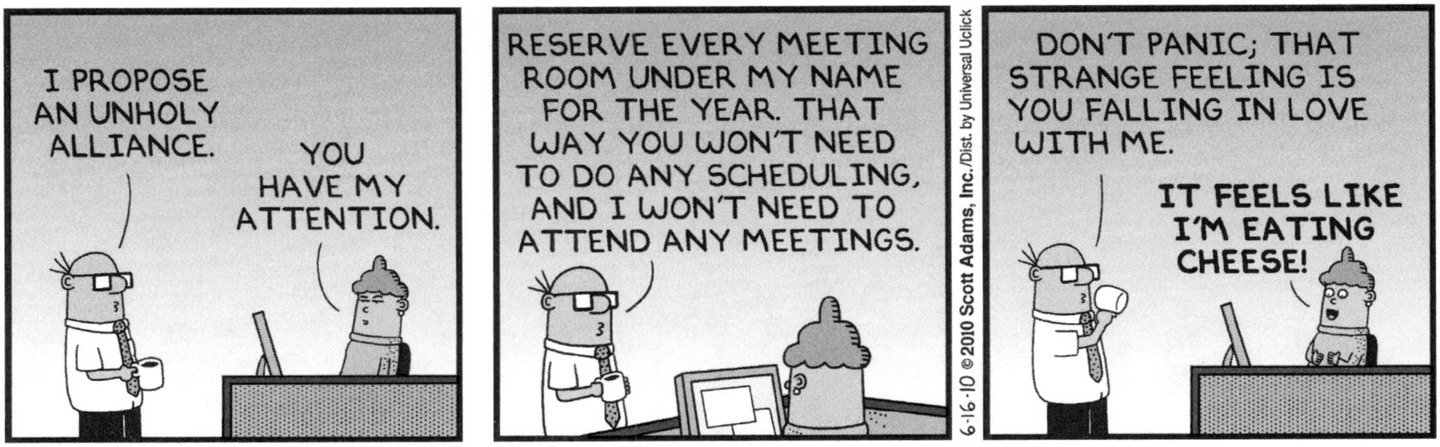
I PROPOSE AN UNHOLY ALLIANCE.
YOU HAVE MY ATTENTION.
RESERVE EVERY MEETING ROOM UNDER MY NAME FOR THE YEAR. THAT WAY YOU WON'T NEED TO DO ANY SCHEDULING, AND I WON'T NEED TO ATTEND ANY MEETINGS.
6-16-10 © 2010 Scott Adams, Inc./Dist. by Universal Uclick
DON'T PANIC; THAT STRANGE FEELING IS YOU FALLING IN LOVE WITH ME.
IT FEELS LIKE I'M EATING CHEESE!

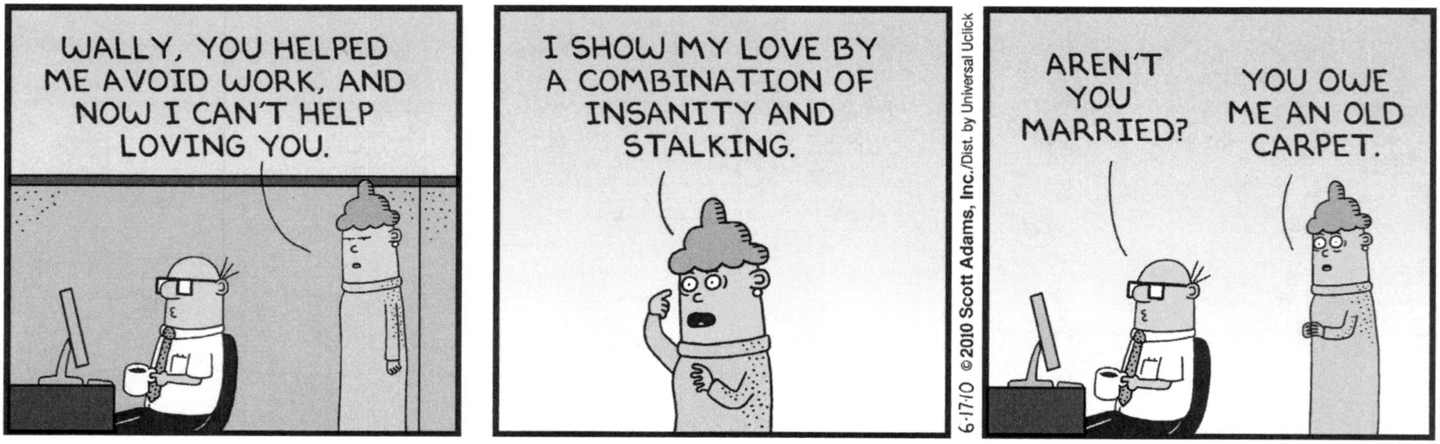
WALLY, YOU HELPED ME AVOID WORK, AND NOW I CAN'T HELP LOVING YOU.
I SHOW MY LOVE BY A COMBINATION OF INSANITY AND STALKING.
6-17-10 © 2010 Scott Adams, Inc./Dist. by Universal Uclick
AREN'T YOU MARRIED?
YOU OWE ME AN OLD CARPET.

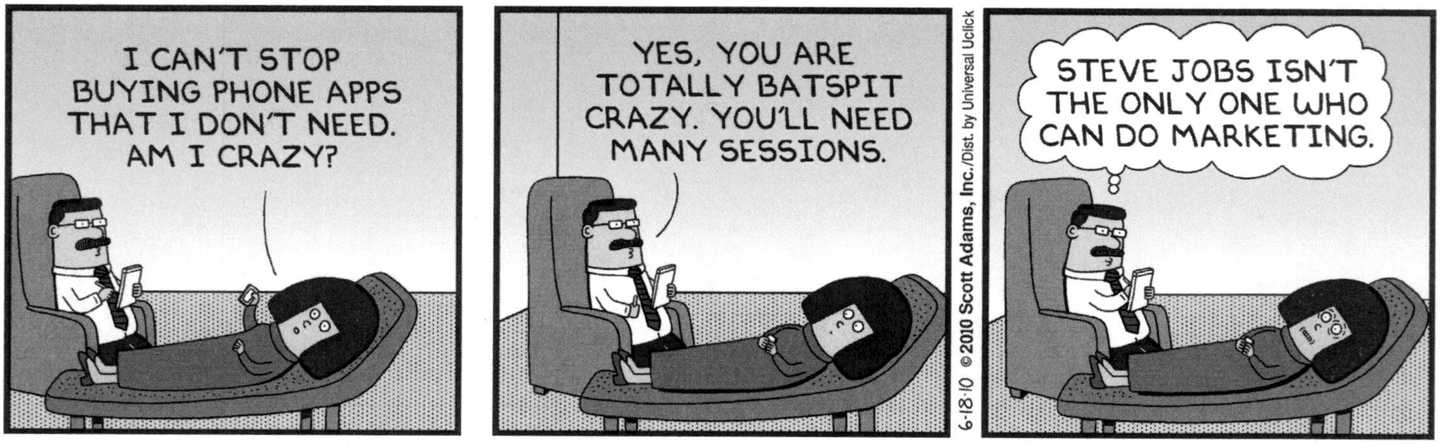
I CAN'T STOP BUYING PHONE APPS THAT I DON'T NEED. AM I CRAZY?
YES, YOU ARE TOTALLY BATSPIT CRAZY. YOU'LL NEED MANY SESSIONS.
6-18-10 © 2010 Scott Adams, Inc./Dist. by Universal Uclick
STEVE JOBS ISN'T THE ONLY ONE WHO CAN DO MARKETING.

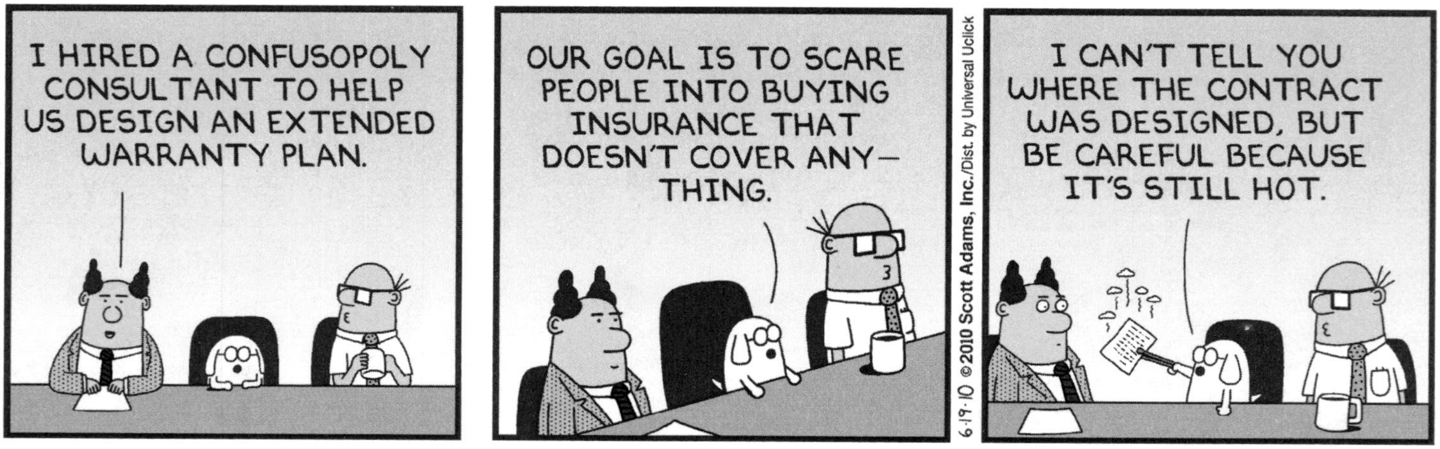
I HIRED A CONFUSOPOLY CONSULTANT TO HELP US DESIGN AN EXTENDED WARRANTY PLAN.
OUR GOAL IS TO SCARE PEOPLE INTO BUYING INSURANCE THAT DOESN'T COVER ANY-THING.
6-19-10 © 2010 Scott Adams, Inc./Dist. by Universal Uclick
I CAN'T TELL YOU WHERE THE CONTRACT WAS DESIGNED, BUT BE CAREFUL BECAUSE IT'S STILL HOT.

A GOOD LEADER USES A PROCESS FOR MAKING DECISIONS.
PROCESS
MAY I TAKE THIS ONE?
GO.
MAKE US PROUD.
QUESTION: IF MAKING A DECISION IS JUST A PROCESS, WHY CAN'T A COMPUTER DO IT?
BECAUSE SOMETIMES I HAVE TO RELY ON MY GUT.
WHICH PART OF YOUR GUT IS THE SMART PART? IS IT THE STOMACH LINING, OR MAYBE THE COLON?
I'M TALKING ABOUT INSTINCT. IT'S AN INDEFINABLE LEADER-SHIP QUALITY.
IS THE INDEFINABLE THING LIKE A SUPER-STITION?
OR COOTIES?
IT'S A PROCESS!
IS THAT YOUR COLON TALKING?
© 2010 Scott Adams, Inc./Dist. by Universal Uclick
6-20-10

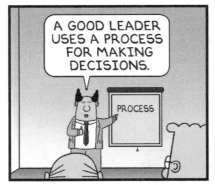

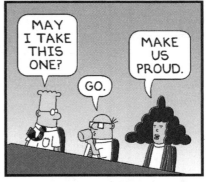

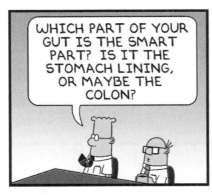

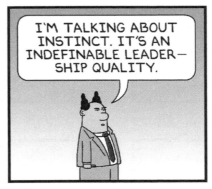

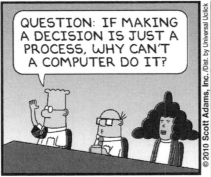

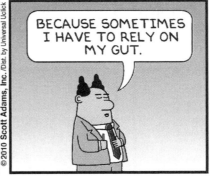

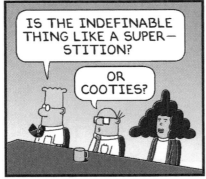

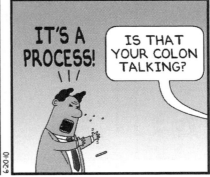

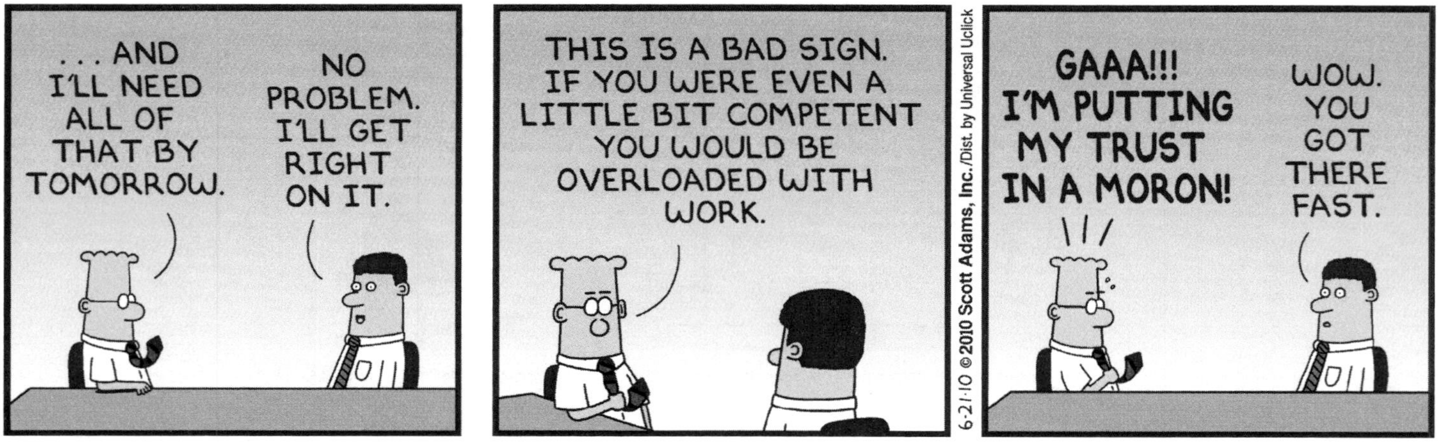
. . . AND I'LL NEED ALL OF THAT BY TOMORROW.
NO PROBLEM. I'LL GET RIGHT ON IT.
THIS IS A BAD SIGN. IF YOU WERE EVEN A LITTLE BIT COMPETENT YOU WOULD BE OVERLOADED WITH WORK.
GAAA!!! I'M PUTTING MY TRUST IN A MORON!
WOW. YOU GOT THERE FAST.
6·21·10 © 2010 Scott Adams, Inc./Dist. by Universal Uclick

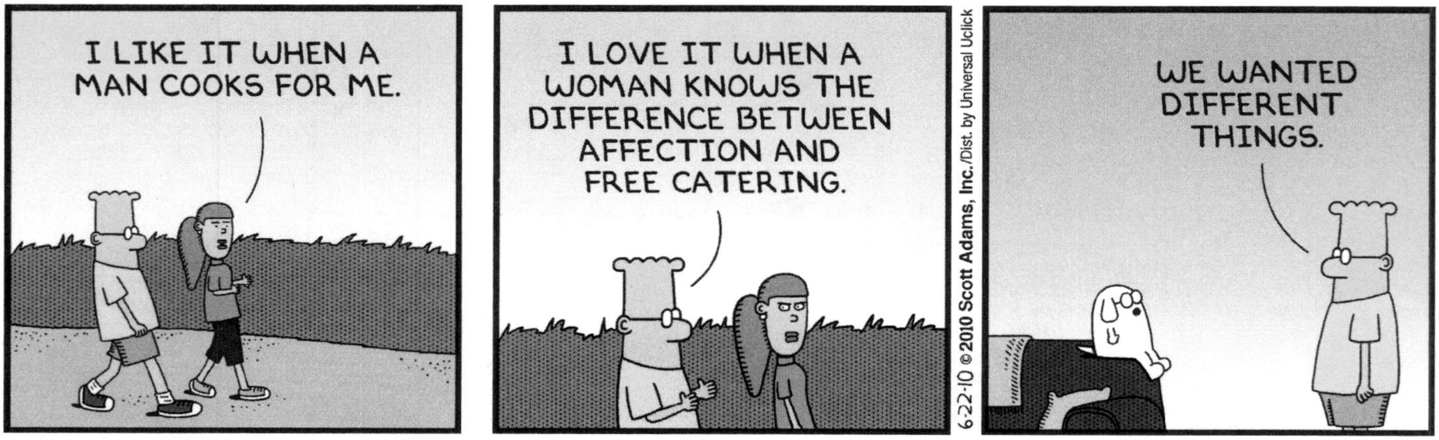
I LIKE IT WHEN A MAN COOKS FOR ME.
I LOVE IT WHEN A WOMAN KNOWS THE DIFFERENCE BETWEEN AFFECTION AND FREE CATERING.
WE WANTED DIFFERENT THINGS.
6·22·10 © 2010 Scott Adams, Inc./Dist. by Universal Uclick

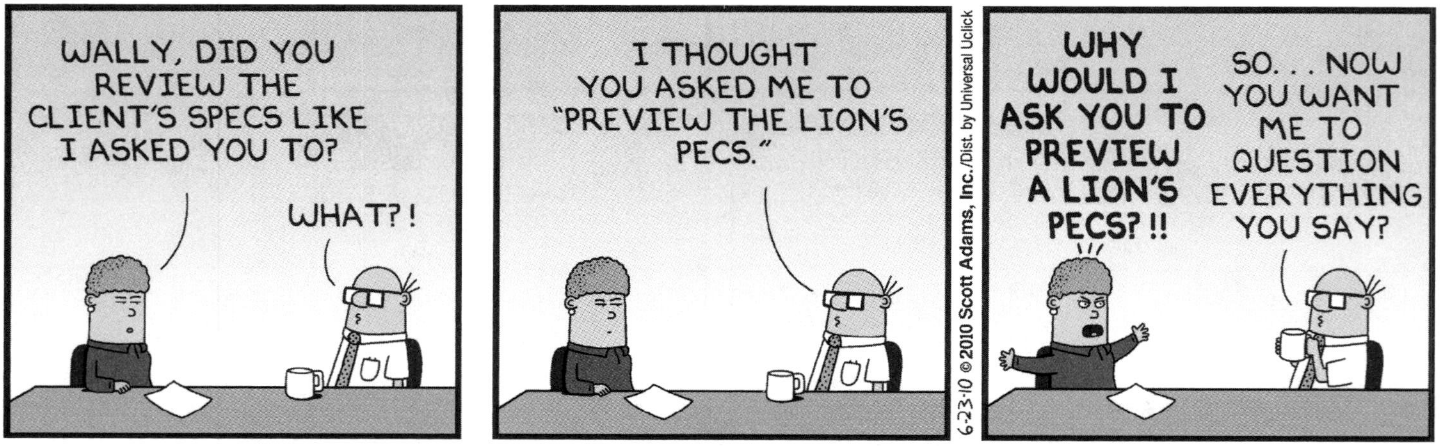
WALLY, DID YOU REVIEW THE CLIENT'S SPECS LIKE I ASKED YOU TO?
WHAT?!
I THOUGHT YOU ASKED ME TO "PREVIEW THE LION'S PECS."
WHY WOULD I ASK YOU TO PREVIEW A LION'S PECS?!!
SO. . . NOW YOU WANT ME TO QUESTION EVERYTHING YOU SAY?
6·23·10 © 2010 Scott Adams, Inc./Dist. by Universal Uclick

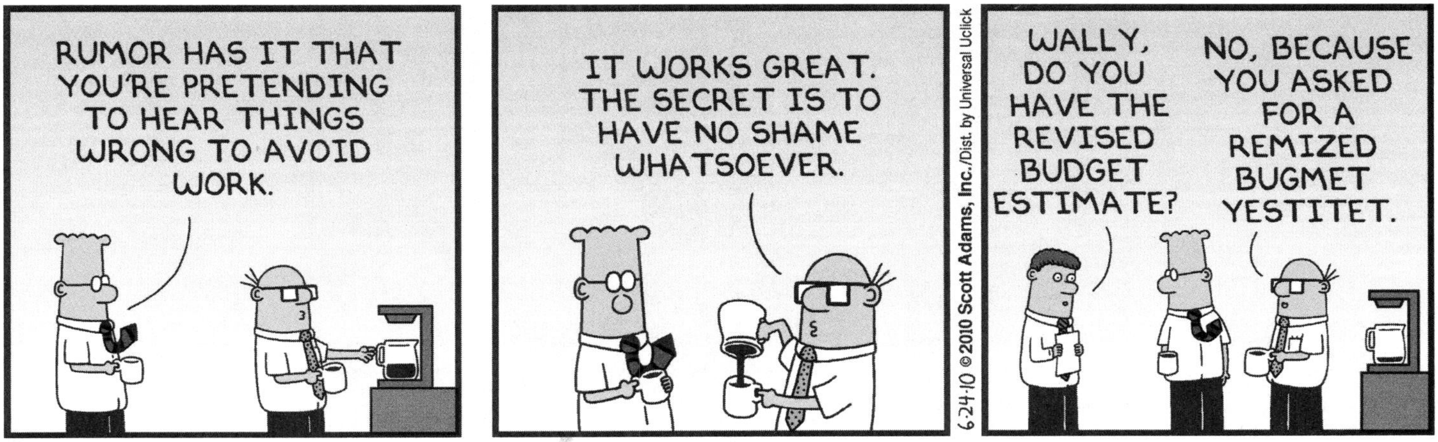
RUMOR HAS IT THAT YOU'RE PRETENDING TO HEAR THINGS WRONG TO AVOID WORK.
IT WORKS GREAT. THE SECRET IS TO HAVE NO SHAME WHATSOEVER.
6·24·10 © 2010 Scott Adams, Inc./Dist. by Universal Uclick
WALLY, DO YOU HAVE THE REVISED BUDGET ESTIMATE?
NO, BECAUSE YOU ASKED FOR A REMIZED BUGMET YESTITET.

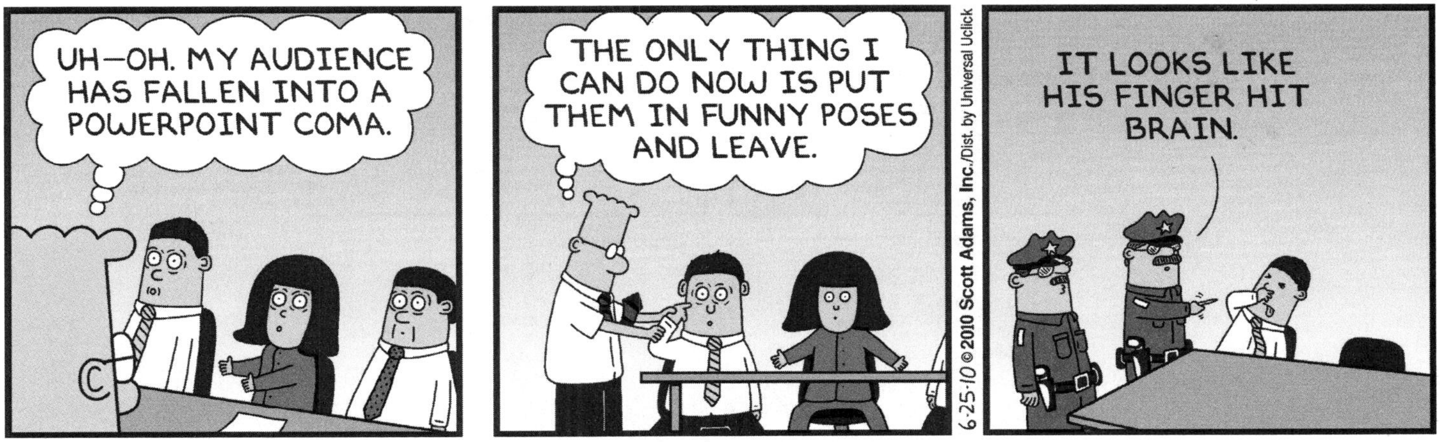
UH-OH. MY AUDIENCE HAS FALLEN INTO A POWERPOINT COMA.
THE ONLY THING I CAN DO NOW IS PUT THEM IN FUNNY POSES AND LEAVE.
6·25·10 © 2010 Scott Adams, Inc./Dist. by Universal Uclick
IT LOOKS LIKE HIS FINGER HIT BRAIN.

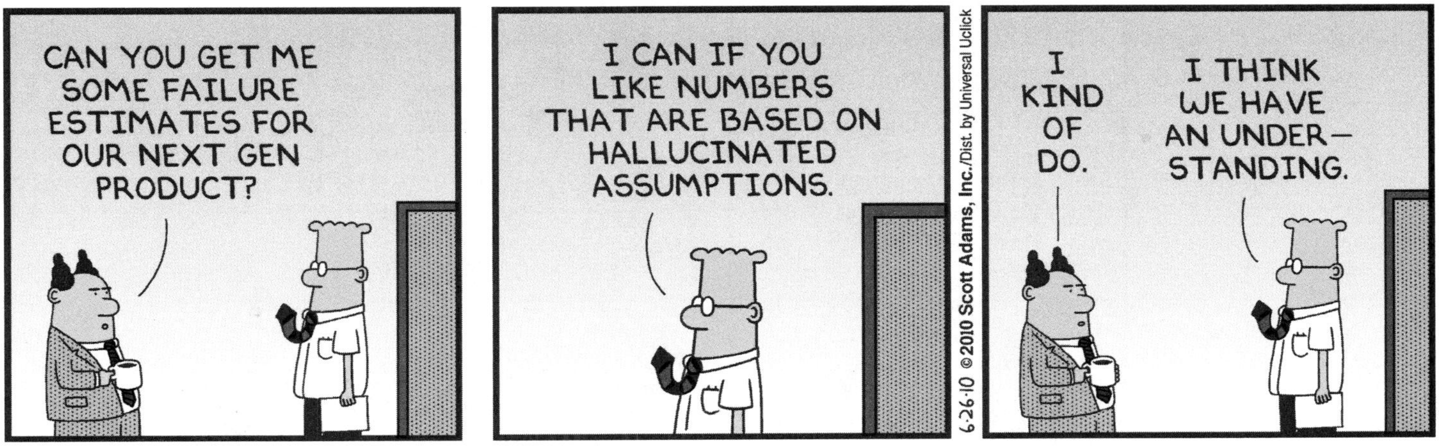
CAN YOU GET ME SOME FAILURE ESTIMATES FOR OUR NEXT GEN PRODUCT?
I CAN IF YOU LIKE NUMBERS THAT ARE BASED ON HALLUCINATED ASSUMPTIONS.
6·26·10 © 2010 Scott Adams, Inc./Dist. by Universal Uclick
I KIND OF DO.
I THINK WE HAVE AN UNDER-STANDING.

I NEED HELP WITH MY COMPUTER.
IT'S A TRAP!
IF I TOUCH YOUR COMPUTER, YOU'LL THINK THAT EVERY FUTURE PROBLEM IS CAUSED BY SOME-THING I DID.
YOU'LL TELL EVERYONE I RUINED YOUR COMPUTER!
I'LL BE OBLIGATED TO SOLVE EVERY COMPUTER PROBLEM YOU HAVE FROM THIS DAY ON.
MY OWN PROJECTS WILL BE LEFT TO WITHER AS I SHOW YOU FOR THE NINETIETH TIME HOW TO SELECT A NEW FONT.
IF I REFUSE TO HELP, YOU'LL TELL MY BOSS I'M NOT A TEAM PLAYER.
DO YOU NEED A HUG?
ONLY IF YOU CAN SQUEEZE HARD ENOUGH TO KILL ME.
©2010 Scott Adams, Inc./Dist. by Universal Uclick
6-27-10

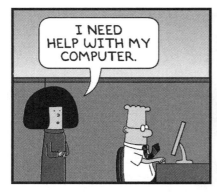

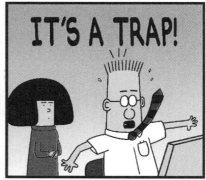

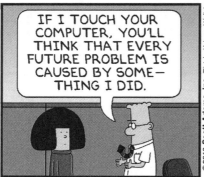

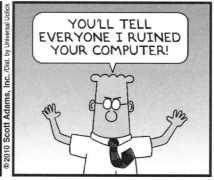

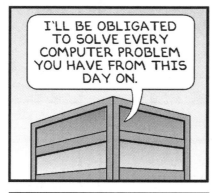

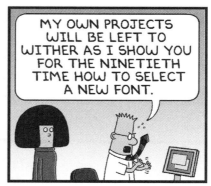

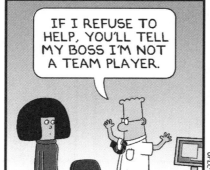

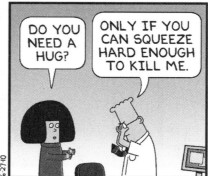

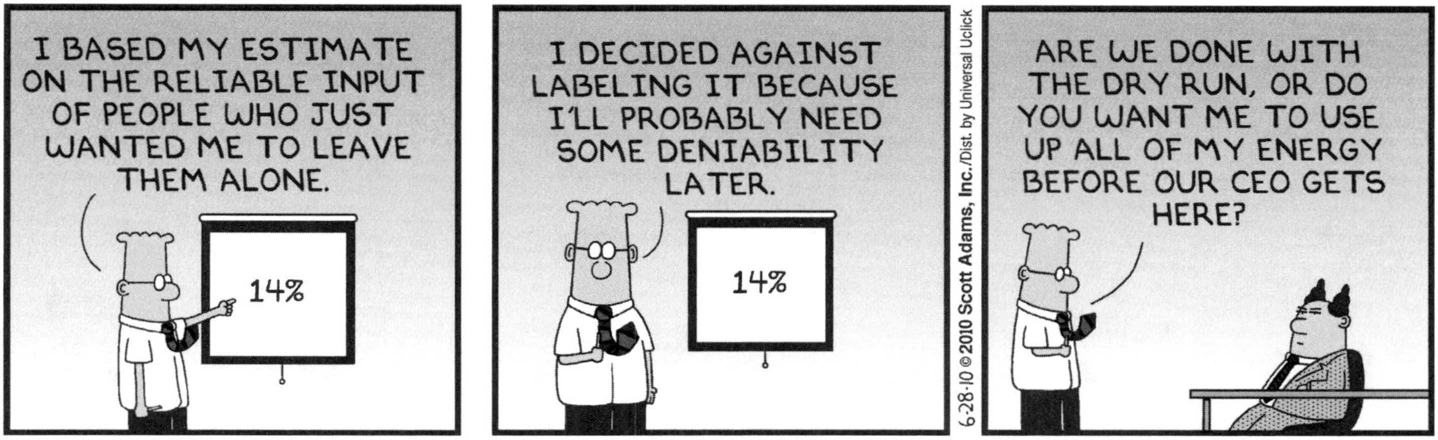
I BASED MY ESTIMATE ON THE RELIABLE INPUT OF PEOPLE WHO JUST WANTED ME TO LEAVE THEM ALONE.
14%
I DECIDED AGAINST LABELING IT BECAUSE I'LL PROBABLY NEED SOME DENIABILITY LATER.
14%
6-28-10 © 2010 Scott Adams, Inc./Dist. by Universal Uclick
ARE WE DONE WITH THE DRY RUN, OR DO YOU WANT ME TO USE UP ALL OF MY ENERGY BEFORE OUR CEO GETS HERE?

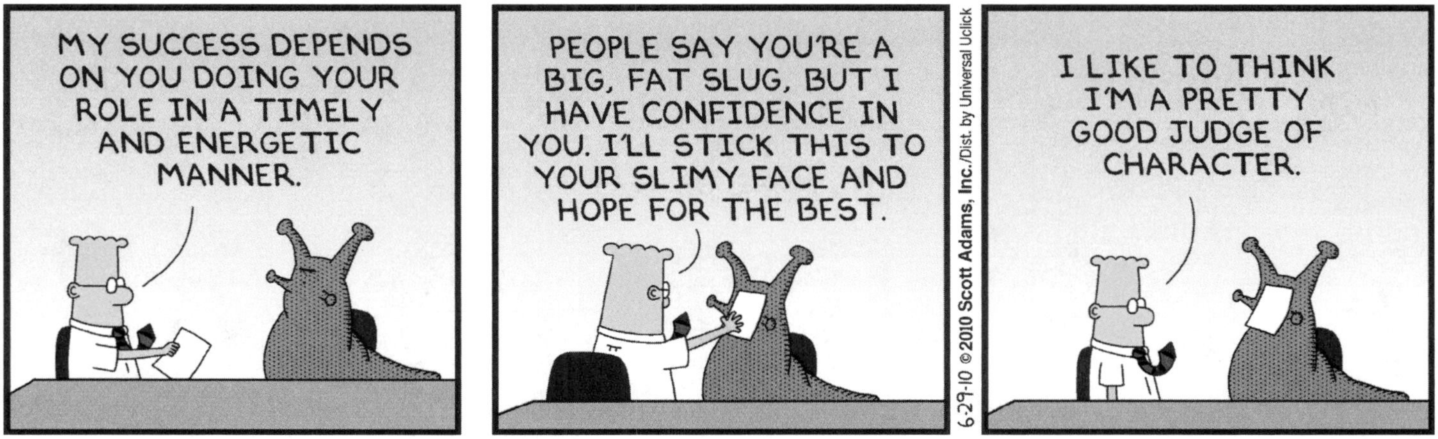
MY SUCCESS DEPENDS ON YOU DOING YOUR ROLE IN A TIMELY AND ENERGETIC MANNER.
PEOPLE SAY YOU'RE A BIG, FAT SLUG, BUT I HAVE CONFIDENCE IN YOU. I'LL STICK THIS TO YOUR SLIMY FACE AND HOPE FOR THE BEST.
6-29-10 © 2010 Scott Adams, Inc./Dist. by Universal Uclick
I LIKE TO THINK I'M A PRETTY GOOD JUDGE OF CHARACTER.

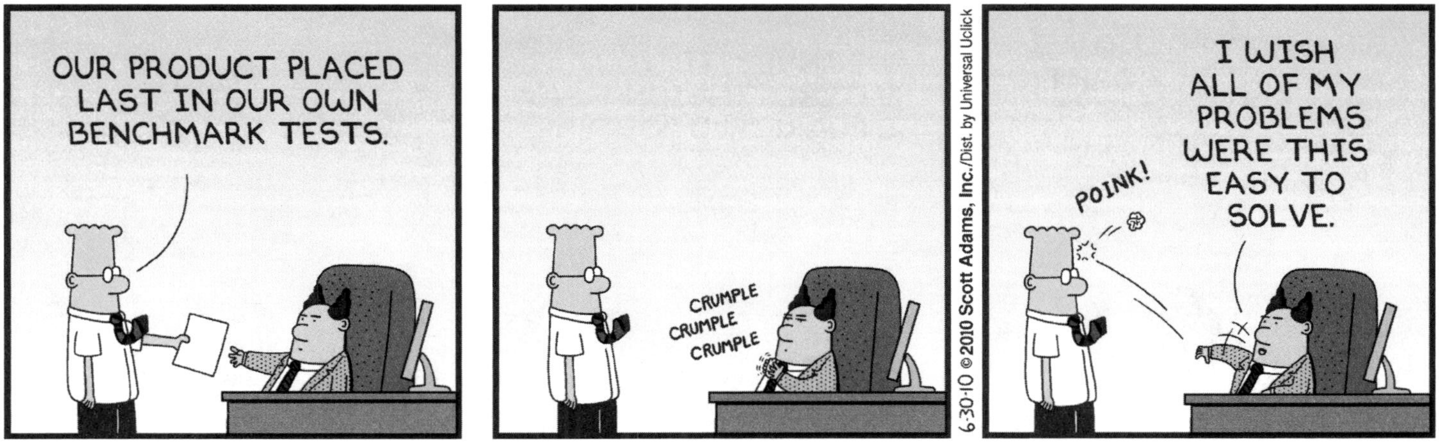
OUR PRODUCT PLACED LAST IN OUR OWN BENCHMARK TESTS.
CRUMPLE
CRUMPLE
CRUMPLE
6-30-10 © 2010 Scott Adams, Inc./Dist. by Universal Uclick
POINK!
I WISH ALL OF MY PROBLEMS WERE THIS EASY TO SOLVE.

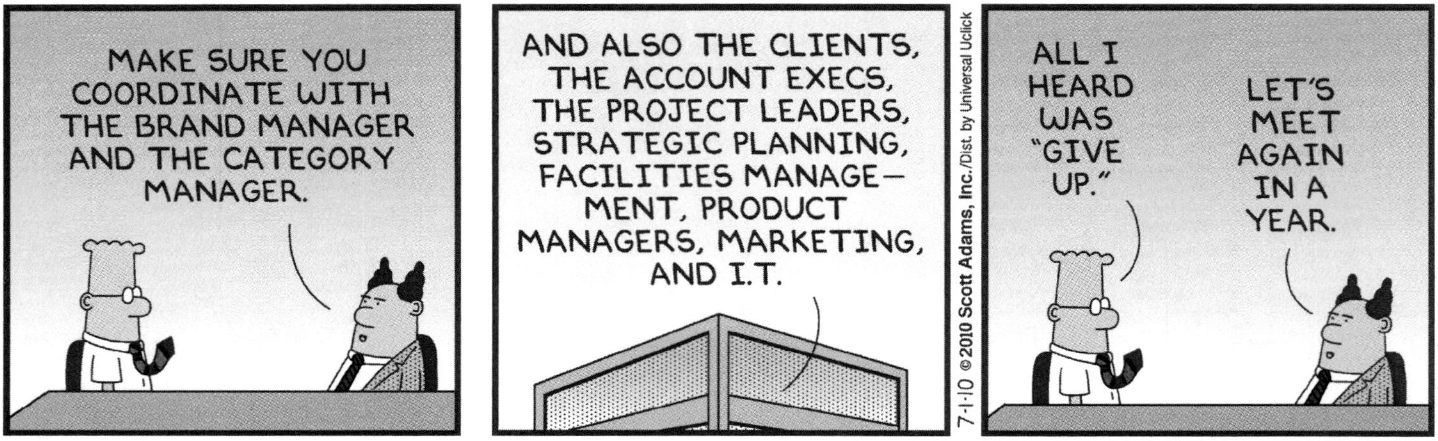
MAKE SURE YOU COORDINATE WITH THE BRAND MANAGER AND THE CATEGORY MANAGER.
AND ALSO THE CLIENTS, THE ACCOUNT EXECS, THE PROJECT LEADERS, STRATEGIC PLANNING, FACILITIES MANAGE-MENT, PRODUCT MANAGERS, MARKETING, AND I.T.
7-1-10 ©2010 Scott Adams, Inc./Dist. by Universal Uclick
ALL I HEARD WAS "GIVE UP."
LET'S MEET AGAIN IN A YEAR.

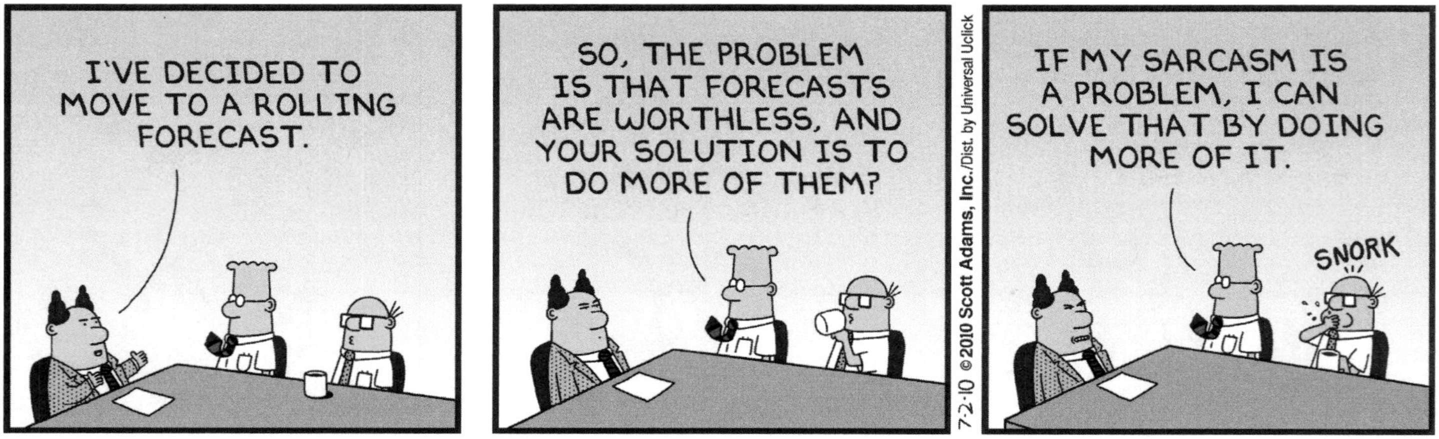
I'VE DECIDED TO MOVE TO A ROLLING FORECAST.
SO, THE PROBLEM IS THAT FORECASTS ARE WORTHLESS, AND YOUR SOLUTION IS TO DO MORE OF THEM?
7-2-10 ©2010 Scott Adams, Inc./Dist. by Universal Uclick
IF MY SARCASM IS A PROBLEM, I CAN SOLVE THAT BY DOING MORE OF IT.
SNORK

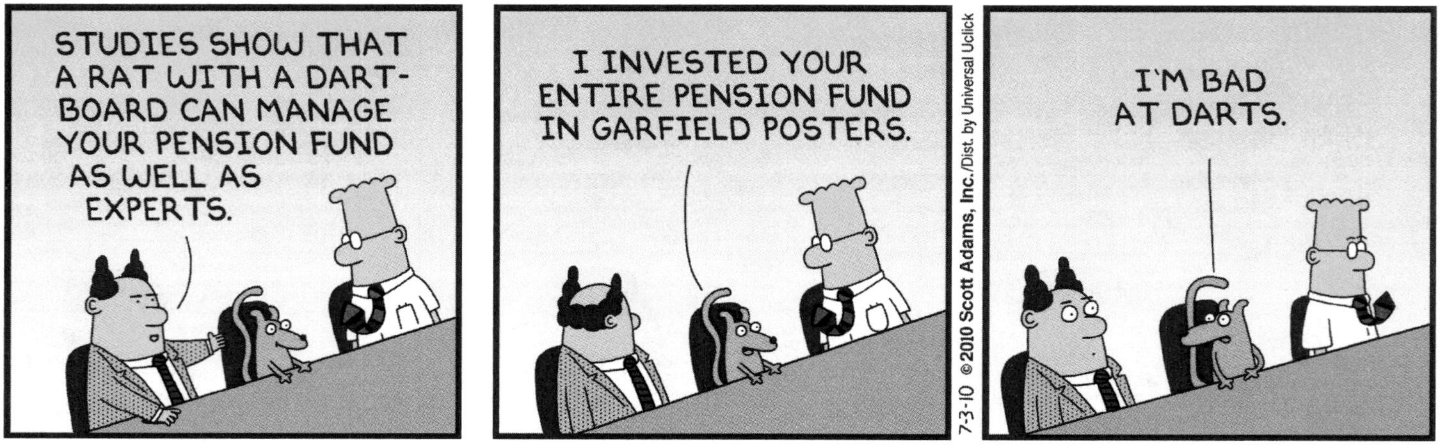
STUDIES SHOW THAT A RAT WITH A DART-BOARD CAN MANAGE YOUR PENSION FUND AS WELL AS EXPERTS.
I INVESTED YOUR ENTIRE PENSION FUND IN GARFIELD POSTERS.
7-3-10 ©2010 Scott Adams, Inc./Dist. by Universal Uclick
I'M BAD AT DARTS.

WALLY, CAN YOU RESPOND TO THIS RFQ BY TOMORROW?
THAT DEPENDS.
I TAKE A DISCIPLINED APPROACH TO ALLOCATING MY LIMITED RESOURCES.
FIRST, I'LL NEED TO EVALUATE ALL OF THE ALTERNATIVE USES FOR MY TIME.
IF DOING THIS RFQ THING COMES OUT ON TOP, THEN YES, I CAN DO IT.
WHEN DO YOU THINK YOU WILL KNOW THAT?
MAYBE NEXT WEEK.
UNLESS SOMETHING COMES UP.
SO. . . YOU'RE USELESS.
I DON'T SEE *YOU* GETTING MUCH DONE RIGHT NOW EITHER.
DID YOU KNOW THAT BEING DISCIPLINED IS ALMOST THE SAME AS BEING USELESS?
YODA? IS THAT YOU?
©2010 Scott Adams, Inc./Dist. by Universal Uclick
7-4-10

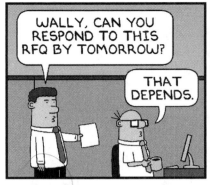

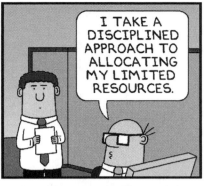

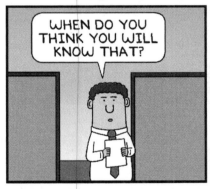

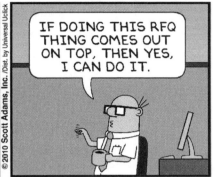

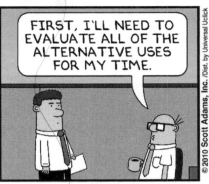

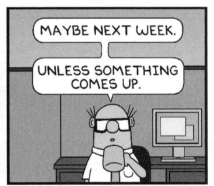

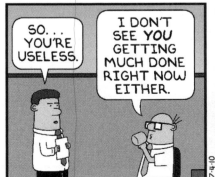

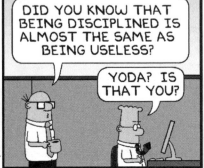

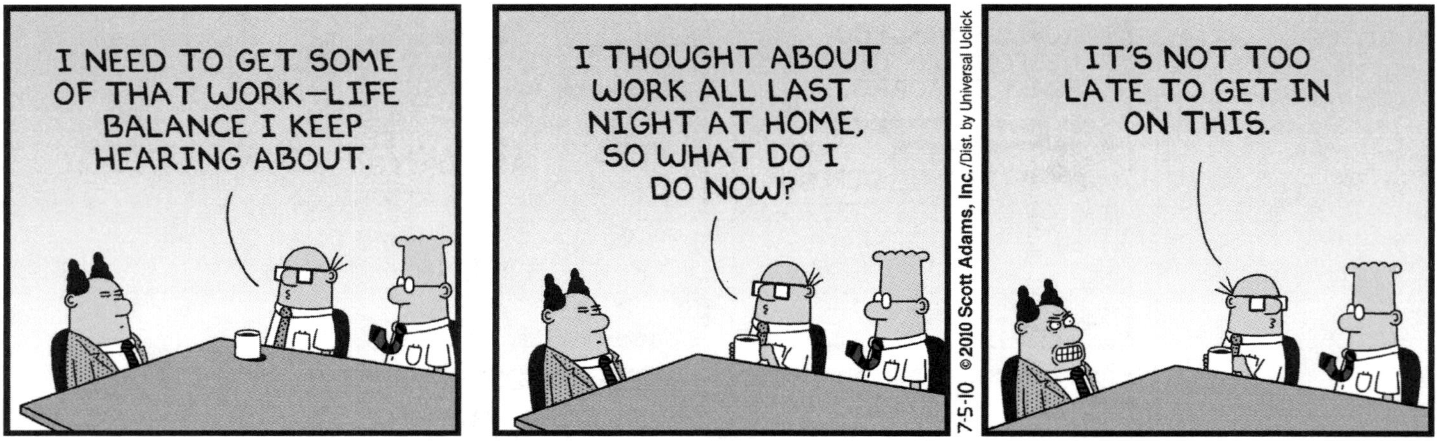
I NEED TO GET SOME OF THAT WORK—LIFE BALANCE I KEEP HEARING ABOUT.
I THOUGHT ABOUT WORK ALL LAST NIGHT AT HOME, SO WHAT DO I DO NOW?
7-5-10 ©2010 Scott Adams, Inc./Dist. by Universal Uclick
IT'S NOT TOO LATE TO GET IN ON THIS.

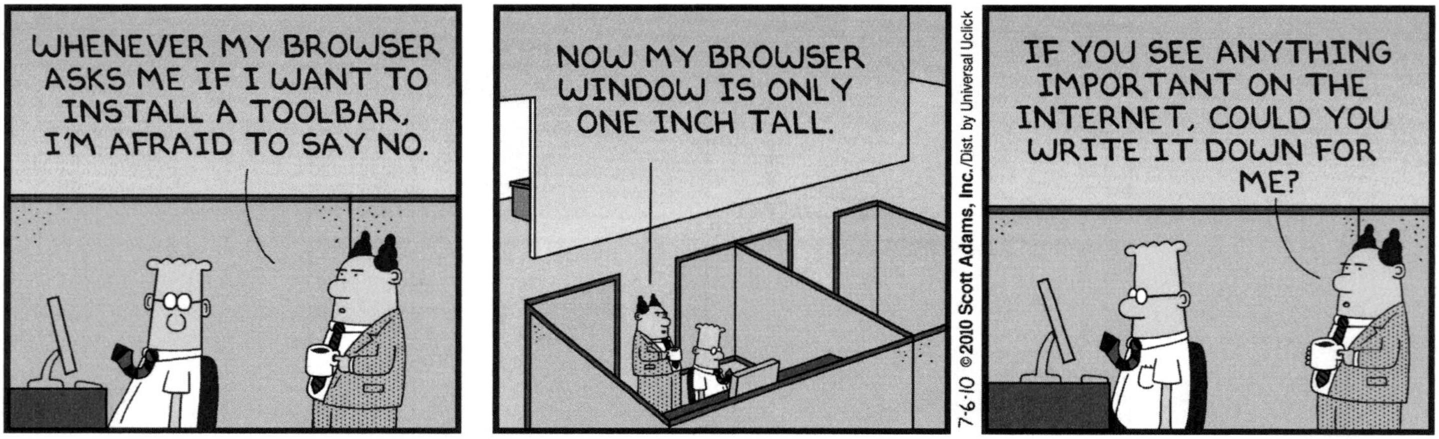
WHENEVER MY BROWSER ASKS ME IF I WANT TO INSTALL A TOOLBAR, I'M AFRAID TO SAY NO.
NOW MY BROWSER WINDOW IS ONLY ONE INCH TALL.
7-6-10 ©2010 Scott Adams, Inc./Dist. by Universal Uclick
IF YOU SEE ANYTHING IMPORTANT ON THE INTERNET, COULD YOU WRITE IT DOWN FOR ME?

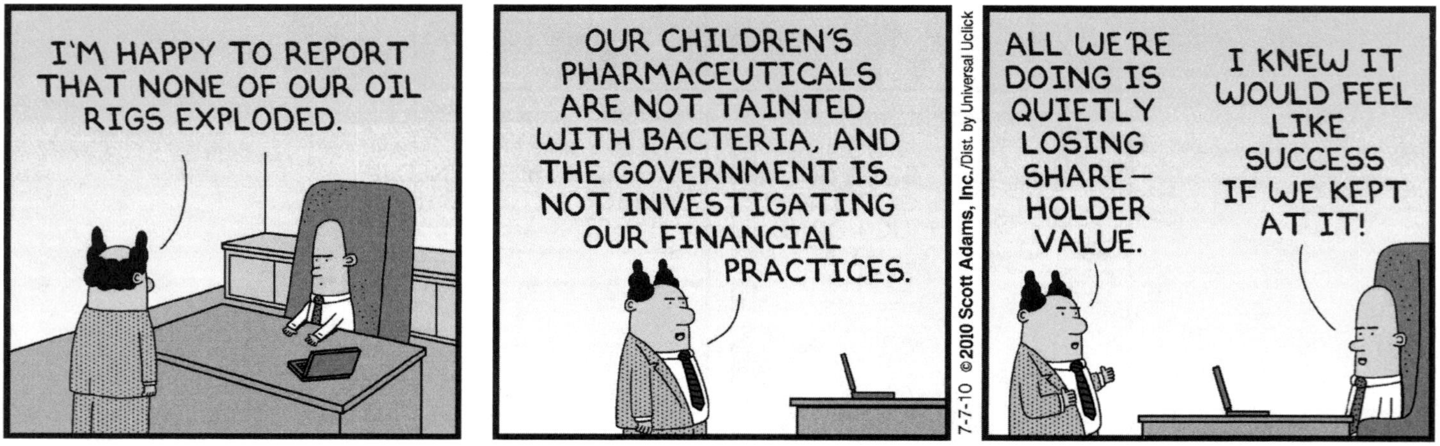
I'M HAPPY TO REPORT THAT NONE OF OUR OIL RIGS EXPLODED.
OUR CHILDREN'S PHARMACEUTICALS ARE NOT TAINTED WITH BACTERIA, AND THE GOVERNMENT IS NOT INVESTIGATING OUR FINANCIAL PRACTICES.
7-7-10 ©2010 Scott Adams, Inc./Dist. by Universal Uclick
ALL WE'RE DOING IS QUIETLY LOSING SHARE-HOLDER VALUE.
I KNEW IT WOULD FEEL LIKE SUCCESS IF WE KEPT AT IT!

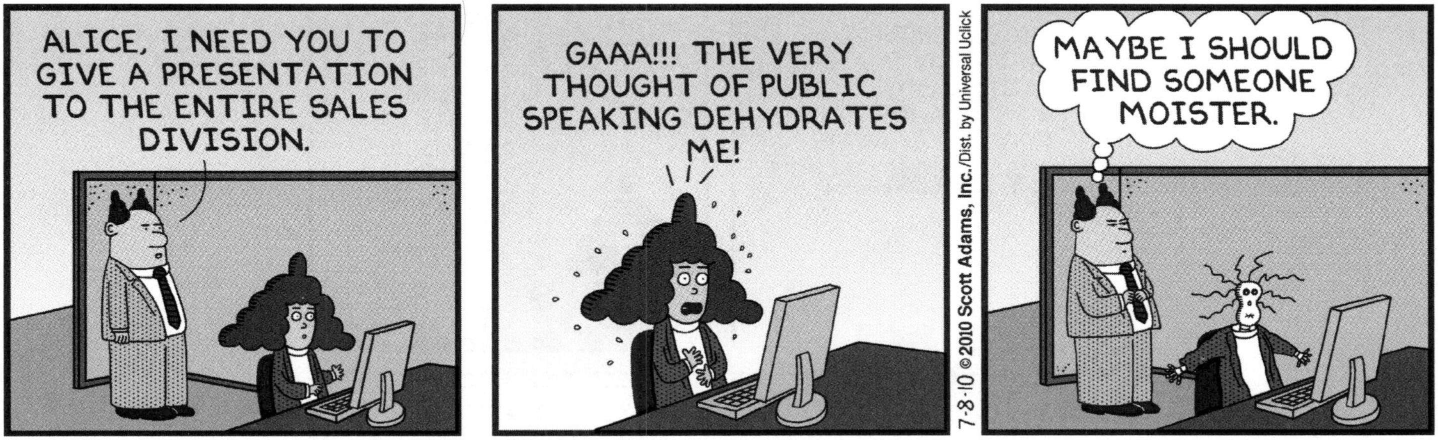
ALICE, I NEED YOU TO GIVE A PRESENTATION TO THE ENTIRE SALES DIVISION.
GAAA!!! THE VERY THOUGHT OF PUBLIC SPEAKING DEHYDRATES ME!
7-8-10 © 2010 Scott Adams, Inc./Dist. by Universal Uclick
MAYBE I SHOULD FIND SOMEONE MOISTER.

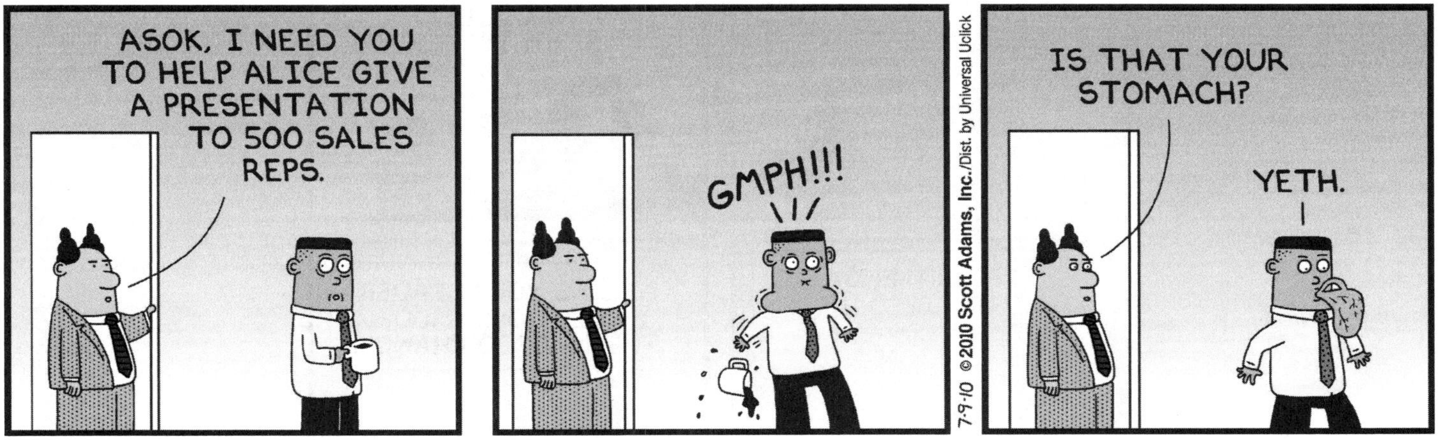
ASOK, I NEED YOU TO HELP ALICE GIVE A PRESENTATION TO 500 SALES REPS.
GMPH!!!
7-9-10 © 2010 Scott Adams, Inc./Dist. by Universal Uclick
IS THAT YOUR STOMACH?
YETH.

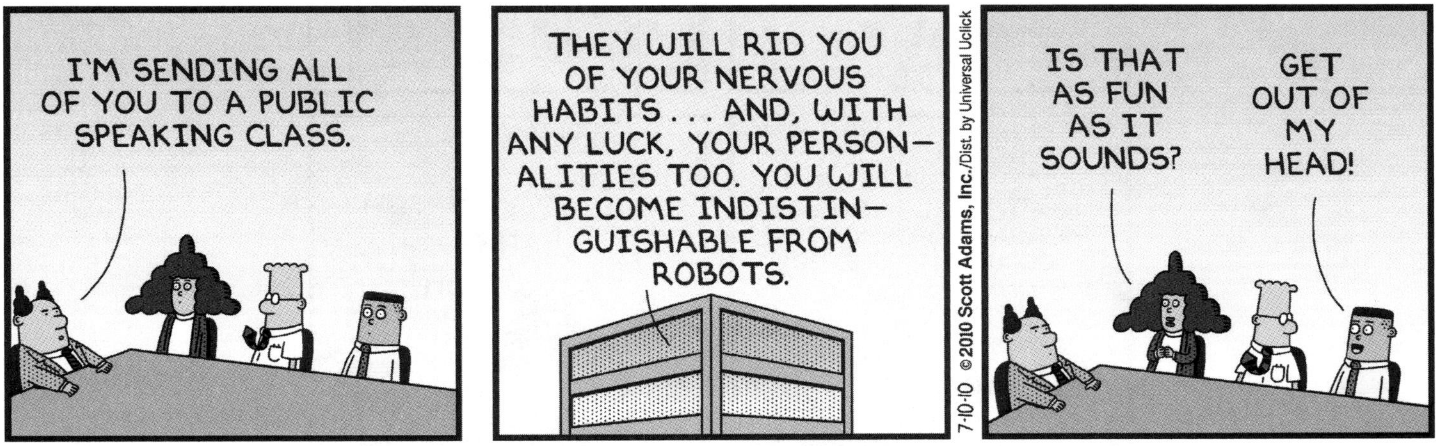
I'M SENDING ALL OF YOU TO A PUBLIC SPEAKING CLASS.
THEY WILL RID YOU OF YOUR NERVOUS HABITS . . . AND, WITH ANY LUCK, YOUR PERSON-ALITIES TOO. YOU WILL BECOME INDISTIN-GUISHABLE FROM ROBOTS.
7-10-10 © 2010 Scott Adams, Inc./Dist. by Universal Uclick
IS THAT AS FUN AS IT SOUNDS?
GET OUT OF MY HEAD!

A SUCCESSFUL TRANSFORMATION REQUIRES EMPLOYEES TO FEEL OWNERSHIP FOR THE CHANGE.
CHANGE
CHANGE? WHAT CHANGE?
IS THERE SOME-THING WE DON'T KNOW?
IT'S IMPORTANT THAT EVERYONE HAS CLEAR ROLES AND RESPONSIBILITIES.
WHAT ARE YOU TRYING TO TELL US? SHOULD WE STOP WORKING ON OUR PROJECTS?
I'LL KEEP YOU ENGAGED AND ENERGIZED WITH MY CLEAR COMMUNI-CATION.
AND AS YOUR LEADER, I WILL ROLE-MODEL THE DESIRED CHANGE.
IF HE'S OUR ROLE MODEL, I GUESS WE NEED TO ACT LIKE MORONS WHO CAN'T COMMUNICATE.
I NEED NEW PEOPLE.
FUH FUH FUH FUH FUH FUH
©2010 Scott Adams, Inc./Dist. by Universal Uclick
7-11-10

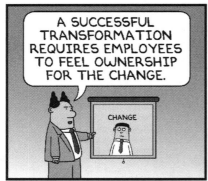

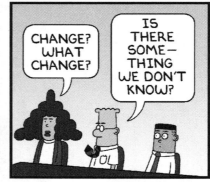

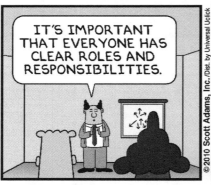

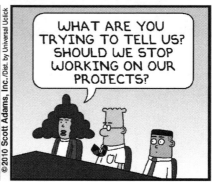

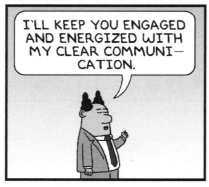

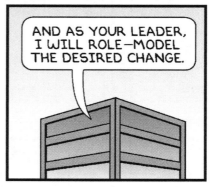

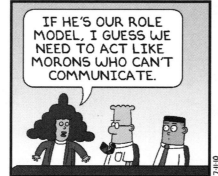

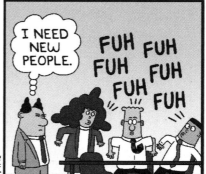

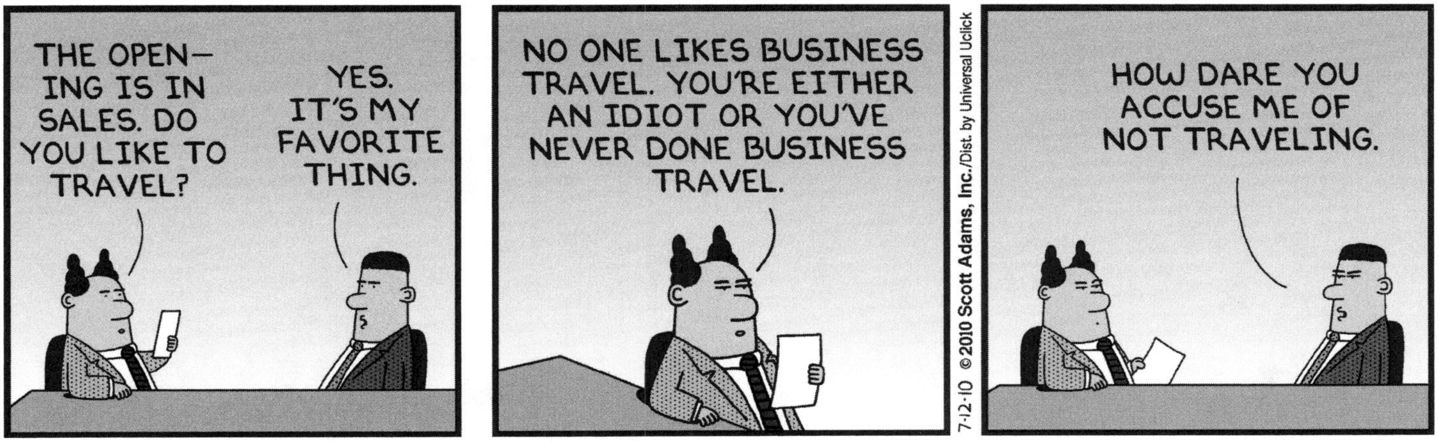
THE OPEN-ING IS IN SALES. DO YOU LIKE TO TRAVEL?
YES. IT'S MY FAVORITE THING.
NO ONE LIKES BUSINESS TRAVEL. YOU'RE EITHER AN IDIOT OR YOU'VE NEVER DONE BUSINESS TRAVEL.
7-12-10 © 2010 Scott Adams, Inc./Dist. by Universal Uclick
HOW DARE YOU ACCUSE ME OF NOT TRAVELING.

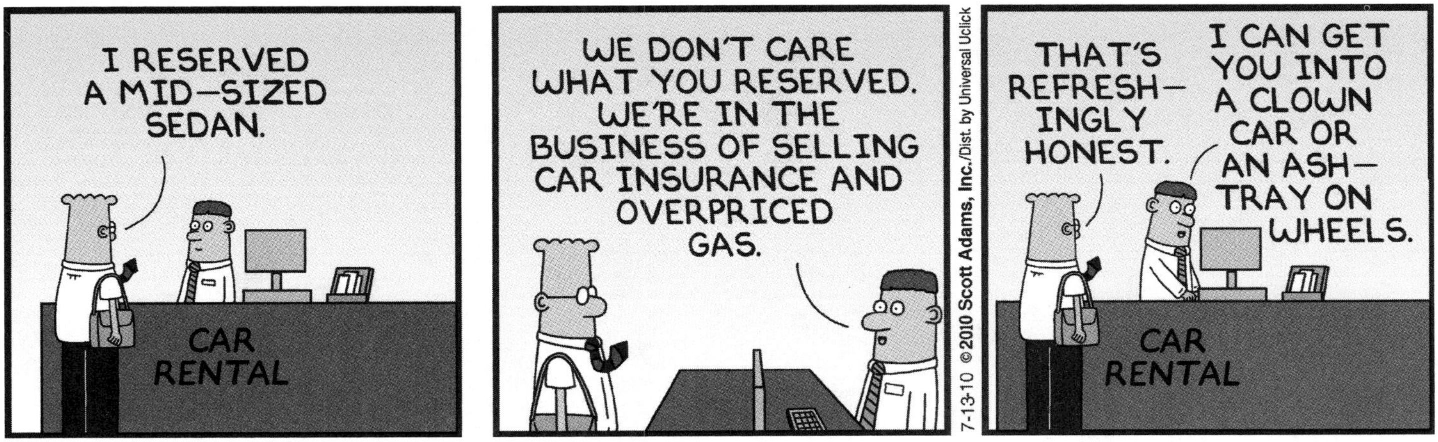
I RESERVED A MID-SIZED SEDAN.
CAR RENTAL
WE DON'T CARE WHAT YOU RESERVED. WE'RE IN THE BUSINESS OF SELLING CAR INSURANCE AND OVERPRICED GAS.
7-13-10 © 2010 Scott Adams, Inc./Dist. by Universal Uclick
THAT'S REFRESH-INGLY HONEST.
I CAN GET YOU INTO A CLOWN CAR OR AN ASH-TRAY ON WHEELS.
CAR RENTAL

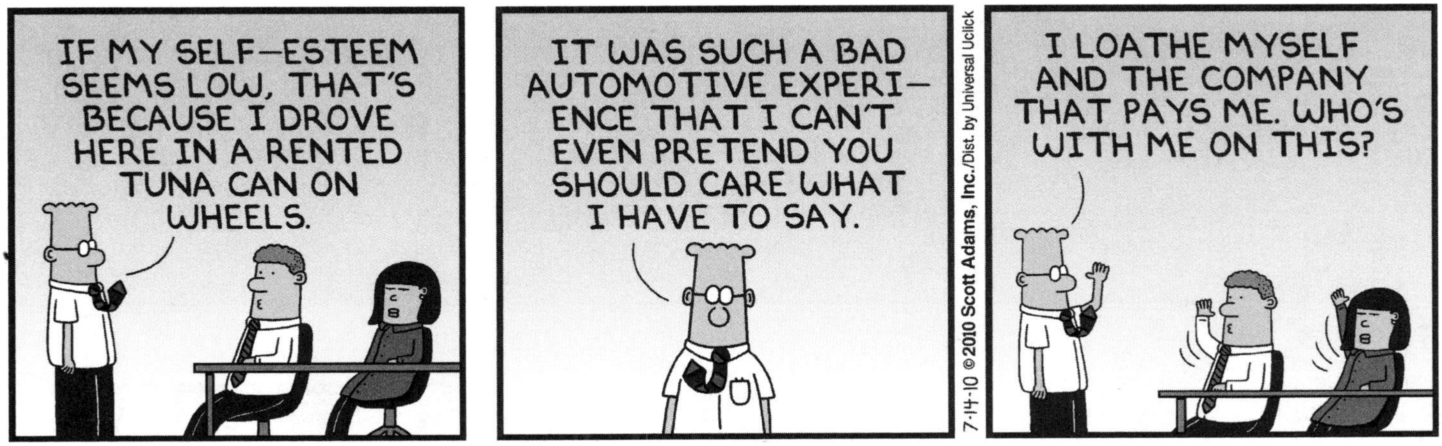
IF MY SELF-ESTEEM SEEMS LOW, THAT'S BECAUSE I DROVE HERE IN A RENTED TUNA CAN ON WHEELS.
IT WAS SUCH A BAD AUTOMOTIVE EXPERI-ENCE THAT I CAN'T EVEN PRETEND YOU SHOULD CARE WHAT I HAVE TO SAY.
7-14-10 © 2010 Scott Adams, Inc./Dist. by Universal Uclick
I LOATHE MYSELF AND THE COMPANY THAT PAYS ME. WHO'S WITH ME ON THIS?

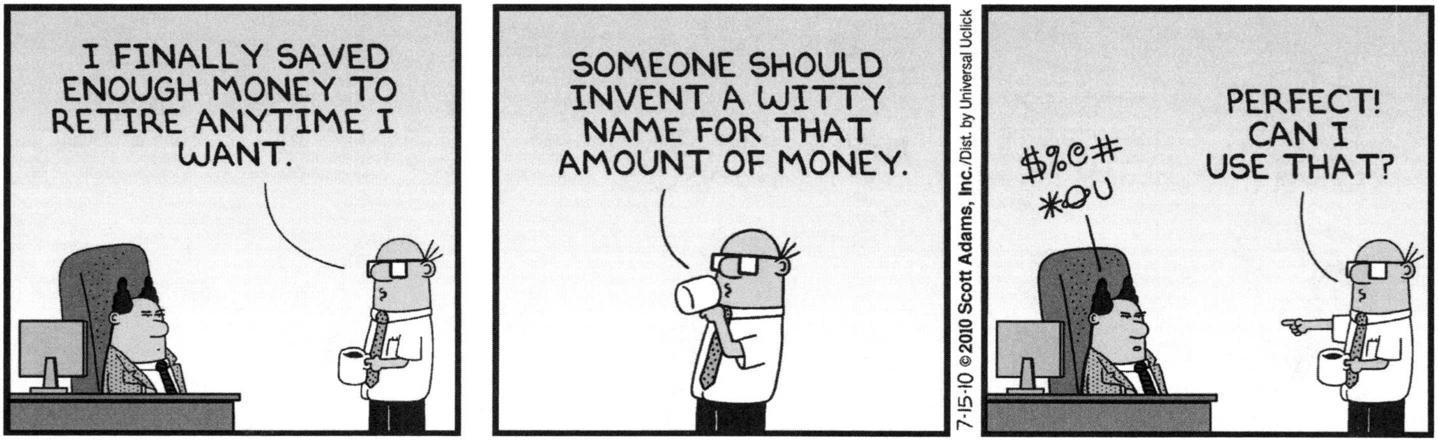
I FINALLY SAVED ENOUGH MONEY TO RETIRE ANYTIME I WANT.
SOMEONE SHOULD INVENT A WITTY NAME FOR THAT AMOUNT OF MONEY.
7-15-10 ©2010 Scott Adams, Inc./Dist. by Universal Uclick
$%@# *@U
PERFECT! CAN I USE THAT?

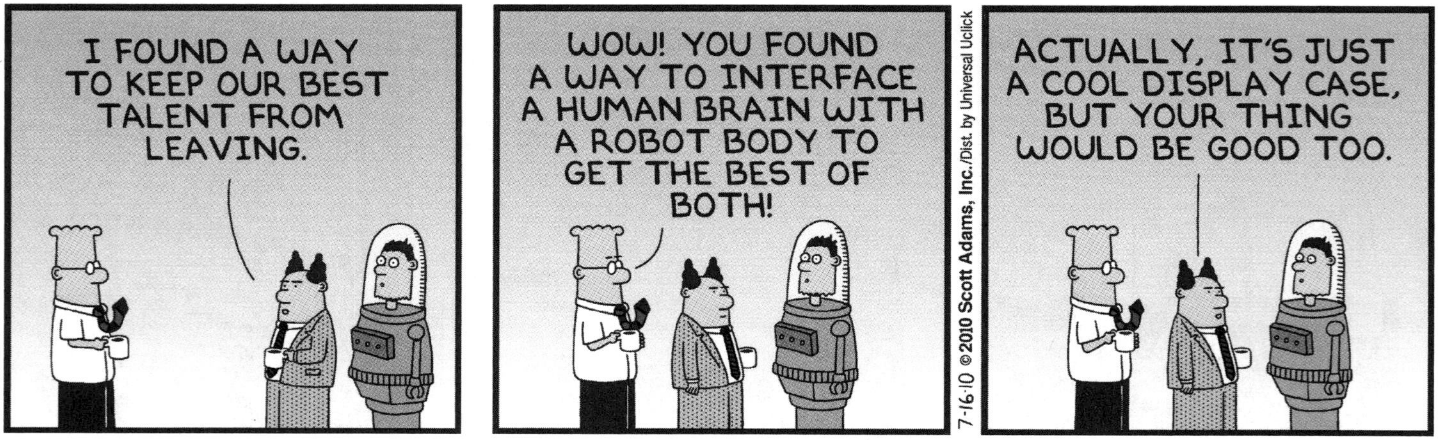
I FOUND A WAY TO KEEP OUR BEST TALENT FROM LEAVING.
WOW! YOU FOUND A WAY TO INTERFACE A HUMAN BRAIN WITH A ROBOT BODY TO GET THE BEST OF BOTH!
7-16-10 ©2010 Scott Adams, Inc./Dist. by Universal Uclick
ACTUALLY, IT'S JUST A COOL DISPLAY CASE, BUT YOUR THING WOULD BE GOOD TOO.

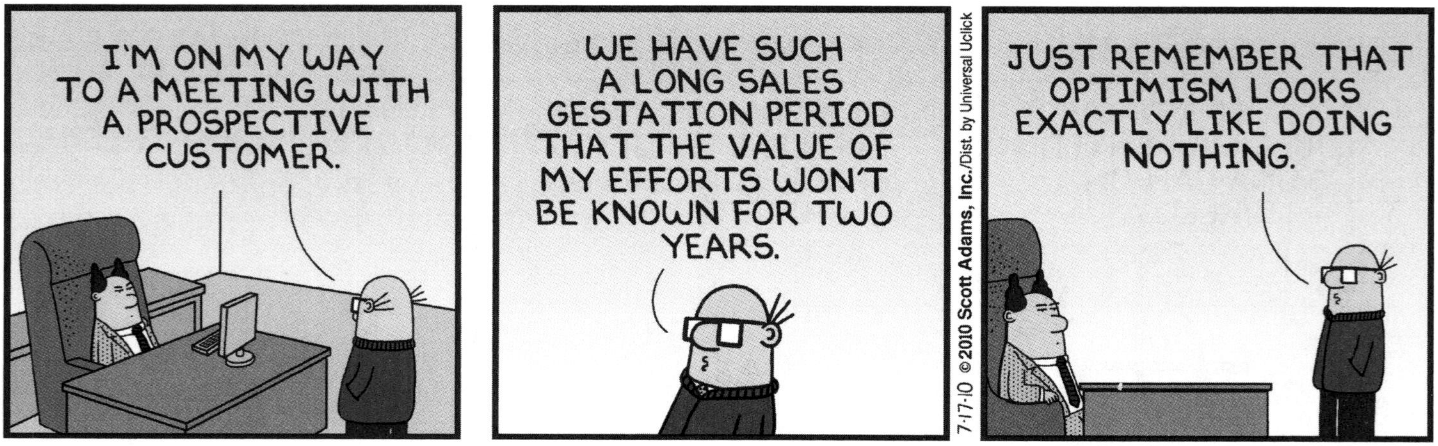
I'M ON MY WAY TO A MEETING WITH A PROSPECTIVE CUSTOMER.
WE HAVE SUCH A LONG SALES GESTATION PERIOD THAT THE VALUE OF MY EFFORTS WON'T BE KNOWN FOR TWO YEARS.
7-17-10 ©2010 Scott Adams, Inc./Dist. by Universal Uclick
JUST REMEMBER THAT OPTIMISM LOOKS EXACTLY LIKE DOING NOTHING.

AND THAT'S OUR NEW MARKETING VIDEO. WE HOPE IT WILL GO VIRAL.
YOU'LL HAVE OUR COMMENTS BY TOMORROW.
I'M NOT ASKING FOR COMMENTS. THE VIDEO IS ALREADY FINISHED.
THE TECHNOLOGY CLAIMS IN THE VIDEO ARE CRIMINALLY INACCURATE.
I SENT THE SCRIPT TO ENGINEERING FOR COMMENTS THREE MONTHS AGO!
I GOT AN EMAIL BACK FROM SOMEONE NAMED WALLY WHO SAID IT WAS GREAT.
I THOUGHT SHE WAS ASKING IF IT WAS FUNNY.
©2010 Scott Adams, Inc./Dist. by Universal Uclick
7-18-10

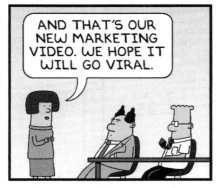

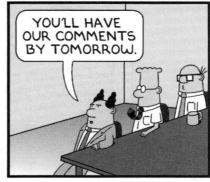

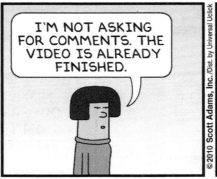

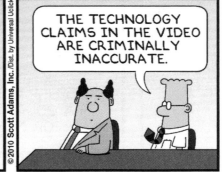

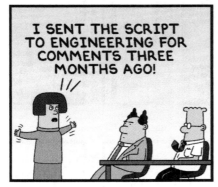

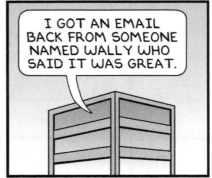

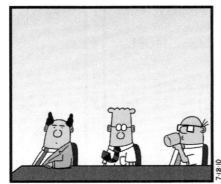

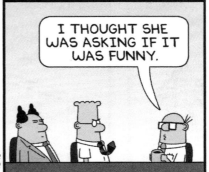

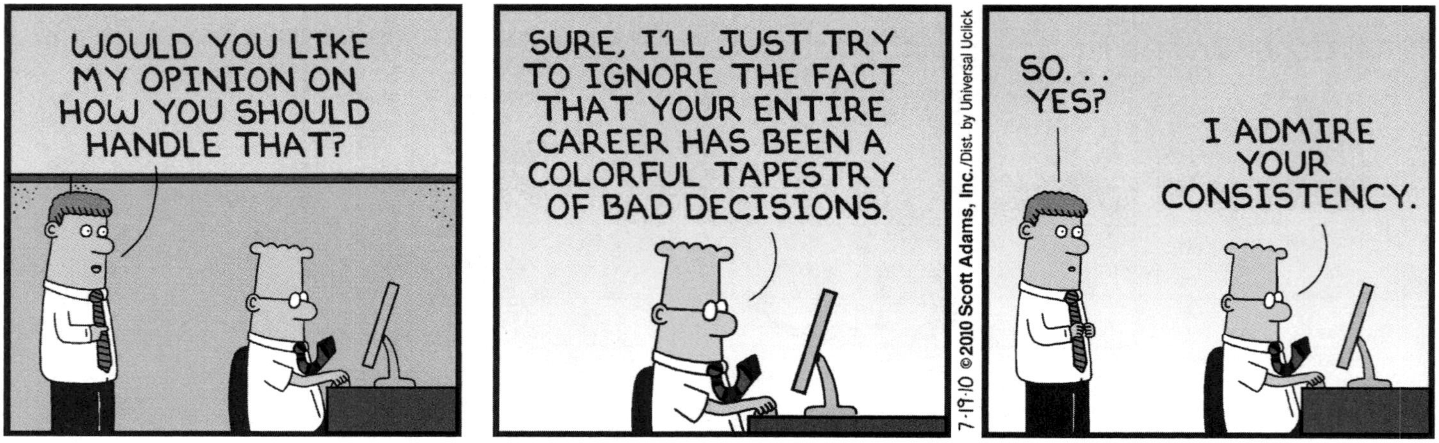
WOULD YOU LIKE MY OPINION ON HOW YOU SHOULD HANDLE THAT?
SURE, I'LL JUST TRY TO IGNORE THE FACT THAT YOUR ENTIRE CAREER HAS BEEN A COLORFUL TAPESTRY OF BAD DECISIONS.
7·19·10 © 2010 Scott Adams, Inc./Dist. by Universal Uclick
SO. . . YES?
I ADMIRE YOUR CONSISTENCY.

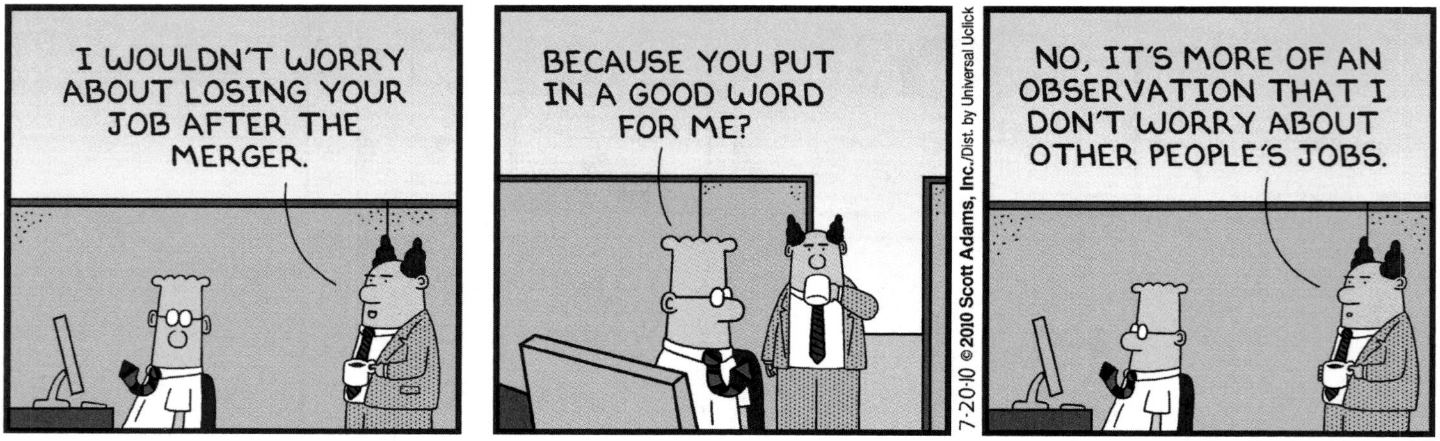
I WOULDN'T WORRY ABOUT LOSING YOUR JOB AFTER THE MERGER.
BECAUSE YOU PUT IN A GOOD WORD FOR ME?
7·20·10 © 2010 Scott Adams, Inc./Dist. by Universal Uclick
NO, IT'S MORE OF AN OBSERVATION THAT I DON'T WORRY ABOUT OTHER PEOPLE'S JOBS.

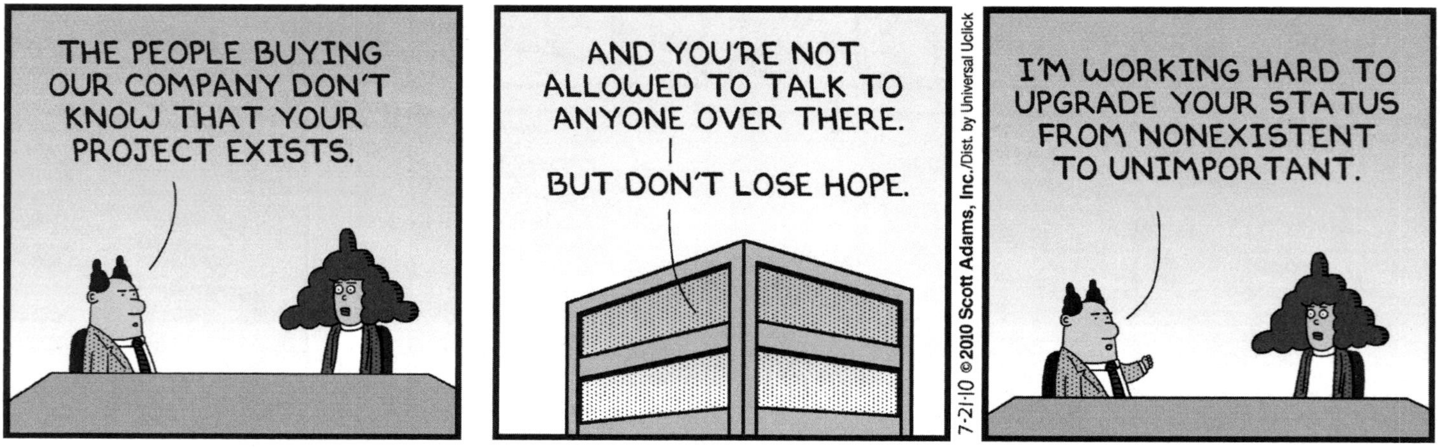
THE PEOPLE BUYING OUR COMPANY DON'T KNOW THAT YOUR PROJECT EXISTS.
AND YOU'RE NOT ALLOWED TO TALK TO ANYONE OVER THERE.
BUT DON'T LOSE HOPE.
7·21·10 © 2010 Scott Adams, Inc./Dist. by Universal Uclick
I'M WORKING HARD TO UPGRADE YOUR STATUS FROM NONEXISTENT TO UNIMPORTANT.

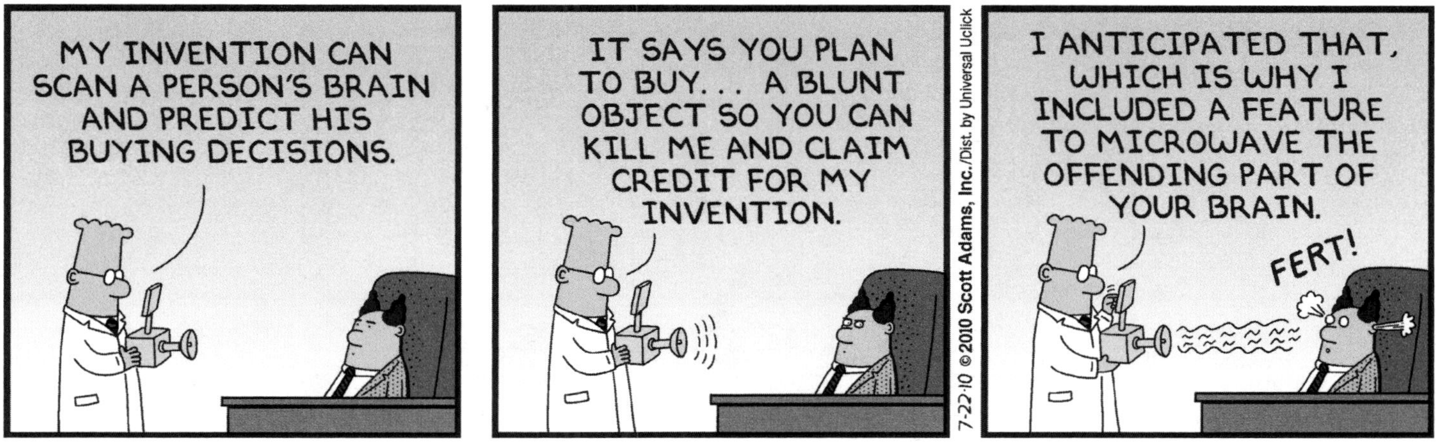
MY INVENTION CAN SCAN A PERSON'S BRAIN AND PREDICT HIS BUYING DECISIONS.
IT SAYS YOU PLAN TO BUY. . . A BLUNT OBJECT SO YOU CAN KILL ME AND CLAIM CREDIT FOR MY INVENTION.
I ANTICIPATED THAT, WHICH IS WHY I INCLUDED A FEATURE TO MICROWAVE THE OFFENDING PART OF YOUR BRAIN.
FERT!
7-22-10 © 2010 Scott Adams, Inc./Dist. by Universal Uclick

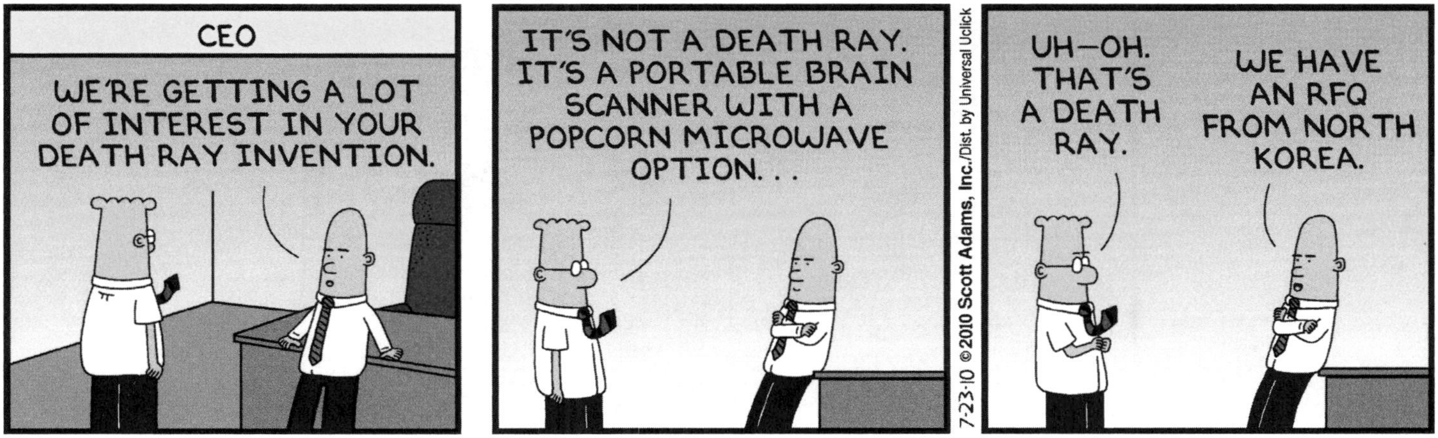
CEO
WE'RE GETTING A LOT OF INTEREST IN YOUR DEATH RAY INVENTION.
IT'S NOT A DEATH RAY. IT'S A PORTABLE BRAIN SCANNER WITH A POPCORN MICROWAVE OPTION. . .
UH—OH. THAT'S A DEATH RAY.
WE HAVE AN RFQ FROM NORTH KOREA.
7-23-10 © 2010 Scott Adams, Inc./Dist. by Universal Uclick

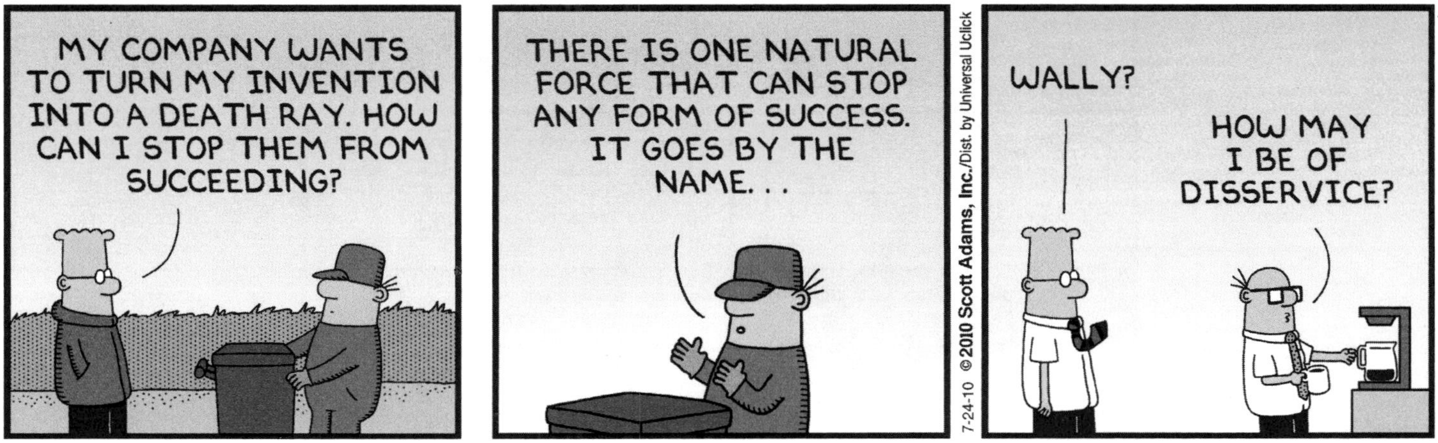
MY COMPANY WANTS TO TURN MY INVENTION INTO A DEATH RAY. HOW CAN I STOP THEM FROM SUCCEEDING?
THERE IS ONE NATURAL FORCE THAT CAN STOP ANY FORM OF SUCCESS. IT GOES BY THE NAME. . .
WALLY?
HOW MAY I BE OF DISSERVICE?
7-24-10 © 2010 Scott Adams, Inc./Dist. by Universal Uclick

I'M GLAD YOUR PROJECT WAS TRANSFERRED TO MY DEPARTMENT, RONALD.
YOUR PROJECT IS FLASHY! IT'S SEXY!
BUT IT'S NOT WORTH FUNDING BECAUSE THE REVENUE PROJECTIONS ARE PUNY.
UNTIL SOMETHING CHANGES, YOU'LL BE IN THE LIMBO CUBE.
LIMBO
I'LL TROT YOU OUT WHENEVER A CUSTOMER OR AN EXECUTIVE VISITS.
YOU CAN SHOW YOUR SEXY—FLASHY POWERPOINT SLIDES WHILE DREAMING OF BEING RELEVANT.
IF YOU WORK HARD, SOMEDAY YOU'LL BE TOTALLY FORGOTTEN.
DID YOU KNOW THAT HONESTY MAKES PEOPLE SAD?
©2010 Scott Adams, Inc./Dist. by Universal Uclick
7-25-10

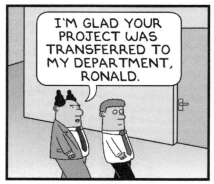

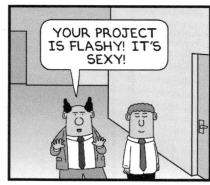

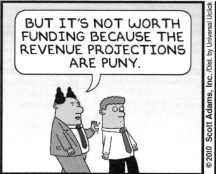

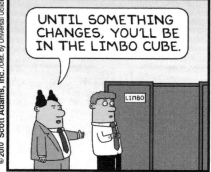

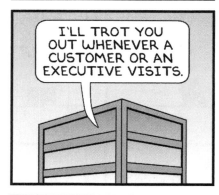

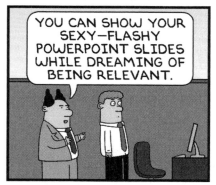

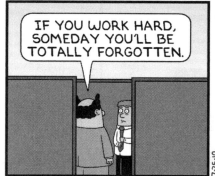

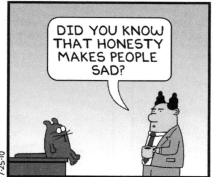

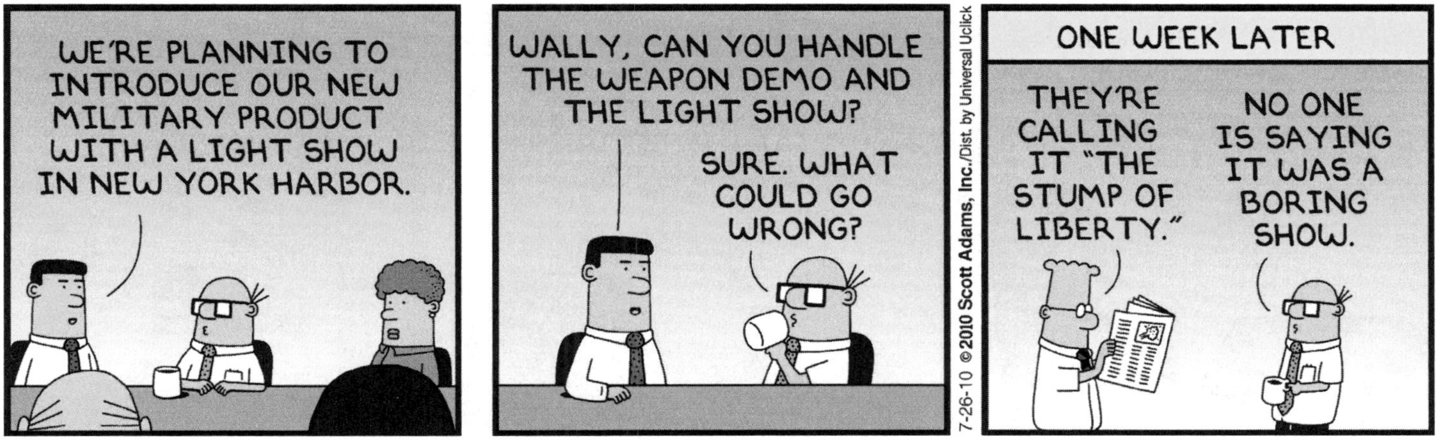
WE'RE PLANNING TO INTRODUCE OUR NEW MILITARY PRODUCT WITH A LIGHT SHOW IN NEW YORK HARBOR.
WALLY, CAN YOU HANDLE THE WEAPON DEMO AND THE LIGHT SHOW?
SURE. WHAT COULD GO WRONG?
7-26-10 © 2010 Scott Adams, Inc./Dist. by Universal Uclick
ONE WEEK LATER
THEY'RE CALLING IT "THE STUMP OF LIBERTY."
NO ONE IS SAYING IT WAS A BORING SHOW.

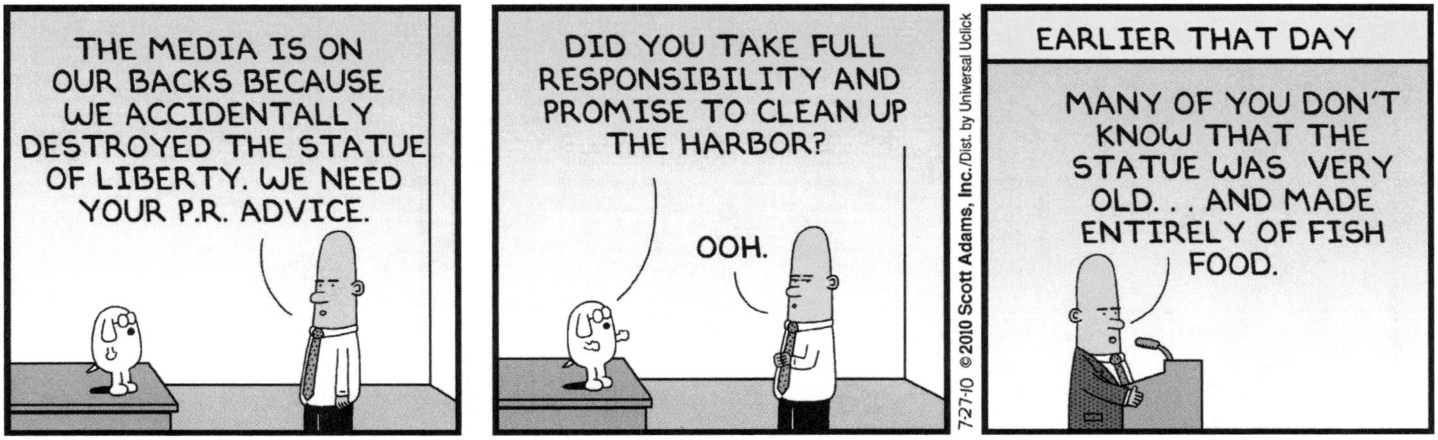
THE MEDIA IS ON OUR BACKS BECAUSE WE ACCIDENTALLY DESTROYED THE STATUE OF LIBERTY. WE NEED YOUR P.R. ADVICE.
DID YOU TAKE FULL RESPONSIBILITY AND PROMISE TO CLEAN UP THE HARBOR?
OOH.
7-27-10 © 2010 Scott Adams, Inc./Dist. by Universal Uclick
EARLIER THAT DAY
MANY OF YOU DON'T KNOW THAT THE STATUE WAS VERY OLD. . . AND MADE ENTIRELY OF FISH FOOD.

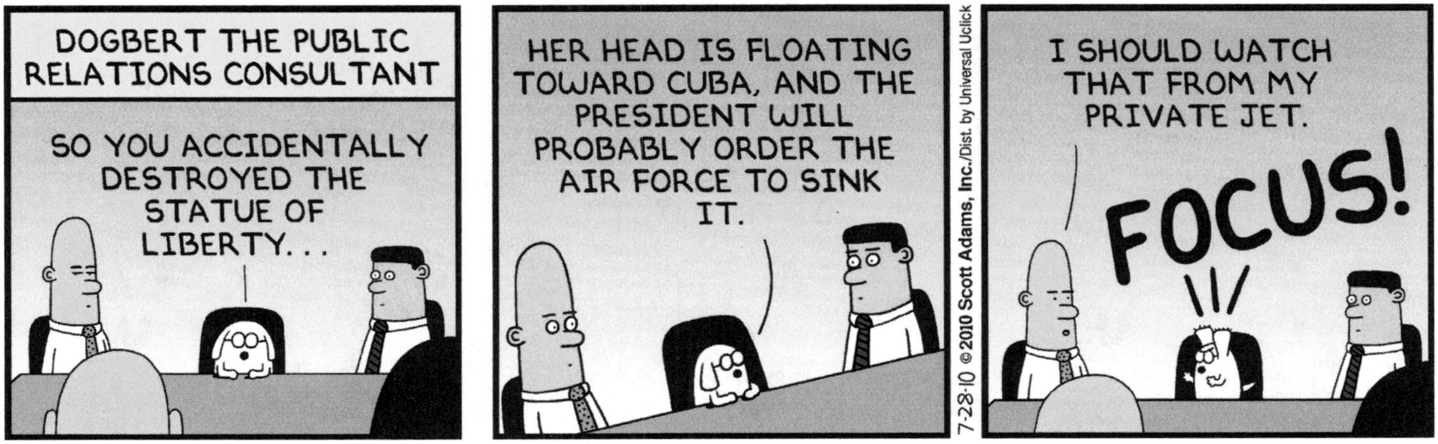
DOGBERT THE PUBLIC RELATIONS CONSULTANT
SO YOU ACCIDENTALLY DESTROYED THE STATUE OF LIBERTY. . .
HER HEAD IS FLOATING TOWARD CUBA, AND THE PRESIDENT WILL PROBABLY ORDER THE AIR FORCE TO SINK IT.
7-28-10 © 2010 Scott Adams, Inc./Dist. by Universal Uclick
I SHOULD WATCH THAT FROM MY PRIVATE JET.
FOCUS!

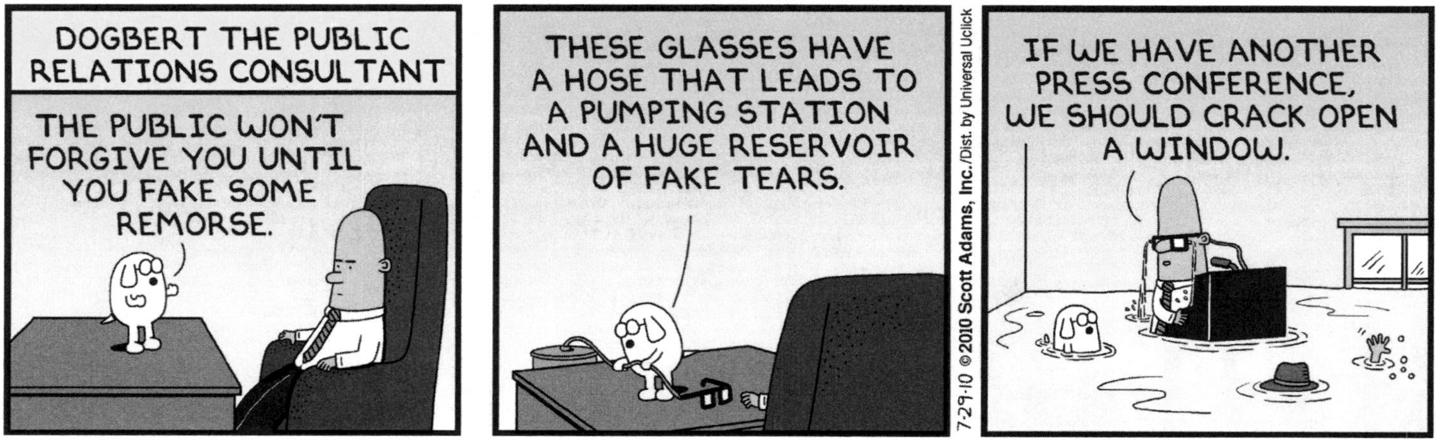
DOGBERT THE PUBLIC RELATIONS CONSULTANT
THE PUBLIC WON'T FORGIVE YOU UNTIL YOU FAKE SOME REMORSE.
THESE GLASSES HAVE A HOSE THAT LEADS TO A PUMPING STATION AND A HUGE RESERVOIR OF FAKE TEARS.
7-29-10 © 2010 Scott Adams, Inc./Dist. by Universal Uclick
IF WE HAVE ANOTHER PRESS CONFERENCE, WE SHOULD CRACK OPEN A WINDOW.

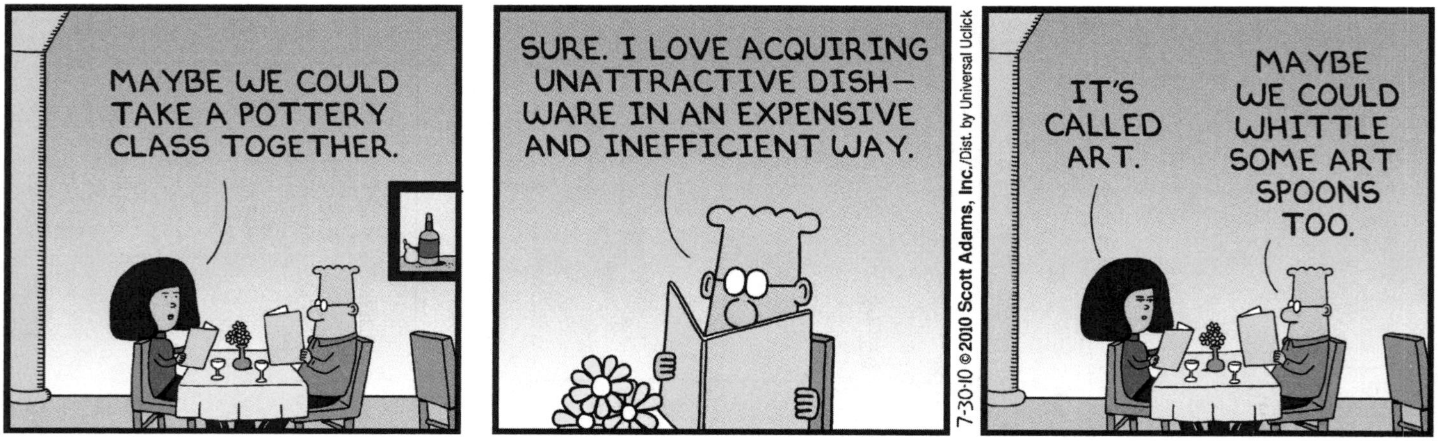
MAYBE WE COULD TAKE A POTTERY CLASS TOGETHER.
SURE. I LOVE ACQUIRING UNATTRACTIVE DISH-WARE IN AN EXPENSIVE AND INEFFICIENT WAY.
7-30-10 © 2010 Scott Adams, Inc./Dist. by Universal Uclick
IT'S CALLED ART.
MAYBE WE COULD WHITTLE SOME ART SPOONS TOO.

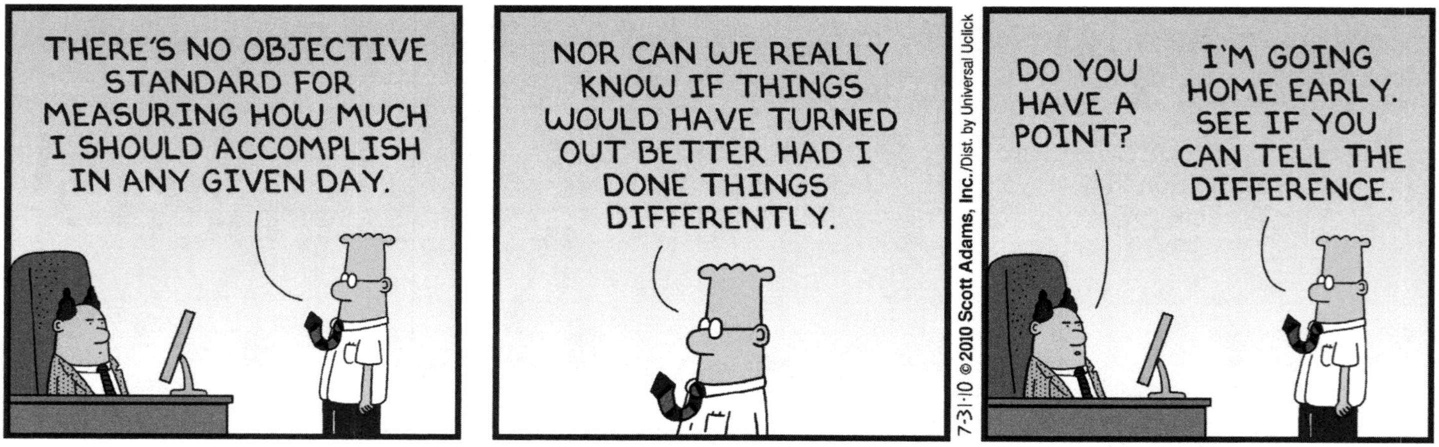
THERE'S NO OBJECTIVE STANDARD FOR MEASURING HOW MUCH I SHOULD ACCOMPLISH IN ANY GIVEN DAY.
NOR CAN WE REALLY KNOW IF THINGS WOULD HAVE TURNED OUT BETTER HAD I DONE THINGS DIFFERENTLY.
7-31-10 © 2010 Scott Adams, Inc./Dist. by Universal Uclick
DO YOU HAVE A POINT?
I'M GOING HOME EARLY. SEE IF YOU CAN TELL THE DIFFERENCE.

DILBERT, COULD YOU HELP ME FILL OUT THIS REBATE FORM THE NEXT TIME YOU VISIT?
SURE, MOM.
ALSO, MY LAPTOP KEEPS CRASHING.
I'LL TAKE A LOOK AT IT.
MY TV IS ACTING UP AGAIN TOO.
AND MAYBE YOU COULD SHOW ME HOW TO CHANGE MY RINGTONE.
DO YOU REALLY NEED ALL OF THAT HELP?
OR IS THIS AN ELABORATE SCHEME TO INOCULATE AGAINST ME EVER WANTING TO MOVE BACK HOME?
WE HAVE A BAD CONNECTION! WHAT? WHAT? WHAT?
THAT SHOULD BUY ME ANOTHER SIX MONTHS.
CLICK
Scott Adams, Inc./Dist. by Universal Uclick
8-1-10

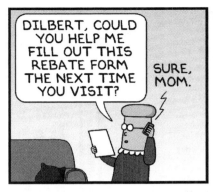

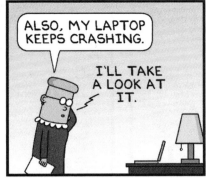

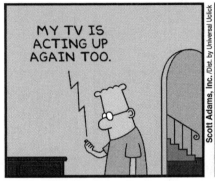

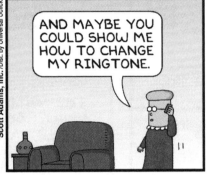

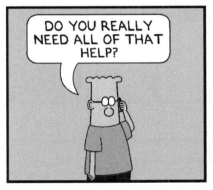

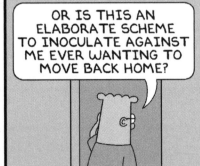

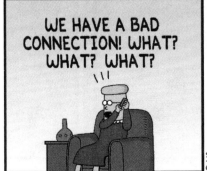

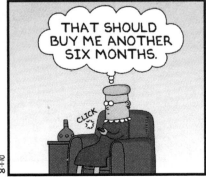

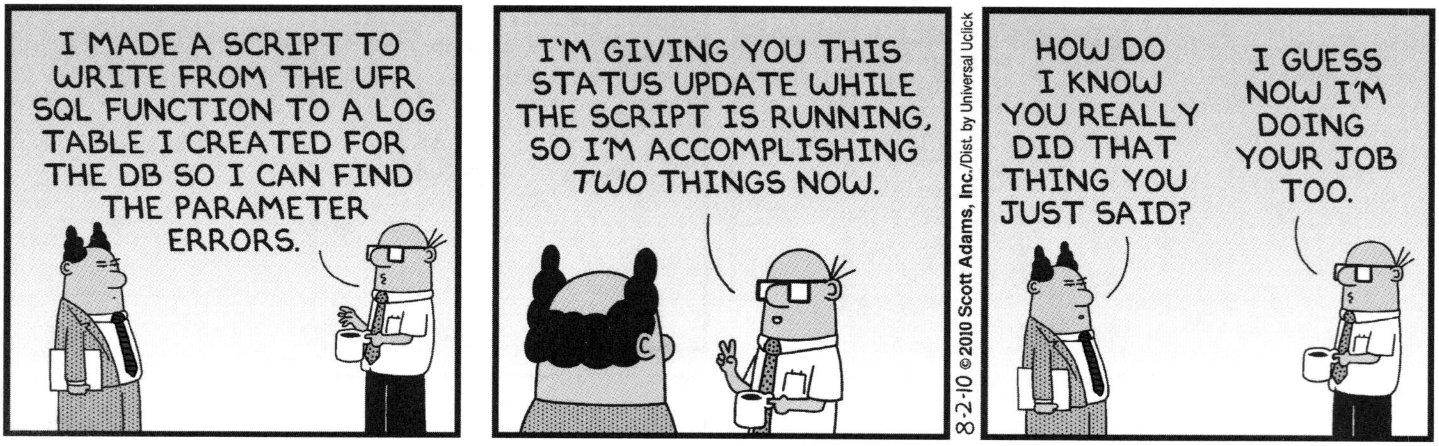
I MADE A SCRIPT TO WRITE FROM THE UFR SQL FUNCTION TO A LOG TABLE I CREATED FOR THE DB SO I CAN FIND THE PARAMETER ERRORS.
I'M GIVING YOU THIS STATUS UPDATE WHILE THE SCRIPT IS RUNNING, SO I'M ACCOMPLISHING *TWO* THINGS NOW.
8-2-10 © 2010 Scott Adams, Inc./Dist. by Universal Uclick
HOW DO I KNOW YOU REALLY DID THAT THING YOU JUST SAID?
I GUESS NOW I'M DOING YOUR JOB TOO.

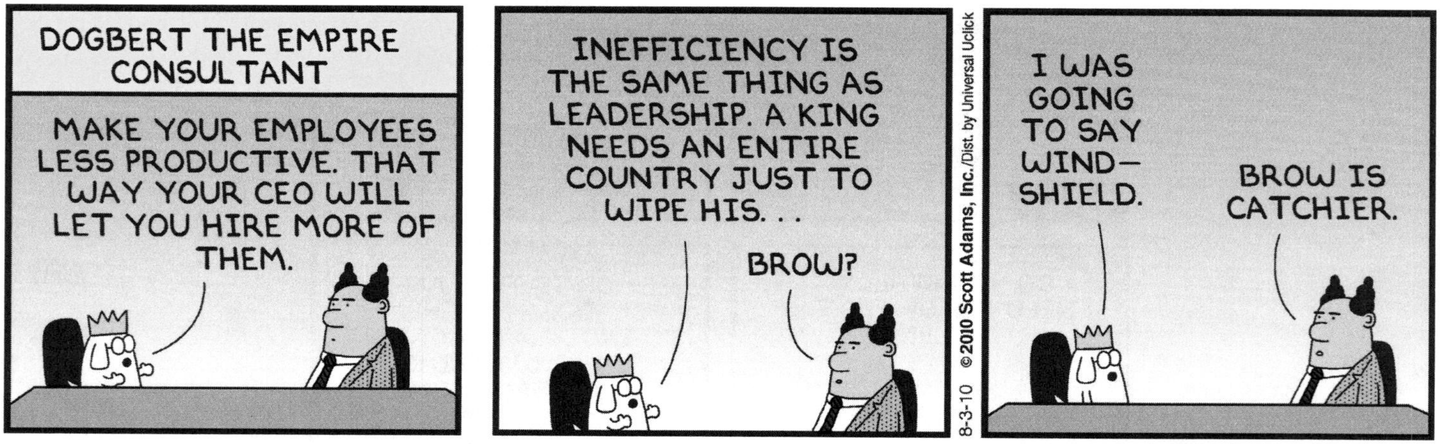
DOGBERT THE EMPIRE CONSULTANT
MAKE YOUR EMPLOYEES LESS PRODUCTIVE. THAT WAY YOUR CEO WILL LET YOU HIRE MORE OF THEM.
INEFFICIENCY IS THE SAME THING AS LEADERSHIP. A KING NEEDS AN ENTIRE COUNTRY JUST TO WIPE HIS. . .
BROW?
8-3-10 © 2010 Scott Adams, Inc./Dist. by Universal Uclick
I WAS GOING TO SAY WIND-SHIELD.
BROW IS CATCHIER.

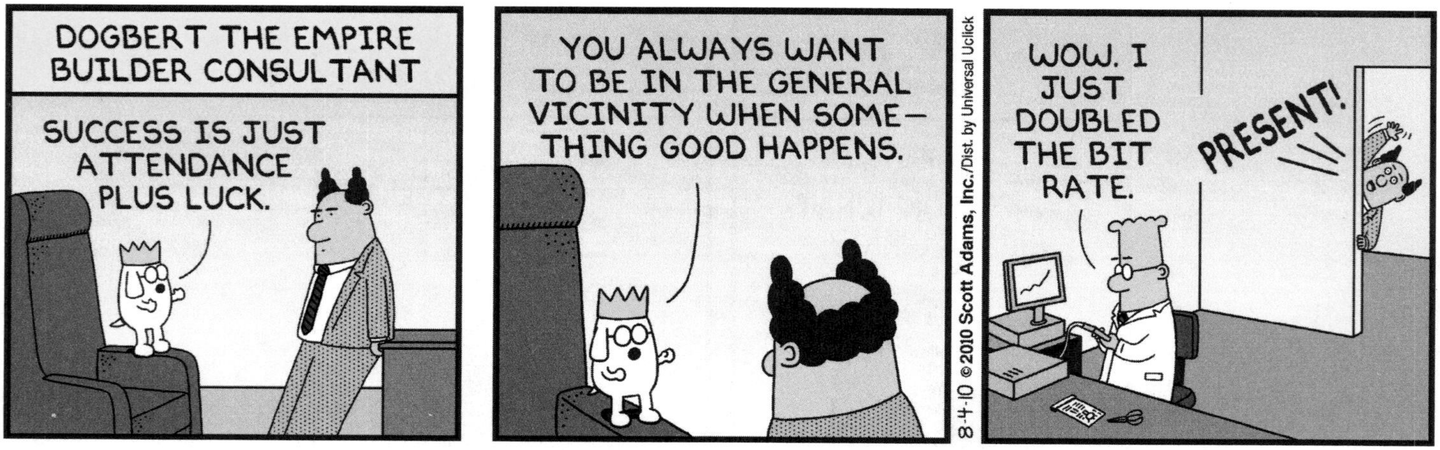
DOGBERT THE EMPIRE BUILDER CONSULTANT
SUCCESS IS JUST ATTENDANCE PLUS LUCK.
YOU ALWAYS WANT TO BE IN THE GENERAL VICINITY WHEN SOME-THING GOOD HAPPENS.
8-4-10 © 2010 Scott Adams, Inc./Dist. by Universal Uclick
WOW. I JUST DOUBLED THE BIT RATE.
PRESENT!

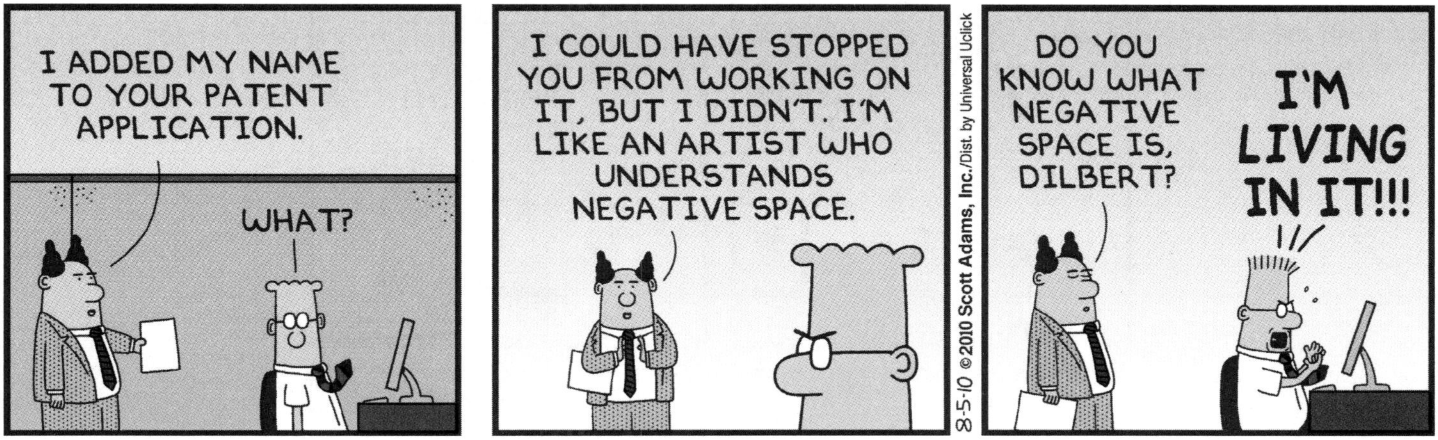
I ADDED MY NAME TO YOUR PATENT APPLICATION.
WHAT?
I COULD HAVE STOPPED YOU FROM WORKING ON IT, BUT I DIDN'T. I'M LIKE AN ARTIST WHO UNDERSTANDS NEGATIVE SPACE.
DO YOU KNOW WHAT NEGATIVE SPACE IS, DILBERT?
I'M LIVING IN IT!!!
8-5-10 © 2010 Scott Adams, Inc./Dist. by Universal Uclick

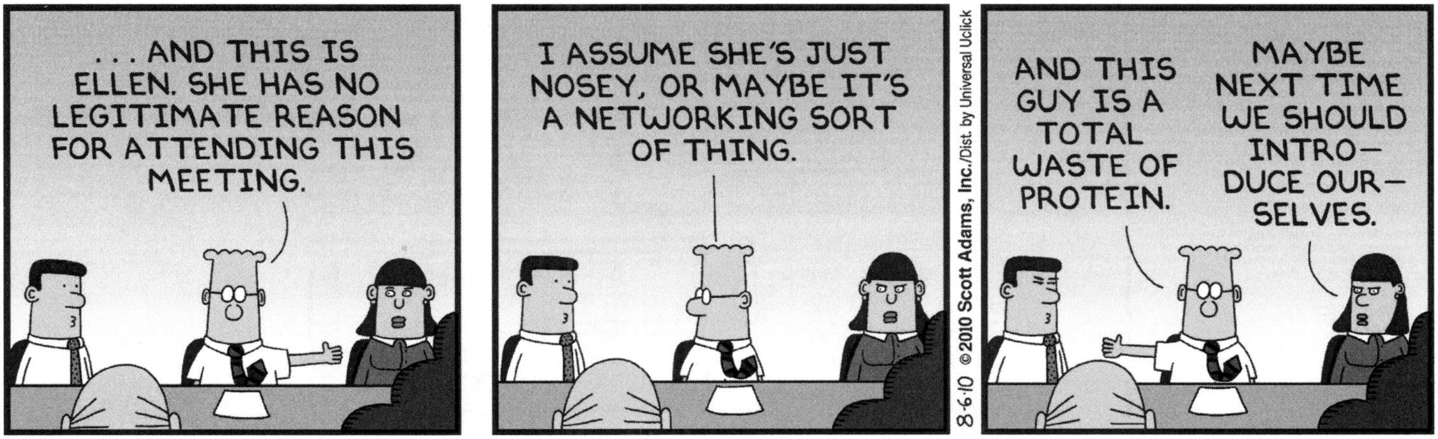
. . . AND THIS IS ELLEN. SHE HAS NO LEGITIMATE REASON FOR ATTENDING THIS MEETING.
I ASSUME SHE'S JUST NOSEY, OR MAYBE IT'S A NETWORKING SORT OF THING.
AND THIS GUY IS A TOTAL WASTE OF PROTEIN.
MAYBE NEXT TIME WE SHOULD INTRO-DUCE OUR-SELVES.
8-6-10 © 2010 Scott Adams, Inc./Dist. by Universal Uclick

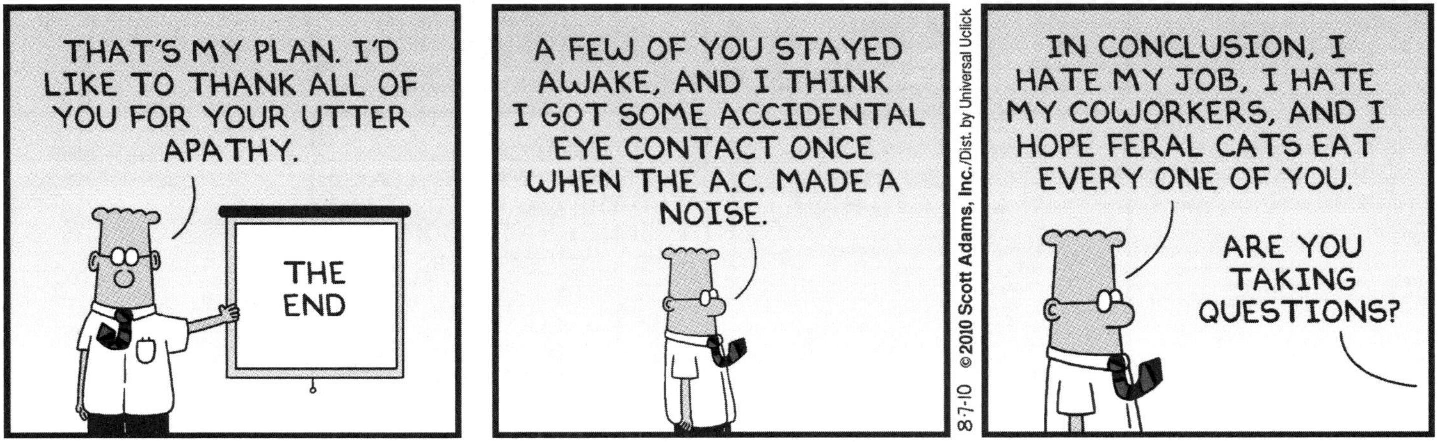
THAT'S MY PLAN. I'D LIKE TO THANK ALL OF YOU FOR YOUR UTTER APATHY.
THE END
A FEW OF YOU STAYED AWAKE, AND I THINK I GOT SOME ACCIDENTAL EYE CONTACT ONCE WHEN THE A.C. MADE A NOISE.
IN CONCLUSION, I HATE MY JOB, I HATE MY COWORKERS, AND I HOPE FERAL CATS EAT EVERY ONE OF YOU.
ARE YOU TAKING QUESTIONS?
8-7-10 © 2010 Scott Adams, Inc./Dist. by Universal Uclick

CAROL, WOULD YOU. . .
RRRING!
HERE'S AN INTERESTING EXPERIMENT. . .
RRRING!
WATCH WHAT HAPPENS TO YOUR BLOOD PRESSURE WHEN I TAKE THIS CALL AND MAKE YOU WAIT.
YEAH? WHAT'S THE PROBLEM NOW?
TELL YOUR BROTHER I SAID TO STOP BITING THE HEADS OFF YOUR DOLLS.
UH—HUH. . . WELL, IF THE MAN WAS WEARING A POSTAL UNIFORM, HE WASN'T THE BOGEYMAN.
YOU DID **WHAT** TO HIM?
LISTEN CAREFULLY. I WANT YOU TO TEAR UP THE CARPET IN THE FANCY BATHROOM. . .
I CAN COME BACK.
©2010 Scott Adams, Inc./Dist. by Universal Uclick
8-8-10

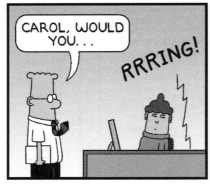

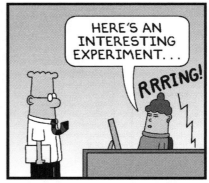

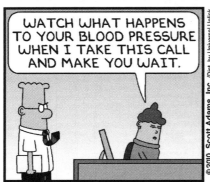

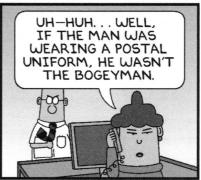

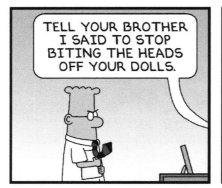

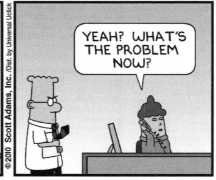

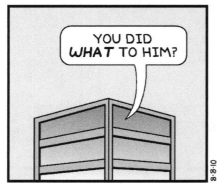

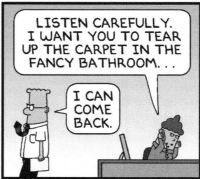

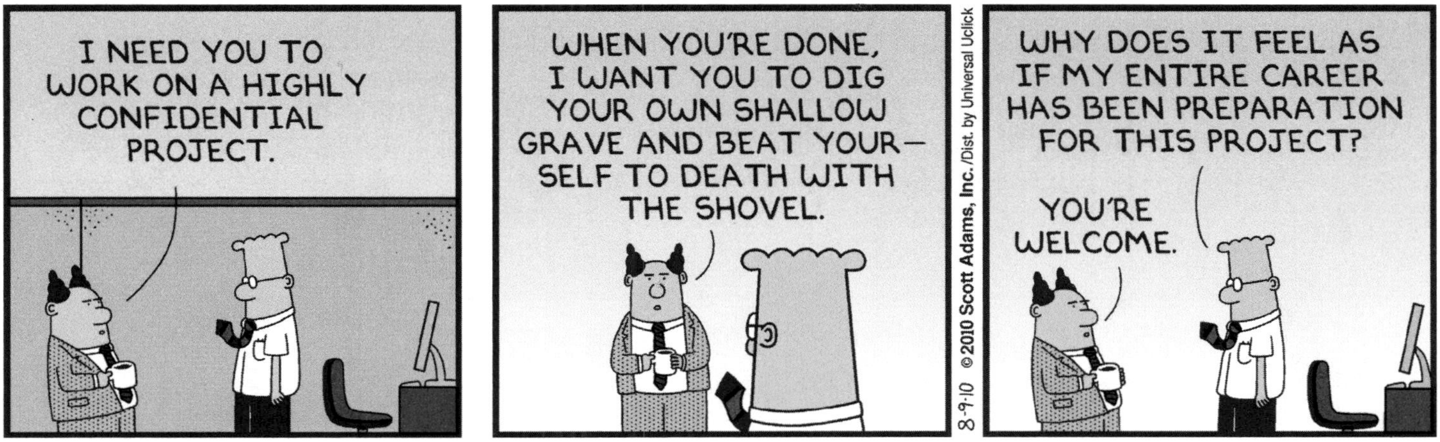
I NEED YOU TO WORK ON A HIGHLY CONFIDENTIAL PROJECT.
WHEN YOU'RE DONE, I WANT YOU TO DIG YOUR OWN SHALLOW GRAVE AND BEAT YOURSELF TO DEATH WITH THE SHOVEL.
8-9-10 ©2010 Scott Adams, Inc./Dist. by Universal Uclick
WHY DOES IT FEEL AS IF MY ENTIRE CAREER HAS BEEN PREPARATION FOR THIS PROJECT?
YOU'RE WELCOME.

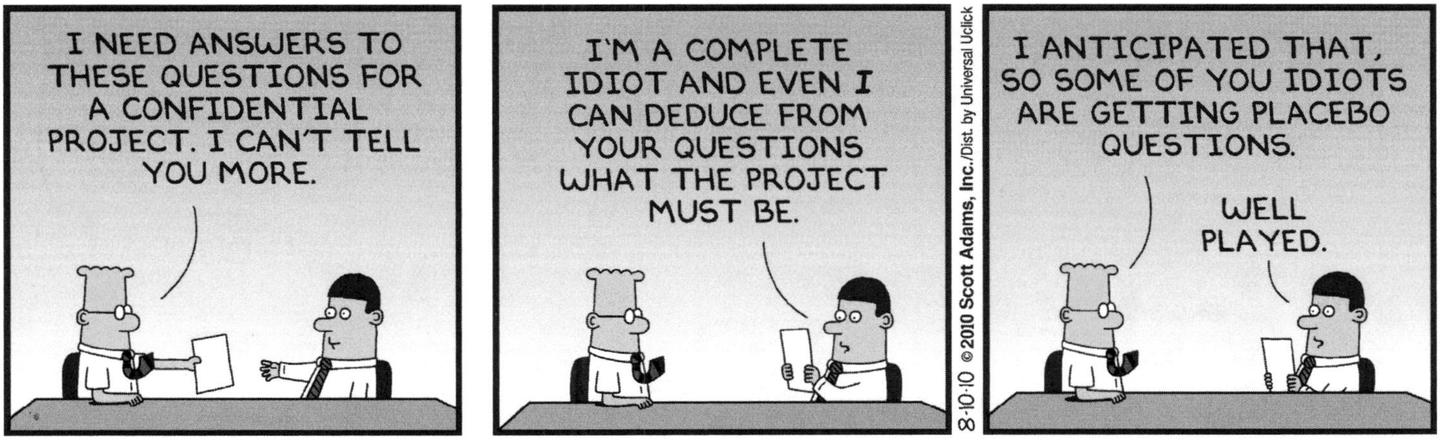
I NEED ANSWERS TO THESE QUESTIONS FOR A CONFIDENTIAL PROJECT. I CAN'T TELL YOU MORE.
I'M A COMPLETE IDIOT AND EVEN *I* CAN DEDUCE FROM YOUR QUESTIONS WHAT THE PROJECT MUST BE.
8-10-10 ©2010 Scott Adams, Inc./Dist. by Universal Uclick
I ANTICIPATED THAT, SO SOME OF YOU IDIOTS ARE GETTING PLACEBO QUESTIONS.
WELL PLAYED.

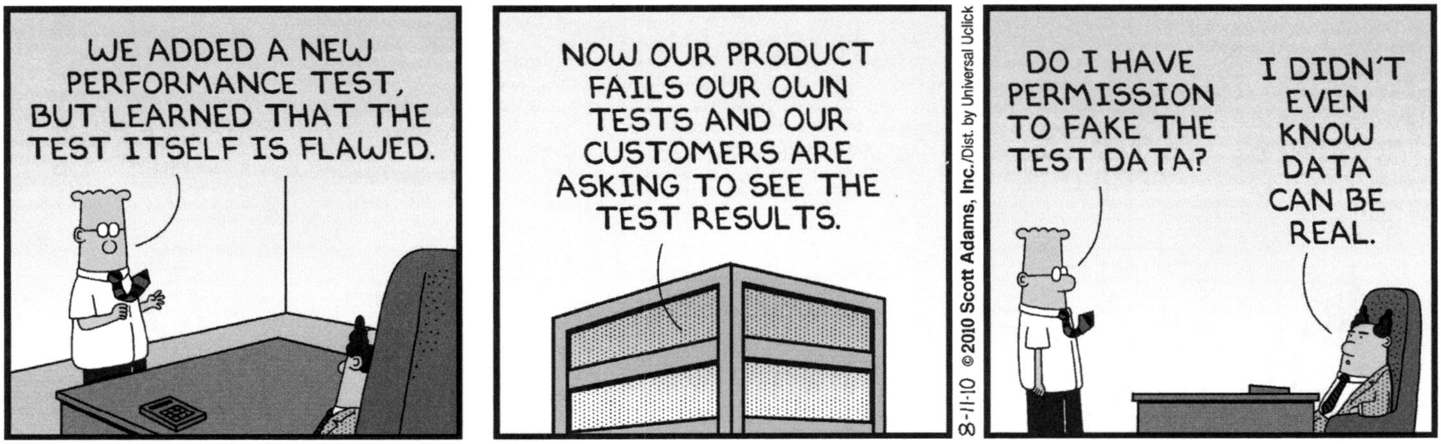
WE ADDED A NEW PERFORMANCE TEST, BUT LEARNED THAT THE TEST ITSELF IS FLAWED.
NOW OUR PRODUCT FAILS OUR OWN TESTS AND OUR CUSTOMERS ARE ASKING TO SEE THE TEST RESULTS.
8-11-10 ©2010 Scott Adams, Inc./Dist. by Universal Uclick
DO I HAVE PERMISSION TO FAKE THE TEST DATA?
I DIDN'T EVEN KNOW DATA CAN BE REAL.

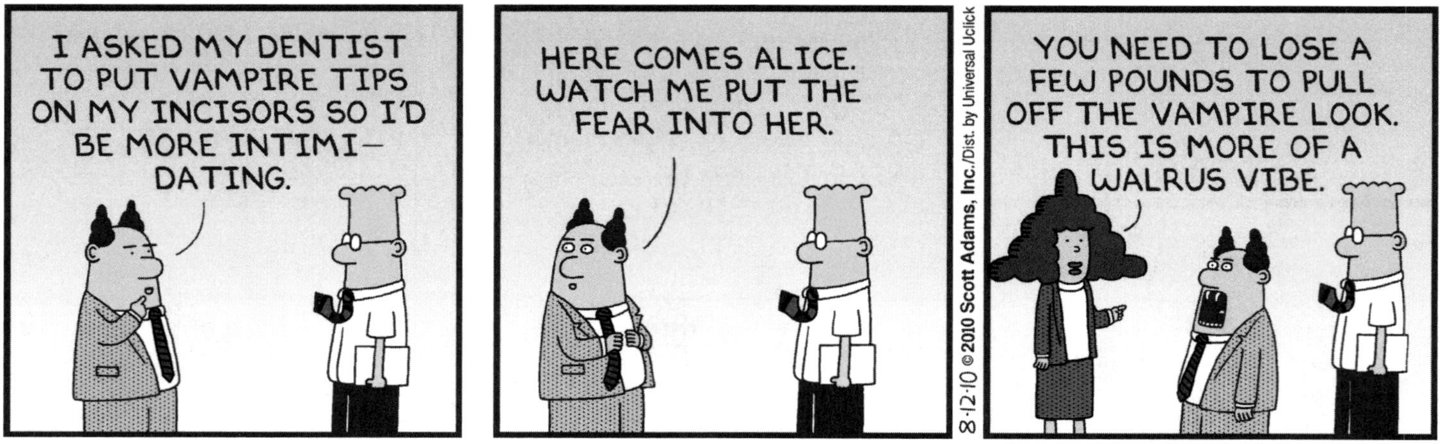
I ASKED MY DENTIST TO PUT VAMPIRE TIPS ON MY INCISORS SO I'D BE MORE INTIMI-DATING.
HERE COMES ALICE. WATCH ME PUT THE FEAR INTO HER.
YOU NEED TO LOSE A FEW POUNDS TO PULL OFF THE VAMPIRE LOOK. THIS IS MORE OF A WALRUS VIBE.
8-12-10 © 2010 Scott Adams, Inc./Dist. by Universal Uclick

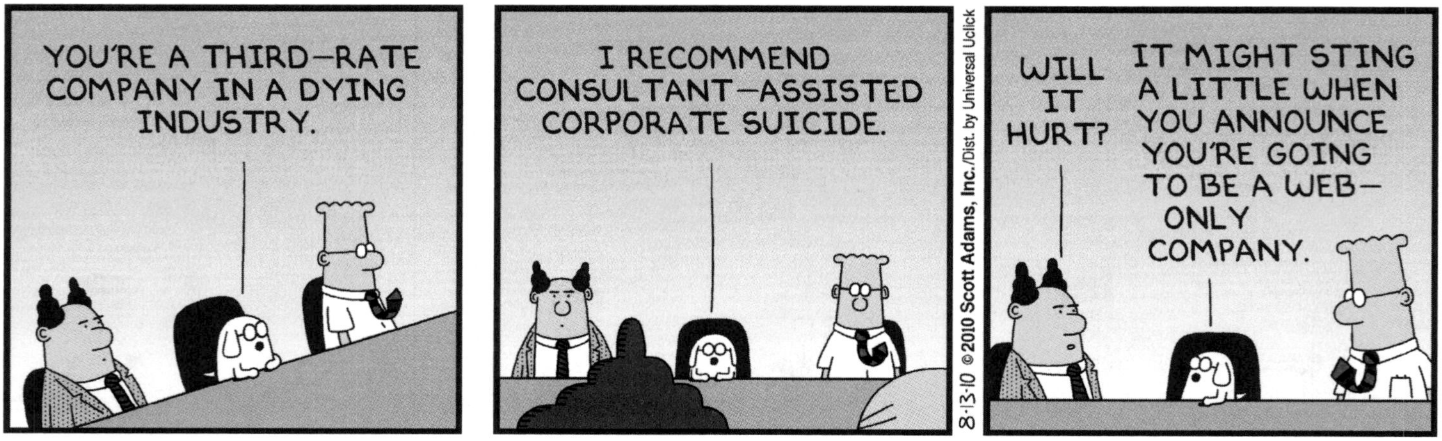
YOU'RE A THIRD-RATE COMPANY IN A DYING INDUSTRY.
I RECOMMEND CONSULTANT-ASSISTED CORPORATE SUICIDE.
WILL IT HURT?
IT MIGHT STING A LITTLE WHEN YOU ANNOUNCE YOU'RE GOING TO BE A WEB-ONLY COMPANY.
8-13-10 © 2010 Scott Adams, Inc./Dist. by Universal Uclick

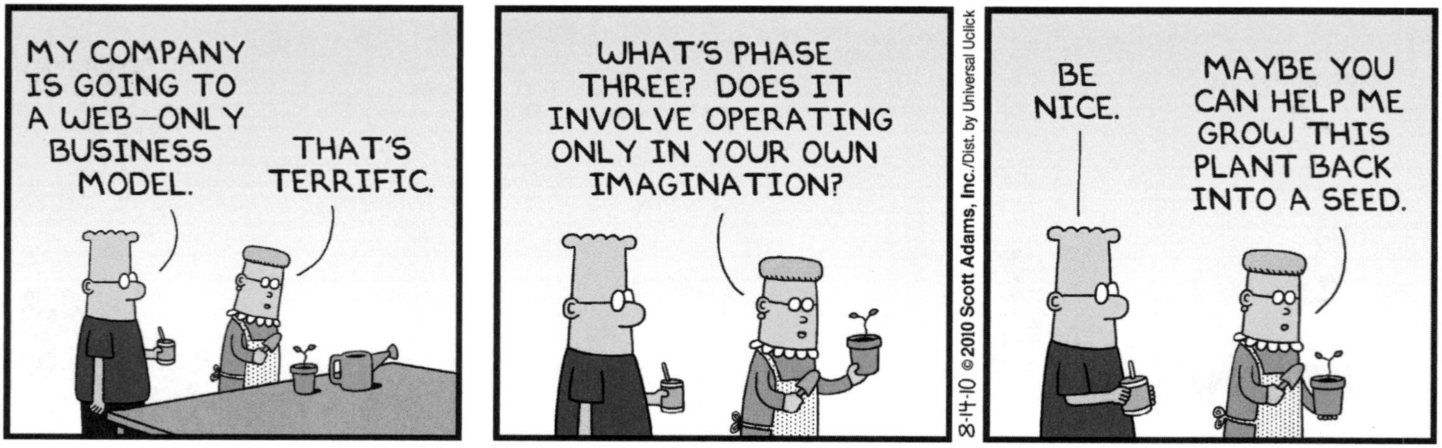
MY COMPANY IS GOING TO A WEB-ONLY BUSINESS MODEL.
THAT'S TERRIFIC.
WHAT'S PHASE THREE? DOES IT INVOLVE OPERATING ONLY IN YOUR OWN IMAGINATION?
BE NICE.
MAYBE YOU CAN HELP ME GROW THIS PLANT BACK INTO A SEED.
8-14-10 © 2010 Scott Adams, Inc./Dist. by Universal Uclick

WE'LL BREAK INTO SMALL GROUPS TO DISCUSS OPTIONS.
WHY? DO YOU THINK WE'LL BE SMARTER WHEN WE'RE IN SMALL GROUPS?
THAT WAY EVERYONE GETS MORE TIME TO TALK.
ACCORDING TO YOUR THEORY, THE IDEAL GROUP SIZE WOULD BE ONE PERSON TALKING TO HIMSELF.
NO, YOU ALSO NEED THE KNOWLEDGE AND PERSPECTIVE THAT EXTRA PEOPLE BRING.
THAT WOULD ARGUE FOR LARGER GROUPS, NOT SMALLER ONES.
FINE! JUST BREAK INTO WHATEVER SIZE GROUPS YOU THINK MAKE SENSE.
I LIKE YOUR STYLE, DILBERT.
THANK YOU FOR NOTICING.
8-15-10

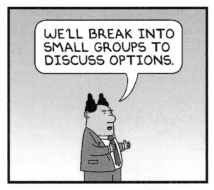

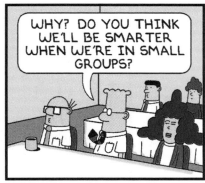

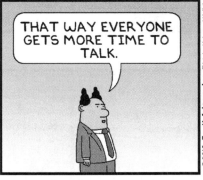

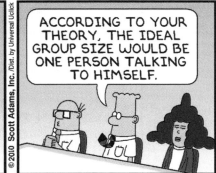

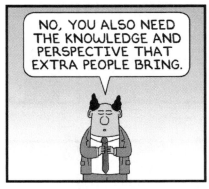

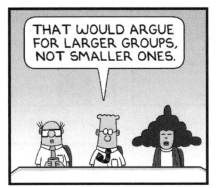

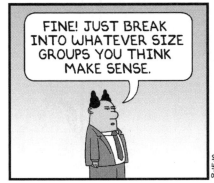

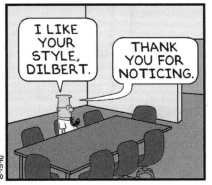

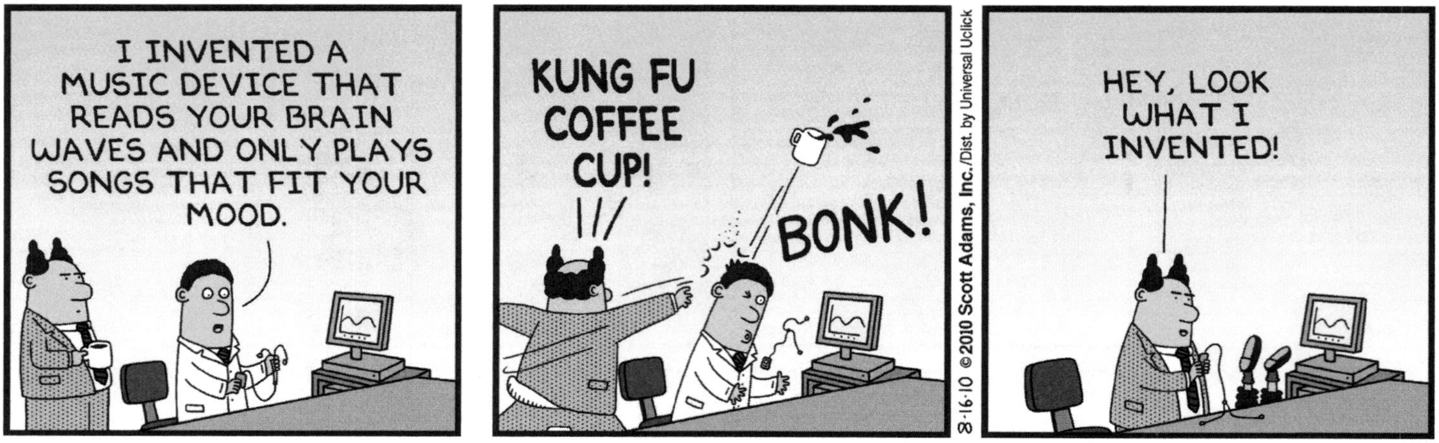
I INVENTED A MUSIC DEVICE THAT READS YOUR BRAIN WAVES AND ONLY PLAYS SONGS THAT FIT YOUR MOOD.
KUNG FU COFFEE CUP!
BONK!
8·16·10 © 2010 Scott Adams, Inc./Dist. by Universal Uclick
HEY, LOOK WHAT I INVENTED!

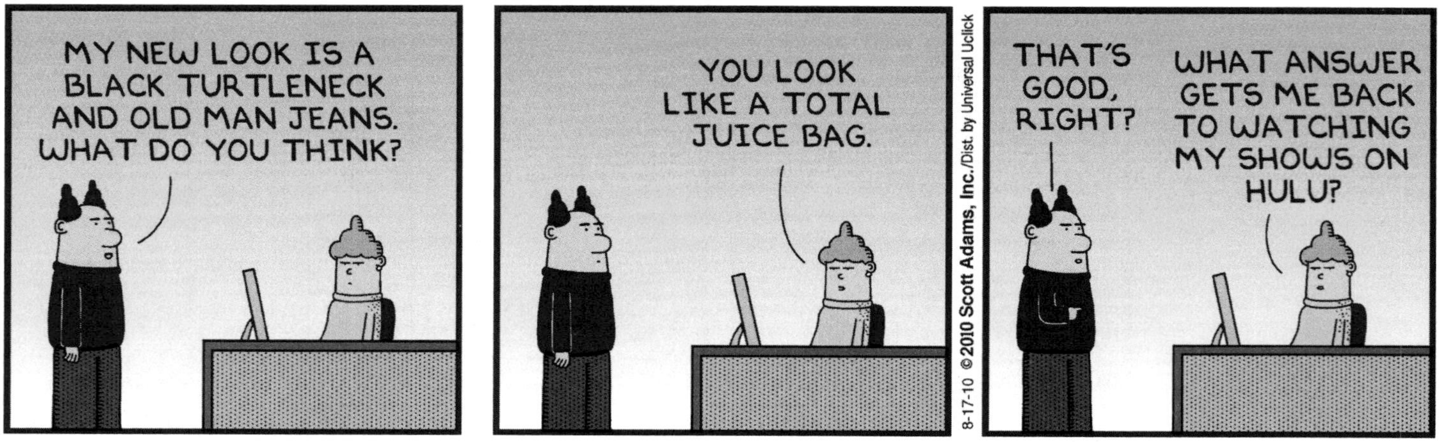
MY NEW LOOK IS A BLACK TURTLENECK AND OLD MAN JEANS. WHAT DO YOU THINK?
YOU LOOK LIKE A TOTAL JUICE BAG.
8-17-10 © 2010 Scott Adams, Inc./Dist. by Universal Uclick
THAT'S GOOD, RIGHT?
WHAT ANSWER GETS ME BACK TO WATCHING MY SHOWS ON HULU?

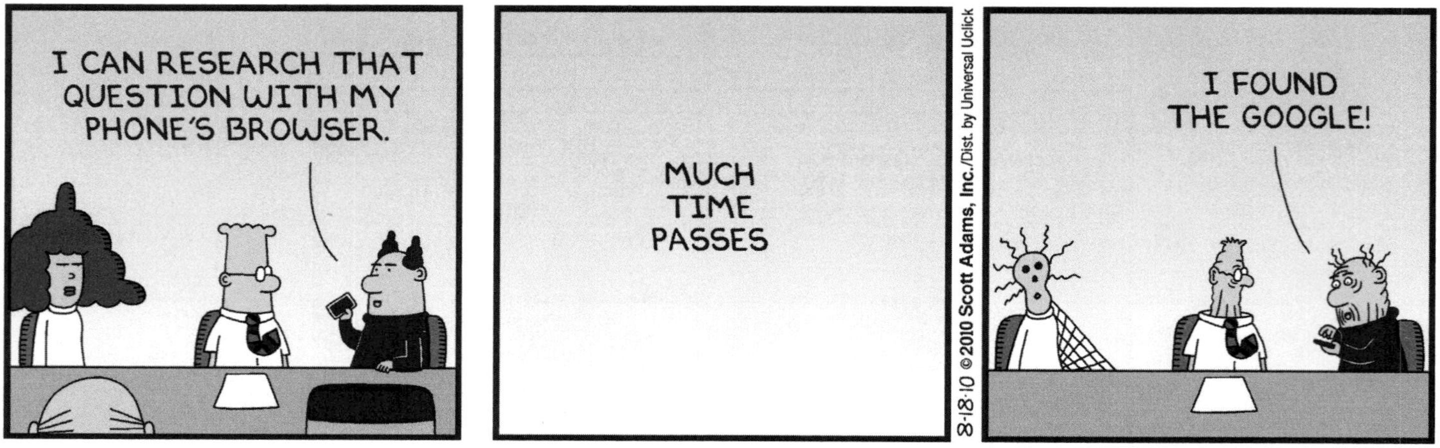
I CAN RESEARCH THAT QUESTION WITH MY PHONE'S BROWSER.
MUCH TIME PASSES
8·18·10 © 2010 Scott Adams, Inc./Dist. by Universal Uclick
I FOUND THE GOOGLE!

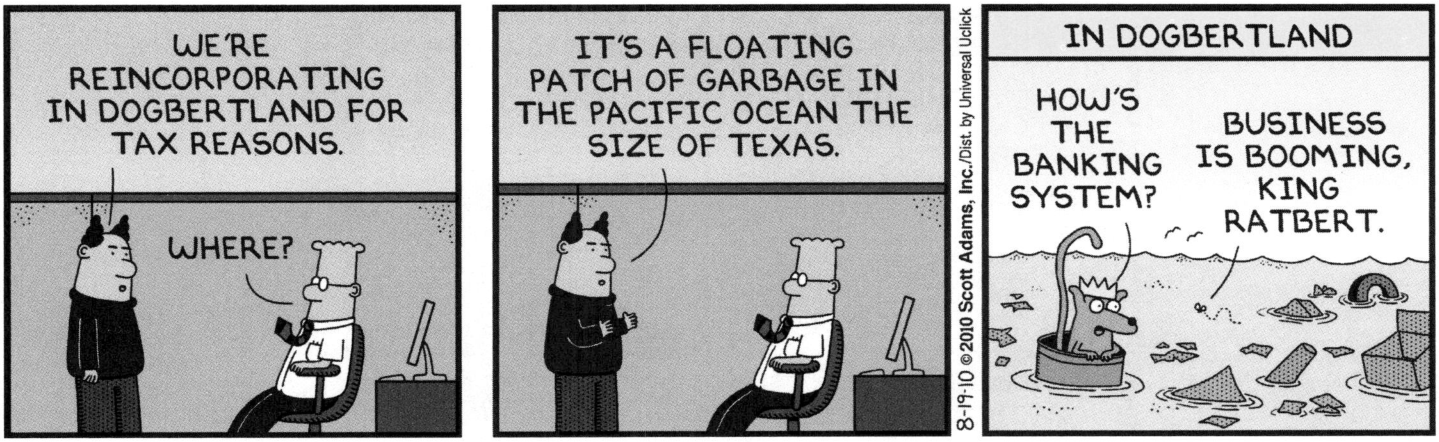
WE'RE REINCORPORATING IN DOGBERTLAND FOR TAX REASONS.
WHERE?
IT'S A FLOATING PATCH OF GARBAGE IN THE PACIFIC OCEAN THE SIZE OF TEXAS.
8-19-10 © 2010 Scott Adams, Inc./Dist. by Universal Uclick
IN DOGBERTLAND
HOW'S THE BANKING SYSTEM?
BUSINESS IS BOOMING, KING RATBERT.

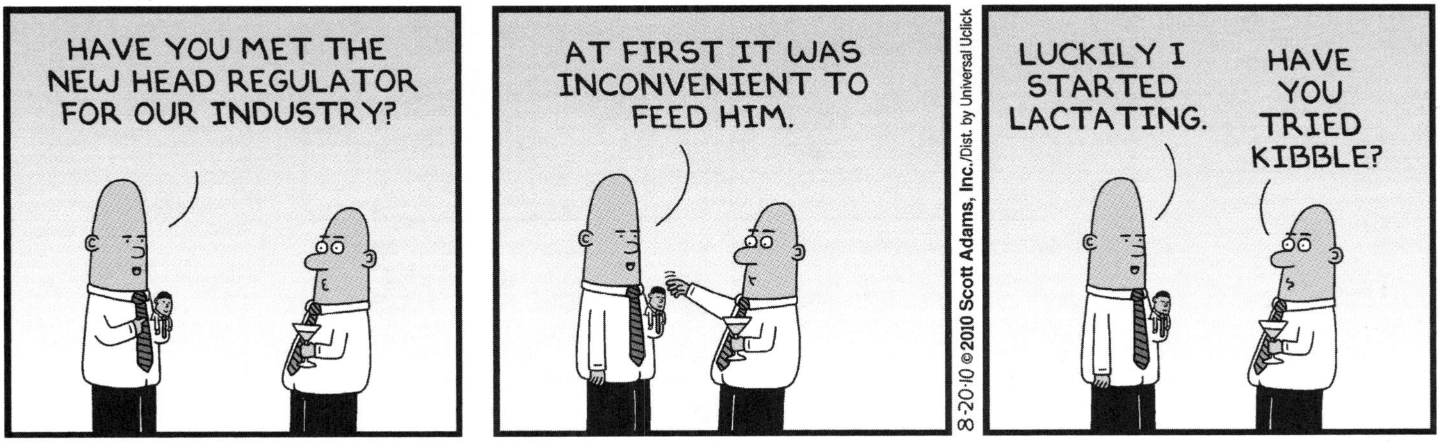
HAVE YOU MET THE NEW HEAD REGULATOR FOR OUR INDUSTRY?
AT FIRST IT WAS INCONVENIENT TO FEED HIM.
8-20-10 © 2010 Scott Adams, Inc./Dist. by Universal Uclick
LUCKILY I STARTED LACTATING.
HAVE YOU TRIED KIBBLE?

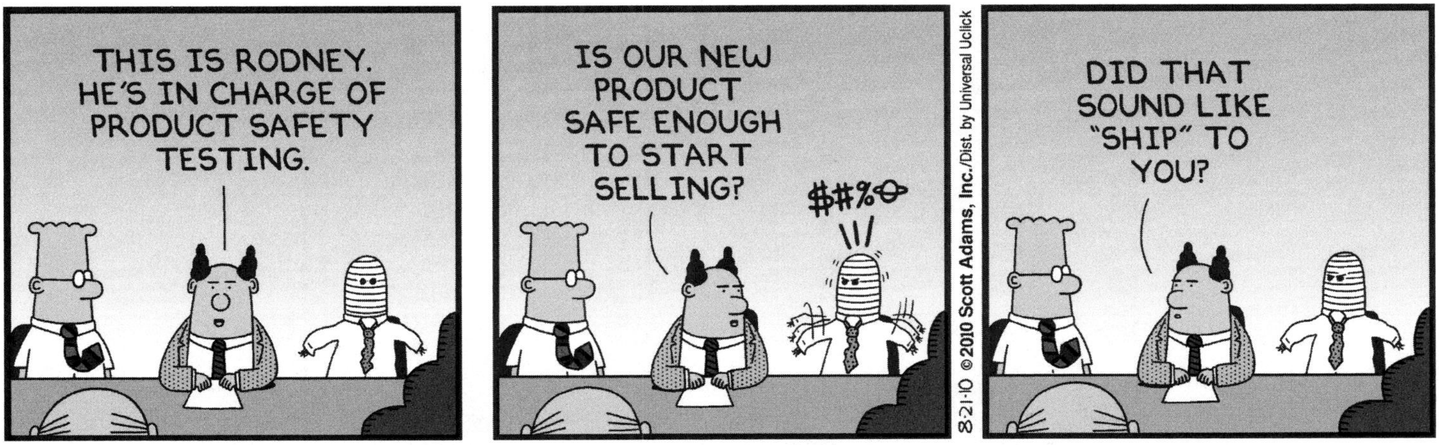
THIS IS RODNEY. HE'S IN CHARGE OF PRODUCT SAFETY TESTING.
IS OUR NEW PRODUCT SAFE ENOUGH TO START SELLING?
$#%
8-21-10 © 2010 Scott Adams, Inc./Dist. by Universal Uclick
DID THAT SOUND LIKE "SHIP" TO YOU?

THE STATUS OF MY PROJECT IS THAT APPARENTLY I DIED AND BECAME A GHOST.
I DON'T REMEMBER DYING, BUT THE EVIDENCE OF MY UNTIMELY DEMISE IS CLEAR.
IN THE PAST WEEK, NO ONE HAS RETURNED MY PHONE CALLS OR REPLIED TO MY EMAILS.
WHEN I TRY TO PRINT A DOCUMENT, I GET NOTHING BUT ERROR MESSAGES.
NOW ALL OF YOU ARE LOOKING AT YOUR PHONES AND READING MATERIALS AS IF NO ONE IS SPEAKING TO YOU.
I WILL NOW TEST MY GHOST THEORY BY RUNNING THROUGH A LIVING PERSON.
BOOOO!!!
GOOD NEWS: I'M ALIVE BUT UNWORTHY OF ATTENTION.
I'M TRYING TO WATCH A SHOW.
©2010 Scott Adams, Inc./Dist. by Universal Uclick
8-22-10

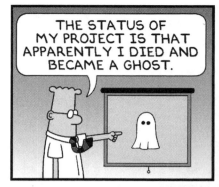

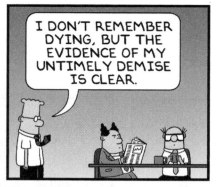

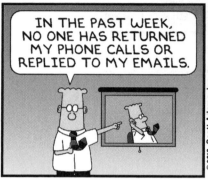

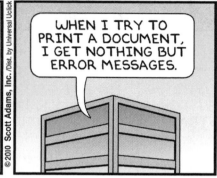

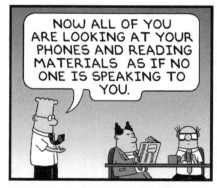

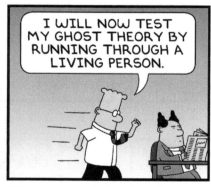

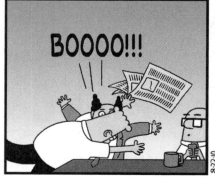

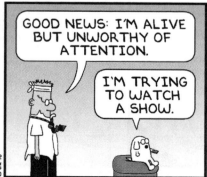

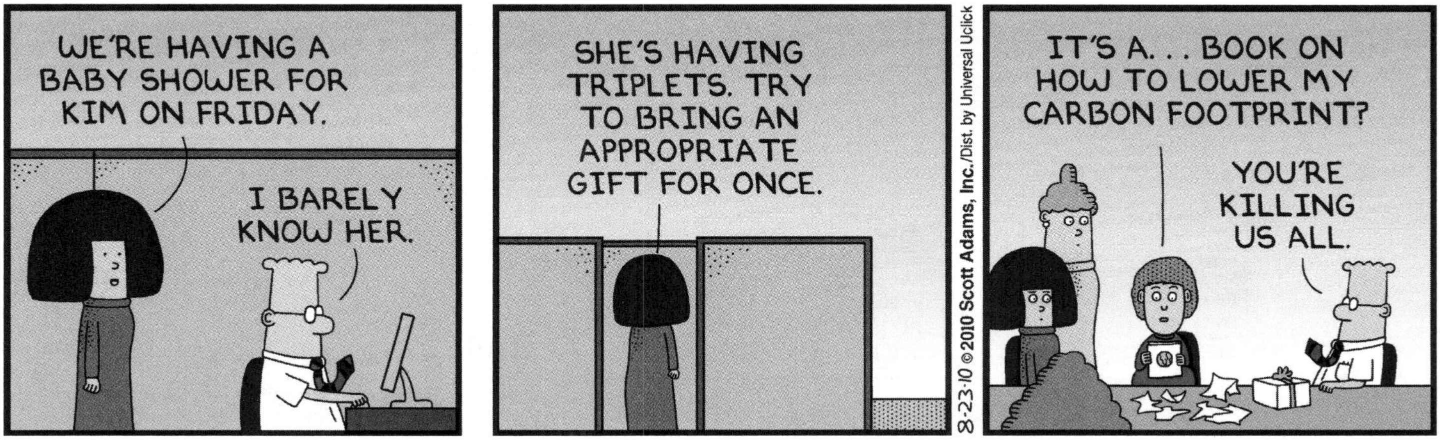
WE'RE HAVING A BABY SHOWER FOR KIM ON FRIDAY.
I BARELY KNOW HER.
SHE'S HAVING TRIPLETS. TRY TO BRING AN APPROPRIATE GIFT FOR ONCE.
8-23-10 © 2010 Scott Adams, Inc./Dist. by Universal Uclick
IT'S A. . . BOOK ON HOW TO LOWER MY CARBON FOOTPRINT?
YOU'RE KILLING US ALL.

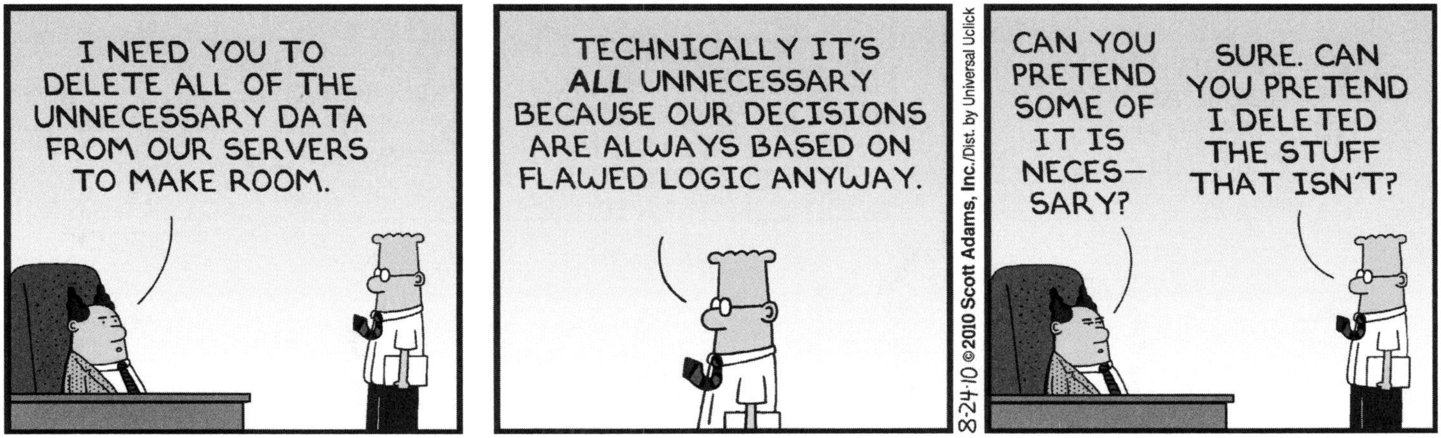
I NEED YOU TO DELETE ALL OF THE UNNECESSARY DATA FROM OUR SERVERS TO MAKE ROOM.
TECHNICALLY IT'S **ALL** UNNECESSARY BECAUSE OUR DECISIONS ARE ALWAYS BASED ON FLAWED LOGIC ANYWAY.
8-24-10 © 2010 Scott Adams, Inc./Dist. by Universal Uclick
CAN YOU PRETEND SOME OF IT IS NECES-SARY?
SURE. CAN YOU PRETEND I DELETED THE STUFF THAT ISN'T?

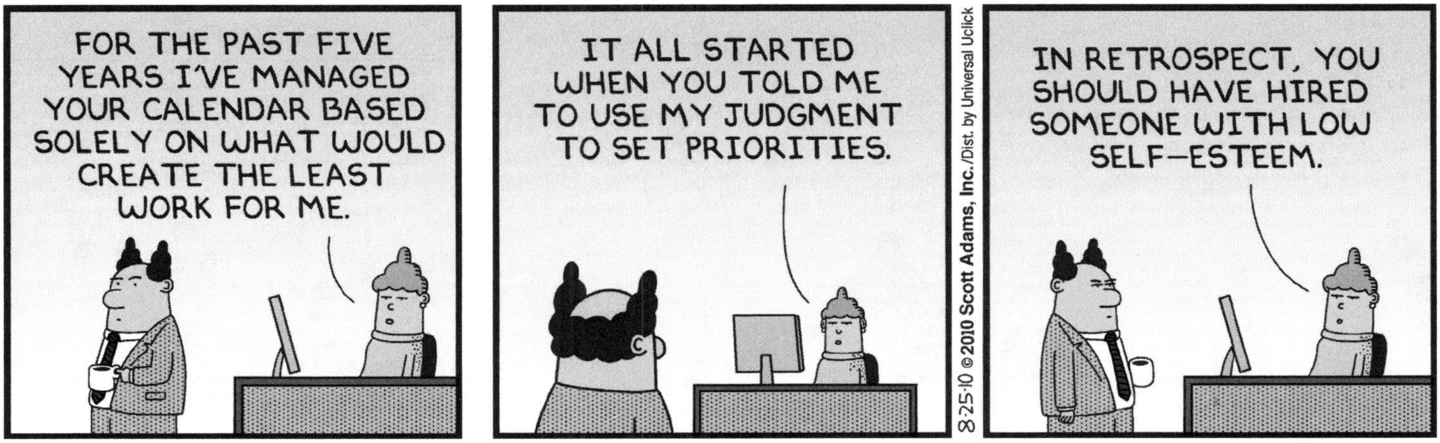
FOR THE PAST FIVE YEARS I'VE MANAGED YOUR CALENDAR BASED SOLELY ON WHAT WOULD CREATE THE LEAST WORK FOR ME.
IT ALL STARTED WHEN YOU TOLD ME TO USE MY JUDGMENT TO SET PRIORITIES.
8-25-10 © 2010 Scott Adams, Inc./Dist. by Universal Uclick
IN RETROSPECT, YOU SHOULD HAVE HIRED SOMEONE WITH LOW SELF-ESTEEM.

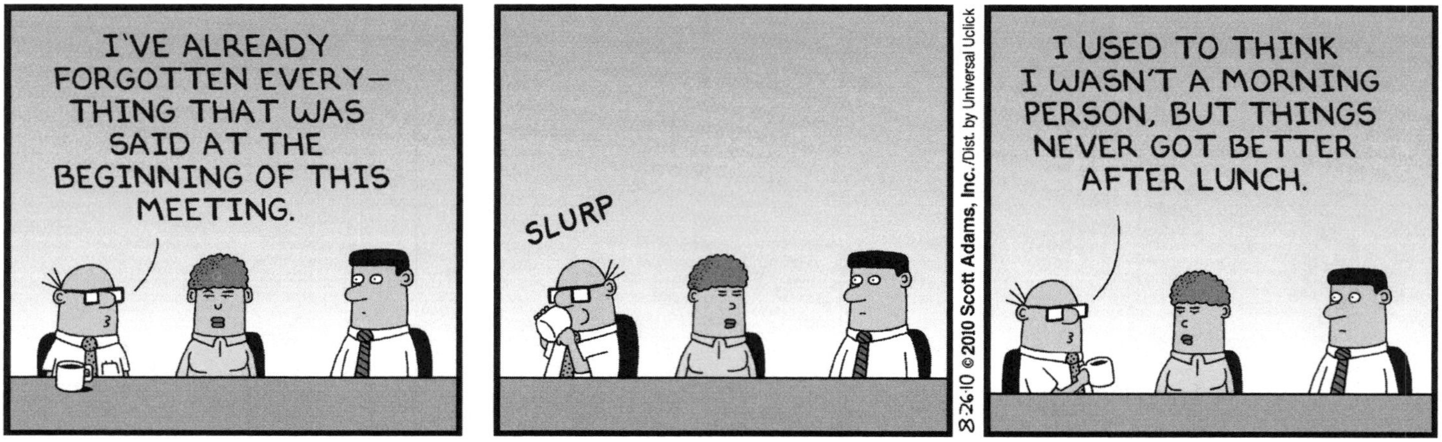
I'VE ALREADY FORGOTTEN EVERY—THING THAT WAS SAID AT THE BEGINNING OF THIS MEETING.
SLURP
I USED TO THINK I WASN'T A MORNING PERSON, BUT THINGS NEVER GOT BETTER AFTER LUNCH.
8·26·10 © 2010 Scott Adams, Inc./Dist. by Universal Uclick

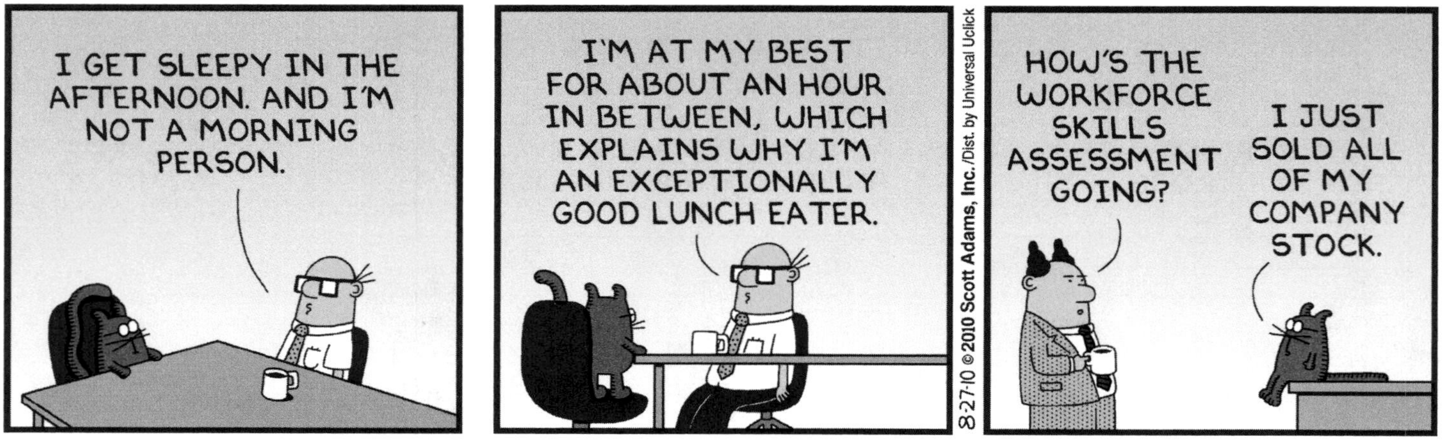
I GET SLEEPY IN THE AFTERNOON. AND I'M NOT A MORNING PERSON.
I'M AT MY BEST FOR ABOUT AN HOUR IN BETWEEN, WHICH EXPLAINS WHY I'M AN EXCEPTIONALLY GOOD LUNCH EATER.
8·27·10 © 2010 Scott Adams, Inc./Dist. by Universal Uclick
HOW'S THE WORKFORCE SKILLS ASSESSMENT GOING?
I JUST SOLD ALL OF MY COMPANY STOCK.

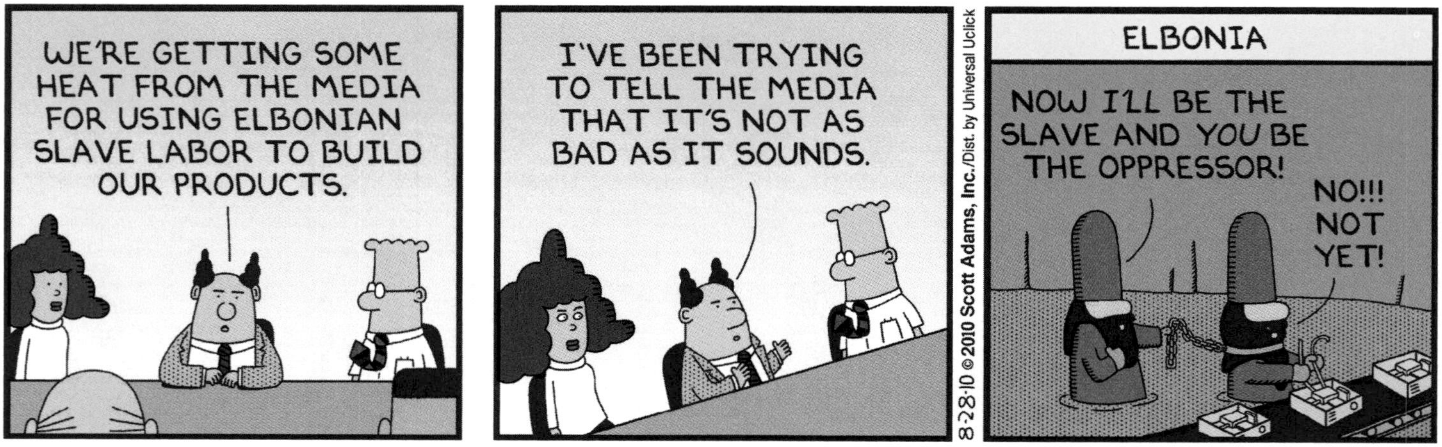
WE'RE GETTING SOME HEAT FROM THE MEDIA FOR USING ELBONIAN SLAVE LABOR TO BUILD OUR PRODUCTS.
I'VE BEEN TRYING TO TELL THE MEDIA THAT IT'S NOT AS BAD AS IT SOUNDS.
8·28·10 © 2010 Scott Adams, Inc./Dist. by Universal Uclick
ELBONIA
NOW I'LL BE THE SLAVE AND YOU BE THE OPPRESSOR!
NO!!! NOT YET!

LET'S HAVE LUNCH SO I CAN TELL YOU ABOUT OUR PRODUCTS.
NO THANKS.
I DON'T LIKE MEETING NEW PEOPLE.
EVERY PERSON I MEET CHIPS AWAY AT MY FREEDOM.
IF I HAVE LUNCH WITH YOU, I'LL FEEL AN OBLIGATION TO RETURN YOUR PESTER-ING PHONE CALLS.
MY LUNCHTIME IS THE ONLY CHANCE I GET DURING THE DAY TO SCRAPE OFF THE LEECHES.
NOTHING PERSONAL.
DO YOU WANT TO HAVE LUNCH AND DISCUSS OUR NEW PRODUCT LINE?
SURE!
CARL, YOU ARE TOTALLY IN THE WRONG PROFESSION.
©2010 Scott Adams, Inc./Dist. by Universal Uclick
8-29-10

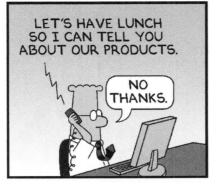

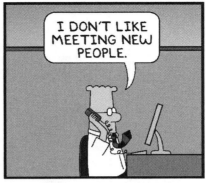

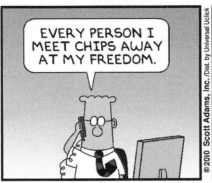

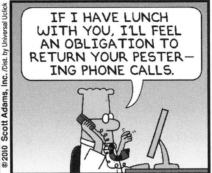

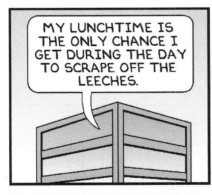

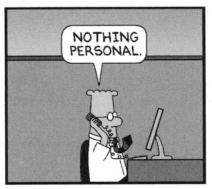

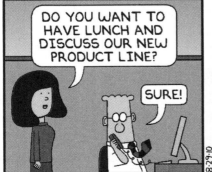

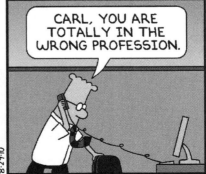

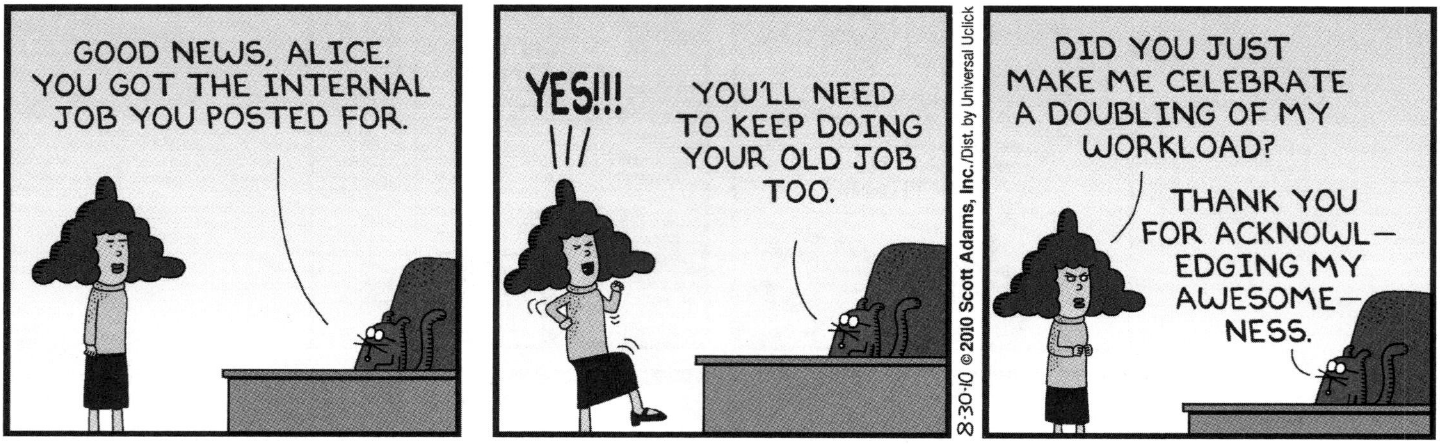
GOOD NEWS, ALICE. YOU GOT THE INTERNAL JOB YOU POSTED FOR.
YES!!!
YOU'LL NEED TO KEEP DOING YOUR OLD JOB TOO.
8-30-10 © 2010 Scott Adams, Inc./Dist. by Universal Uclick
DID YOU JUST MAKE ME CELEBRATE A DOUBLING OF MY WORKLOAD?
THANK YOU FOR ACKNOWL-EDGING MY AWESOME-NESS.

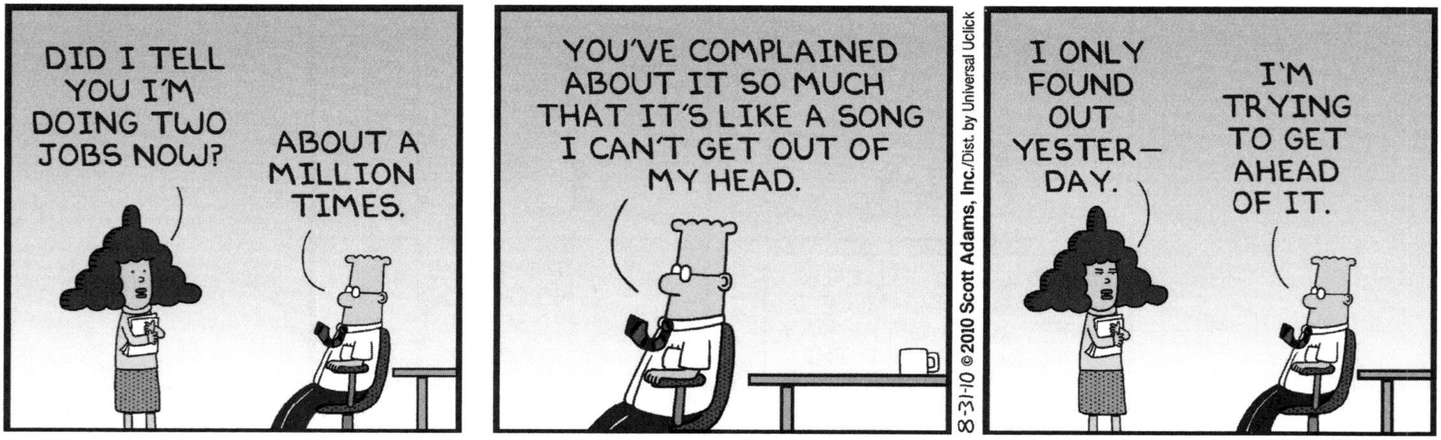
DID I TELL YOU I'M DOING TWO JOBS NOW?
ABOUT A MILLION TIMES.
YOU'VE COMPLAINED ABOUT IT SO MUCH THAT IT'S LIKE A SONG I CAN'T GET OUT OF MY HEAD.
8-31-10 © 2010 Scott Adams, Inc./Dist. by Universal Uclick
I ONLY FOUND OUT YESTER-DAY.
I'M TRYING TO GET AHEAD OF IT.

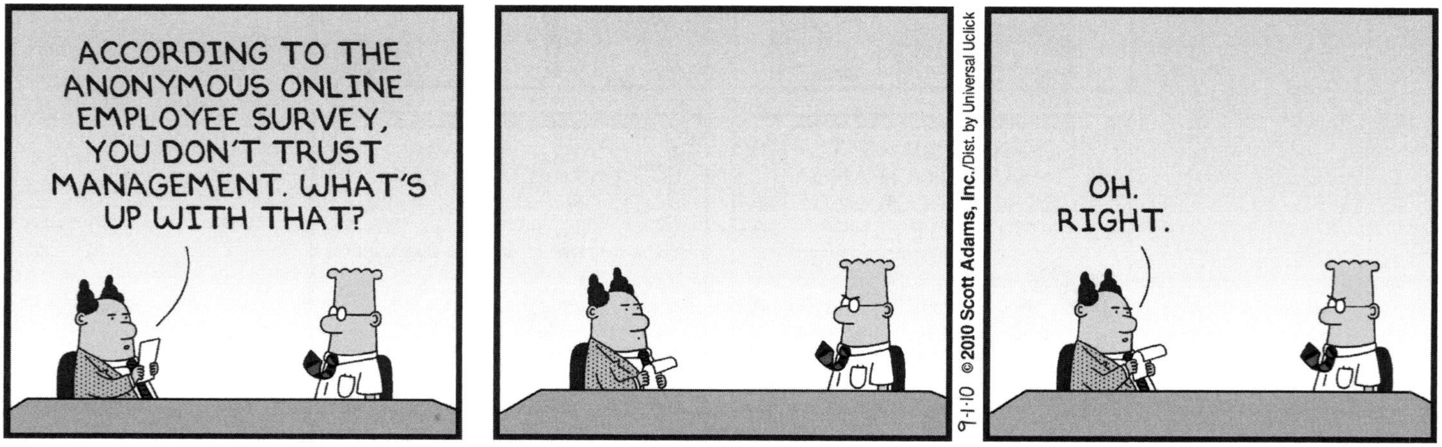
ACCORDING TO THE ANONYMOUS ONLINE EMPLOYEE SURVEY, YOU DON'T TRUST MANAGEMENT. WHAT'S UP WITH THAT?
9-1-10 © 2010 Scott Adams, Inc./Dist. by Universal Uclick
OH. RIGHT.

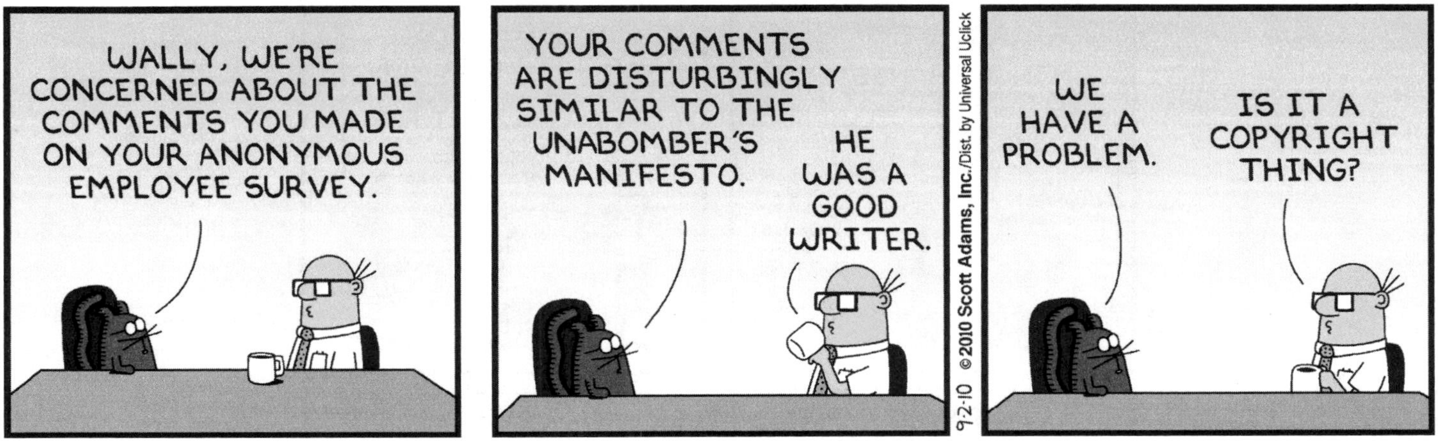
WALLY, WE'RE CONCERNED ABOUT THE COMMENTS YOU MADE ON YOUR ANONYMOUS EMPLOYEE SURVEY.
YOUR COMMENTS ARE DISTURBINGLY SIMILAR TO THE UNABOMBER'S MANIFESTO.
HE WAS A GOOD WRITER.
WE HAVE A PROBLEM.
IS IT A COPYRIGHT THING?
9-2-10 © 2010 Scott Adams, Inc./Dist. by Universal Uclick

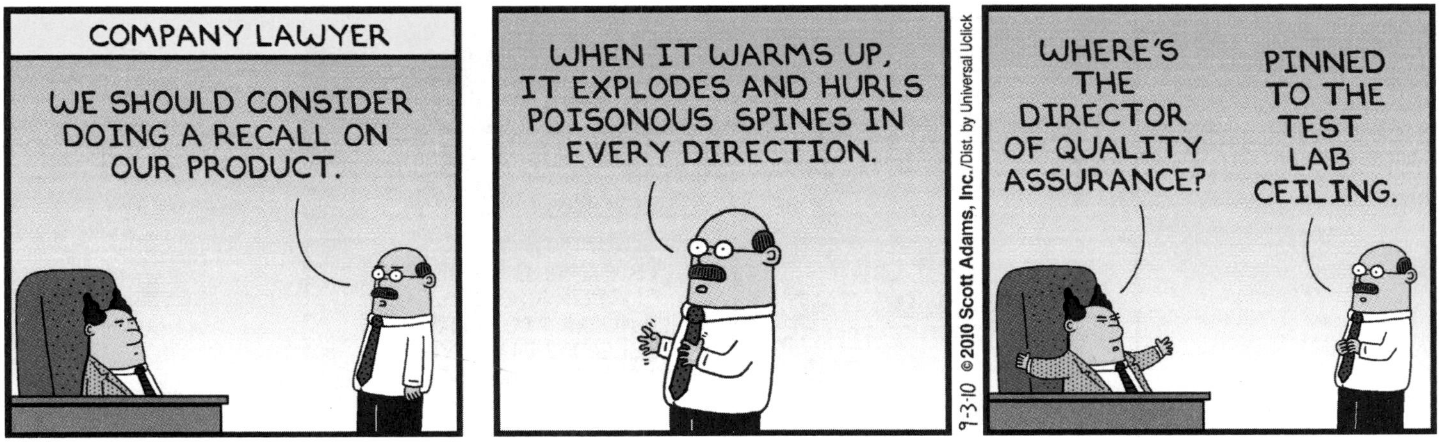
COMPANY LAWYER
WE SHOULD CONSIDER DOING A RECALL ON OUR PRODUCT.
WHEN IT WARMS UP, IT EXPLODES AND HURLS POISONOUS SPINES IN EVERY DIRECTION.
WHERE'S THE DIRECTOR OF QUALITY ASSURANCE?
PINNED TO THE TEST LAB CEILING.
9-3-10 © 2010 Scott Adams, Inc./Dist. by Universal Uclick

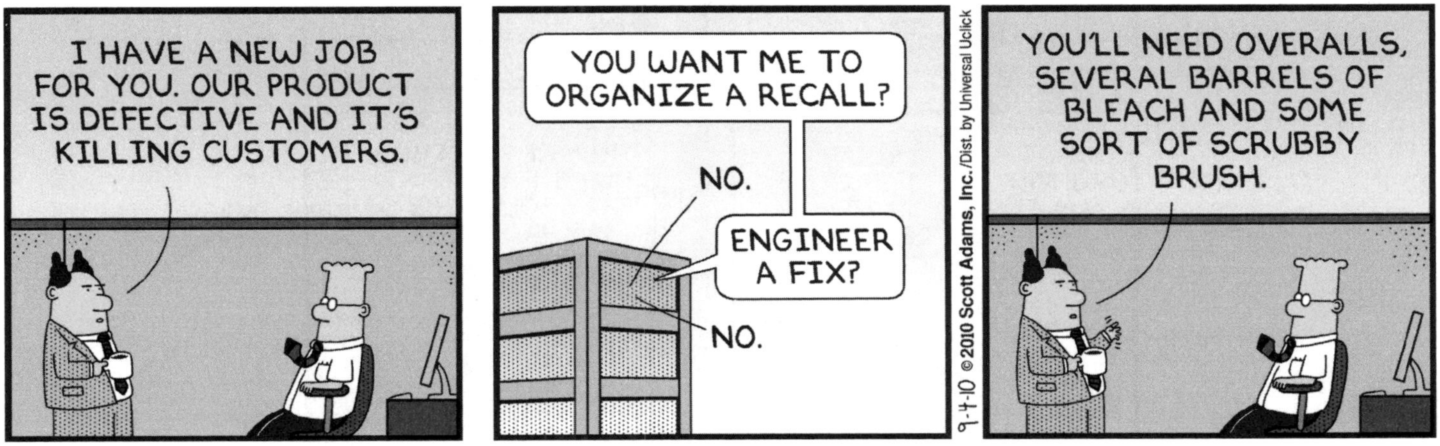
I HAVE A NEW JOB FOR YOU. OUR PRODUCT IS DEFECTIVE AND IT'S KILLING CUSTOMERS.
YOU WANT ME TO ORGANIZE A RECALL?
NO.
ENGINEER A FIX?
NO.
YOU'LL NEED OVERALLS, SEVERAL BARRELS OF BLEACH AND SOME SORT OF SCRUBBY BRUSH.
9-4-10 © 2010 Scott Adams, Inc./Dist. by Universal Uclick

I NEED A MINOR CHANGE TO OUR WEBSITE.
GIVE ME YOUR BUSINESS CASE FOR THE CHANGE AND I'LL PRIORITIZE IT FOR THE QUEUE.
I DON'T HAVE TIME TO WRITE A BUSINESS CASE FOR ONE LITTLE CHANGE.
I CAN'T JUSTIFY CHANGING MY PRIORITIES WITHOUT ONE.
GAAAA!!! WHY CAN'T WE DO THE SIMPLEST THINGS IN THIS STUPID COMPANY???!
TRY ONE OF THESE CORPORATE POST-TRAUMATIC STRESS PILLS TO DULL YOUR MEMORY OF THESE EVENTS.
WHAT? WHERE AM I? WHO ARE YOU?
YOU WERE JUST LEAVING.
THEY'RE PLACEBOS, BUT I FIND THAT THEY SOLVE 20% OF MY PROBLEMS.
© 2010 Scott Adams, Inc./Dist. by Universal Uclick
9-5-10

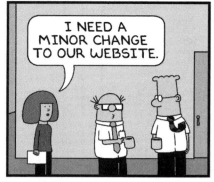

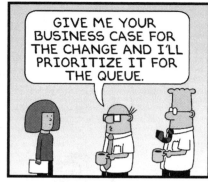

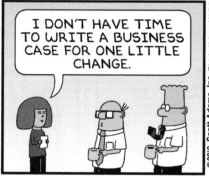

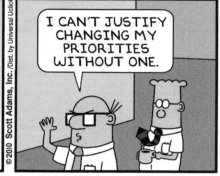

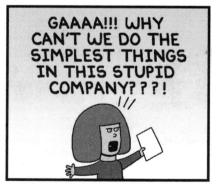

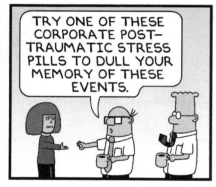

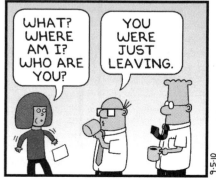

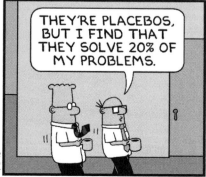

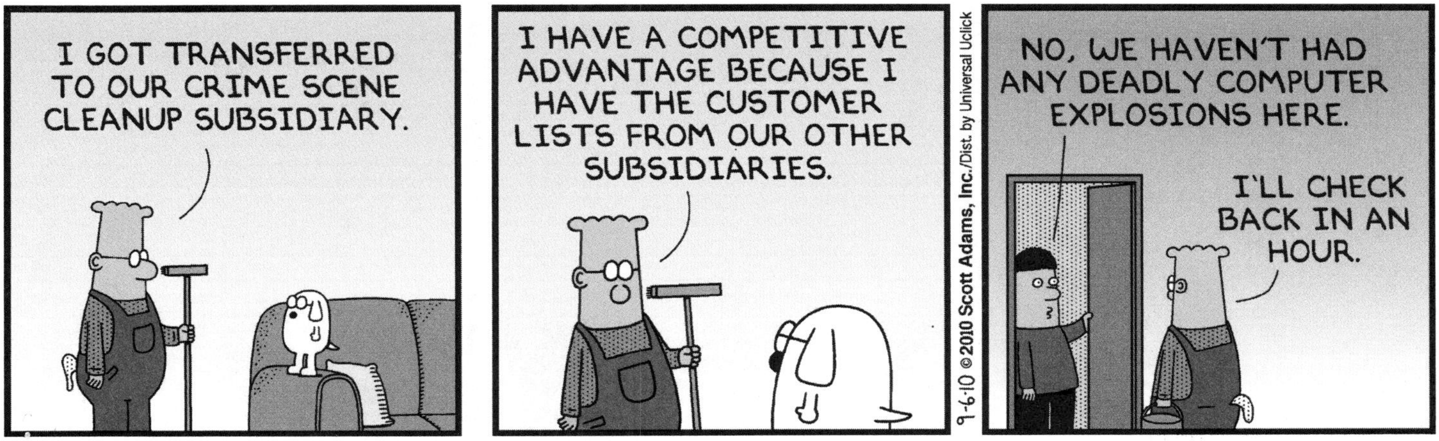
I GOT TRANSFERRED TO OUR CRIME SCENE CLEANUP SUBSIDIARY.
I HAVE A COMPETITIVE ADVANTAGE BECAUSE I HAVE THE CUSTOMER LISTS FROM OUR OTHER SUBSIDIARIES.
9-6-10 © 2010 Scott Adams, Inc./Dist. by Universal Uclick
NO, WE HAVEN'T HAD ANY DEADLY COMPUTER EXPLOSIONS HERE.
I'LL CHECK BACK IN AN HOUR.

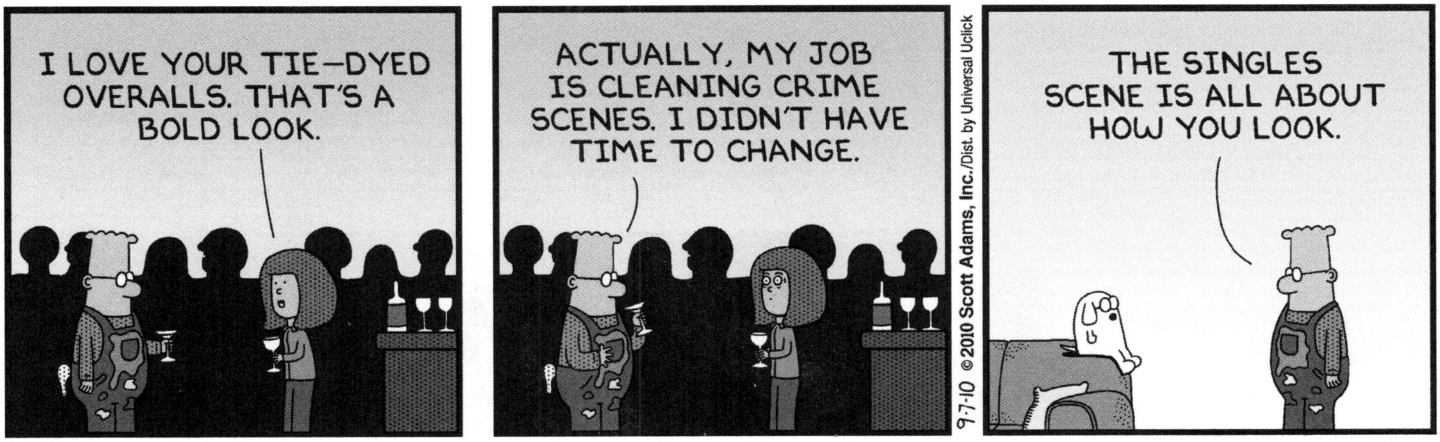
I LOVE YOUR TIE-DYED OVERALLS. THAT'S A BOLD LOOK.
ACTUALLY, MY JOB IS CLEANING CRIME SCENES. I DIDN'T HAVE TIME TO CHANGE.
9-7-10 © 2010 Scott Adams, Inc./Dist. by Universal Uclick
THE SINGLES SCENE IS ALL ABOUT HOW YOU LOOK.

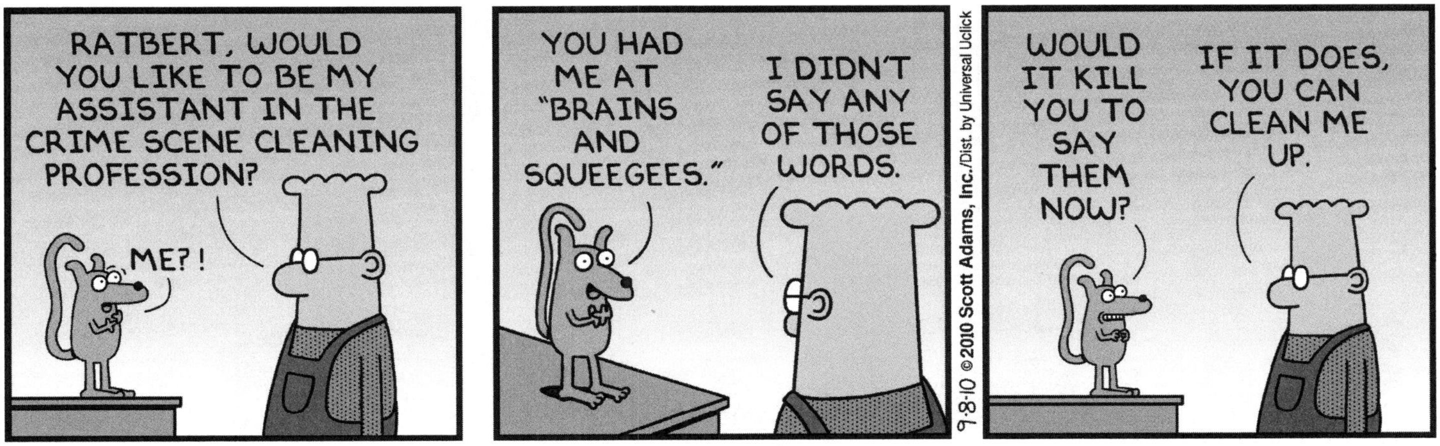
RATBERT, WOULD YOU LIKE TO BE MY ASSISTANT IN THE CRIME SCENE CLEANING PROFESSION?
ME?!
YOU HAD ME AT "BRAINS AND SQUEEGEES."
I DIDN'T SAY ANY OF THOSE WORDS.
9-8-10 © 2010 Scott Adams, Inc./Dist. by Universal Uclick
WOULD IT KILL YOU TO SAY THEM NOW?
IF IT DOES, YOU CAN CLEAN ME UP.

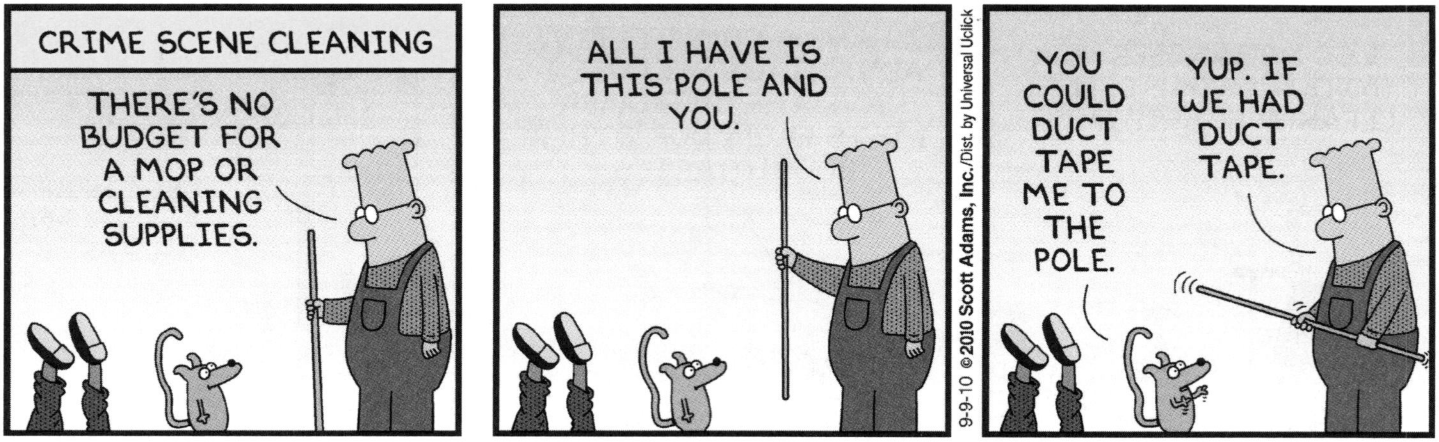
CRIME SCENE CLEANING
THERE'S NO BUDGET FOR A MOP OR CLEANING SUPPLIES.
ALL I HAVE IS THIS POLE AND YOU.
9-9-10 © 2010 Scott Adams, Inc./Dist. by Universal Uclick
YOU COULD DUCT TAPE ME TO THE POLE.
YUP. IF WE HAD DUCT TAPE.

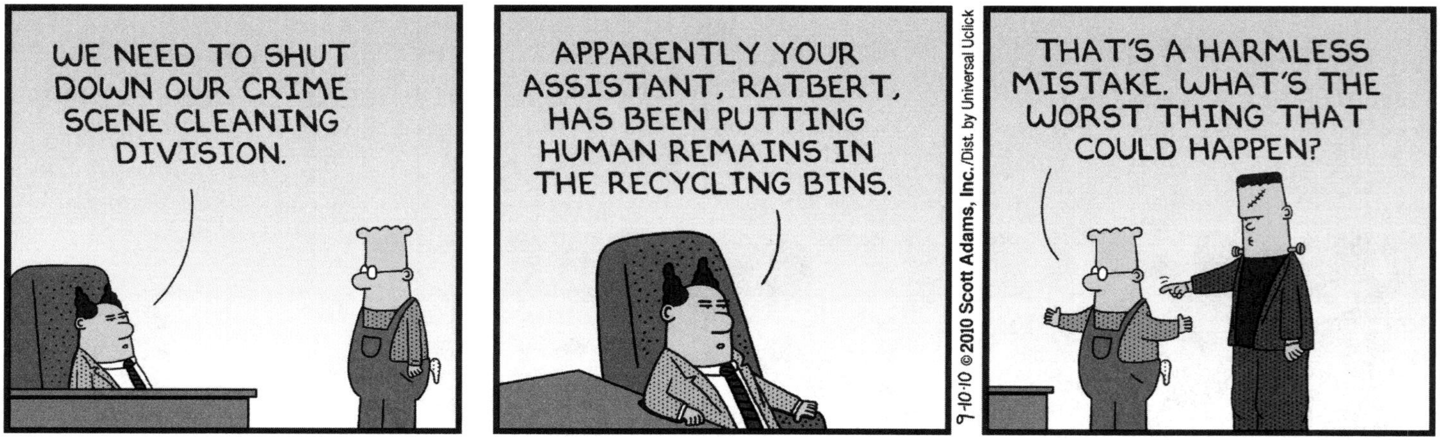
WE NEED TO SHUT DOWN OUR CRIME SCENE CLEANING DIVISION.
APPARENTLY YOUR ASSISTANT, RATBERT, HAS BEEN PUTTING HUMAN REMAINS IN THE RECYCLING BINS.
9-10-10 © 2010 Scott Adams, Inc./Dist. by Universal Uclick
THAT'S A HARMLESS MISTAKE. WHAT'S THE WORST THING THAT COULD HAPPEN?

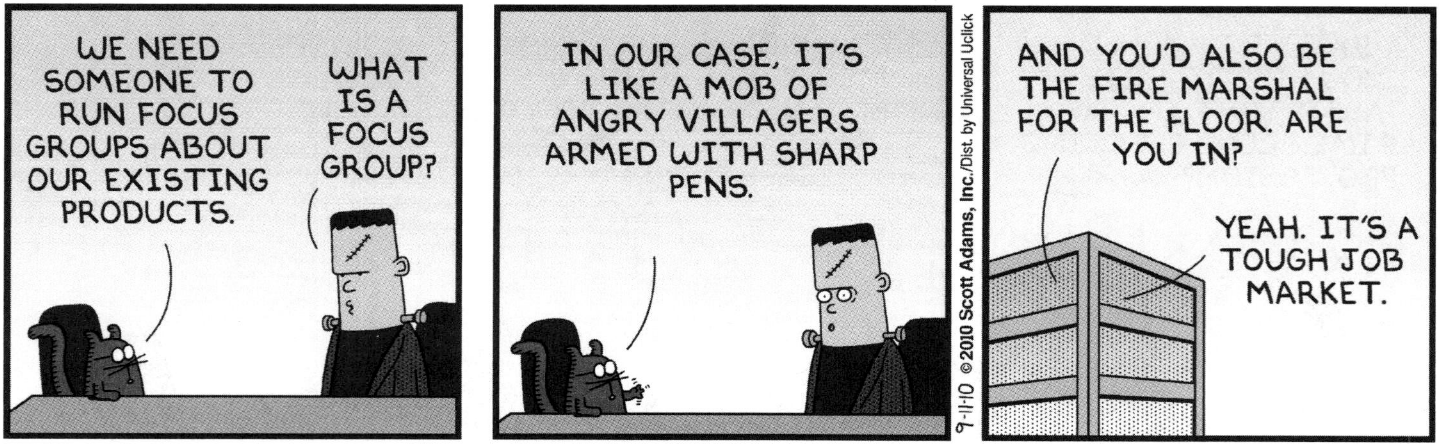
WE NEED SOMEONE TO RUN FOCUS GROUPS ABOUT OUR EXISTING PRODUCTS.
WHAT IS A FOCUS GROUP?
IN OUR CASE, IT'S LIKE A MOB OF ANGRY VILLAGERS ARMED WITH SHARP PENS.
9-11-10 © 2010 Scott Adams, Inc./Dist. by Universal Uclick
AND YOU'D ALSO BE THE FIRE MARSHAL FOR THE FLOOR. ARE YOU IN?
YEAH. IT'S A TOUGH JOB MARKET.

I NEED THIS ROOM FOR MY MEETING.
WOULDN'T IT MAKE MORE SENSE FOR YOU TO GET A DIFFERENT ROOM SINCE WE'RE ALREADY HERE?
ALL OF THE CONFERENCE ROOMS ARE BOOKED.
OKAY, THEN I GUESS WE SHOULD COMPARE THE IMPORTANCE OF YOUR MEETING VERSUS THIS ONE.
THAT'S NOT HOW IT WORKS.
CONFERENCE ROOMS GO TO THE HIGHEST RANKED MANAGER.
IT TOOK ME MONTHS TO SCHEDULE THIS MEETING!
SCRAM.
THE GOAL OF THIS MEETING IS TO FIGURE OUT WHY NOTHING EVER GETS DONE AROUND HERE.
© 2010 Scott Adams, Inc. /Dist. by Universal Uclick
9-12-10

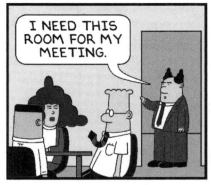

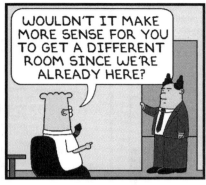

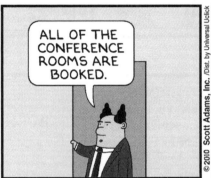

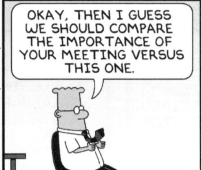

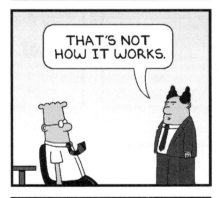

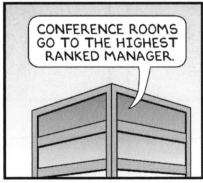

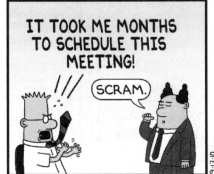

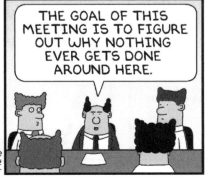

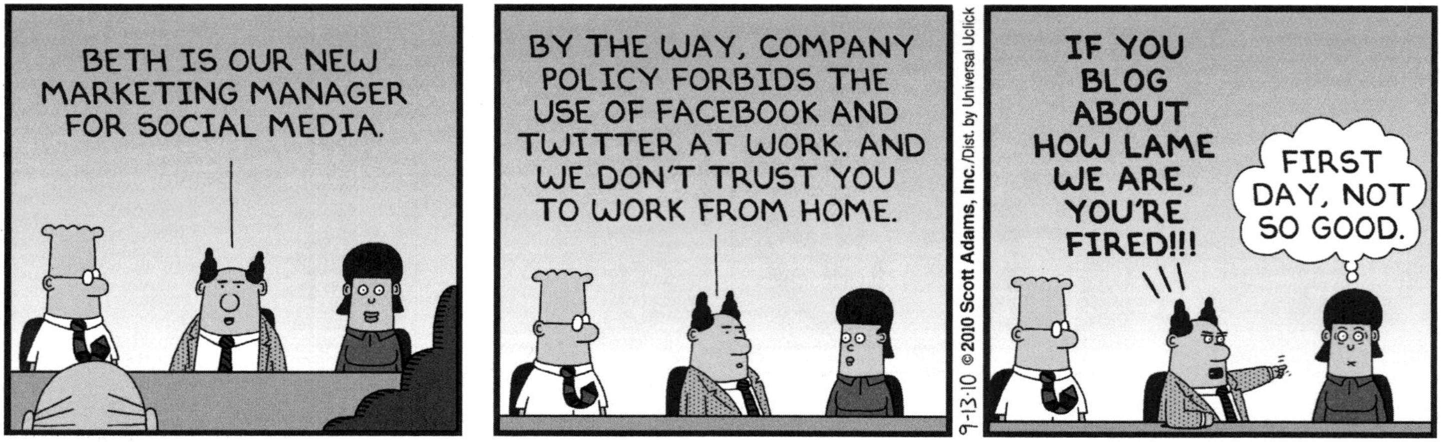
BETH IS OUR NEW MARKETING MANAGER FOR SOCIAL MEDIA.
BY THE WAY, COMPANY POLICY FORBIDS THE USE OF FACEBOOK AND TWITTER AT WORK. AND WE DON'T TRUST YOU TO WORK FROM HOME.
9-13-10 © 2010 Scott Adams, Inc./Dist. by Universal Uclick
IF YOU BLOG ABOUT HOW LAME WE ARE, YOU'RE FIRED!!!
FIRST DAY, NOT SO GOOD.

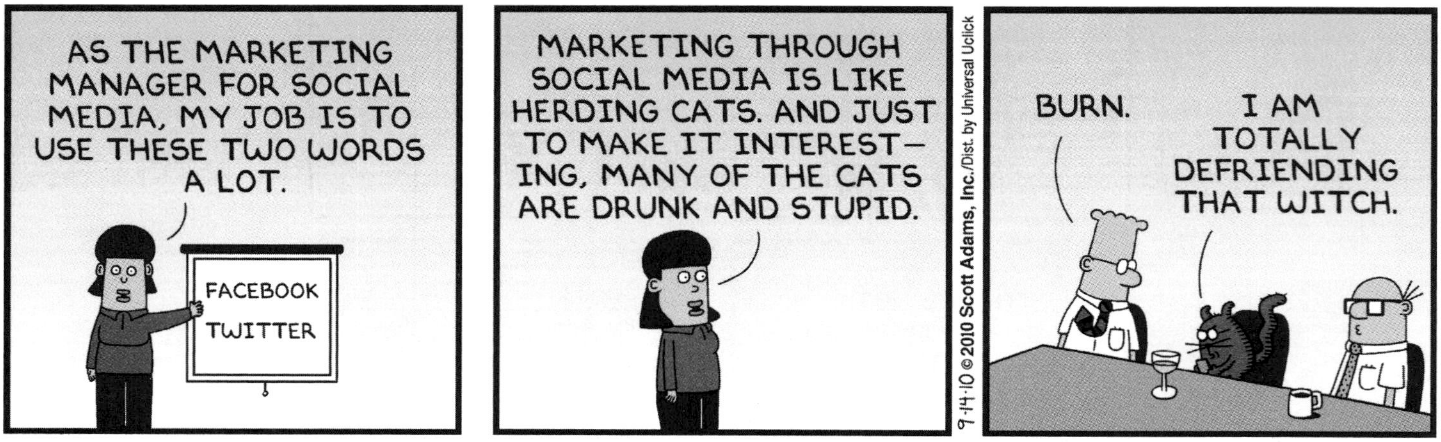
AS THE MARKETING MANAGER FOR SOCIAL MEDIA, MY JOB IS TO USE THESE TWO WORDS A LOT.
FACEBOOK
TWITTER
MARKETING THROUGH SOCIAL MEDIA IS LIKE HERDING CATS. AND JUST TO MAKE IT INTEREST-ING, MANY OF THE CATS ARE DRUNK AND STUPID.
9-14-10 © 2010 Scott Adams, Inc./Dist. by Universal Uclick
BURN.
I AM TOTALLY DEFRIENDING THAT WITCH.

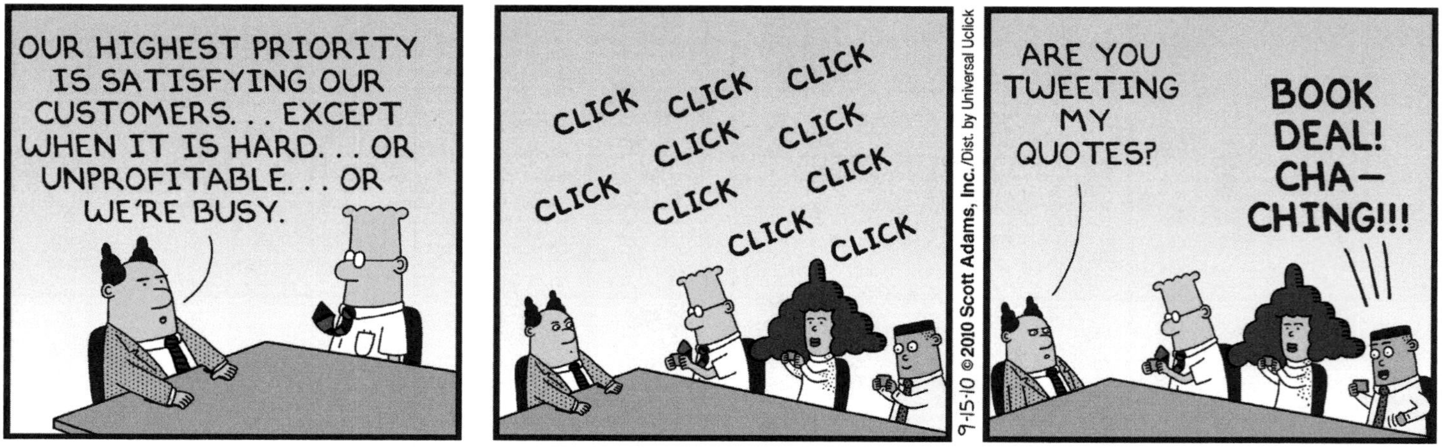
OUR HIGHEST PRIORITY IS SATISFYING OUR CUSTOMERS. . . EXCEPT WHEN IT IS HARD. . . OR UNPROFITABLE. . . OR WE'RE BUSY.
CLICK CLICK CLICK CLICK CLICK CLICK CLICK CLICK CLICK CLICK CLICK
9-15-10 © 2010 Scott Adams, Inc./Dist. by Universal Uclick
ARE YOU TWEETING MY QUOTES?
BOOK DEAL! CHA-CHING!!!

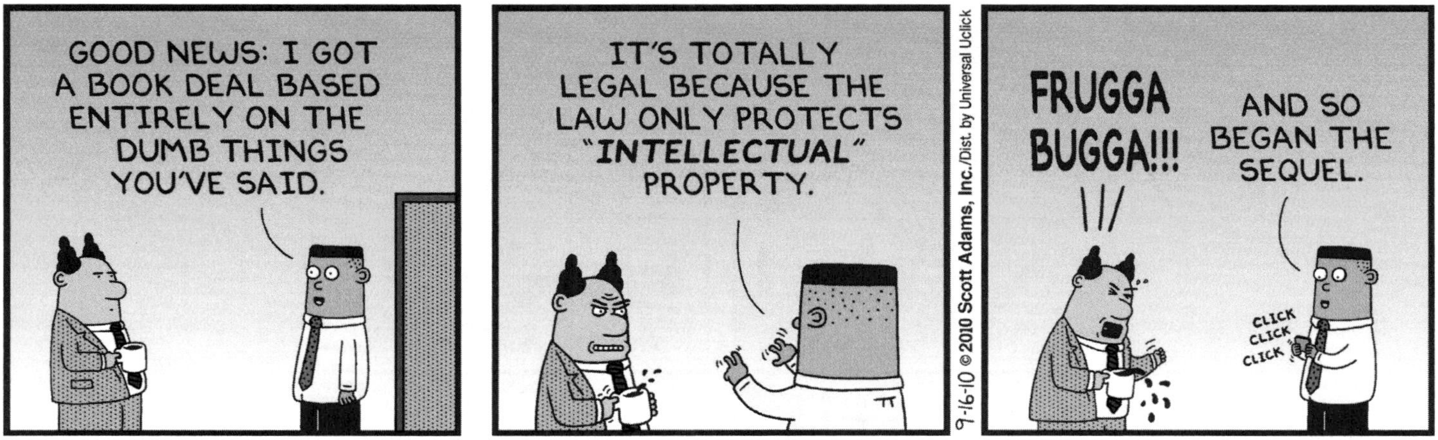
GOOD NEWS: I GOT A BOOK DEAL BASED ENTIRELY ON THE DUMB THINGS YOU'VE SAID.
IT'S TOTALLY LEGAL BECAUSE THE LAW ONLY PROTECTS "*INTELLECTUAL*" PROPERTY.
9-16-10 © 2010 Scott Adams, Inc./Dist. by Universal Uclick
FRUGGA BUGGA!!!
AND SO BEGAN THE SEQUEL.
CLICK CLICK CLICK

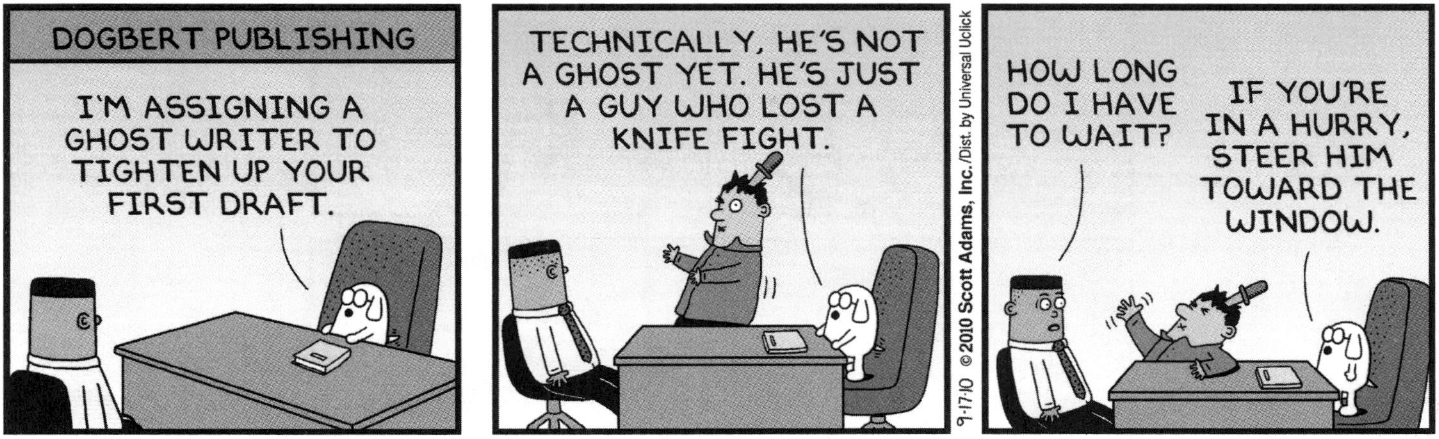
DOGBERT PUBLISHING
I'M ASSIGNING A GHOST WRITER TO TIGHTEN UP YOUR FIRST DRAFT.
TECHNICALLY, HE'S NOT A GHOST YET. HE'S JUST A GUY WHO LOST A KNIFE FIGHT.
9-17-10 © 2010 Scott Adams, Inc./Dist. by Universal Uclick
HOW LONG DO I HAVE TO WAIT?
IF YOU'RE IN A HURRY, STEER HIM TOWARD THE WINDOW.

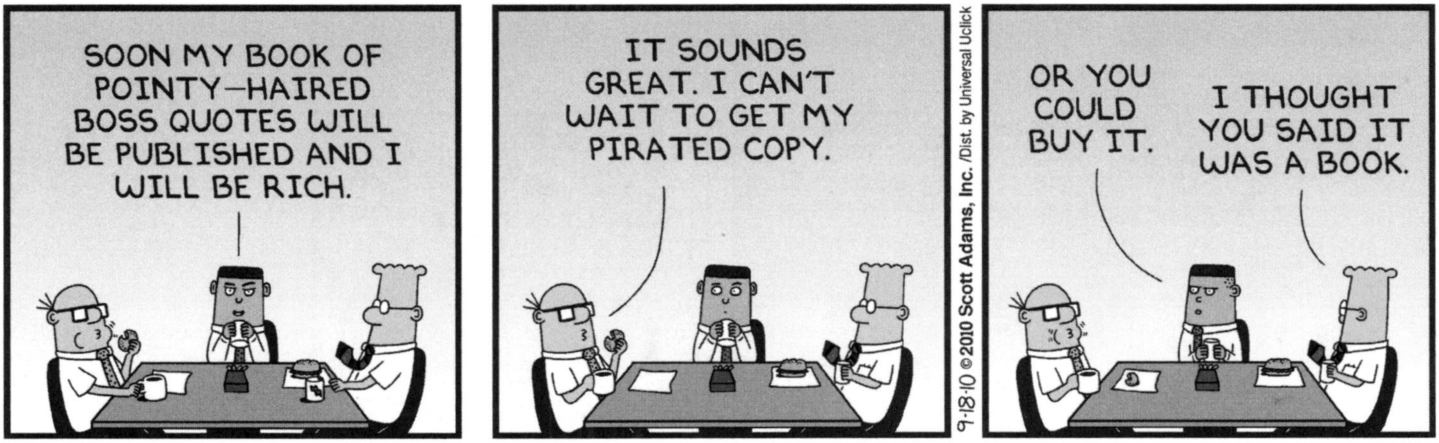
SOON MY BOOK OF POINTY-HAIRED BOSS QUOTES WILL BE PUBLISHED AND I WILL BE RICH.
IT SOUNDS GREAT. I CAN'T WAIT TO GET MY PIRATED COPY.
9-18-10 © 2010 Scott Adams, Inc./Dist. by Universal Uclick
OR YOU COULD BUY IT.
I THOUGHT YOU SAID IT WAS A BOOK.

I DON'T UNDERSTAND EITHER OF YOUR TECHNICAL PROPOSALS, AND I NEED TO PICK ONE.
NORMALLY I'D USE FAVORITISM, BUT I DON'T LIKE EITHER ONE OF YOU.
SO I'LL GIVE YOU AN INTELLIGENCE TEST, AND I'LL APPROVE THE PROPOSAL OF WHOEVER IS THE SMARTEST.
©2010 Scott Adams, Inc./Dist. by Universal Uclick
IF YOU SHOOT AN ARROW AT A MONKEY FROM AN AIRPLANE. . .
AND THE MONKEY THROWS A COCONUT AT THE INCOMING ARROW TO STOP IT, BUT HE MISSES. . .
HOW CAN YOU TELL WHAT TIME IT IS?
THERE'S NOT ENOUGH DATA.
YOU LOOK AT YOUR WATCH?
9·19·10
THE CORRECT ANSWER IS "ASK THE MONKEY AND HOPE HE DOESN'T HOLD A GRUDGE."

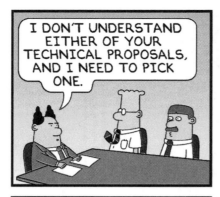

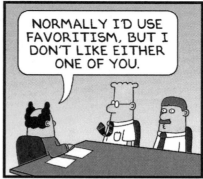

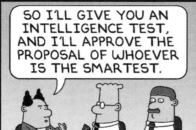

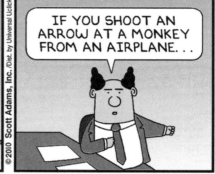

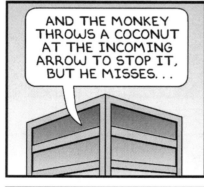

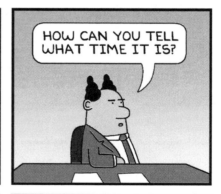

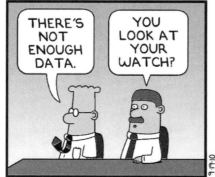

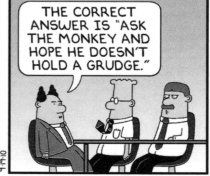

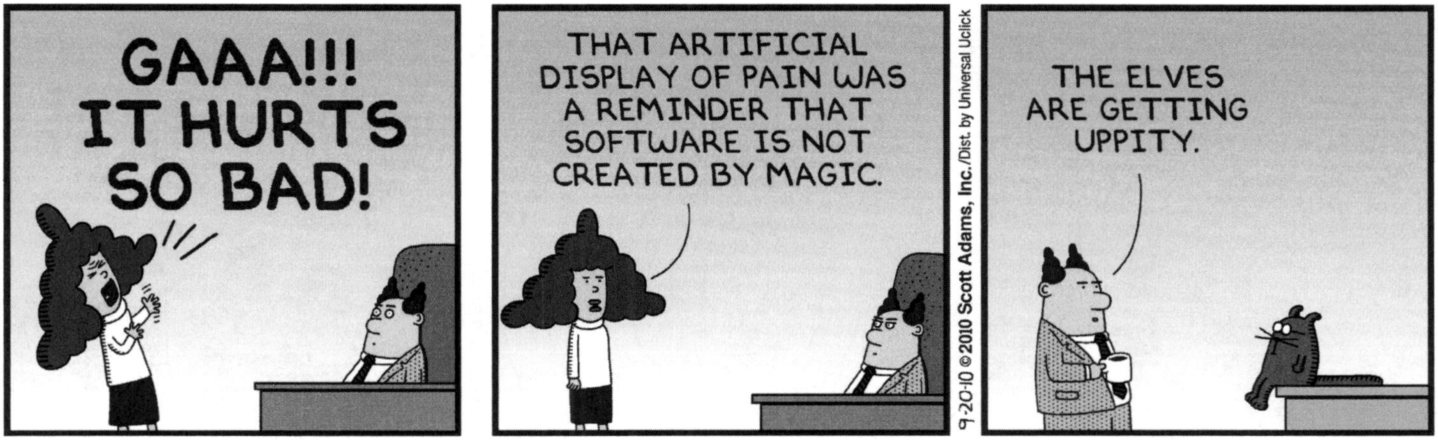
GAAA!!! IT HURTS SO BAD!
THAT ARTIFICIAL DISPLAY OF PAIN WAS A REMINDER THAT SOFTWARE IS NOT CREATED BY MAGIC.
9-20-10 © 2010 Scott Adams, Inc./Dist. by Universal Uclick
THE ELVES ARE GETTING UPPITY.

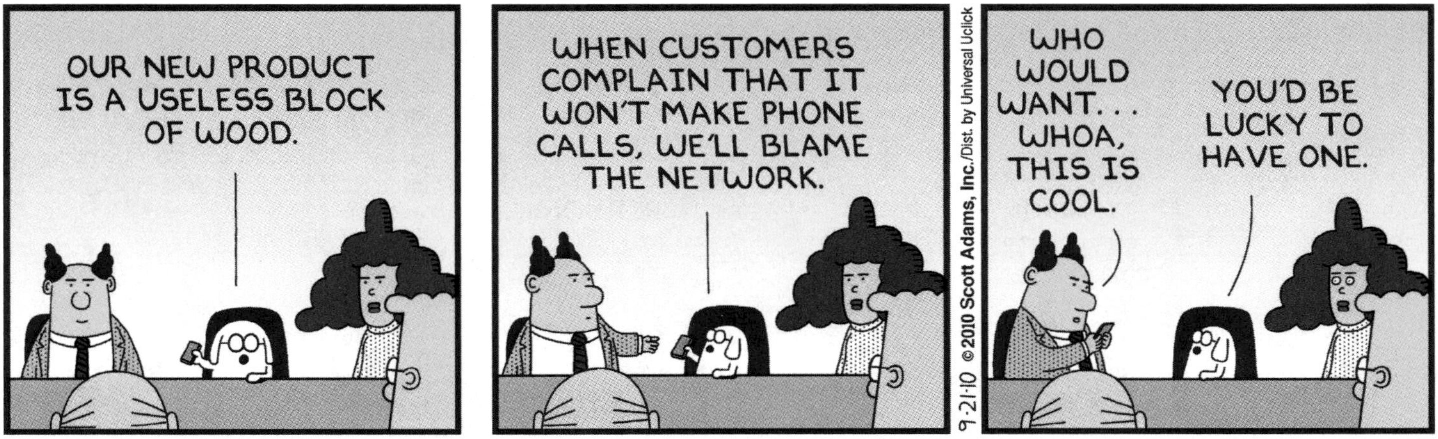
OUR NEW PRODUCT IS A USELESS BLOCK OF WOOD.
WHEN CUSTOMERS COMPLAIN THAT IT WON'T MAKE PHONE CALLS, WE'LL BLAME THE NETWORK.
9-21-10 © 2010 Scott Adams, Inc./Dist. by Universal Uclick
WHO WOULD WANT... WHOA, THIS IS COOL.
YOU'D BE LUCKY TO HAVE ONE.

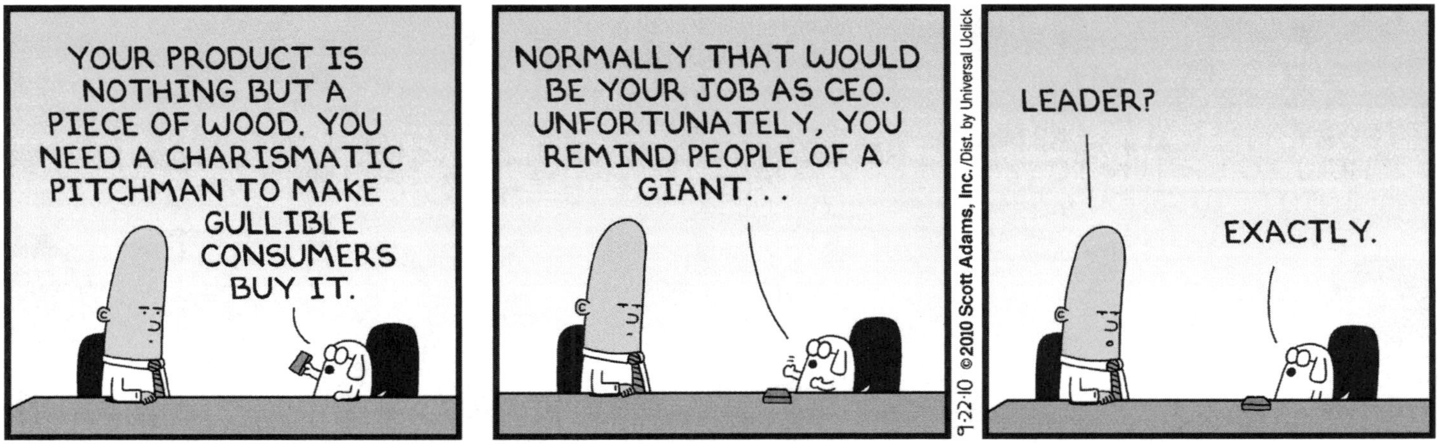
YOUR PRODUCT IS NOTHING BUT A PIECE OF WOOD. YOU NEED A CHARISMATIC PITCHMAN TO MAKE GULLIBLE CONSUMERS BUY IT.
NORMALLY THAT WOULD BE YOUR JOB AS CEO. UNFORTUNATELY, YOU REMIND PEOPLE OF A GIANT...
9-22-10 © 2010 Scott Adams, Inc./Dist. by Universal Uclick
LEADER?
EXACTLY.

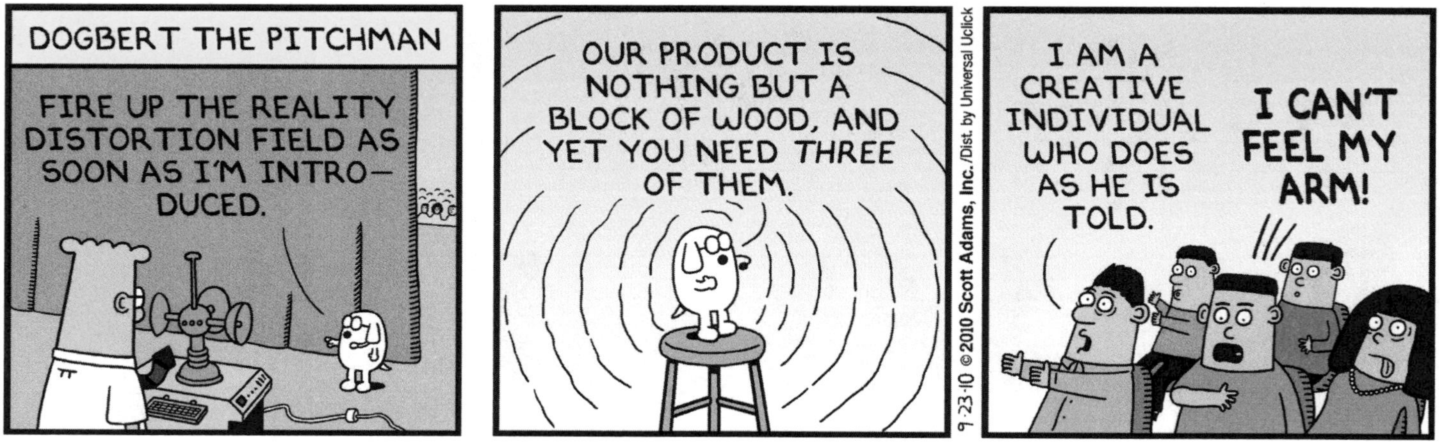
DOGBERT THE PITCHMAN
FIRE UP THE REALITY DISTORTION FIELD AS SOON AS I'M INTRO-DUCED.
OUR PRODUCT IS NOTHING BUT A BLOCK OF WOOD, AND YET YOU NEED *THREE* OF THEM.
I AM A CREATIVE INDIVIDUAL WHO DOES AS HE IS TOLD.
I CAN'T FEEL MY ARM!
9·23·10 © 2010 Scott Adams, Inc./Dist. by Universal Uclick

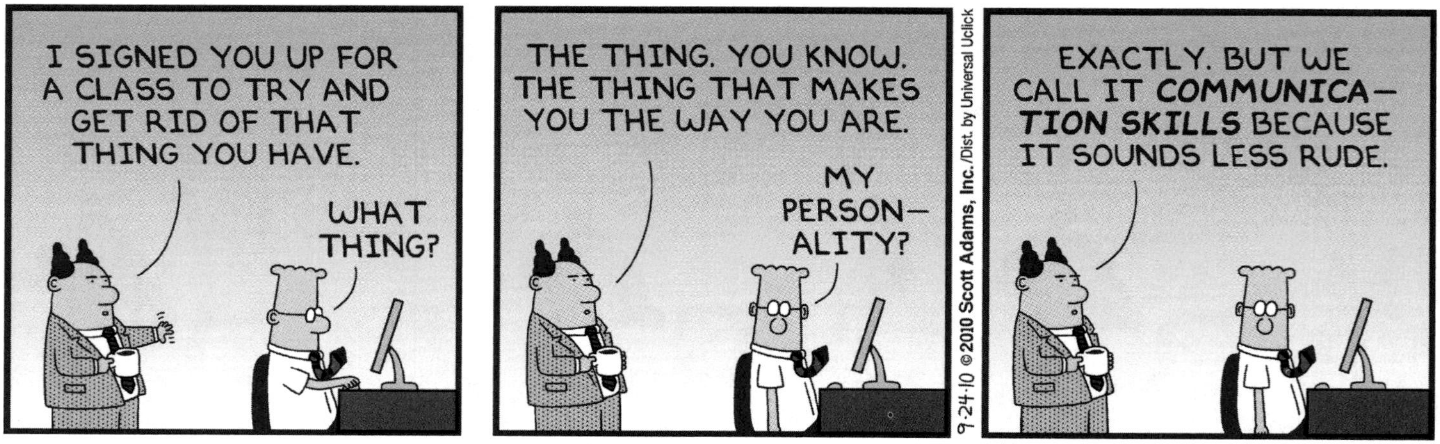
I SIGNED YOU UP FOR A CLASS TO TRY AND GET RID OF THAT THING YOU HAVE.
WHAT THING?
THE THING. YOU KNOW. THE THING THAT MAKES YOU THE WAY YOU ARE.
MY PERSON-ALITY?
EXACTLY. BUT WE CALL IT ***COMMUNICA-TION SKILLS*** BECAUSE IT SOUNDS LESS RUDE.
9·24·10 © 2010 Scott Adams, Inc./Dist. by Universal Uclick

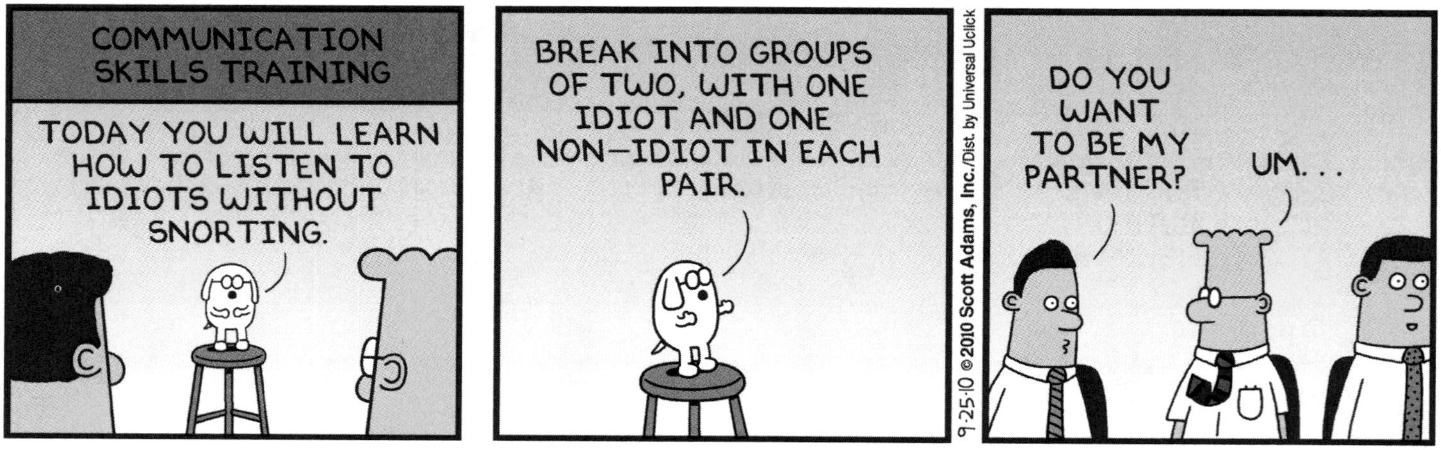
COMMUNICATION SKILLS TRAINING
TODAY YOU WILL LEARN HOW TO LISTEN TO IDIOTS WITHOUT SNORTING.
BREAK INTO GROUPS OF TWO, WITH ONE IDIOT AND ONE NON-IDIOT IN EACH PAIR.
DO YOU WANT TO BE MY PARTNER?
UM. . .
9·25·10 © 2010 Scott Adams, Inc./Dist. by Universal Uclick

INTERVIEW THIS APPLICANT AND TELL ME IF HE'S RIGHT FOR OUR COMPANY.
TIM, WE DON'T SET THE BAR AS HIGH AS WE USED TO.
IN OUR GOLDEN DAYS, WE INSISTED ON EMPLOYEES WHO COULD WORK TIRELESSLY THROUGH THE NIGHT.
AS BUSINESS SLOWED, WE WERE HAPPY WITH ANYONE WHO PUT IN EIGHT HOURS A DAY.
THEN OUR BEST PEOPLE LEFT.
NOW OUR CUBICLES ARE MOSTLY USED FOR NAPPING.
SO MY QUESTION IS THIS: WOULD A RINGING PHONE WAKE YOU UP?
PROBABLY.
HE COMES ACROSS AS A BRAGGART.
© 2010 Scott Adams, Inc. /Dist. by Universal Uclick
9-26-10

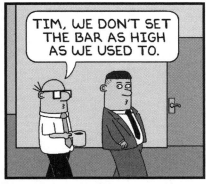

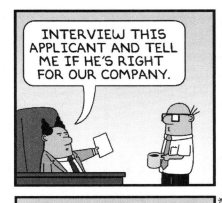

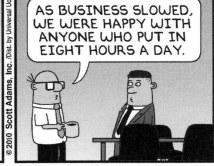

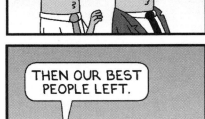

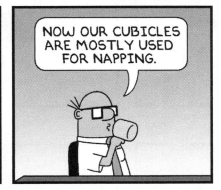

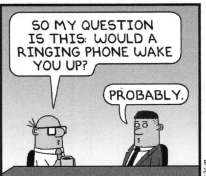

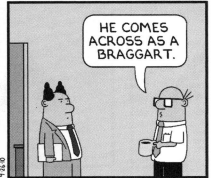

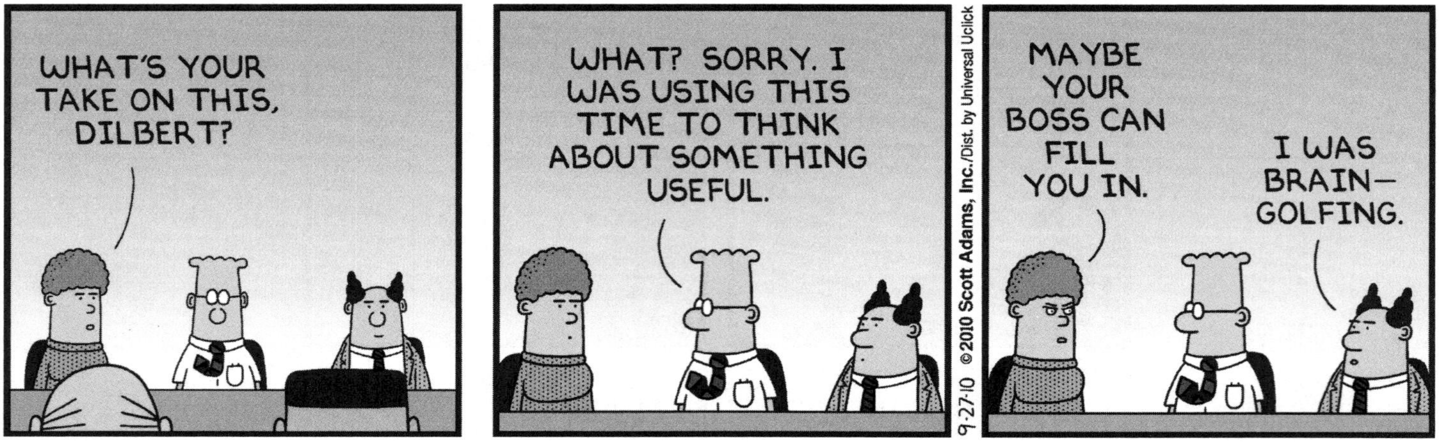
WHAT'S YOUR TAKE ON THIS, DILBERT?
WHAT? SORRY. I WAS USING THIS TIME TO THINK ABOUT SOMETHING USEFUL.
9·27·10 © 2010 Scott Adams, Inc./Dist. by Universal Uclick
MAYBE YOUR BOSS CAN FILL YOU IN.
I WAS BRAIN–GOLFING.

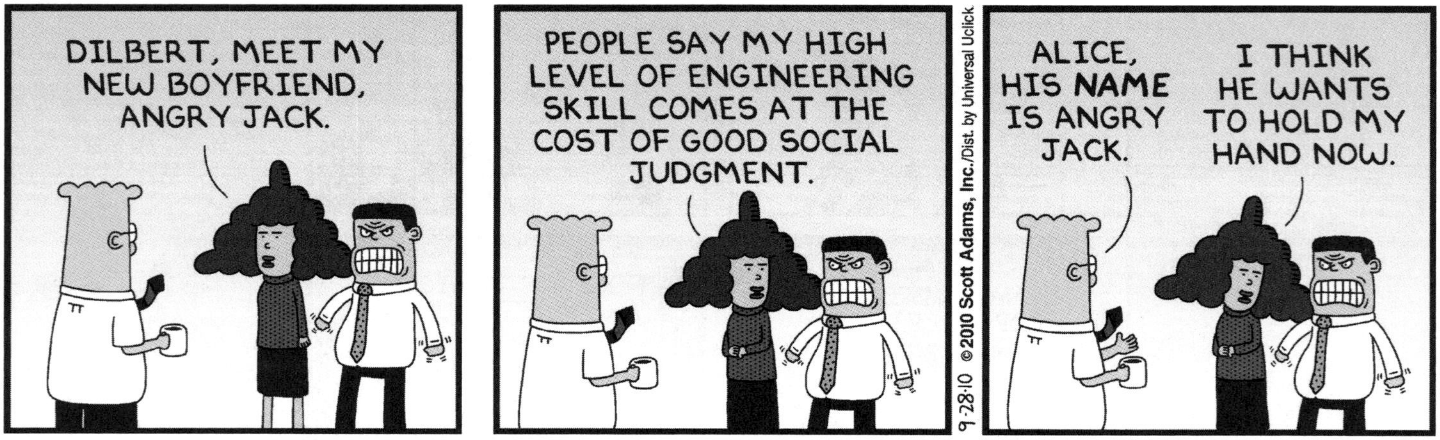
DILBERT, MEET MY NEW BOYFRIEND, ANGRY JACK.
PEOPLE SAY MY HIGH LEVEL OF ENGINEERING SKILL COMES AT THE COST OF GOOD SOCIAL JUDGMENT.
9·28·10 © 2010 Scott Adams, Inc./Dist. by Universal Uclick
ALICE, HIS **NAME** IS ANGRY JACK.
I THINK HE WANTS TO HOLD MY HAND NOW.

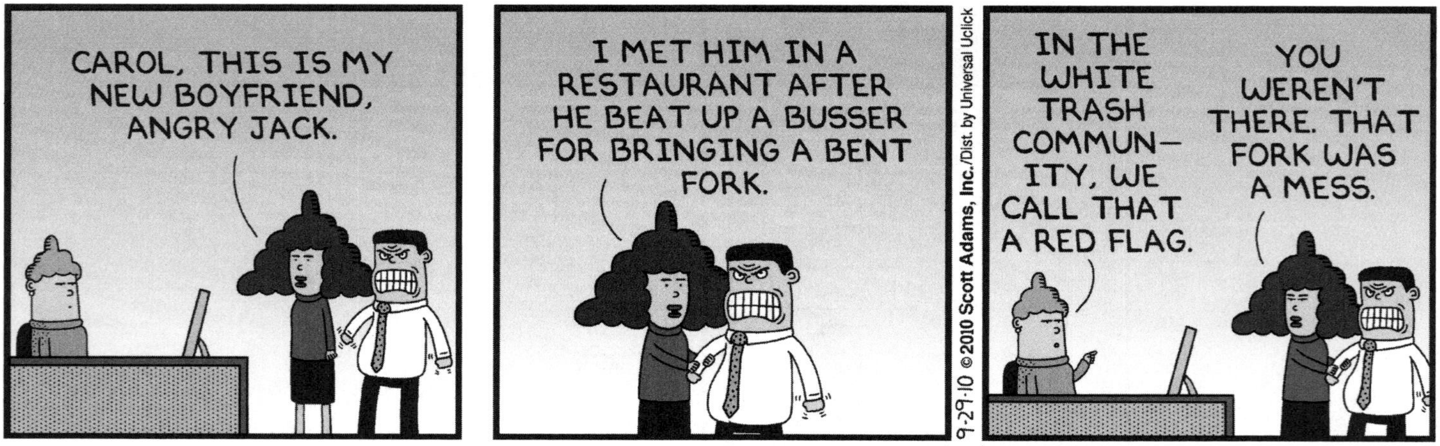
CAROL, THIS IS MY NEW BOYFRIEND, ANGRY JACK.
I MET HIM IN A RESTAURANT AFTER HE BEAT UP A BUSSER FOR BRINGING A BENT FORK.
9·29·10 © 2010 Scott Adams, Inc./Dist. by Universal Uclick
IN THE WHITE TRASH COMMUN–ITY, WE CALL THAT A RED FLAG.
YOU WEREN'T THERE. THAT FORK WAS A MESS.

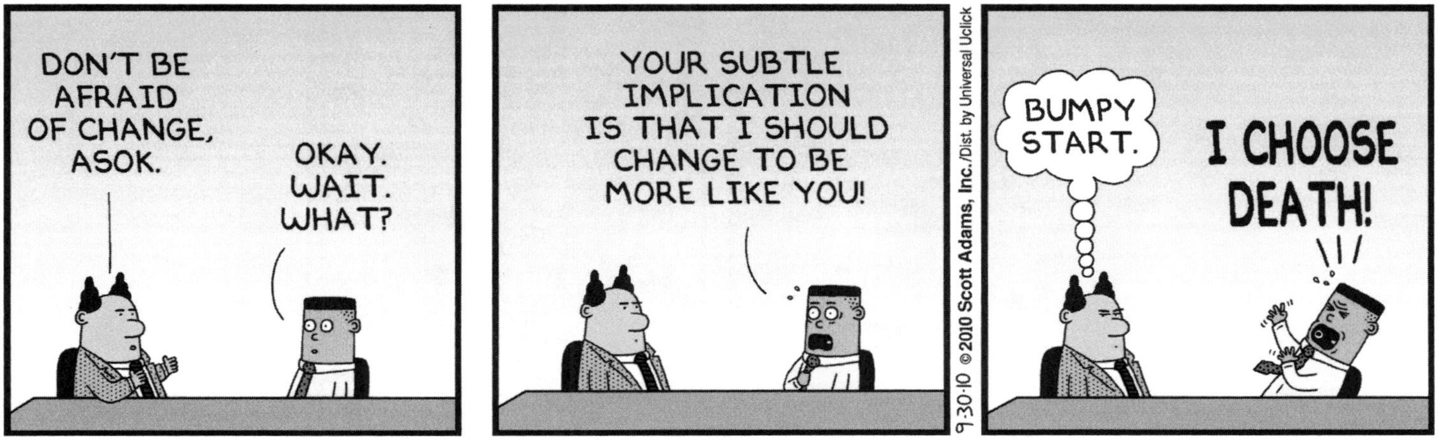
DON'T BE AFRAID OF CHANGE, ASOK.
OKAY. WAIT. WHAT?
YOUR SUBTLE IMPLICATION IS THAT I SHOULD CHANGE TO BE MORE LIKE YOU!
9·30·10 © 2010 Scott Adams, Inc./Dist. by Universal Uclick
BUMPY START.
I CHOOSE DEATH!

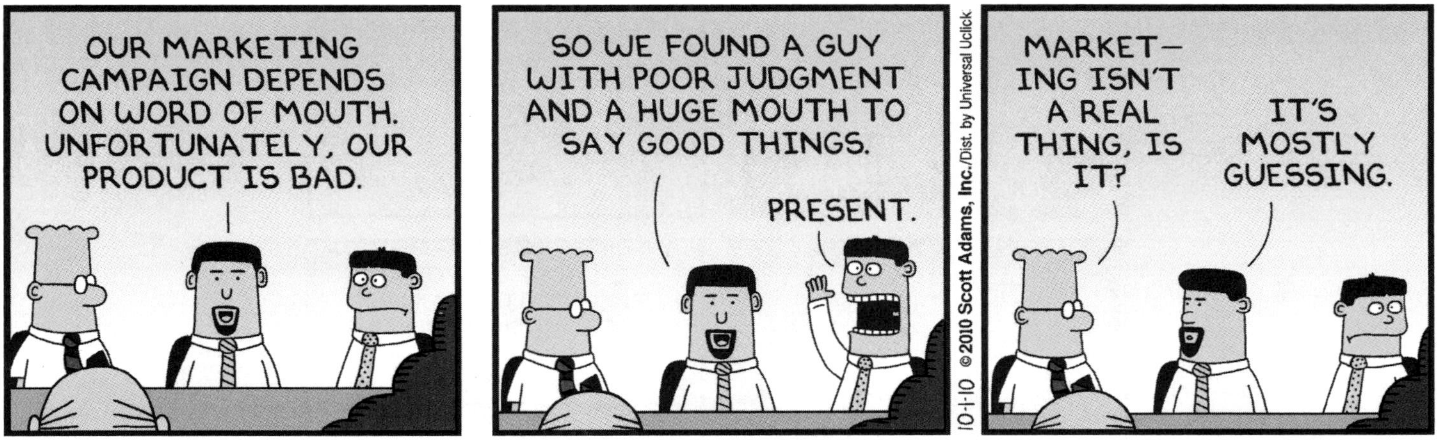
OUR MARKETING CAMPAIGN DEPENDS ON WORD OF MOUTH. UNFORTUNATELY, OUR PRODUCT IS BAD.
SO WE FOUND A GUY WITH POOR JUDGMENT AND A HUGE MOUTH TO SAY GOOD THINGS.
PRESENT.
10·1·10 © 2010 Scott Adams, Inc./Dist. by Universal Uclick
MARKET–ING ISN'T A REAL THING, IS IT?
IT'S MOSTLY GUESSING.

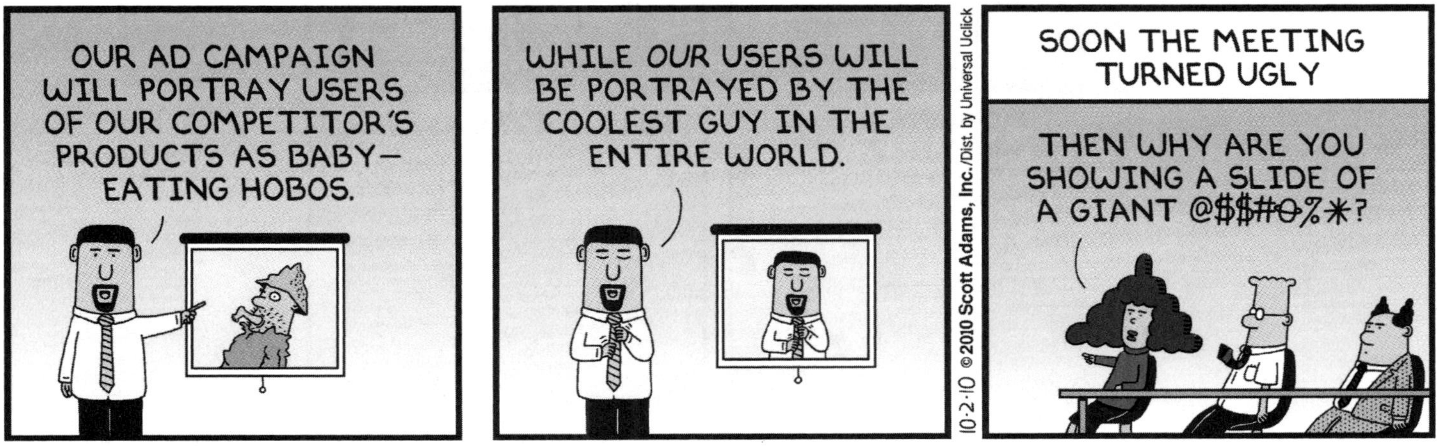
OUR AD CAMPAIGN WILL PORTRAY USERS OF OUR COMPETITOR'S PRODUCTS AS BABY–EATING HOBOS.
WHILE *OUR* USERS WILL BE PORTRAYED BY THE COOLEST GUY IN THE ENTIRE WORLD.
10·2·10 © 2010 Scott Adams, Inc./Dist. by Universal Uclick
SOON THE MEETING TURNED UGLY
THEN WHY ARE YOU SHOWING A SLIDE OF A GIANT @$$#0%*?

. . . AND OF COURSE WE'LL ASSESS OUR PROGRESS ALONG THE WAY.
PROGRESS
WILL YOU BE USING AN ENHANCED ASSESSMENT METHODOLOGY?
I HOPE THAT MEANS SOMETHING. ALL I DID WAS STRING TOGETHER SOME WORDS I HEARD IN THE HALLWAY.
UM. . . I'LL BE ASSESSING. . . BY MEASURING. . . AND UM. . .
I'D BETTER GET IN ON THIS.
I CAN'T SUPPORT THIS PROJECT UNTIL I SEE YOUR ADVANCED ASSESSMENT METHOD-OLOGY PLAN.
I'LL HAVE IT IN TEN MINUTES, ASSUMING YOU DON'T KNOW WHAT IT'S SUPPOSED TO LOOK LIKE.
VERY GOOD.
I'LL BE IN THE SHOWER TRYING TO WASH MY SOUL.
©2010 Scott Adams, Inc. /Dist. by Universal Uclick
10-3-10

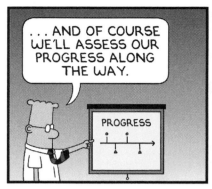

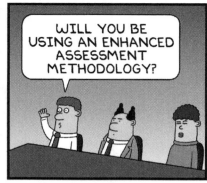

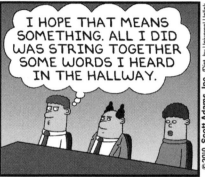

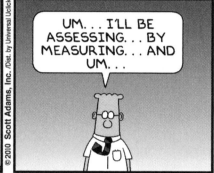

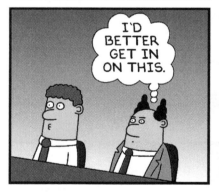

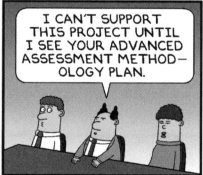

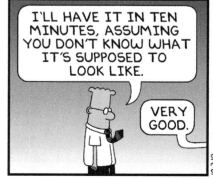

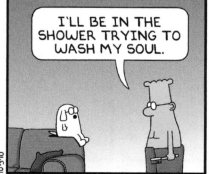

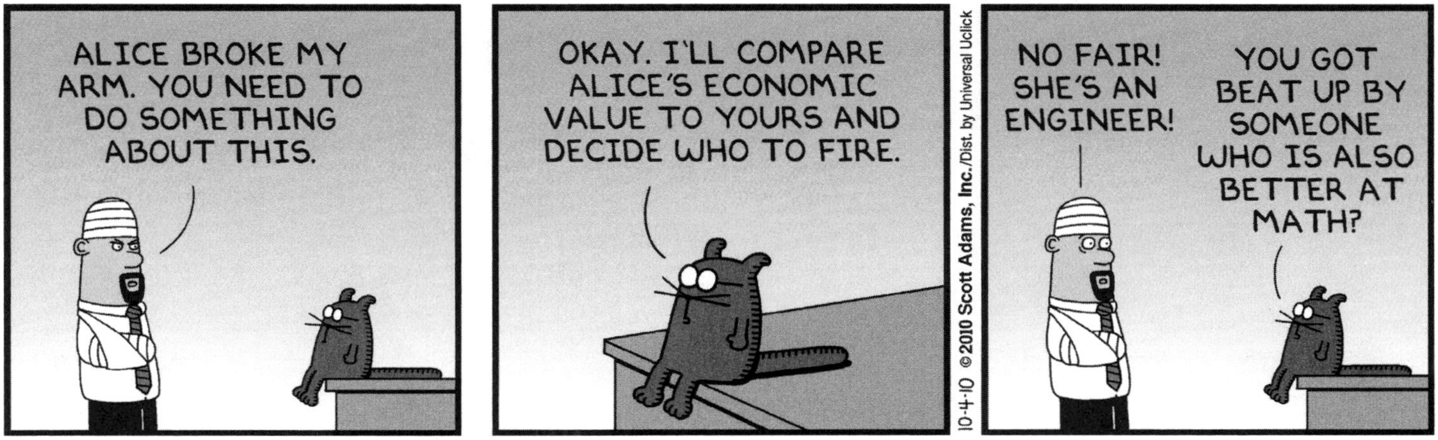
ALICE BROKE MY ARM. YOU NEED TO DO SOMETHING ABOUT THIS.
OKAY. I'LL COMPARE ALICE'S ECONOMIC VALUE TO YOURS AND DECIDE WHO TO FIRE.
10-4-10 © 2010 Scott Adams, Inc./Dist. by Universal Uclick
NO FAIR! SHE'S AN ENGINEER!
YOU GOT BEAT UP BY SOMEONE WHO IS ALSO BETTER AT MATH?

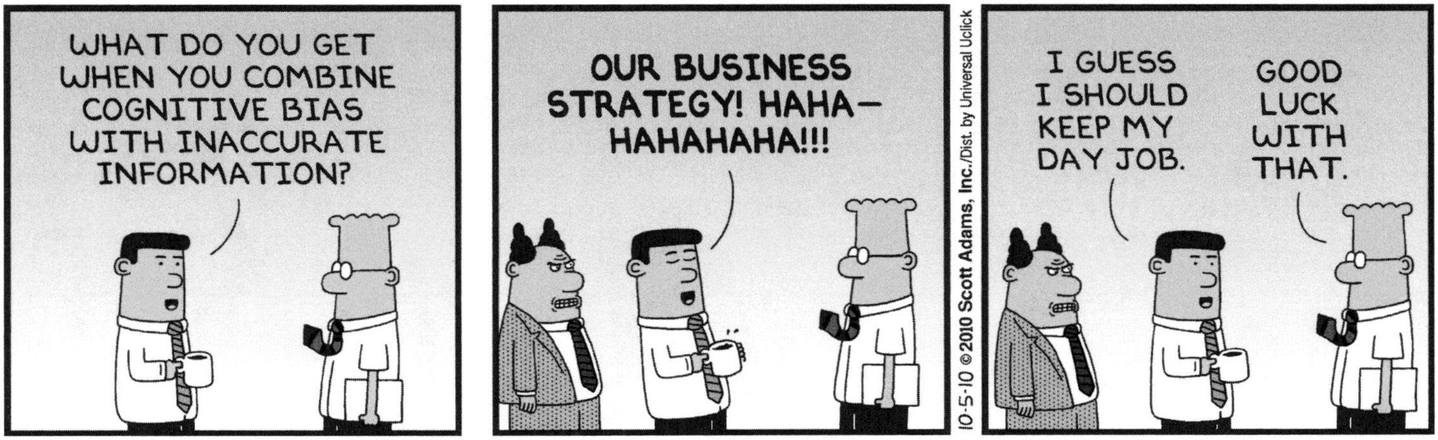
WHAT DO YOU GET WHEN YOU COMBINE COGNITIVE BIAS WITH INACCURATE INFORMATION?
OUR BUSINESS STRATEGY! HAHA-HAHAHAHA!!!
10-5-10 © 2010 Scott Adams, Inc./Dist. by Universal Uclick
I GUESS I SHOULD KEEP MY DAY JOB.
GOOD LUCK WITH THAT.

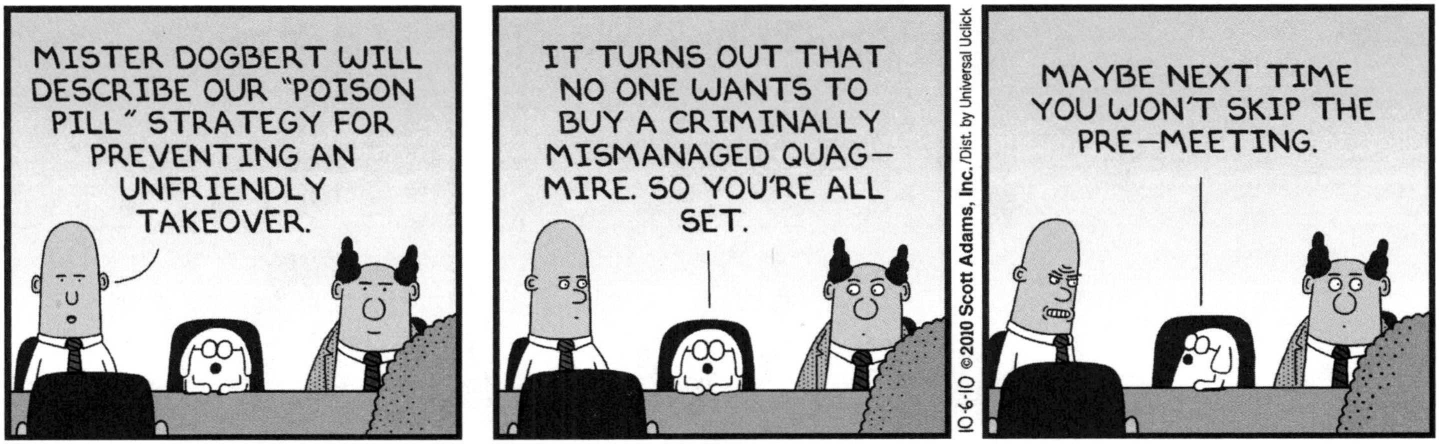
MISTER DOGBERT WILL DESCRIBE OUR "POISON PILL" STRATEGY FOR PREVENTING AN UNFRIENDLY TAKEOVER.
IT TURNS OUT THAT NO ONE WANTS TO BUY A CRIMINALLY MISMANAGED QUAG-MIRE. SO YOU'RE ALL SET.
10-6-10 © 2010 Scott Adams, Inc./Dist. by Universal Uclick
MAYBE NEXT TIME YOU WON'T SKIP THE PRE-MEETING.

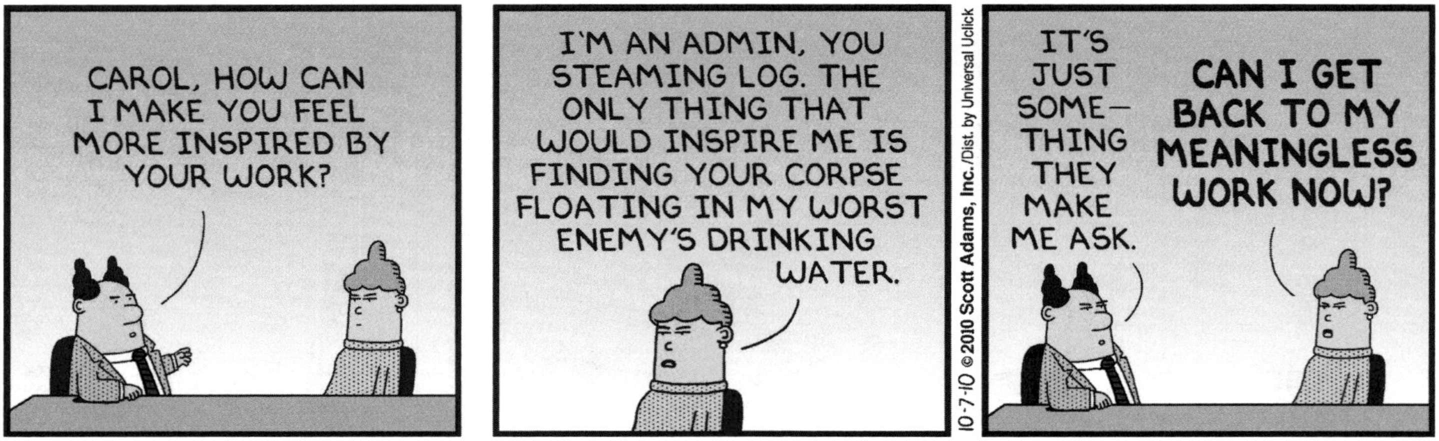
CAROL, HOW CAN I MAKE YOU FEEL MORE INSPIRED BY YOUR WORK?
I'M AN ADMIN, YOU STEAMING LOG. THE ONLY THING THAT WOULD INSPIRE ME IS FINDING YOUR CORPSE FLOATING IN MY WORST ENEMY'S DRINKING WATER.
10-7-10 ©2010 Scott Adams, Inc./Dist. by Universal Uclick
IT'S JUST SOME-THING THEY MAKE ME ASK.
CAN I GET BACK TO MY MEANINGLESS WORK NOW?

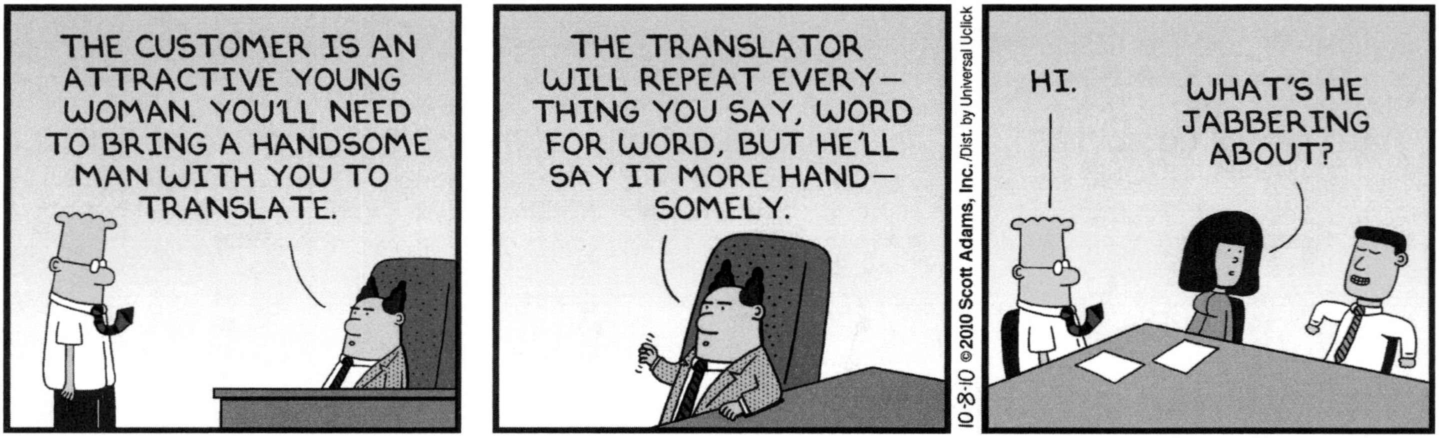
THE CUSTOMER IS AN ATTRACTIVE YOUNG WOMAN. YOU'LL NEED TO BRING A HANDSOME MAN WITH YOU TO TRANSLATE.
THE TRANSLATOR WILL REPEAT EVERY-THING YOU SAY, WORD FOR WORD, BUT HE'LL SAY IT MORE HAND-SOMELY.
10-8-10 ©2010 Scott Adams, Inc./Dist. by Universal Uclick
HI.
WHAT'S HE JABBERING ABOUT?

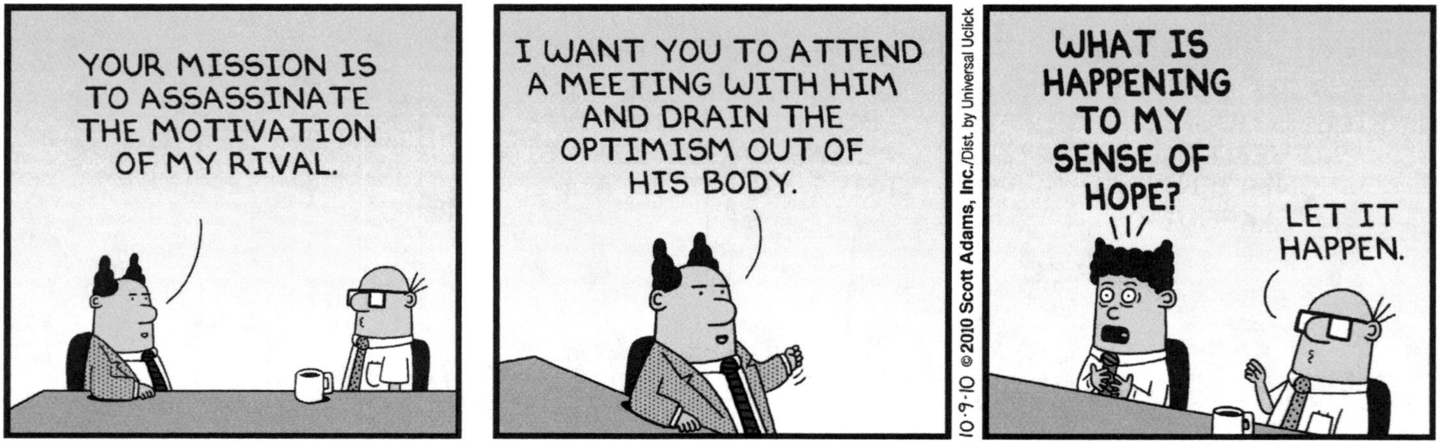
YOUR MISSION IS TO ASSASSINATE THE MOTIVATION OF MY RIVAL.
I WANT YOU TO ATTEND A MEETING WITH HIM AND DRAIN THE OPTIMISM OUT OF HIS BODY.
10-9-10 ©2010 Scott Adams, Inc./Dist. by Universal Uclick
WHAT IS HAPPENING TO MY SENSE OF HOPE?
LET IT HAPPEN.

WALLY, HAVE YOU MADE ANY PROGRESS CODING YOUR MODULE?
PROGRESS IS DIFFICULT TO MEASURE IN THE SOFTWARE REALM.
YOU COULD MEASURE THE LINES OF CODE I PRODUCE, BUT THAT WOULD REWARD INEFFICIENCY.
THE ART OF THIS JOB IS BINDING THE RARE MOMENTS OF INSPIRATION TO KNOWLEDGE AND MACHINES.
IN FACT, JUST A MINUTE AGO I COULD FEEL THE INSPIRATION WELLING UP INSIDE ME.
BUT THEN YOU INTERRUPTED ME WITH YOUR NAIVE QUESTION AND THE MOMENT WAS LOST.
MAYBE YOU SHOULD GO BACK TO YOUR OFFICE AND REFLECT ON THE DAMAGE YOU'VE DONE HERE TODAY.
THERE GOES THE ONE PERSON WHO HAS LESS OF A REAL JOB THAN I DO.
© 2010 Scott Adams, Inc./Dist. by Universal Uclick
10-10-10

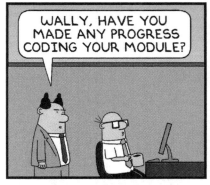

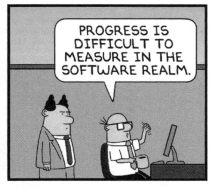

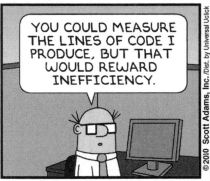

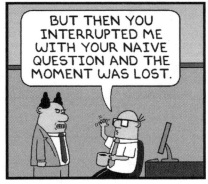

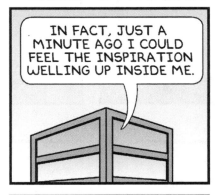

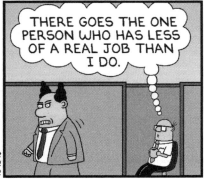

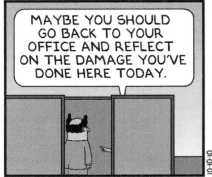

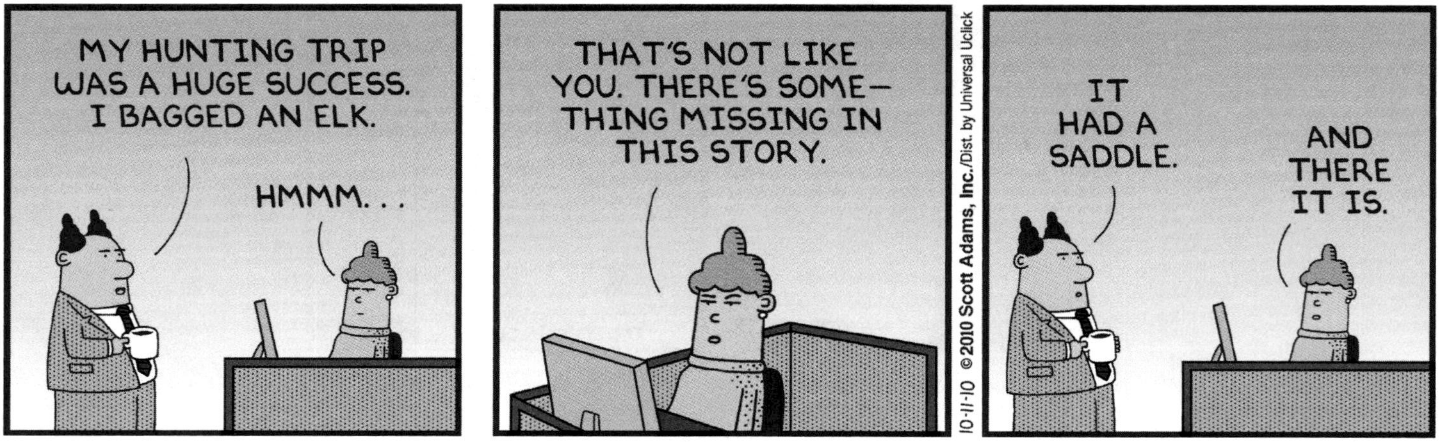
MY HUNTING TRIP WAS A HUGE SUCCESS. I BAGGED AN ELK.
HMMM. . .
THAT'S NOT LIKE YOU. THERE'S SOME—THING MISSING IN THIS STORY.
10-11-10 ©2010 Scott Adams, Inc./Dist. by Universal Uclick
IT HAD A SADDLE.
AND THERE IT IS.

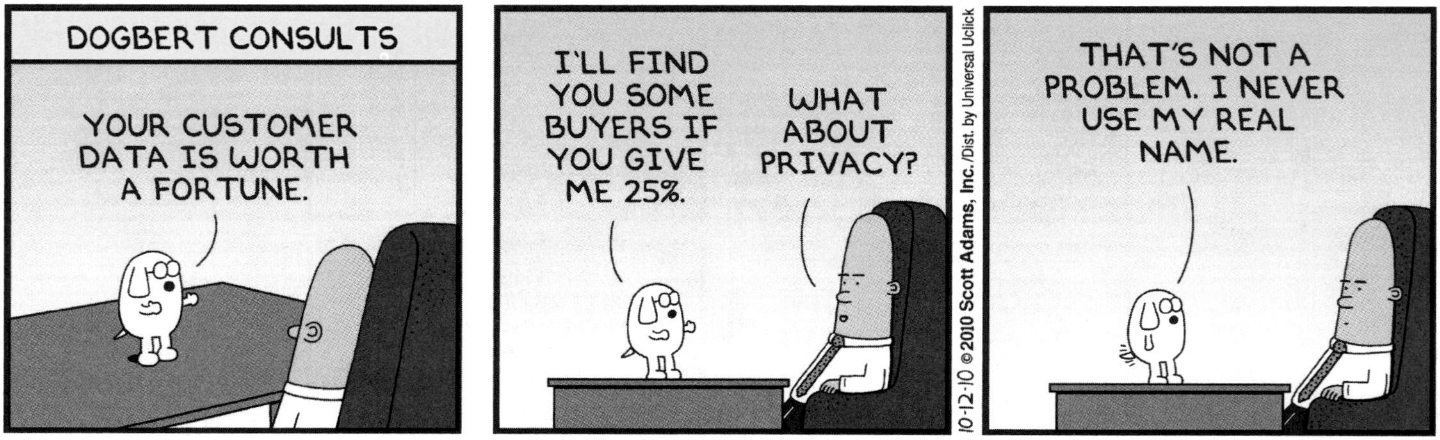
DOGBERT CONSULTS
YOUR CUSTOMER DATA IS WORTH A FORTUNE.
I'LL FIND YOU SOME BUYERS IF YOU GIVE ME 25%.
WHAT ABOUT PRIVACY?
10-12-10 ©2010 Scott Adams, Inc./Dist. by Universal Uclick
THAT'S NOT A PROBLEM. I NEVER USE MY REAL NAME.

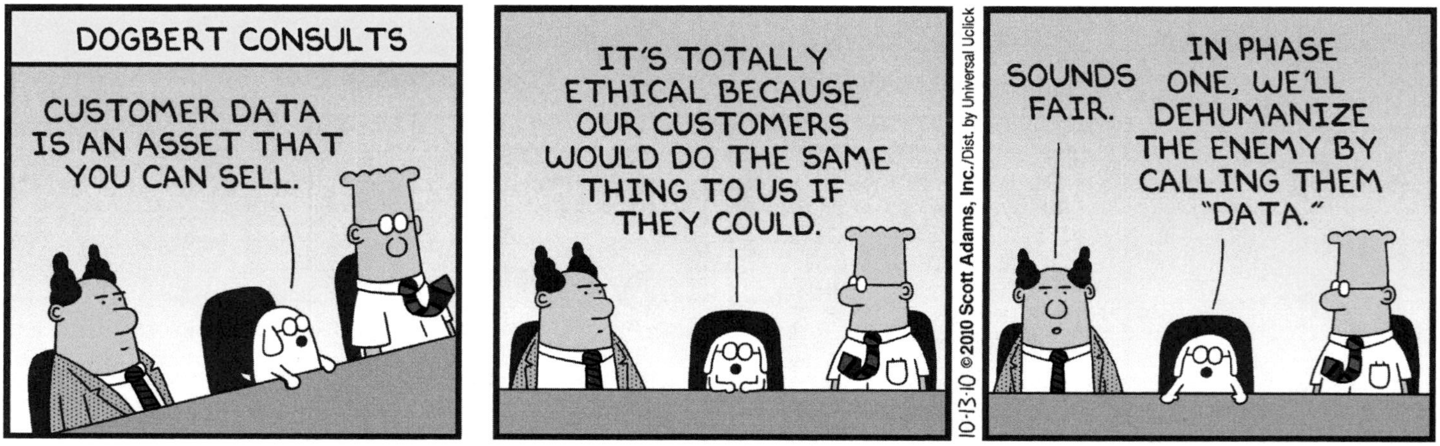
DOGBERT CONSULTS
CUSTOMER DATA IS AN ASSET THAT YOU CAN SELL.
IT'S TOTALLY ETHICAL BECAUSE OUR CUSTOMERS WOULD DO THE SAME THING TO US IF THEY COULD.
10-13-10 ©2010 Scott Adams, Inc./Dist. by Universal Uclick
SOUNDS FAIR.
IN PHASE ONE, WE'LL DEHUMANIZE THE ENEMY BY CALLING THEM "DATA."

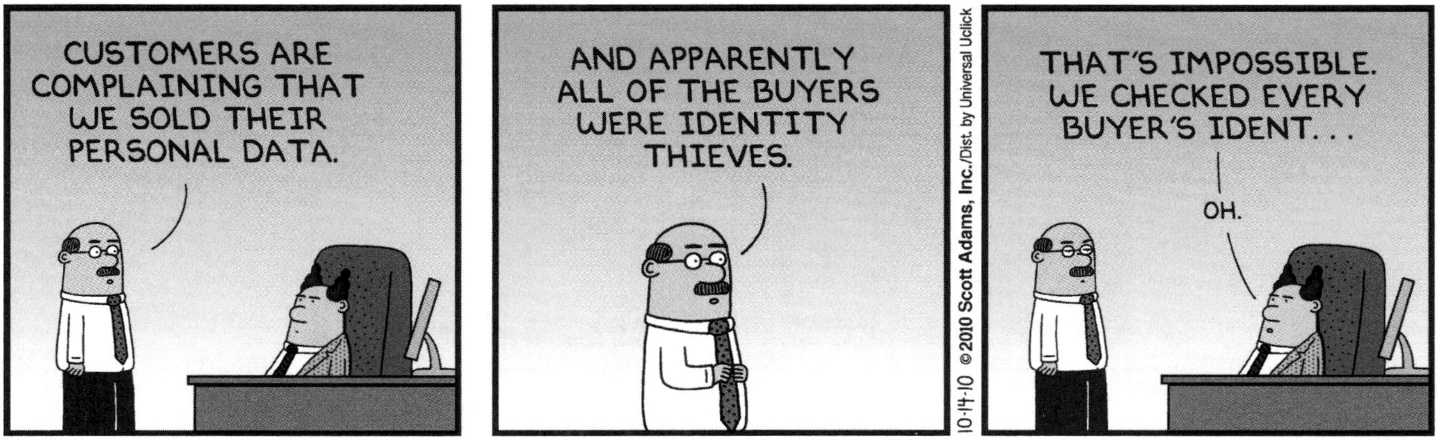
CUSTOMERS ARE COMPLAINING THAT WE SOLD THEIR PERSONAL DATA.
AND APPARENTLY ALL OF THE BUYERS WERE IDENTITY THIEVES.
10-14-10 © 2010 Scott Adams, Inc./Dist. by Universal Uclick
THAT'S IMPOSSIBLE. WE CHECKED EVERY BUYER'S IDENT. . .
OH.

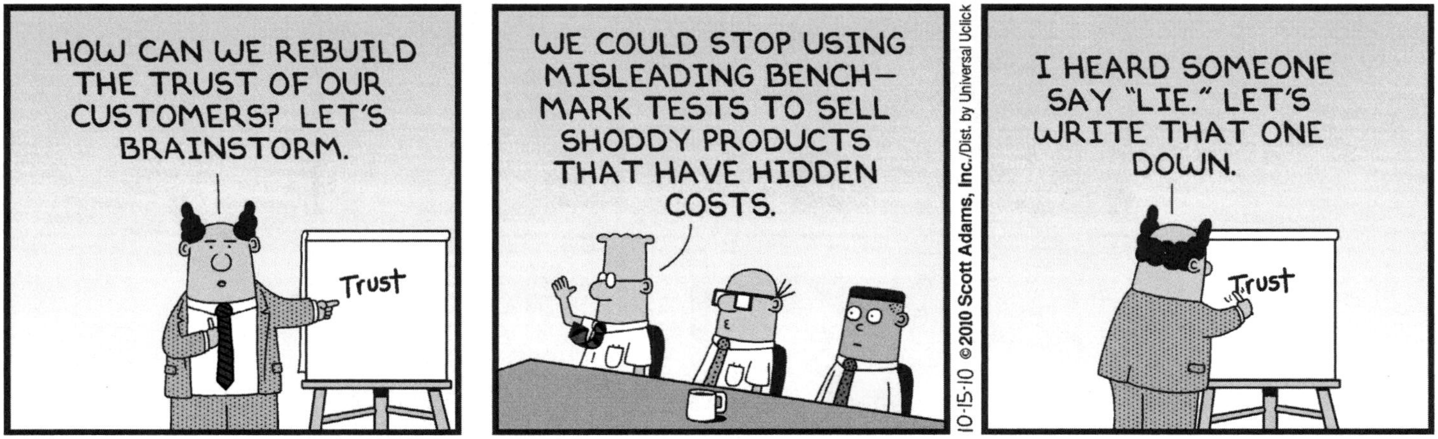
HOW CAN WE REBUILD THE TRUST OF OUR CUSTOMERS? LET'S BRAINSTORM.
Trust
WE COULD STOP USING MISLEADING BENCH-MARK TESTS TO SELL SHODDY PRODUCTS THAT HAVE HIDDEN COSTS.
10-15-10 © 2010 Scott Adams, Inc./Dist. by Universal Uclick
I HEARD SOMEONE SAY "LIE." LET'S WRITE THAT ONE DOWN.
Trust

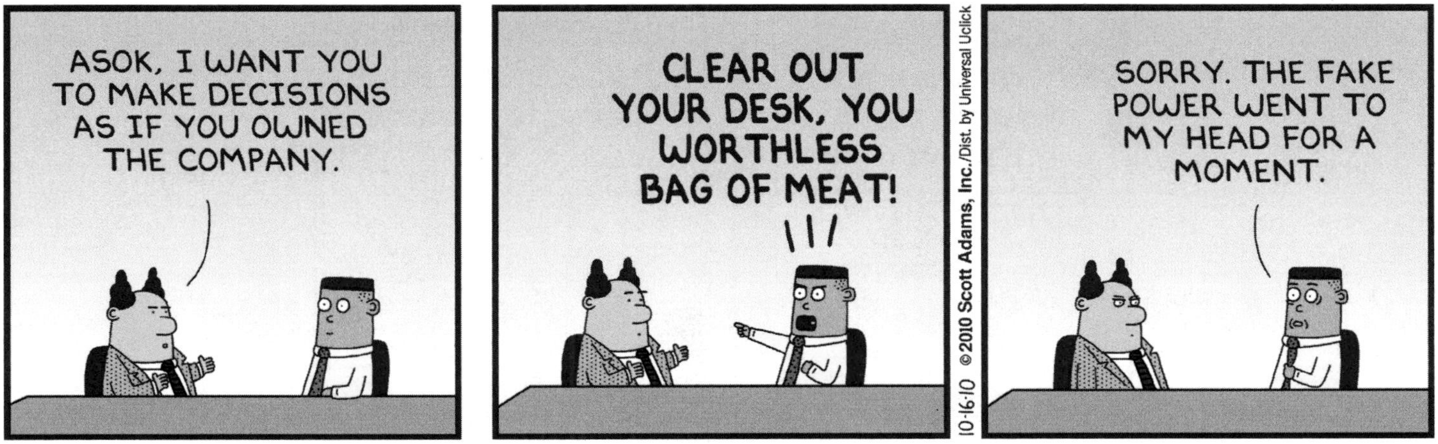
ASOK, I WANT YOU TO MAKE DECISIONS AS IF YOU OWNED THE COMPANY.
CLEAR OUT YOUR DESK, YOU WORTHLESS BAG OF MEAT!
10-16-10 © 2010 Scott Adams, Inc./Dist. by Universal Uclick
SORRY. THE FAKE POWER WENT TO MY HEAD FOR A MOMENT.

WE'LL LOSE THE ELBONIAN PROJECT UNLESS WE GIVE THEIR MINISTER OF MUD SOME. . . INCENTIVE.
YOU MEAN A BRIBE?
NO, A BRIBE WOULD BE ILLEGAL.
TAKE A BAG OF GOLD TO ELBONIA AND LEAVE IT BY THE STATUE OF THE MONKEY GOD, OOBANOOBAH.
©2010 Scott Adams, Inc./Dist. by Universal Uclick
IF OOBANOOBAH DOES NOT ACCEPT YOUR OFFERING, BY ELBONIAN LAW IT BECOMES UNCLAIMED PROPERTY.
TAKE THE GOLD TO THE UNCLAIMED PROPERTY DESK AT THE MINISTRY OF MUD.
RING THE BELL AND ASK FOR THE MINISTER OF MUD. GIVE HIM THE UNCLAIMED PROPERTY AND A COPY OF OUR BID.
WHAT IF THE MONKEY GOD ACCEPTS THE GOLD AND I'M THE ONLY WITNESS?
10-17-10
WHAT?
HOW MUCH MONKEY GOD GOLD ARE WE TALKING ABOUT?

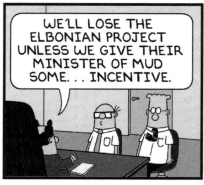

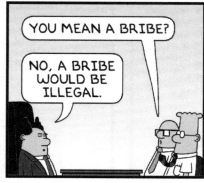

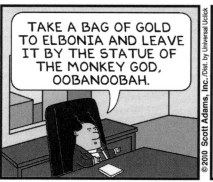

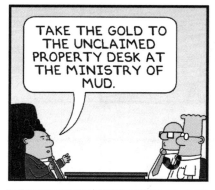

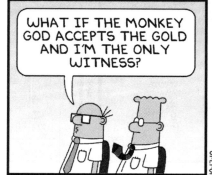

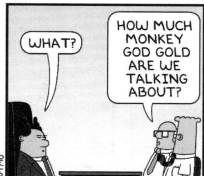

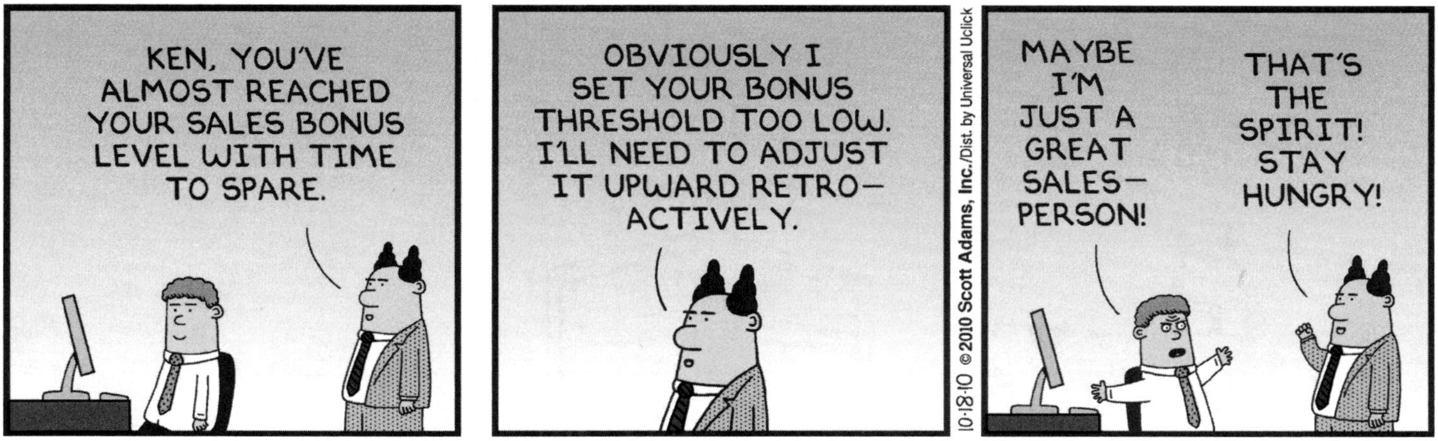
KEN, YOU'VE ALMOST REACHED YOUR SALES BONUS LEVEL WITH TIME TO SPARE.
OBVIOUSLY I SET YOUR BONUS THRESHOLD TOO LOW. I'LL NEED TO ADJUST IT UPWARD RETRO-ACTIVELY.
10·18·10 © 2010 Scott Adams, Inc./Dist. by Universal Uclick
MAYBE I'M JUST A GREAT SALES-PERSON!
THAT'S THE SPIRIT! STAY HUNGRY!

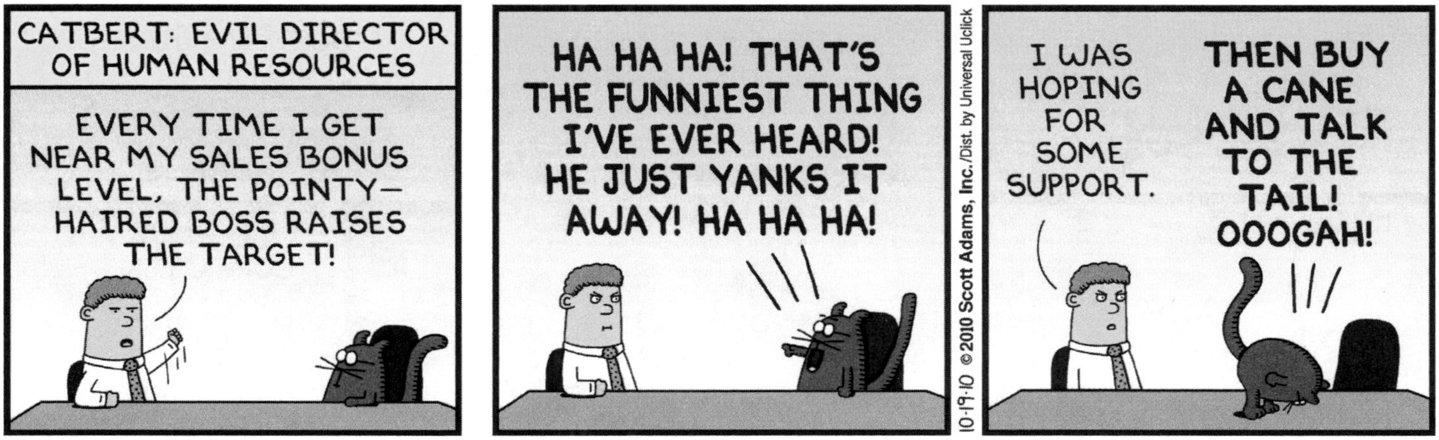
CATBERT: EVIL DIRECTOR OF HUMAN RESOURCES
EVERY TIME I GET NEAR MY SALES BONUS LEVEL, THE POINTY-HAIRED BOSS RAISES THE TARGET!
HA HA HA! THAT'S THE FUNNIEST THING I'VE EVER HEARD! HE JUST YANKS IT AWAY! HA HA HA!
10·19·10 © 2010 Scott Adams, Inc./Dist. by Universal Uclick
I WAS HOPING FOR SOME SUPPORT.
THEN BUY A CANE AND TALK TO THE TAIL! OOOGAH!

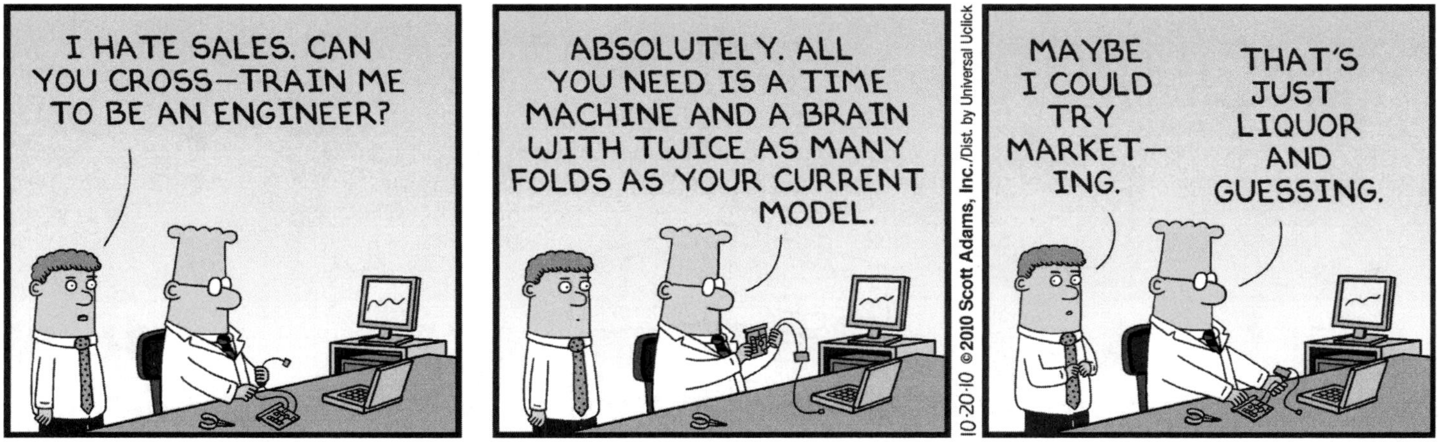
I HATE SALES. CAN YOU CROSS-TRAIN ME TO BE AN ENGINEER?
ABSOLUTELY. ALL YOU NEED IS A TIME MACHINE AND A BRAIN WITH TWICE AS MANY FOLDS AS YOUR CURRENT MODEL.
10·20·10 © 2010 Scott Adams, Inc./Dist. by Universal Uclick
MAYBE I COULD TRY MARKET-ING.
THAT'S JUST LIQUOR AND GUESSING.

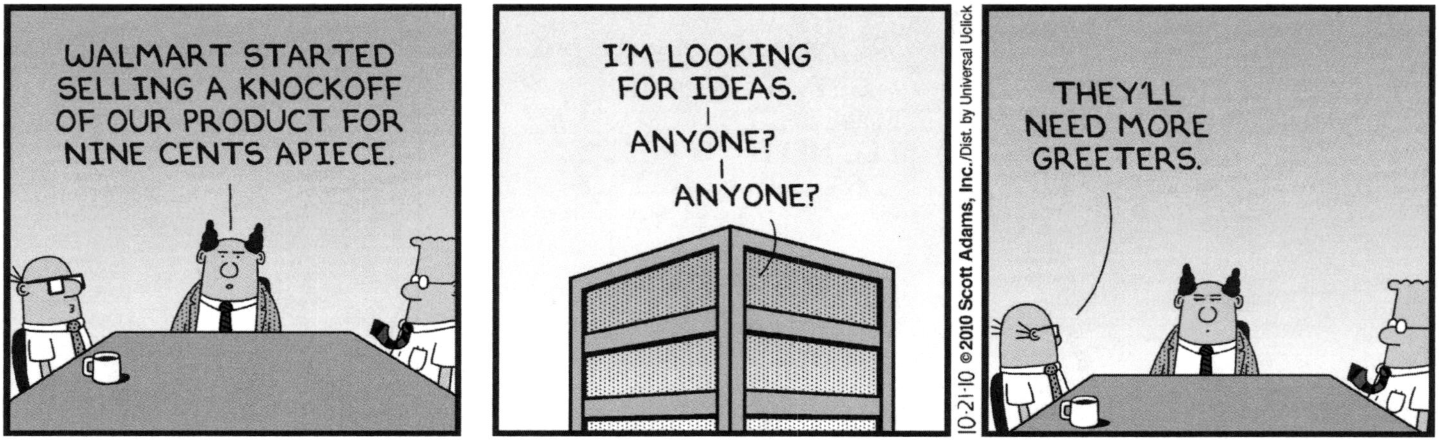
WALMART STARTED SELLING A KNOCKOFF OF OUR PRODUCT FOR NINE CENTS APIECE.
I'M LOOKING FOR IDEAS.
ANYONE?
ANYONE?
THEY'LL NEED MORE GREETERS.
10-21-10 © 2010 Scott Adams, Inc./Dist. by Universal Uclick

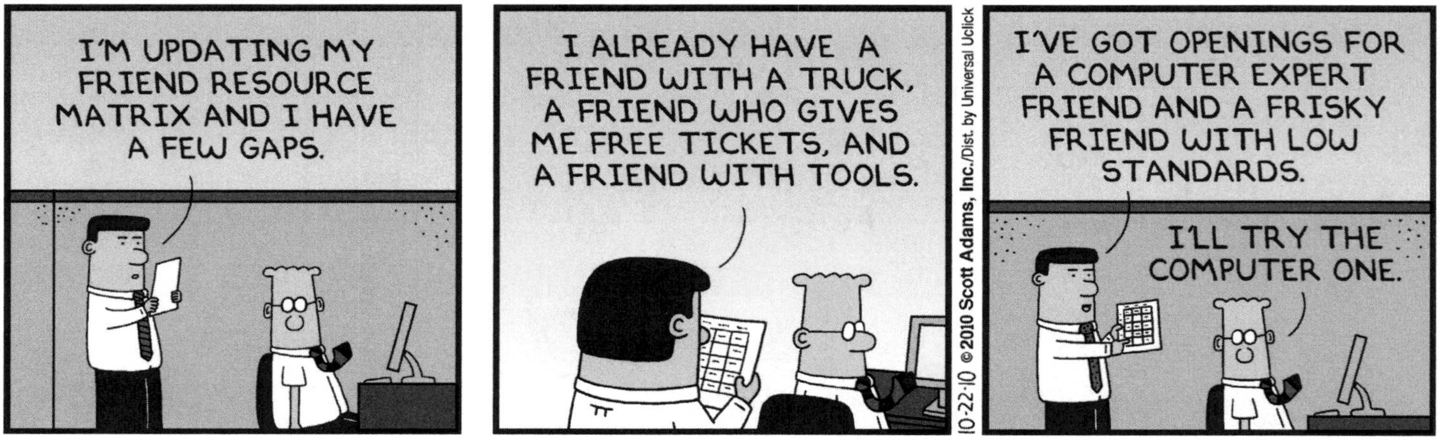
I'M UPDATING MY FRIEND RESOURCE MATRIX AND I HAVE A FEW GAPS.
I ALREADY HAVE A FRIEND WITH A TRUCK, A FRIEND WHO GIVES ME FREE TICKETS, AND A FRIEND WITH TOOLS.
I'VE GOT OPENINGS FOR A COMPUTER EXPERT FRIEND AND A FRISKY FRIEND WITH LOW STANDARDS.
I'LL TRY THE COMPUTER ONE.
10-22-10 © 2010 Scott Adams, Inc./Dist. by Universal Uclick

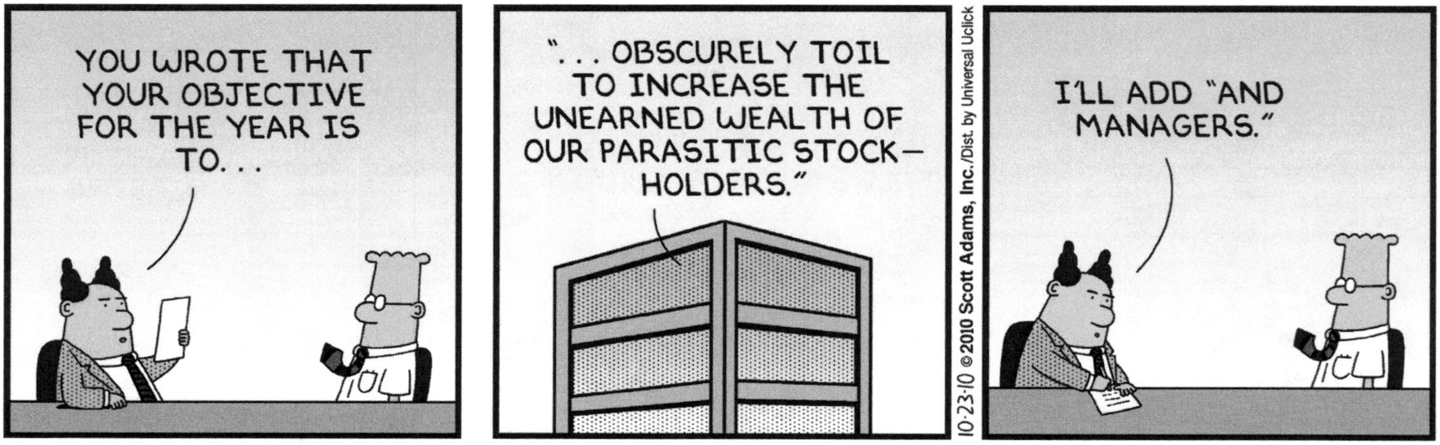
YOU WROTE THAT YOUR OBJECTIVE FOR THE YEAR IS TO...
"...OBSCURELY TOIL TO INCREASE THE UNEARNED WEALTH OF OUR PARASITIC STOCK-HOLDERS."
I'LL ADD "AND MANAGERS."
10-23-10 © 2010 Scott Adams, Inc./Dist. by Universal Uclick

OUR BEST SALES GUY ASKED FOR YOU TO ACCOMPANY HIM ON A SALES CALL.
WHAT'S THE SECRET OF BEING A GOOD SALES PERSON?
YOU NEED TO GIVE CUSTOMERS THE INFORMATION THEY NEED. . .
. . . WITHOUT GETTING IN THEIR FACES SO OFTEN THAT YOU BECOME A NUISANCE.
FOR EXAMPLE, A CUSTOMER WOULD GET SICK OF *YOUR* FACE MUCH SOONER THAN MINE.
SO HALFWAY THROUGH THE SALES CALL, YOU'LL NEED TO PUT THIS BAG OVER YOUR HEAD WHILE I CLOSE THE DEAL.
IT LOOKS AS IF I WIN OUR BET.
NO. . . WAIT FOR IT. . .
WHOA. HOW DO YOU DO THAT?
IT'S CALLED SALES. NOW YOU OWE ME A PURCHASE ORDER.
©2010 Scott Adams, Inc. /Dist. by Universal Uclick
10-24-10

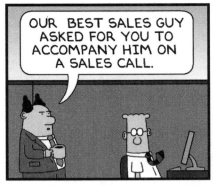

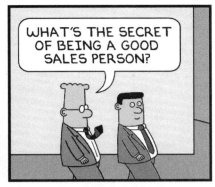

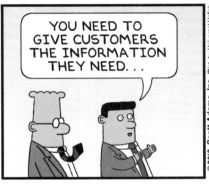

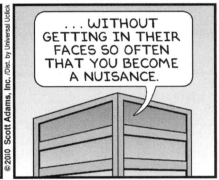

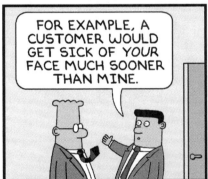

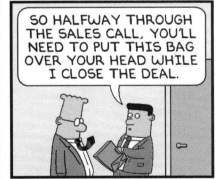

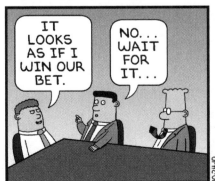

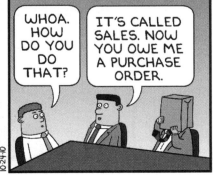

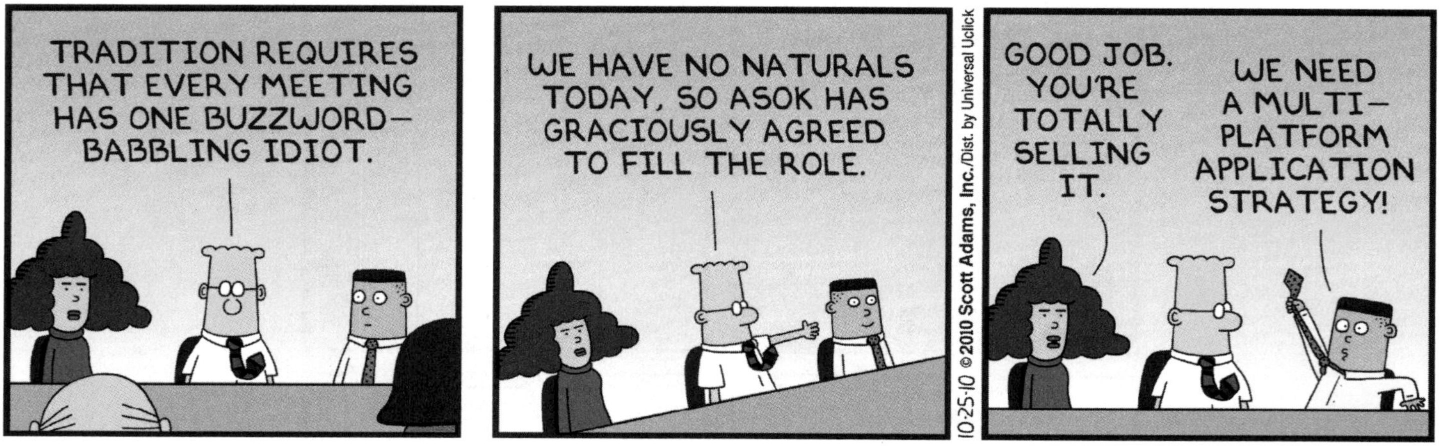
TRADITION REQUIRES THAT EVERY MEETING HAS ONE BUZZWORD-BABBLING IDIOT.
WE HAVE NO NATURALS TODAY, SO ASOK HAS GRACIOUSLY AGREED TO FILL THE ROLE.
GOOD JOB. YOU'RE TOTALLY SELLING IT.
WE NEED A MULTI-PLATFORM APPLICATION STRATEGY!
10-25-10 © 2010 Scott Adams, Inc./Dist. by Universal Uclick

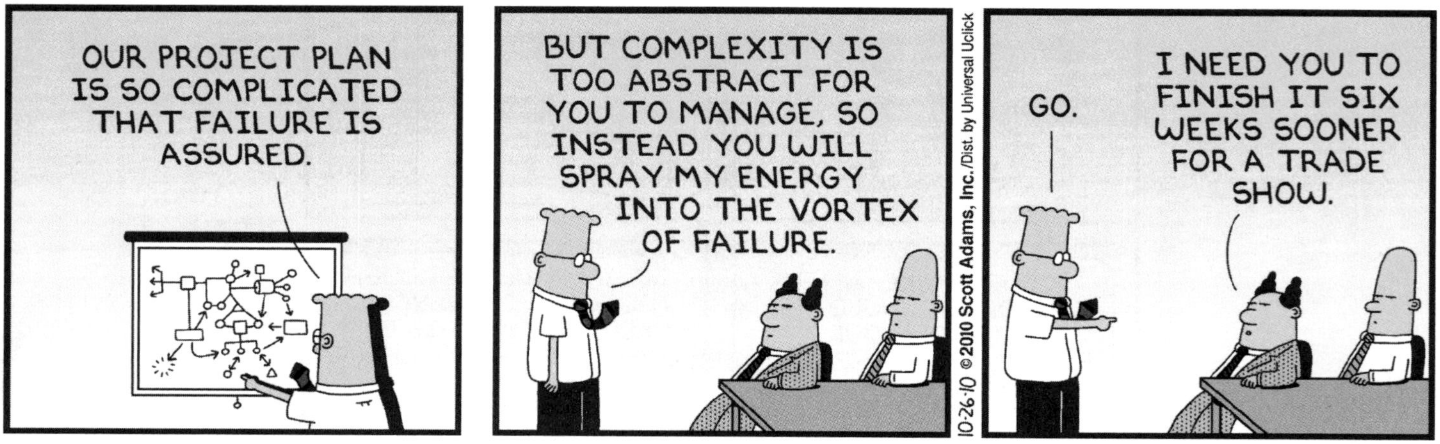
OUR PROJECT PLAN IS SO COMPLICATED THAT FAILURE IS ASSURED.
BUT COMPLEXITY IS TOO ABSTRACT FOR YOU TO MANAGE, SO INSTEAD YOU WILL SPRAY MY ENERGY INTO THE VORTEX OF FAILURE.
GO.
I NEED YOU TO FINISH IT SIX WEEKS SOONER FOR A TRADE SHOW.
10-26-10 © 2010 Scott Adams, Inc./Dist. by Universal Uclick

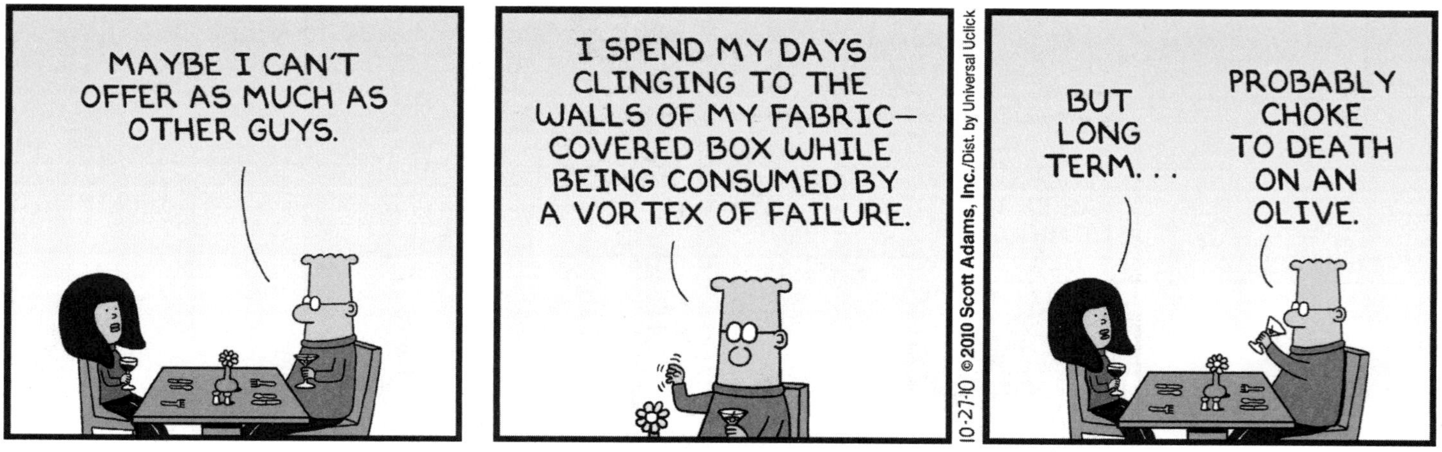
MAYBE I CAN'T OFFER AS MUCH AS OTHER GUYS.
I SPEND MY DAYS CLINGING TO THE WALLS OF MY FABRIC-COVERED BOX WHILE BEING CONSUMED BY A VORTEX OF FAILURE.
BUT LONG TERM. . .
PROBABLY CHOKE TO DEATH ON AN OLIVE.
10-27-10 © 2010 Scott Adams, Inc./Dist. by Universal Uclick

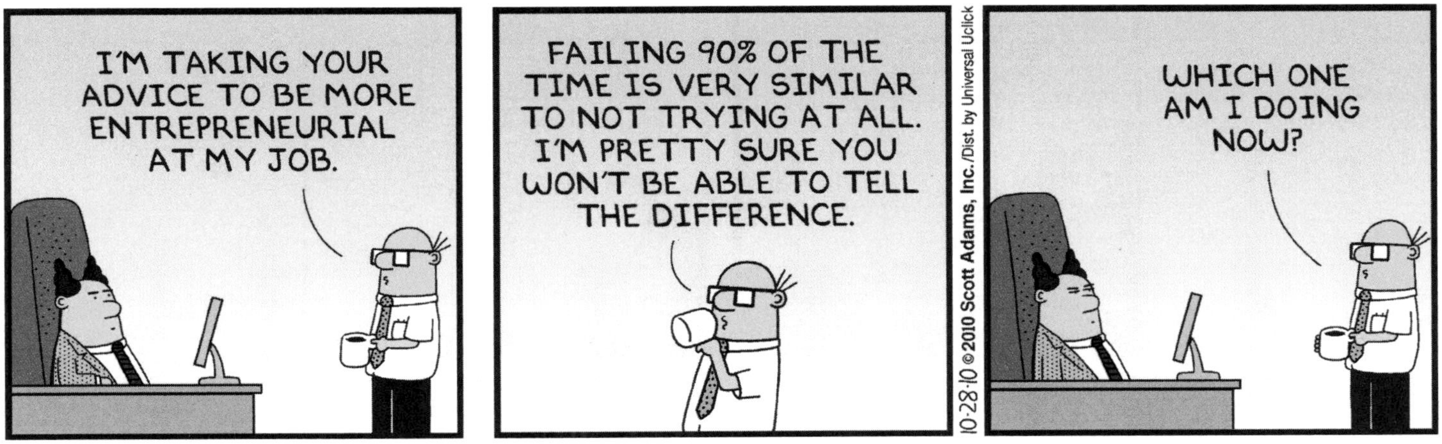
I'M TAKING YOUR ADVICE TO BE MORE ENTREPRENEURIAL AT MY JOB.
FAILING 90% OF THE TIME IS VERY SIMILAR TO NOT TRYING AT ALL. I'M PRETTY SURE YOU WON'T BE ABLE TO TELL THE DIFFERENCE.
10-28-10 ©2010 Scott Adams, Inc./Dist. by Universal Uclick
WHICH ONE AM I DOING NOW?

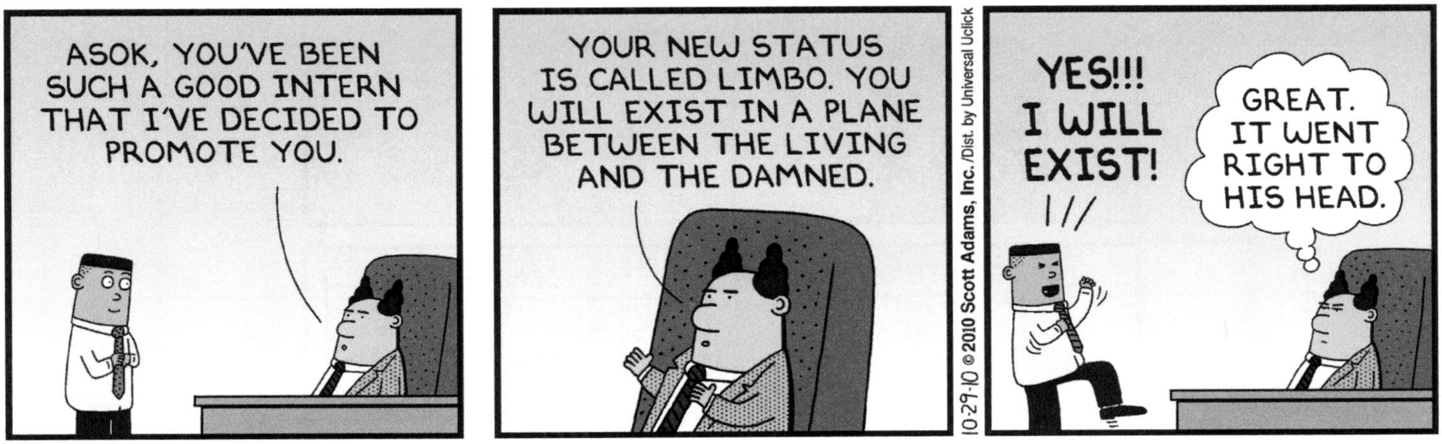
ASOK, YOU'VE BEEN SUCH A GOOD INTERN THAT I'VE DECIDED TO PROMOTE YOU.
YOUR NEW STATUS IS CALLED LIMBO. YOU WILL EXIST IN A PLANE BETWEEN THE LIVING AND THE DAMNED.
10-29-10 ©2010 Scott Adams, Inc./Dist. by Universal Uclick
YES!!! I WILL EXIST!
GREAT. IT WENT RIGHT TO HIS HEAD.

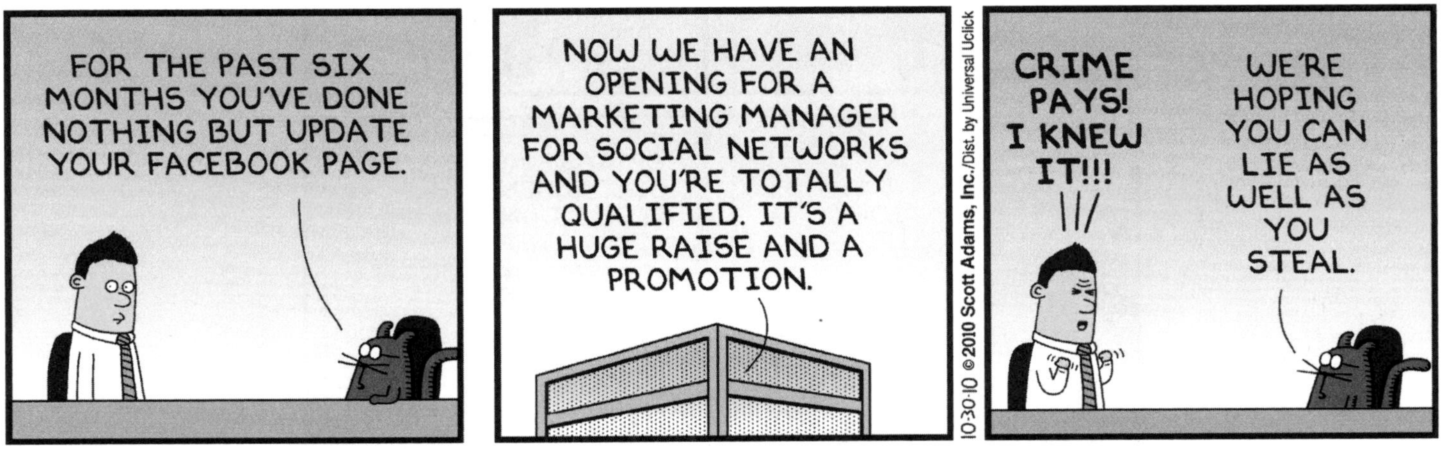
FOR THE PAST SIX MONTHS YOU'VE DONE NOTHING BUT UPDATE YOUR FACEBOOK PAGE.
NOW WE HAVE AN OPENING FOR A MARKETING MANAGER FOR SOCIAL NETWORKS AND YOU'RE TOTALLY QUALIFIED. IT'S A HUGE RAISE AND A PROMOTION.
10-30-10 ©2010 Scott Adams, Inc./Dist. by Universal Uclick
CRIME PAYS! I KNEW IT!!!
WE'RE HOPING YOU CAN LIE AS WELL AS YOU STEAL.

I NEED THIS CLASS TO UPDATE MY SKILLS. WILL YOU APPROVE THE EXPENSE?
WHERE'S THE ANALYSIS OF ALTERNATIVES?
WHAT?
WHEN YOU ASK FOR FUNDING, YOU NEED TO TELL ME WHAT MY OPTIONS ARE.
WELL, OKAY. THAT SEEMS LOGICAL.
OPTION TWO: DO NOTHING WHILE I BECOME INCREASINGLY UNQUALIFIED FOR MY JOB.
OPTION THREE: REPLACE ME WITH SOMEONE YOUNGER WHO EARNS LESS THAN I DO AND ALREADY HAS THE SKILLS.
OH.
OPTIONS ARE ONLY GOOD WHEN OTHER PEOPLE DON'T HAVE THEM.
© 2010 Scott Adams, Inc. /Dist. by Universal Uclick
10-31-10

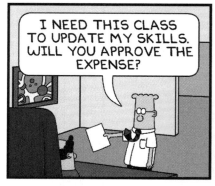

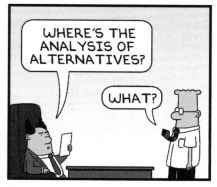

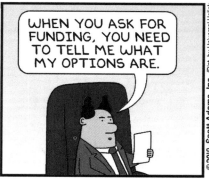

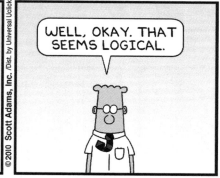

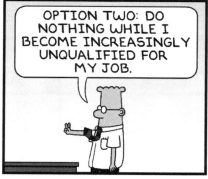

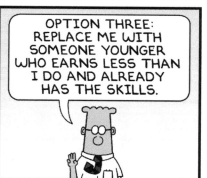

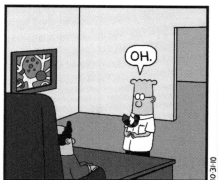

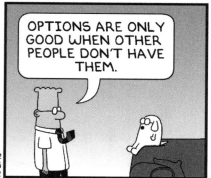

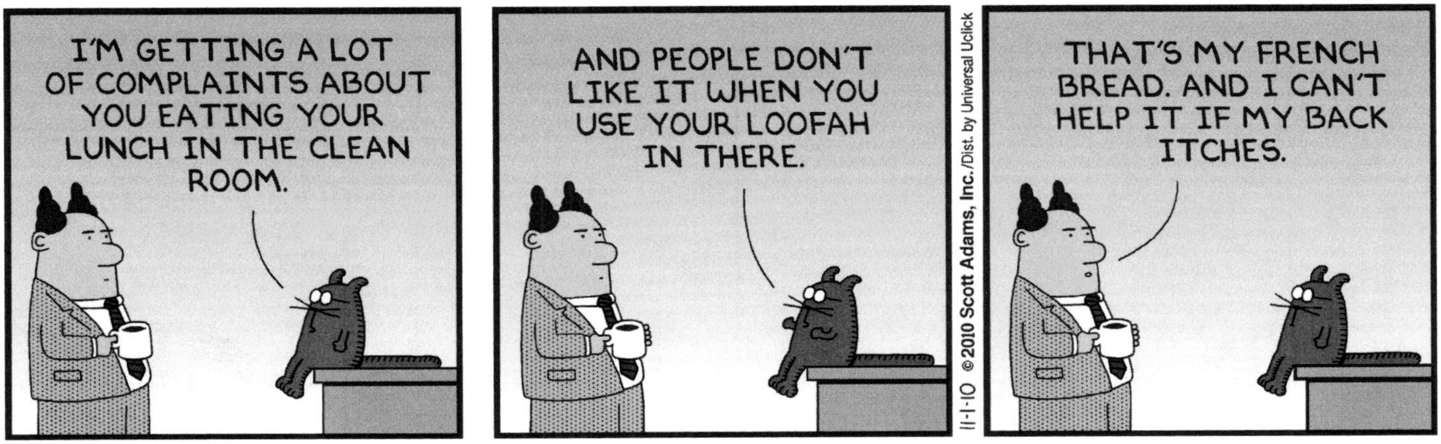
I'M GETTING A LOT OF COMPLAINTS ABOUT YOU EATING YOUR LUNCH IN THE CLEAN ROOM.
AND PEOPLE DON'T LIKE IT WHEN YOU USE YOUR LOOFAH IN THERE.
11-1-10 ©2010 Scott Adams, Inc./Dist. by Universal Uclick
THAT'S MY FRENCH BREAD. AND I CAN'T HELP IT IF MY BACK ITCHES.

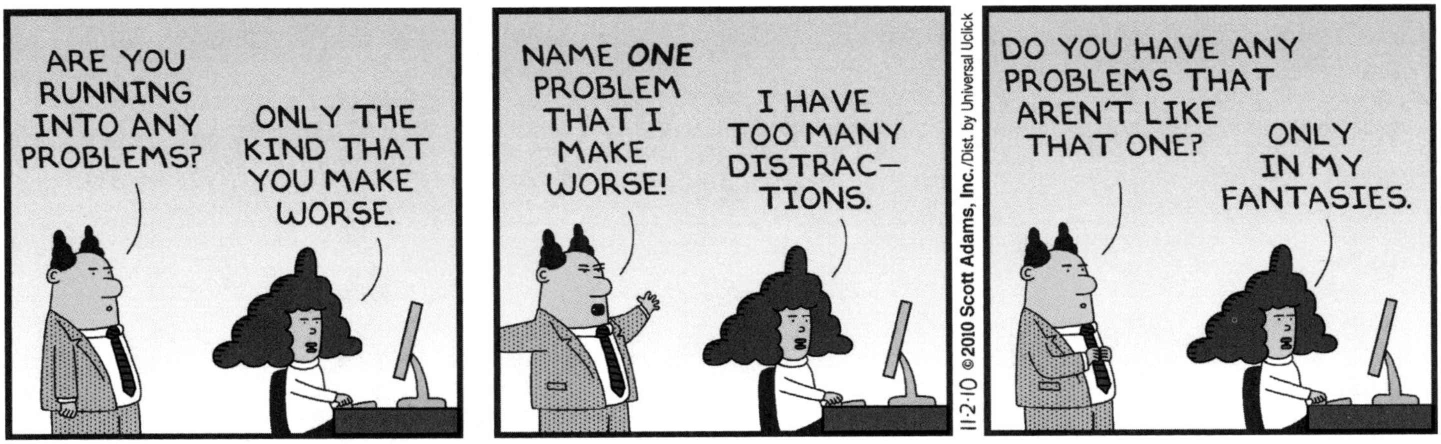
ARE YOU RUNNING INTO ANY PROBLEMS?
ONLY THE KIND THAT YOU MAKE WORSE.
NAME ONE PROBLEM THAT I MAKE WORSE!
I HAVE TOO MANY DISTRAC– TIONS.
11-2-10 ©2010 Scott Adams, Inc./Dist. by Universal Uclick
DO YOU HAVE ANY PROBLEMS THAT AREN'T LIKE THAT ONE?
ONLY IN MY FANTASIES.

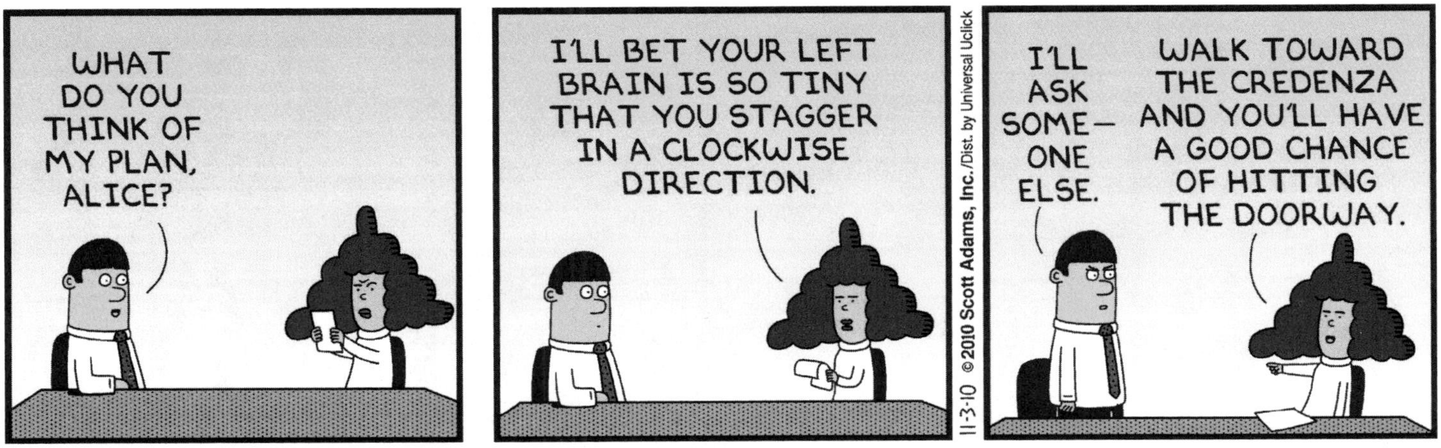
WHAT DO YOU THINK OF MY PLAN, ALICE?
I'LL BET YOUR LEFT BRAIN IS SO TINY THAT YOU STAGGER IN A CLOCKWISE DIRECTION.
11-3-10 ©2010 Scott Adams, Inc./Dist. by Universal Uclick
I'LL ASK SOME– ONE ELSE.
WALK TOWARD THE CREDENZA AND YOU'LL HAVE A GOOD CHANCE OF HITTING THE DOORWAY.

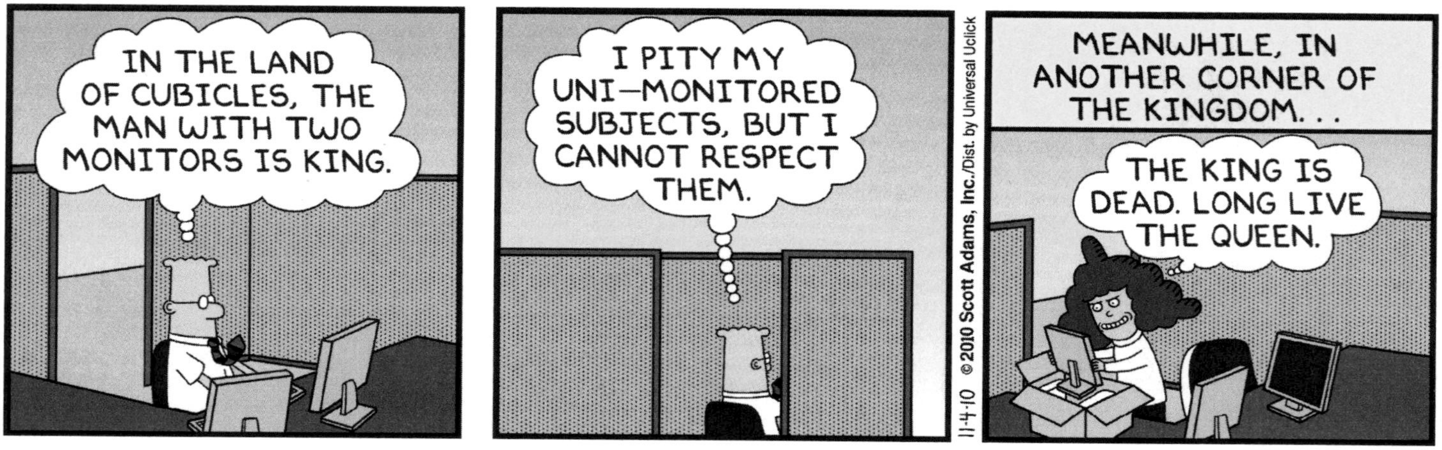
IN THE LAND OF CUBICLES, THE MAN WITH TWO MONITORS IS KING.
I PITY MY UNI—MONITORED SUBJECTS, BUT I CANNOT RESPECT THEM.
11·4·10 ©2010 Scott Adams, Inc./Dist. by Universal Uclick
MEANWHILE, IN ANOTHER CORNER OF THE KINGDOM. . .
THE KING IS DEAD. LONG LIVE THE QUEEN.

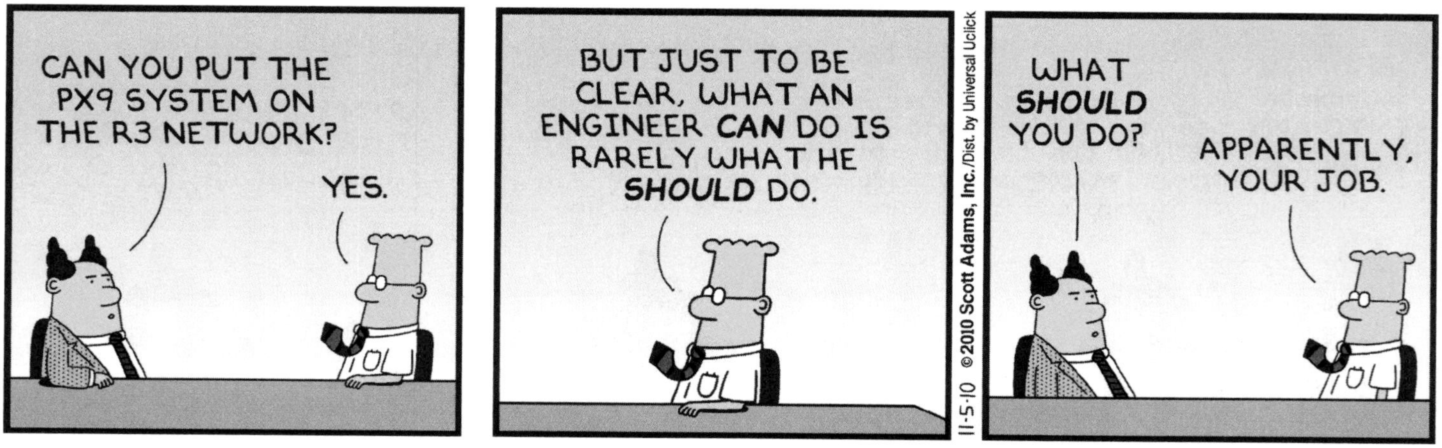
CAN YOU PUT THE PX9 SYSTEM ON THE R3 NETWORK?
YES.
BUT JUST TO BE CLEAR, WHAT AN ENGINEER CAN DO IS RARELY WHAT HE SHOULD DO.
11·5·10 ©2010 Scott Adams, Inc./Dist. by Universal Uclick
WHAT SHOULD YOU DO?
APPARENTLY, YOUR JOB.

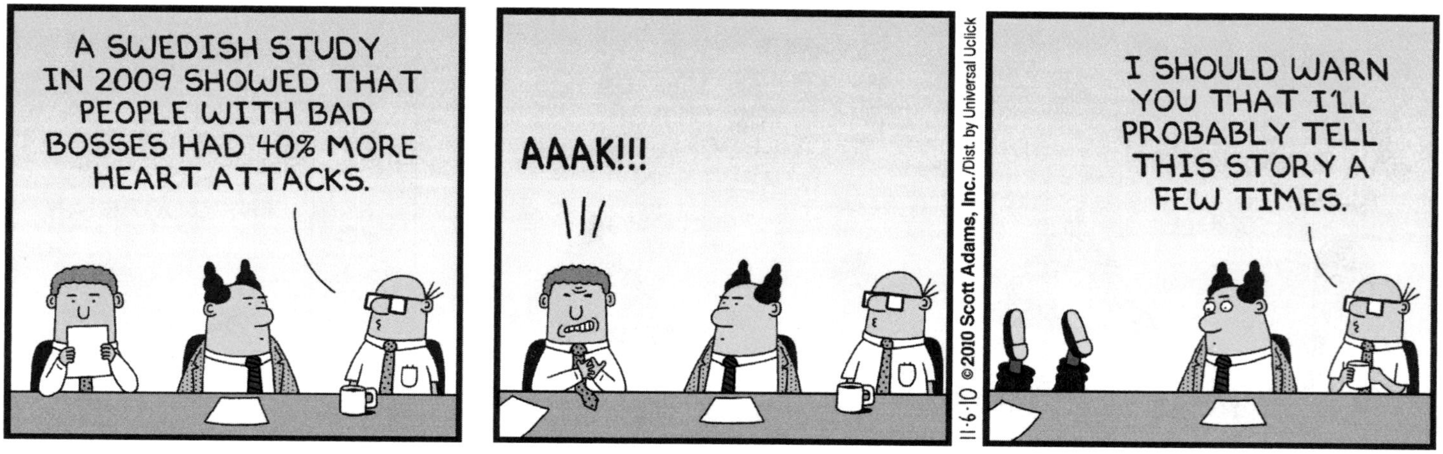
A SWEDISH STUDY IN 2009 SHOWED THAT PEOPLE WITH BAD BOSSES HAD 40% MORE HEART ATTACKS.
AAAK!!!
11·6·10 ©2010 Scott Adams, Inc./Dist. by Universal Uclick
I SHOULD WARN YOU THAT I'LL PROBABLY TELL THIS STORY A FEW TIMES.

I'D LIKE TO THANK ALL OF THE PEOPLE WHO HELPED DESIGN THE TECHNOLOGY TEST PARAMETERS.
THANKS TO YOUR INPUT, THE TEST HAD NOTHING IN COMMON WITH HOW THINGS WORK IN THE REAL WORLD.
SO I WASTED TWO WEEKS OF MY LIFE ON A TEST THAT IS NOT ONLY MEANINGLESS. . .
. . . BUT ALSO DANGEROUSLY MISLEADING.
THIS SLIDE SHOWS THE GAP BETWEEN THE TEST RESULTS AND REALITY.
WE'LL USE THE TEST RESULTS ANYWAY BECAUSE IT'S THE ONLY DATA WE HAVE.
FINE. I HOPE YOU ALL CHOKE TO DEATH ON YOUR LUNCHES.
WHY'S HE SO CRANKY?
SOME—THING ABOUT DATA.
© 2010 Scott Adams, Inc. /Dist. by Universal Uclick
11-7-10

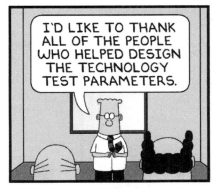

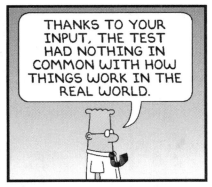

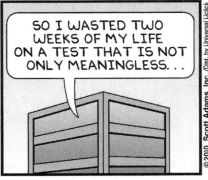

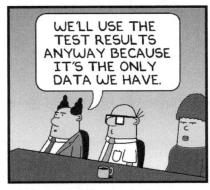

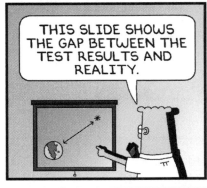

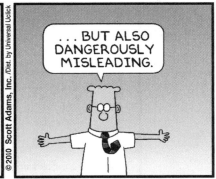

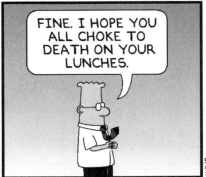

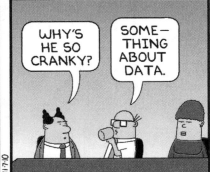

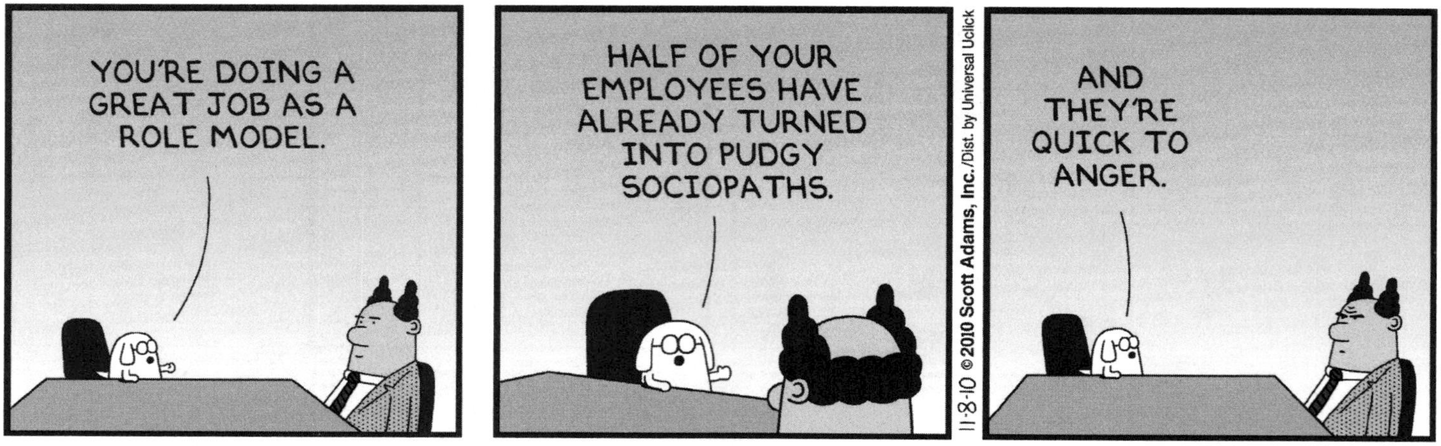
YOU'RE DOING A GREAT JOB AS A ROLE MODEL.
HALF OF YOUR EMPLOYEES HAVE ALREADY TURNED INTO PUDGY SOCIOPATHS.
AND THEY'RE QUICK TO ANGER.
11-8-10 © 2010 Scott Adams, Inc./Dist. by Universal Uclick

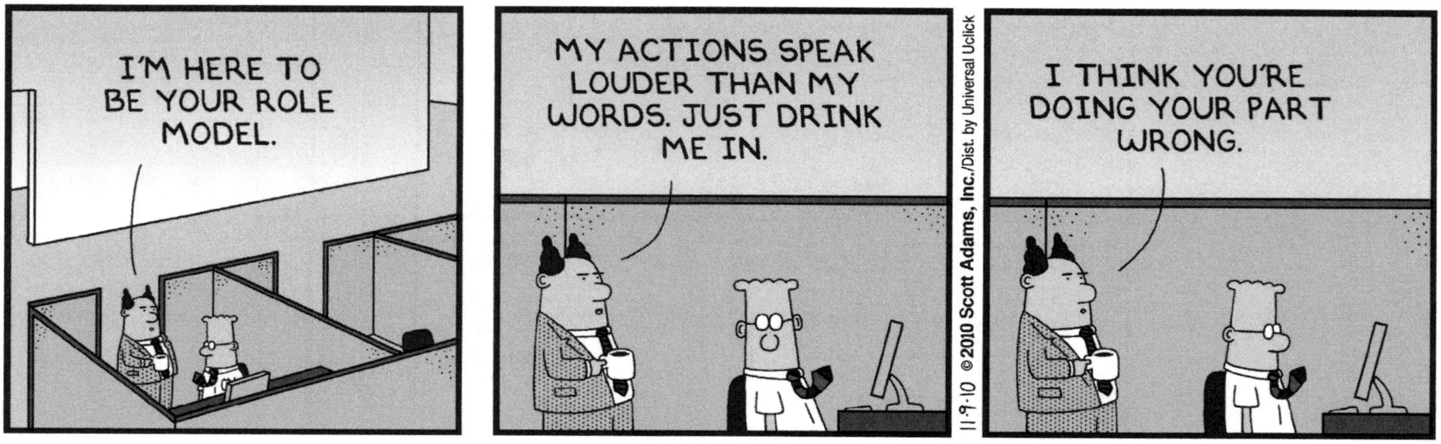
I'M HERE TO BE YOUR ROLE MODEL.
MY ACTIONS SPEAK LOUDER THAN MY WORDS. JUST DRINK ME IN.
I THINK YOU'RE DOING YOUR PART WRONG.
11-9-10 © 2010 Scott Adams, Inc./Dist. by Universal Uclick

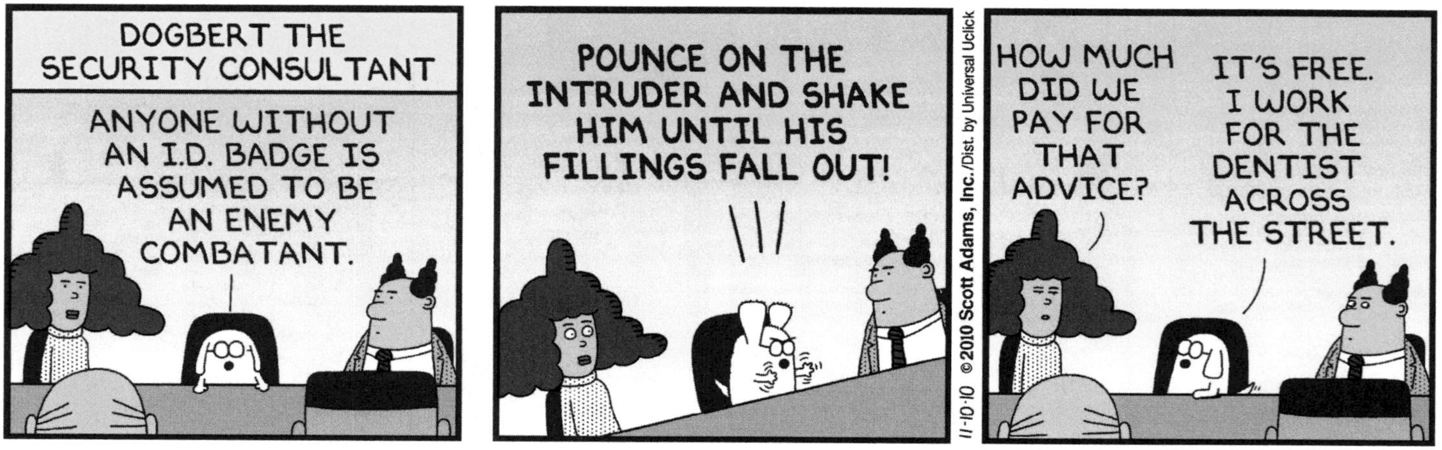
DOGBERT THE SECURITY CONSULTANT
ANYONE WITHOUT AN I.D. BADGE IS ASSUMED TO BE AN ENEMY COMBATANT.
POUNCE ON THE INTRUDER AND SHAKE HIM UNTIL HIS FILLINGS FALL OUT!
HOW MUCH DID WE PAY FOR THAT ADVICE?
IT'S FREE. I WORK FOR THE DENTIST ACROSS THE STREET.
11-10-10 © 2010 Scott Adams, Inc./Dist. by Universal Uclick

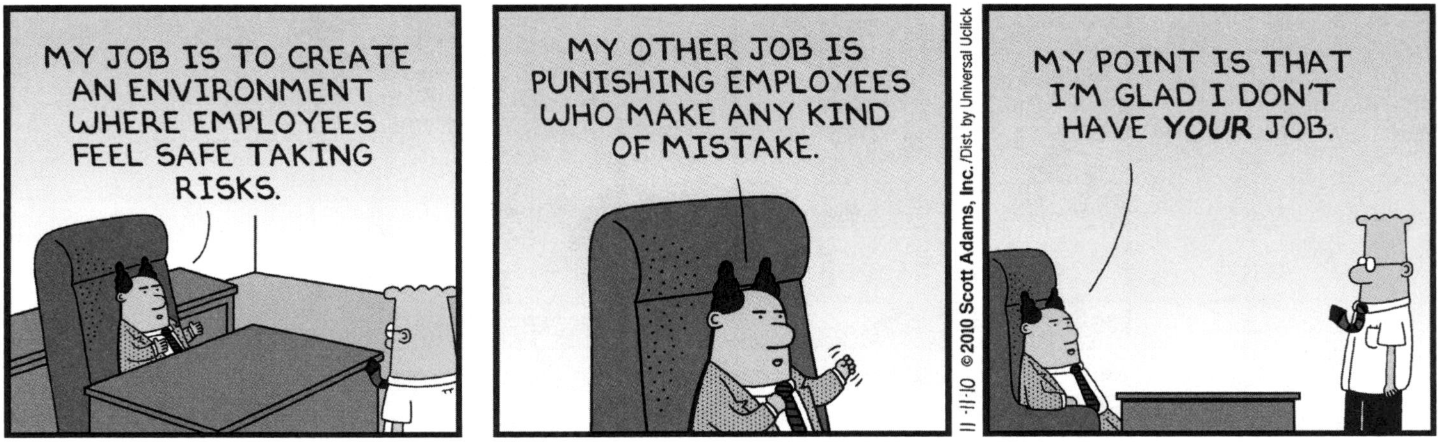
MY JOB IS TO CREATE AN ENVIRONMENT WHERE EMPLOYEES FEEL SAFE TAKING RISKS.
MY OTHER JOB IS PUNISHING EMPLOYEES WHO MAKE ANY KIND OF MISTAKE.
11-11-10 © 2010 Scott Adams, Inc./Dist. by Universal Uclick
MY POINT IS THAT I'M GLAD I DON'T HAVE **YOUR** JOB.

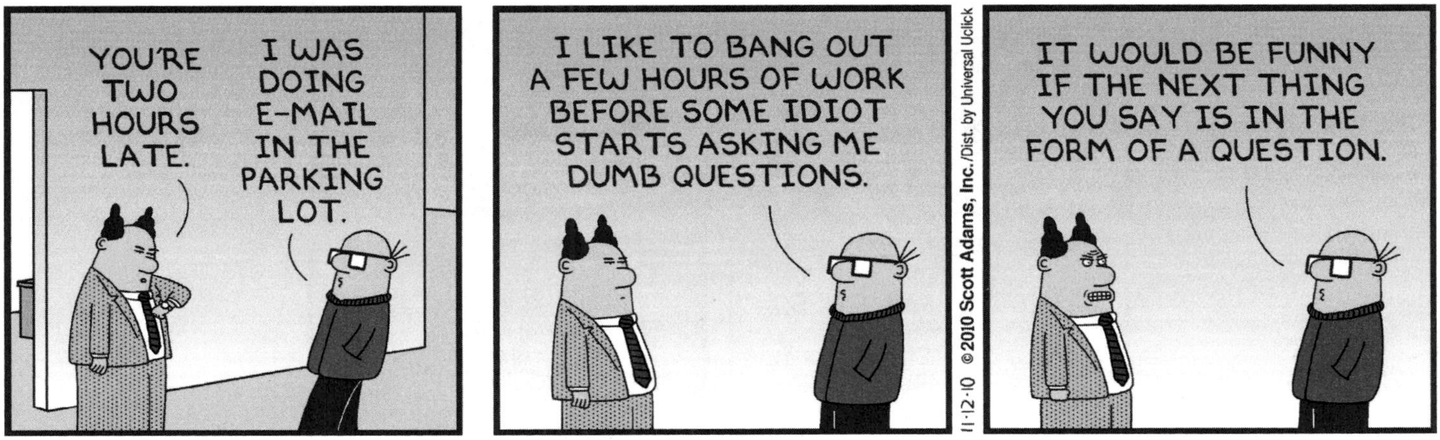
YOU'RE TWO HOURS LATE.
I WAS DOING E-MAIL IN THE PARKING LOT.
I LIKE TO BANG OUT A FEW HOURS OF WORK BEFORE SOME IDIOT STARTS ASKING ME DUMB QUESTIONS.
11-12-10 © 2010 Scott Adams, Inc./Dist. by Universal Uclick
IT WOULD BE FUNNY IF THE NEXT THING YOU SAY IS IN THE FORM OF A QUESTION.

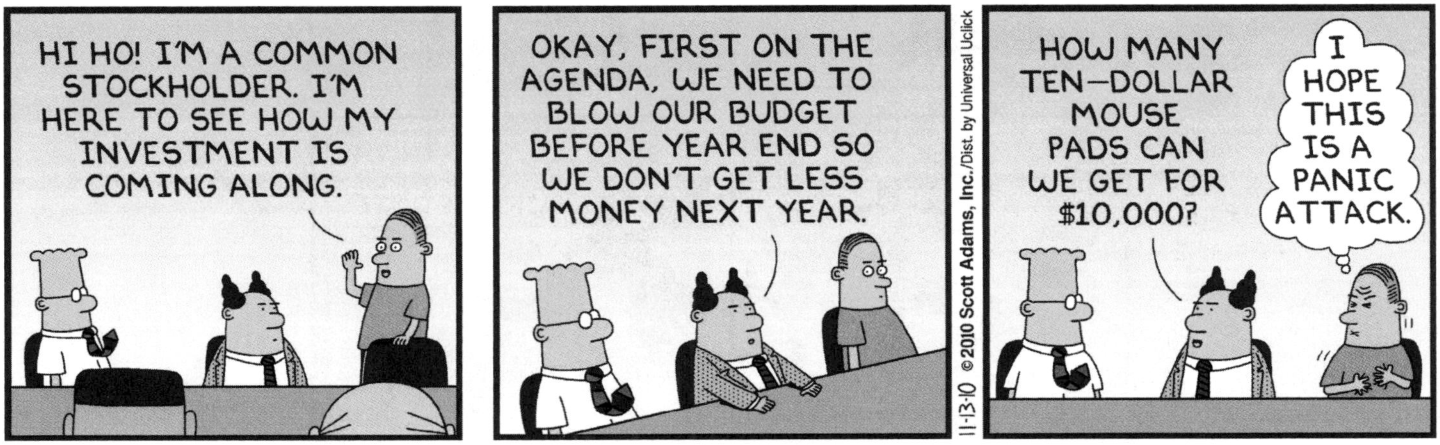
HI HO! I'M A COMMON STOCKHOLDER. I'M HERE TO SEE HOW MY INVESTMENT IS COMING ALONG.
OKAY, FIRST ON THE AGENDA, WE NEED TO BLOW OUR BUDGET BEFORE YEAR END SO WE DON'T GET LESS MONEY NEXT YEAR.
11-13-10 © 2010 Scott Adams, Inc./Dist. by Universal Uclick
HOW MANY TEN-DOLLAR MOUSE PADS CAN WE GET FOR $10,000?
I HOPE THIS IS A PANIC ATTACK.

YOU DIDN'T ANSWER MY E-MAIL.
I DON'T CHECK E-MAIL OFTEN.
THE WHOLE POINT OF E-MAIL IS THAT YOU CHECK IT OFTEN.
ARE YOU AN IDIOT OR SOME SORT OF DIGITAL SOCIOPATH?
© 2010 Scott Adams, Inc. /Dist. by Universal Uclick
SOMETIMES I DON'T REMEMBER TO CHECK IT.
YOU SEEM LIKE A VISUAL LEARNER, SO LET ME SHOW YOU HOW TO KEEP E-MAIL IN THE FRONT OF YOUR MIND.
IS THIS YOUR SMART-PHONE?
YES.
BAM!
11-14-10
NOW IT'S IN THE FRONT OF YOUR MIND. GET IT?

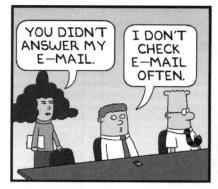

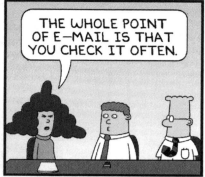

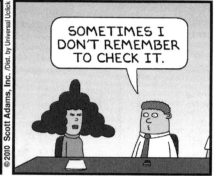

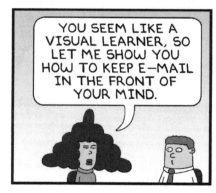

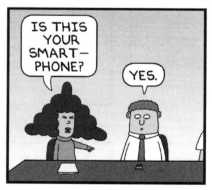

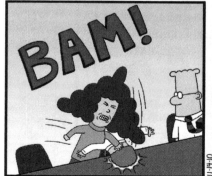

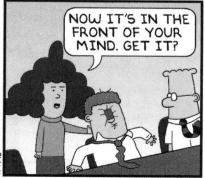

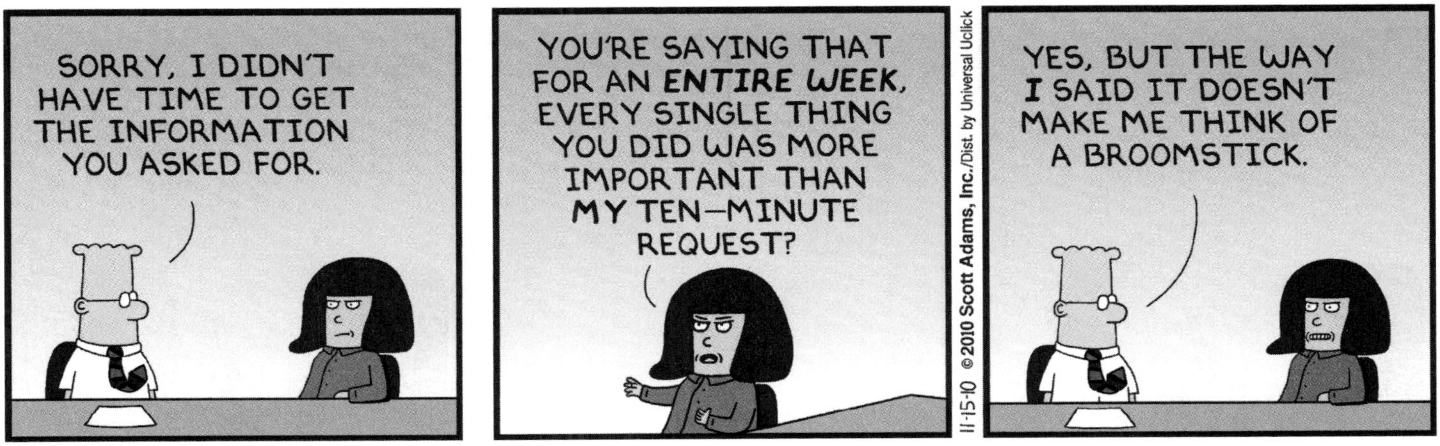
SORRY, I DIDN'T HAVE TIME TO GET THE INFORMATION YOU ASKED FOR.
YOU'RE SAYING THAT FOR AN ENTIRE WEEK, EVERY SINGLE THING YOU DID WAS MORE IMPORTANT THAN MY TEN-MINUTE REQUEST?
YES, BUT THE WAY I SAID IT DOESN'T MAKE ME THINK OF A BROOMSTICK.
11-15-10 ©2010 Scott Adams, Inc./Dist. by Universal Uclick

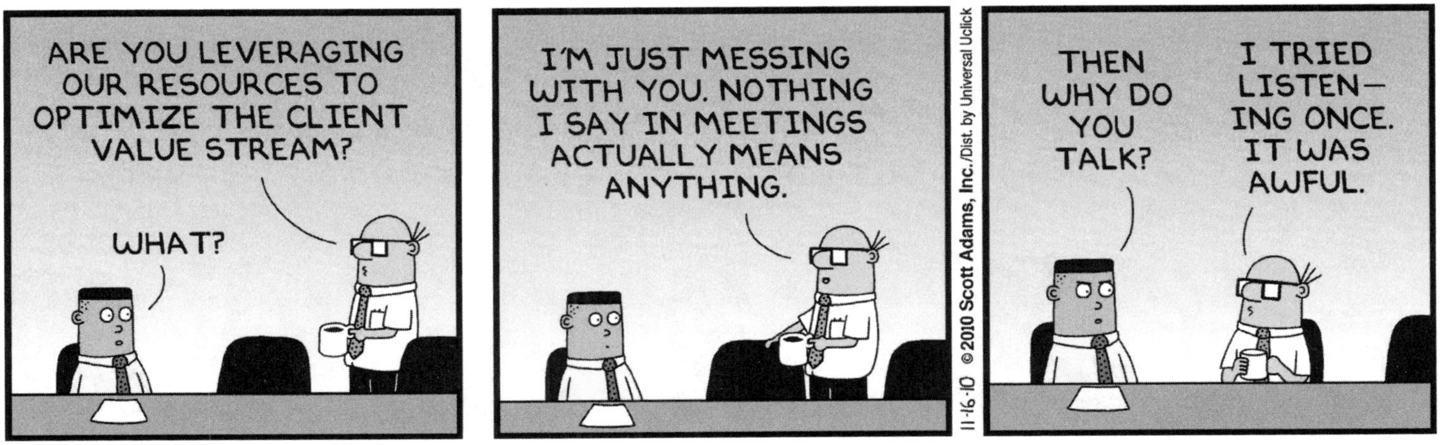
ARE YOU LEVERAGING OUR RESOURCES TO OPTIMIZE THE CLIENT VALUE STREAM?
WHAT?
I'M JUST MESSING WITH YOU. NOTHING I SAY IN MEETINGS ACTUALLY MEANS ANYTHING.
THEN WHY DO YOU TALK?
I TRIED LISTEN-ING ONCE. IT WAS AWFUL.
11-16-10 ©2010 Scott Adams, Inc./Dist. by Universal Uclick

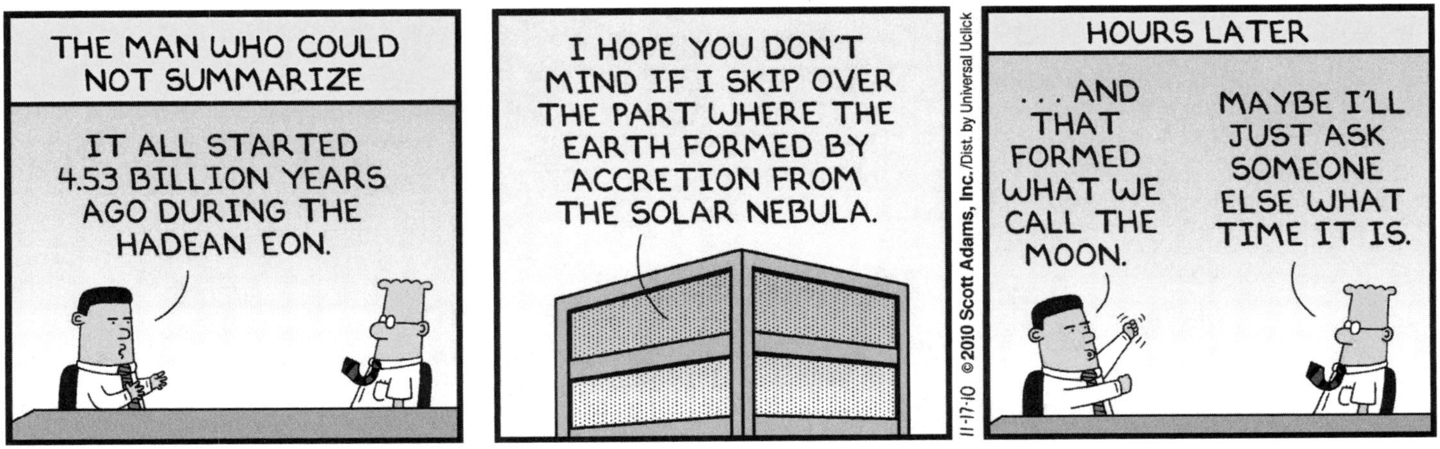
THE MAN WHO COULD NOT SUMMARIZE
IT ALL STARTED 4.53 BILLION YEARS AGO DURING THE HADEAN EON.
I HOPE YOU DON'T MIND IF I SKIP OVER THE PART WHERE THE EARTH FORMED BY ACCRETION FROM THE SOLAR NEBULA.
HOURS LATER
. . . AND THAT FORMED WHAT WE CALL THE MOON.
MAYBE I'LL JUST ASK SOMEONE ELSE WHAT TIME IT IS.
11-17-10 ©2010 Scott Adams, Inc./Dist. by Universal Uclick

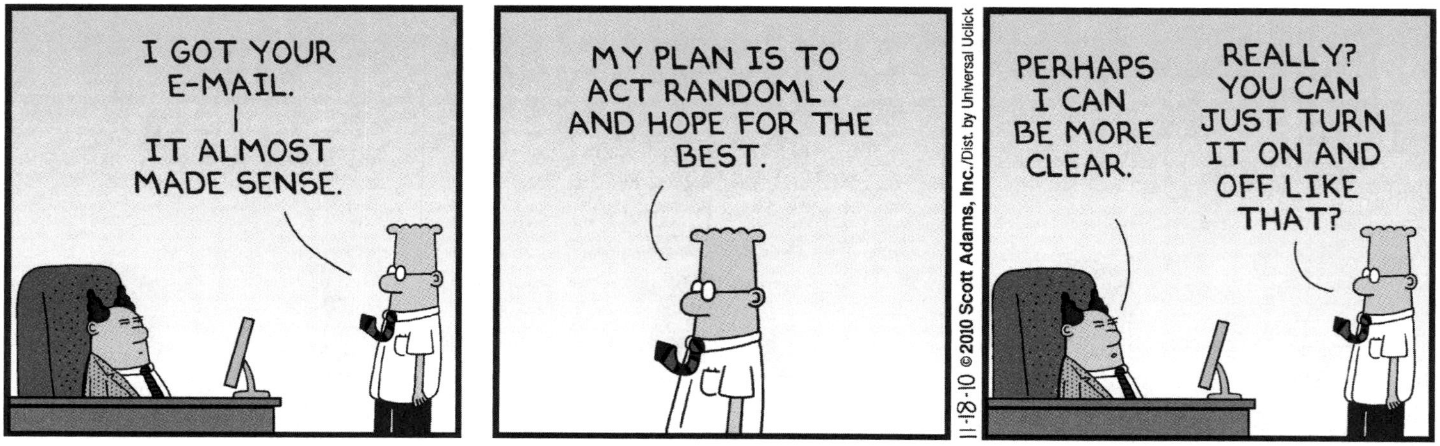
I GOT YOUR E-MAIL.
IT ALMOST MADE SENSE.
MY PLAN IS TO ACT RANDOMLY AND HOPE FOR THE BEST.
PERHAPS I CAN BE MORE CLEAR.
REALLY? YOU CAN JUST TURN IT ON AND OFF LIKE THAT?
11-18-10 © 2010 Scott Adams, Inc./Dist. by Universal Uclick

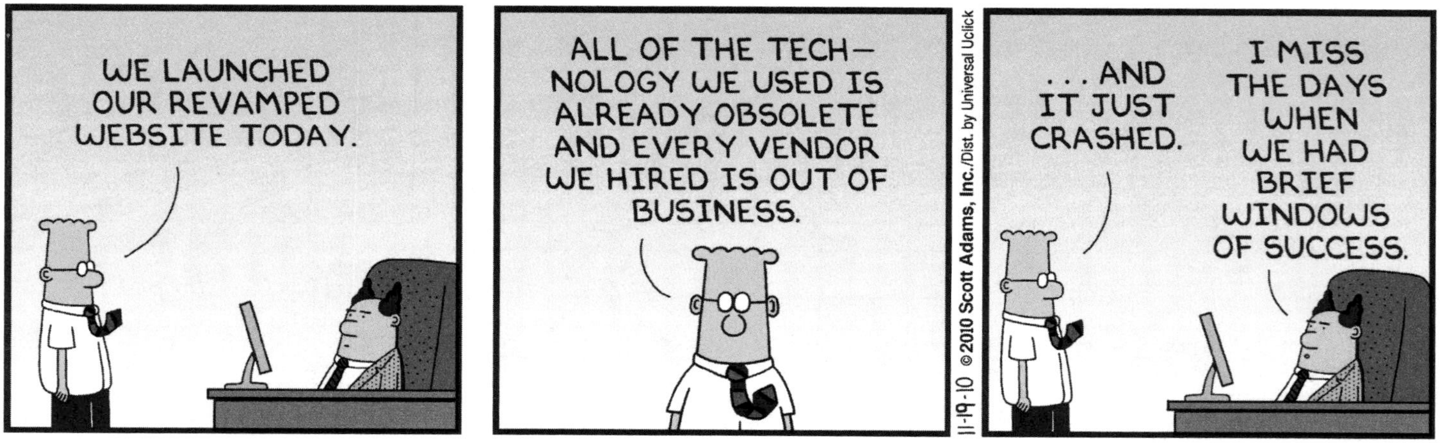
WE LAUNCHED OUR REVAMPED WEBSITE TODAY.
ALL OF THE TECH–NOLOGY WE USED IS ALREADY OBSOLETE AND EVERY VENDOR WE HIRED IS OUT OF BUSINESS.
. . . AND IT JUST CRASHED.
I MISS THE DAYS WHEN WE HAD BRIEF WINDOWS OF SUCCESS.
11-19-10 © 2010 Scott Adams, Inc./Dist. by Universal Uclick

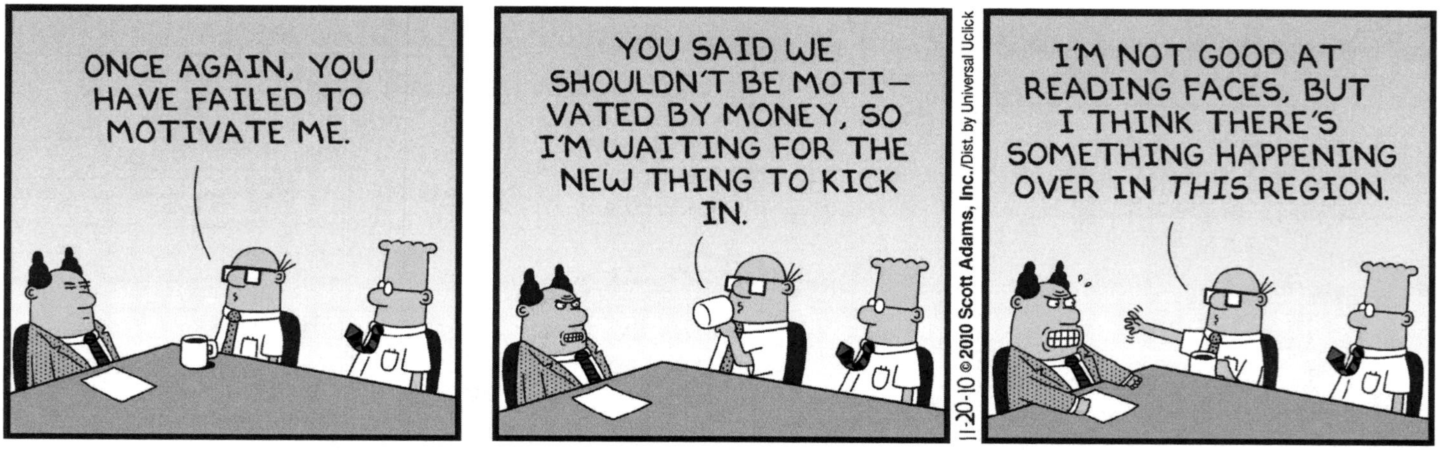
ONCE AGAIN, YOU HAVE FAILED TO MOTIVATE ME.
YOU SAID WE SHOULDN'T BE MOTI–VATED BY MONEY, SO I'M WAITING FOR THE NEW THING TO KICK IN.
I'M NOT GOOD AT READING FACES, BUT I THINK THERE'S SOMETHING HAPPENING OVER IN *THIS* REGION.
11-20-10 © 2010 Scott Adams, Inc./Dist. by Universal Uclick

IS IT MY IMAGINATION OR IS YOUR PRICING INTENTIONALLY CONFUSING?
IT'S INTENTIONALLY CONFUSING.
THAT WAY YOU CAN'T COMPARE OUR PRICES TO OUR COMPETITORS' PRICES.
OUR COMPETITORS DO THE SAME THING. IT'S CALLED A CONFUSOPOLY.
WE ALL GET OUR FAIR SHARE OF CONFUSED CUSTOMERS AND WE DON'T NEED TO LOWER OUR PRICES TO COMPETE.
WE USE THE PROFITS FROM OUR ANTI-COMPETITIVE BEHAVIOR TO FUND INNOVATION.
SO DON'T RUIN A GOOD SYSTEM BY TRYING TO UNDER-STAND WHAT YOU'RE BUYING.
THAT ALMOST SOUNDS REASON-ABLE.
NOW SPANK YOURSELF AND THANK ME!
©2010 Scott Adams, Inc./Dist. by Universal Uclick
11-21-10

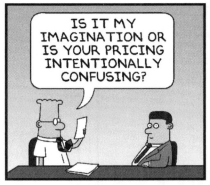

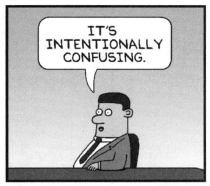

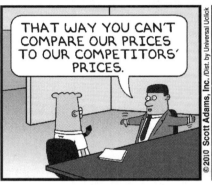

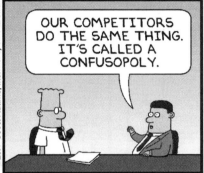

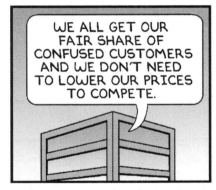

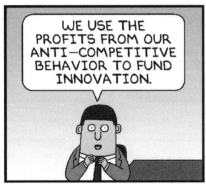

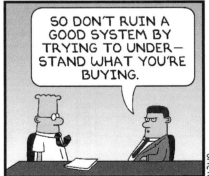

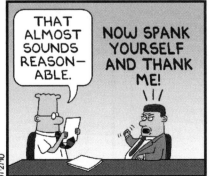

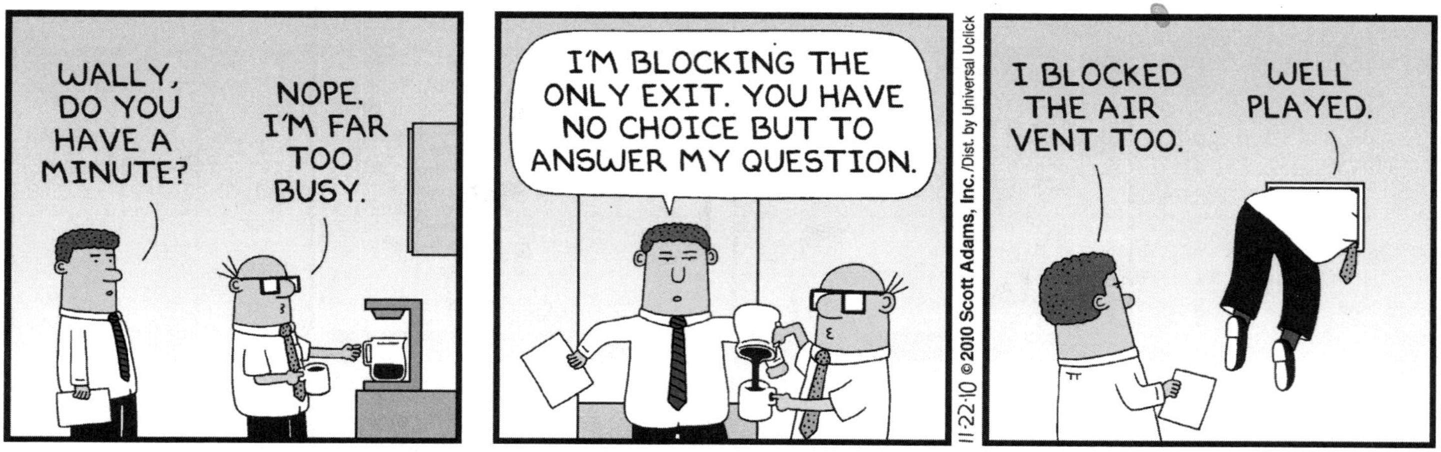
WALLY, DO YOU HAVE A MINUTE?
NOPE. I'M FAR TOO BUSY.
I'M BLOCKING THE ONLY EXIT. YOU HAVE NO CHOICE BUT TO ANSWER MY QUESTION.
11-22-10 © 2010 Scott Adams, Inc./Dist. by Universal Uclick
I BLOCKED THE AIR VENT TOO.
WELL PLAYED.

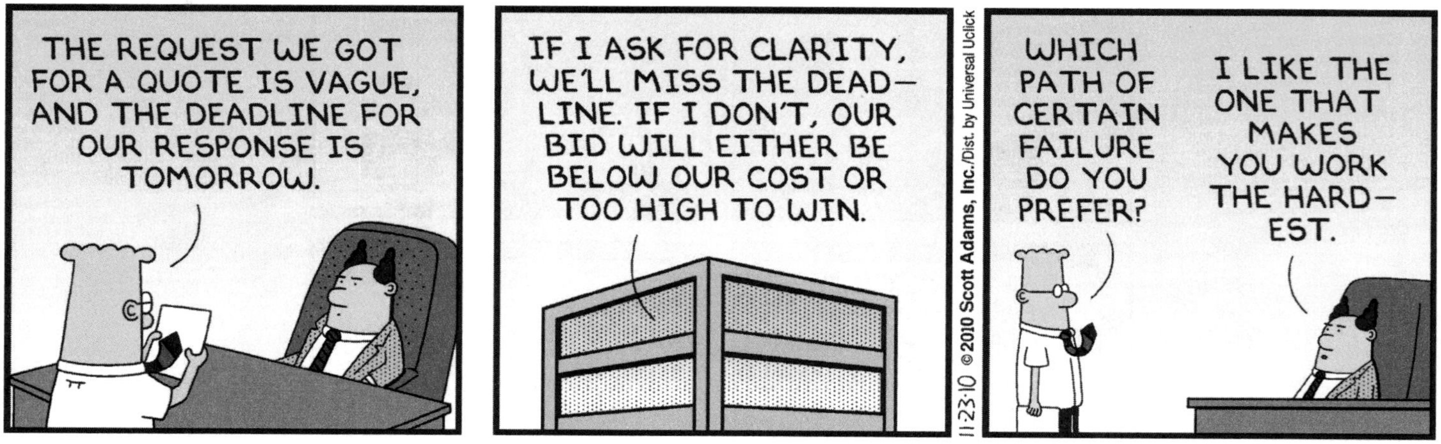
THE REQUEST WE GOT FOR A QUOTE IS VAGUE, AND THE DEADLINE FOR OUR RESPONSE IS TOMORROW.
IF I ASK FOR CLARITY, WE'LL MISS THE DEAD-LINE. IF I DON'T, OUR BID WILL EITHER BE BELOW OUR COST OR TOO HIGH TO WIN.
11-23-10 © 2010 Scott Adams, Inc./Dist. by Universal Uclick
WHICH PATH OF CERTAIN FAILURE DO YOU PREFER?
I LIKE THE ONE THAT MAKES YOU WORK THE HARD-EST.

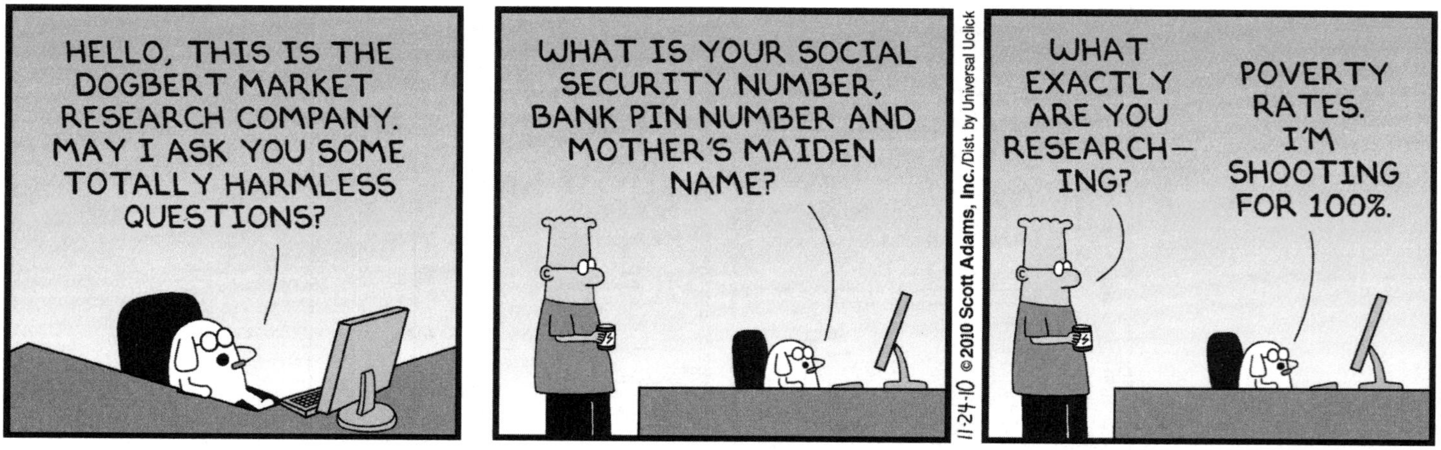
HELLO, THIS IS THE DOGBERT MARKET RESEARCH COMPANY. MAY I ASK YOU SOME TOTALLY HARMLESS QUESTIONS?
WHAT IS YOUR SOCIAL SECURITY NUMBER, BANK PIN NUMBER AND MOTHER'S MAIDEN NAME?
11-24-10 © 2010 Scott Adams, Inc./Dist. by Universal Uclick
WHAT EXACTLY ARE YOU RESEARCH-ING?
POVERTY RATES. I'M SHOOTING FOR 100%.

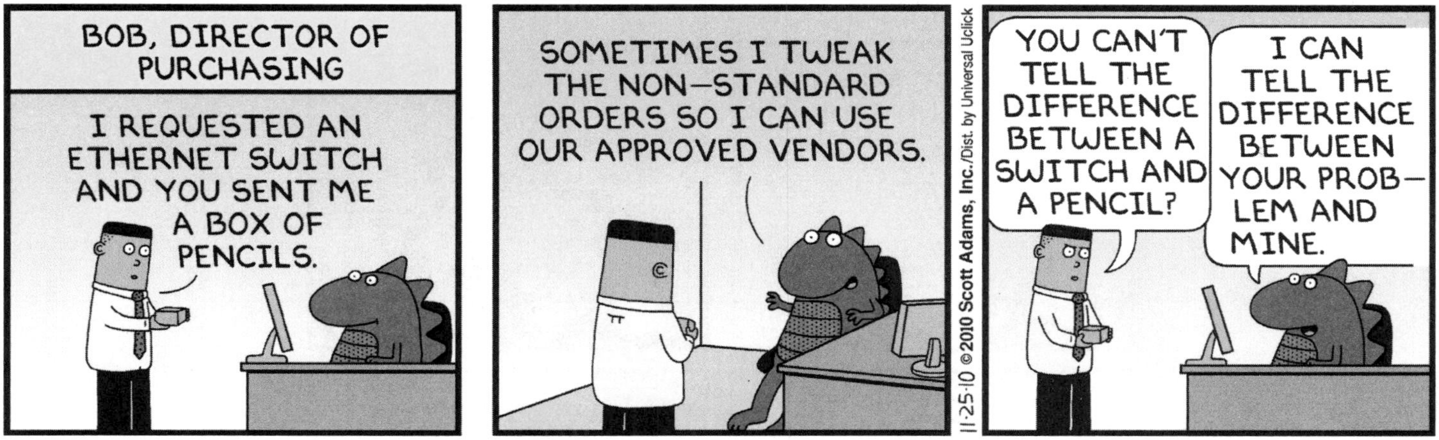
BOB, DIRECTOR OF PURCHASING
I REQUESTED AN ETHERNET SWITCH AND YOU SENT ME A BOX OF PENCILS.
SOMETIMES I TWEAK THE NON-STANDARD ORDERS SO I CAN USE OUR APPROVED VENDORS.
11-25-10 © 2010 Scott Adams, Inc./Dist. by Universal Uclick
YOU CAN'T TELL THE DIFFERENCE BETWEEN A SWITCH AND A PENCIL?
I CAN TELL THE DIFFERENCE BETWEEN YOUR PROB-LEM AND MINE.

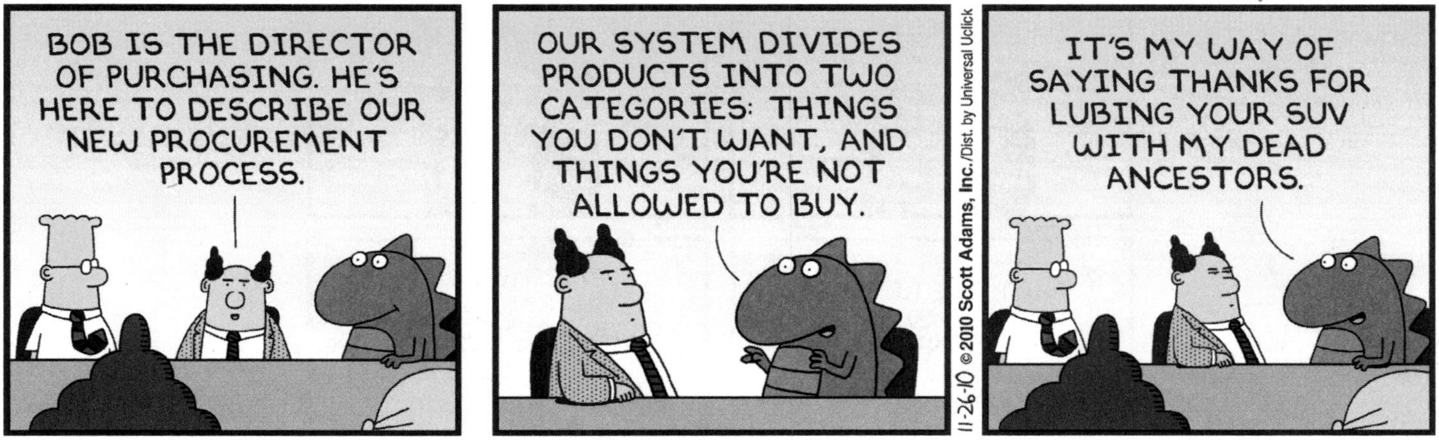
BOB IS THE DIRECTOR OF PURCHASING. HE'S HERE TO DESCRIBE OUR NEW PROCUREMENT PROCESS.
OUR SYSTEM DIVIDES PRODUCTS INTO TWO CATEGORIES: THINGS YOU DON'T WANT, AND THINGS YOU'RE NOT ALLOWED TO BUY.
11-26-10 © 2010 Scott Adams, Inc./Dist. by Universal Uclick
IT'S MY WAY OF SAYING THANKS FOR LUBING YOUR SUV WITH MY DEAD ANCESTORS.

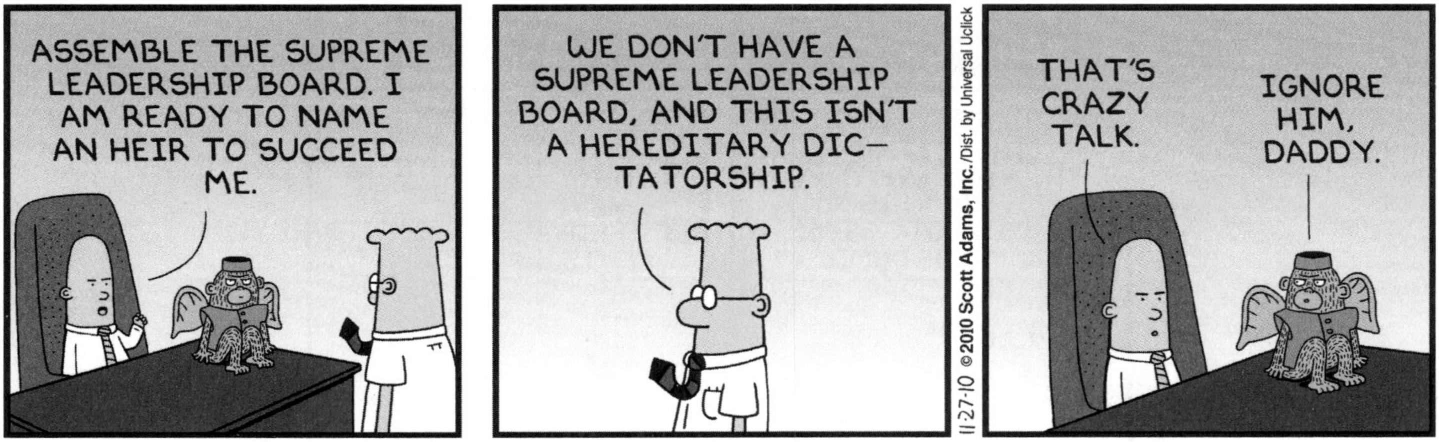
ASSEMBLE THE SUPREME LEADERSHIP BOARD. I AM READY TO NAME AN HEIR TO SUCCEED ME.
WE DON'T HAVE A SUPREME LEADERSHIP BOARD, AND THIS ISN'T A HEREDITARY DIC-TATORSHIP.
11-27-10 © 2010 Scott Adams, Inc./Dist. by Universal Uclick
THAT'S CRAZY TALK.
IGNORE HIM, DADDY.

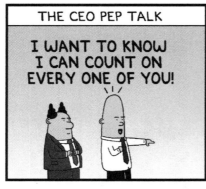

THE CEO PEP TALK
I WANT TO KNOW I CAN COUNT ON EVERY ONE OF YOU!
WHAT'S WRONG WITH THESE PEOPLE?
WELL. . . I FIRED THAT GUY THIS MORNING. HIS LAST DAY IS TOMORROW.
THAT ONE RETIRES AT THE END OF THE MONTH.
THOSE THREE ARE CONTRACTORS. I DIDN'T RENEW THEIR CONTRACTS.
THE REST OF THEM BELIEVE THAT MOTIVATION IS HOW THE POWERFUL STEAL FROM THE DUMB.
TELL THEM I HATE THEIR GUTS.
I DID THAT IN THE PRE–MEETING.
©2010 Scott Adams, Inc. /Dist. by Universal Uclick
11-28-10

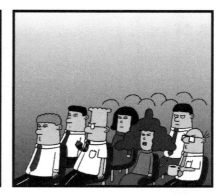

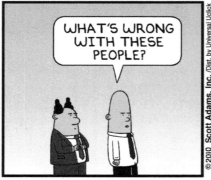

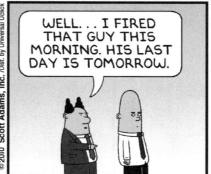

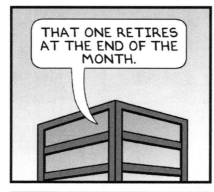

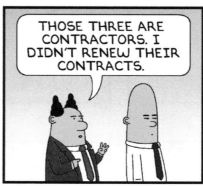

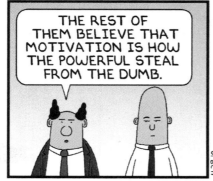

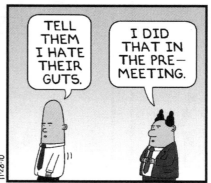

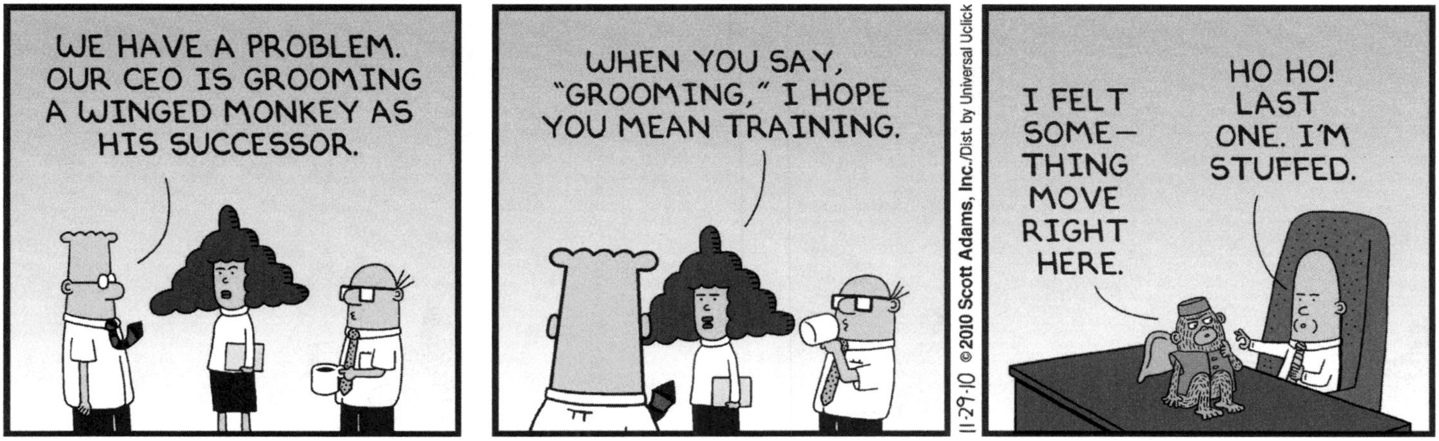
WE HAVE A PROBLEM. OUR CEO IS GROOMING A WINGED MONKEY AS HIS SUCCESSOR.
WHEN YOU SAY, "GROOMING," I HOPE YOU MEAN TRAINING.
11-29-10 © 2010 Scott Adams, Inc./Dist. by Universal Uclick
I FELT SOME-THING MOVE RIGHT HERE.
HO HO! LAST ONE. I'M STUFFED.

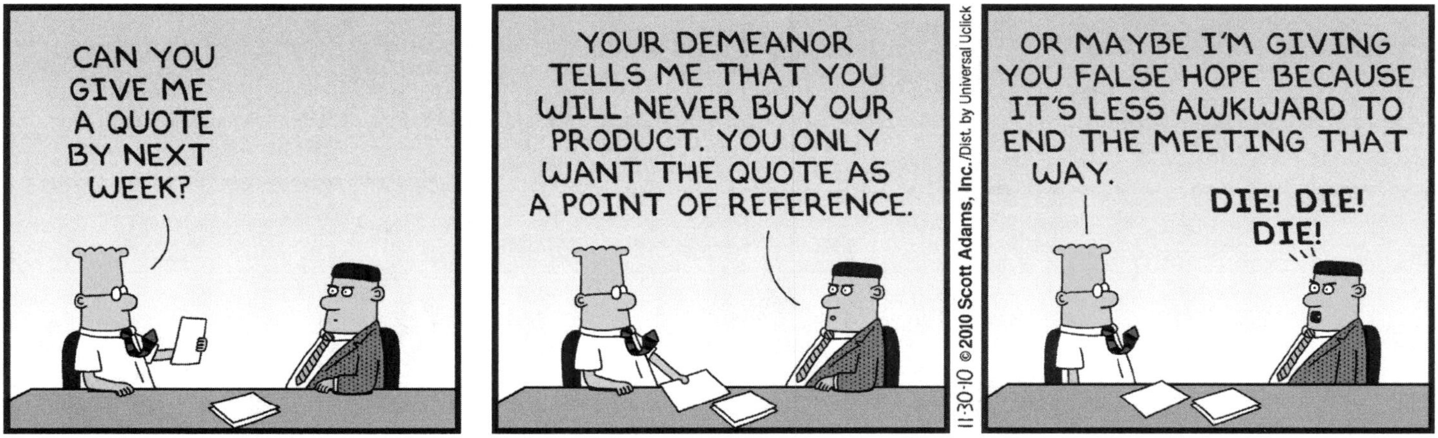
CAN YOU GIVE ME A QUOTE BY NEXT WEEK?
YOUR DEMEANOR TELLS ME THAT YOU WILL NEVER BUY OUR PRODUCT. YOU ONLY WANT THE QUOTE AS A POINT OF REFERENCE.
11-30-10 © 2010 Scott Adams, Inc./Dist. by Universal Uclick
OR MAYBE I'M GIVING YOU FALSE HOPE BECAUSE IT'S LESS AWKWARD TO END THE MEETING THAT WAY.
DIE! DIE! DIE!

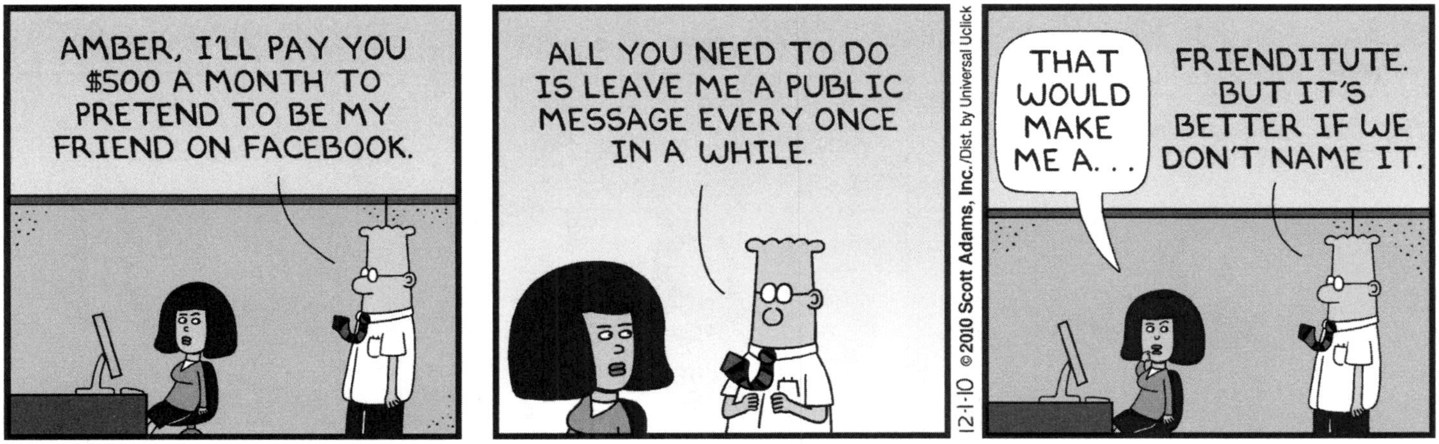
AMBER, I'LL PAY YOU $500 A MONTH TO PRETEND TO BE MY FRIEND ON FACEBOOK.
ALL YOU NEED TO DO IS LEAVE ME A PUBLIC MESSAGE EVERY ONCE IN A WHILE.
12-1-10 © 2010 Scott Adams, Inc./Dist. by Universal Uclick
THAT WOULD MAKE ME A. . .
FRIENDITUTE. BUT IT'S BETTER IF WE DON'T NAME IT.

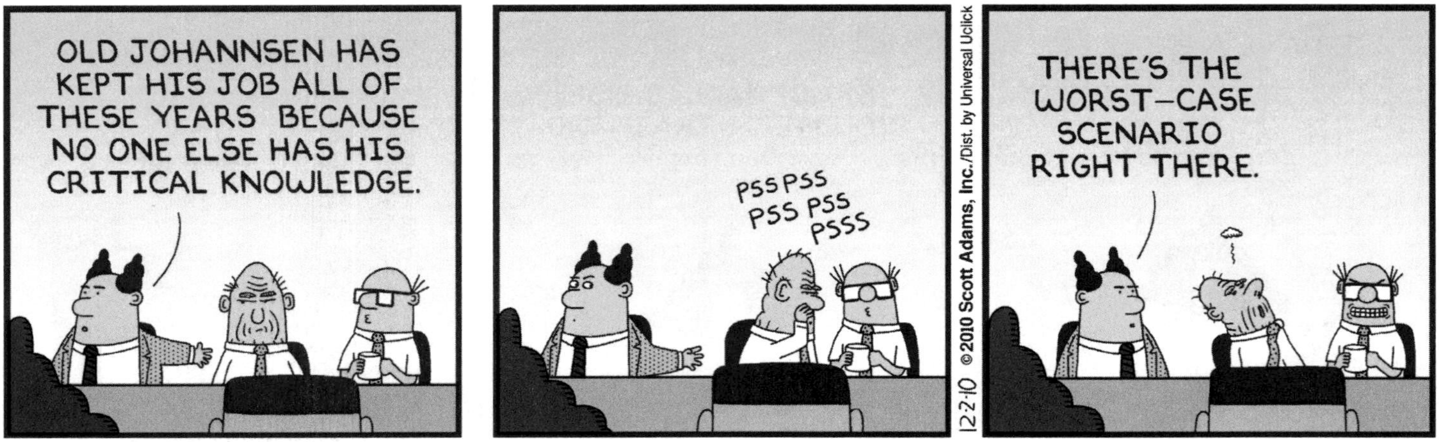
OLD JOHANNSEN HAS KEPT HIS JOB ALL OF THESE YEARS BECAUSE NO ONE ELSE HAS HIS CRITICAL KNOWLEDGE.
PSS PSS PSS PSS PSSS
12·2·10 ©2010 Scott Adams, Inc./Dist. by Universal Uclick
THERE'S THE WORST-CASE SCENARIO RIGHT THERE.

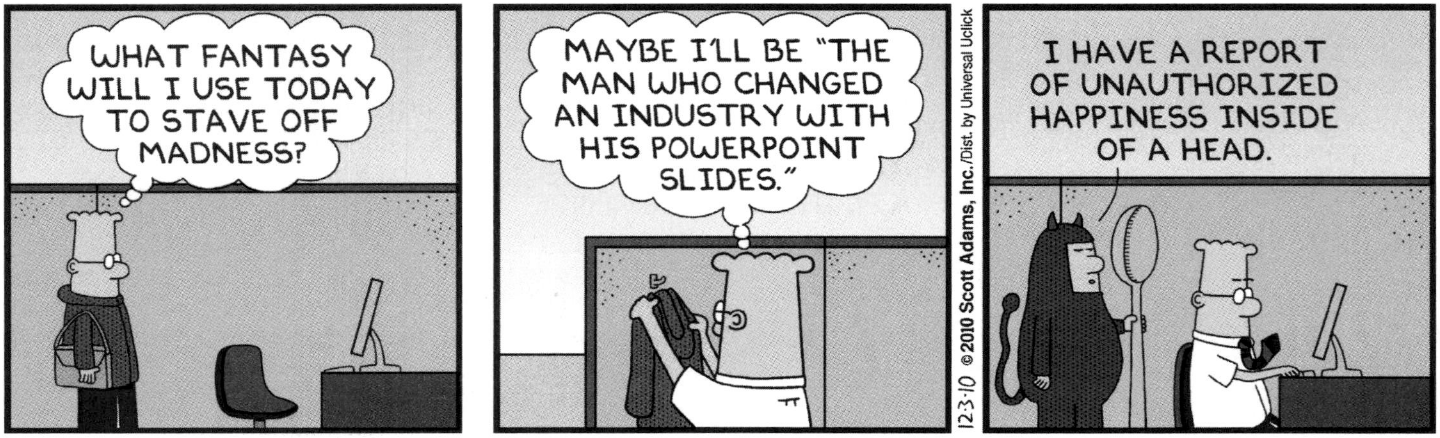
WHAT FANTASY WILL I USE TODAY TO STAVE OFF MADNESS?
MAYBE I'LL BE "THE MAN WHO CHANGED AN INDUSTRY WITH HIS POWERPOINT SLIDES."
12·3·10 ©2010 Scott Adams, Inc./Dist. by Universal Uclick
I HAVE A REPORT OF UNAUTHORIZED HAPPINESS INSIDE OF A HEAD.

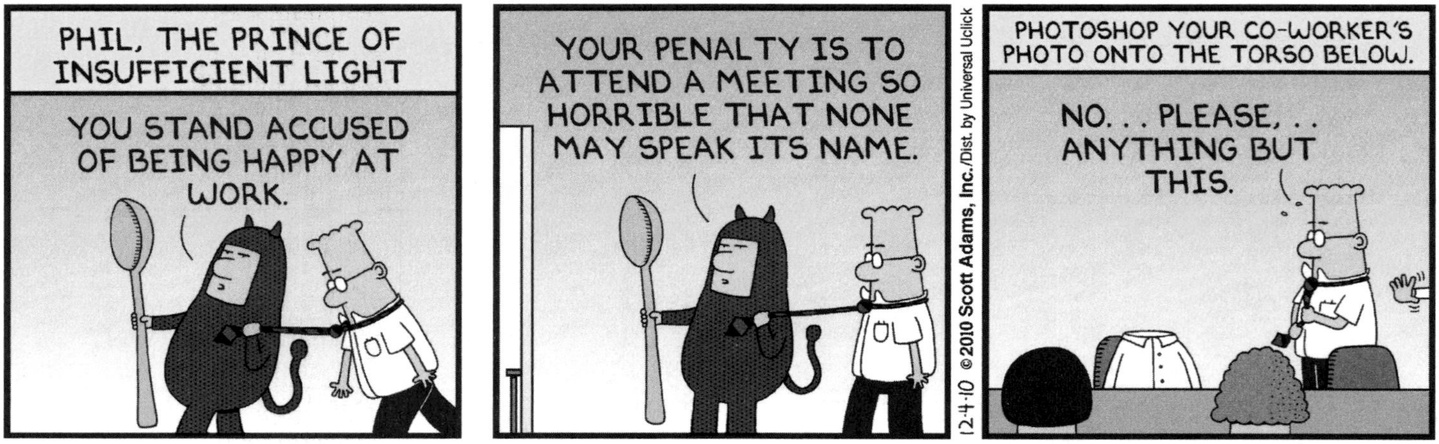
PHIL, THE PRINCE OF INSUFFICIENT LIGHT
YOU STAND ACCUSED OF BEING HAPPY AT WORK.
YOUR PENALTY IS TO ATTEND A MEETING SO HORRIBLE THAT NONE MAY SPEAK ITS NAME.
12·4·10 ©2010 Scott Adams, Inc./Dist. by Universal Uclick
PHOTOSHOP YOUR CO-WORKER'S PHOTO ONTO THE TORSO BELOW.
NO. . . PLEASE, . . ANYTHING BUT THIS.

MY DESIGN PLAN IS OBVIOUSLY TOO COMPLEX FOR A MANAGER TO UNDERSTAND.
SO I HIGHLIGHTED A FEW AREAS THAT ARE INTENTIONALLY SUBOPTIMAL.
JUST POINT TO THE HIGHLIGHTED ITEMS AND DEMAND THAT I FIX THEM.
©2010 Scott Adams, Inc./Dist. by Universal Uclick
THAT WILL GIVE YOU THE ILLUSION OF USEFULNESS.
PRETEND THIS IS OLDEN TIMES WHEN BOSSES KNEW WHAT THEIR EMPLOYEES DID FOR A LIVING.
TO ROUND OUT THE FANTASY, WEAR THIS HAT MADE FROM A DEAD ANIMAL.
NOW MANAGE ME LIKE IT'S THE 1800'S!
12/5
DO YOU HAVE A SMALLER HAT?
IMAGINE THAT WE'RE OUT OF CANDLES.

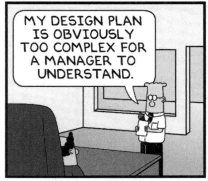

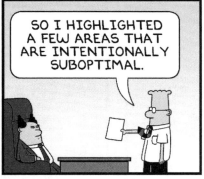

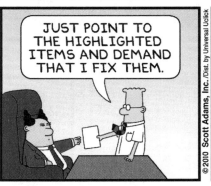

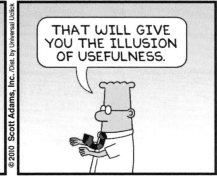

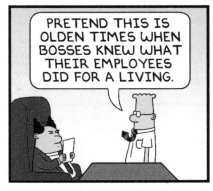

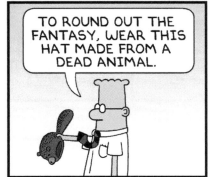

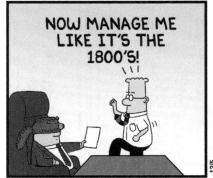

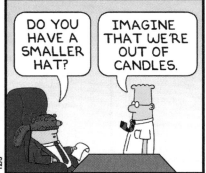

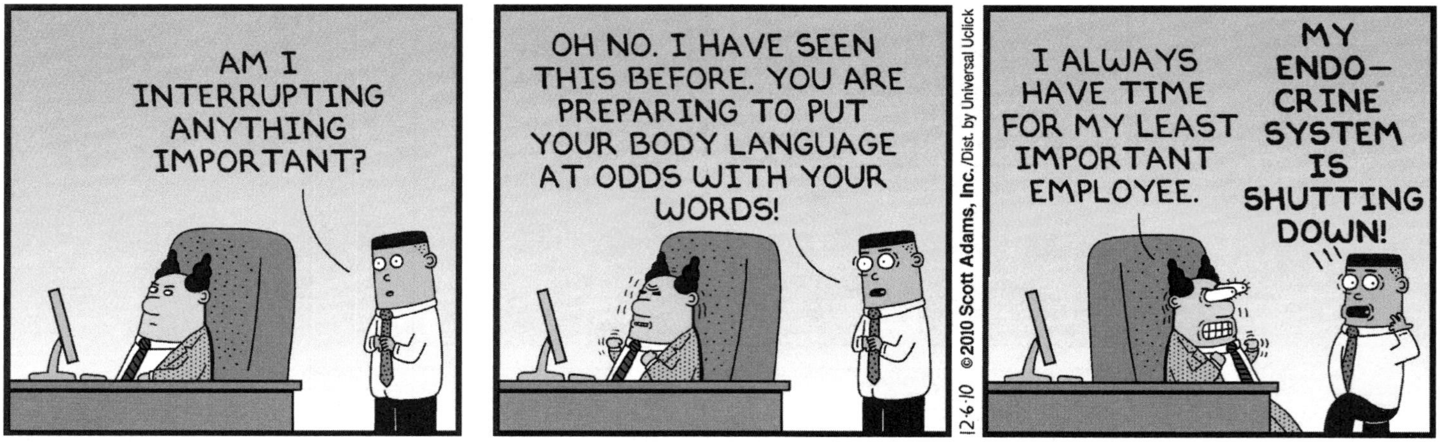
AM I INTERRUPTING ANYTHING IMPORTANT?
OH NO. I HAVE SEEN THIS BEFORE. YOU ARE PREPARING TO PUT YOUR BODY LANGUAGE AT ODDS WITH YOUR WORDS!
12·6·10 © 2010 Scott Adams, Inc./Dist. by Universal Uclick
I ALWAYS HAVE TIME FOR MY LEAST IMPORTANT EMPLOYEE.
MY ENDO-CRINE SYSTEM IS SHUTTING DOWN!

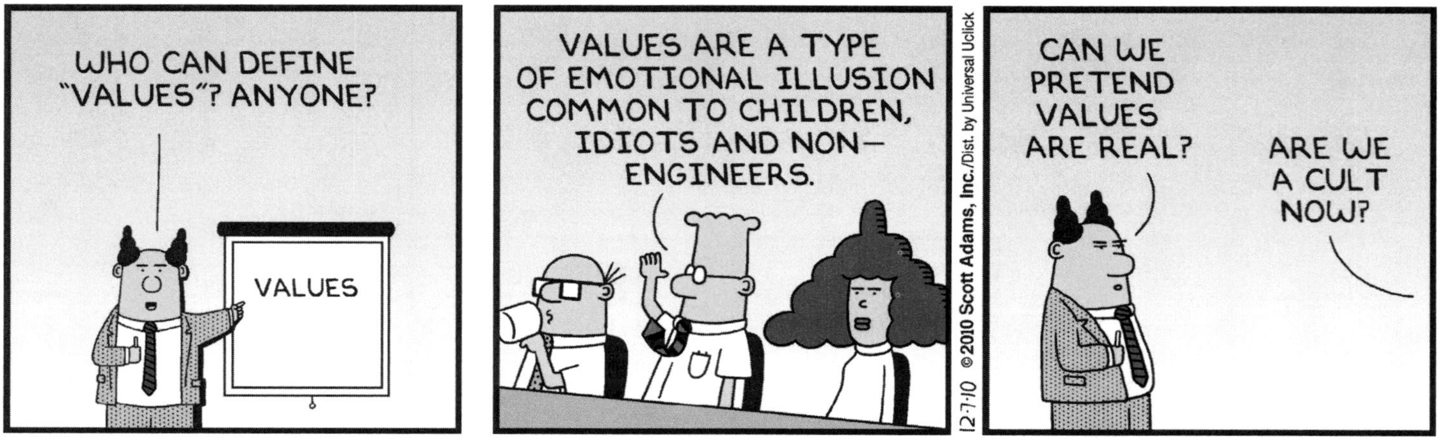
WHO CAN DEFINE "VALUES"? ANYONE?
VALUES
VALUES ARE A TYPE OF EMOTIONAL ILLUSION COMMON TO CHILDREN, IDIOTS AND NON-ENGINEERS.
12·7·10 © 2010 Scott Adams, Inc./Dist. by Universal Uclick
CAN WE PRETEND VALUES ARE REAL?
ARE WE A CULT NOW?

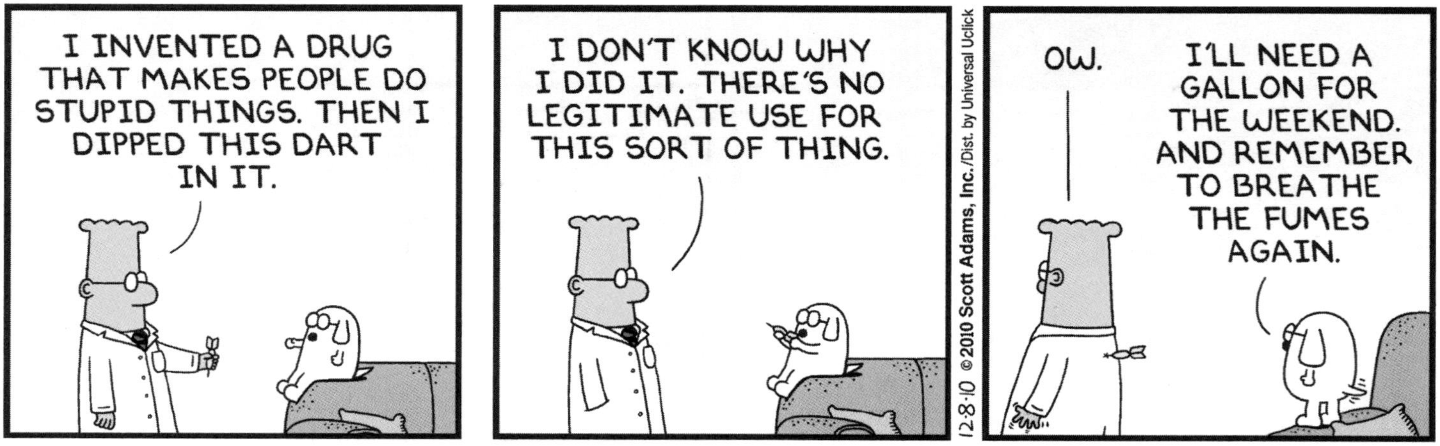
I INVENTED A DRUG THAT MAKES PEOPLE DO STUPID THINGS. THEN I DIPPED THIS DART IN IT.
I DON'T KNOW WHY I DID IT. THERE'S NO LEGITIMATE USE FOR THIS SORT OF THING.
12·8·10 © 2010 Scott Adams, Inc./Dist. by Universal Uclick
OW.
I'LL NEED A GALLON FOR THE WEEKEND. AND REMEMBER TO BREATHE THE FUMES AGAIN.

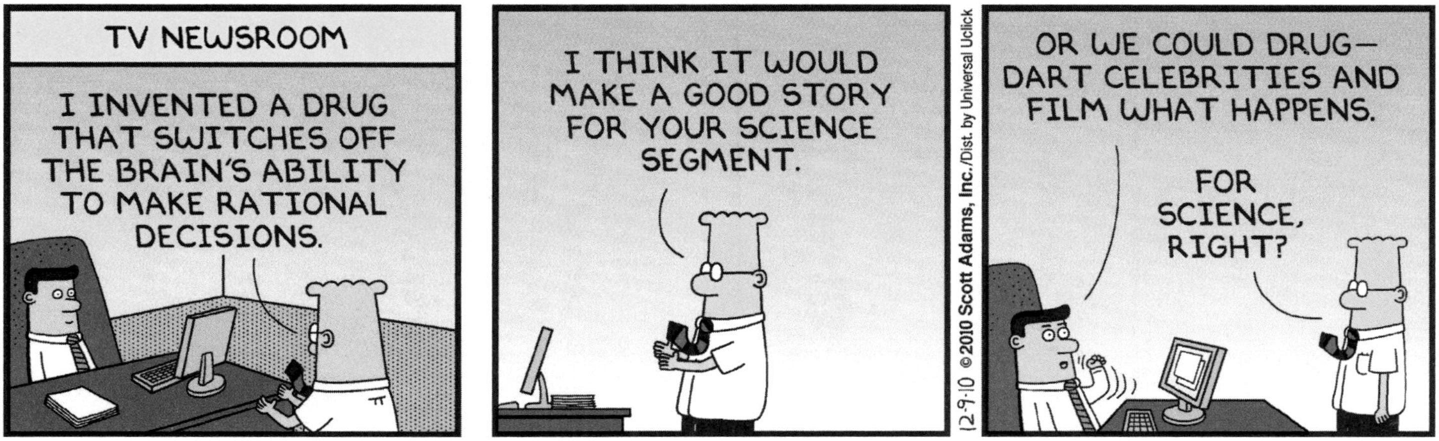
TV NEWSROOM
I INVENTED A DRUG THAT SWITCHES OFF THE BRAIN'S ABILITY TO MAKE RATIONAL DECISIONS.
I THINK IT WOULD MAKE A GOOD STORY FOR YOUR SCIENCE SEGMENT.
12-9-10 © 2010 Scott Adams, Inc./Dist. by Universal Uclick
OR WE COULD DRUG-DART CELEBRITIES AND FILM WHAT HAPPENS.
FOR SCIENCE, RIGHT?

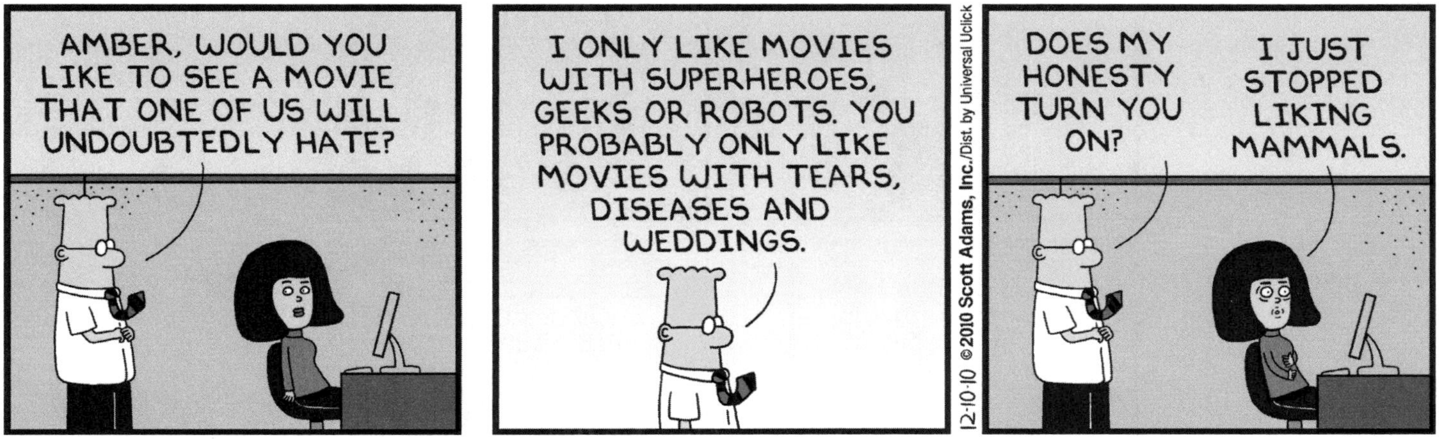
AMBER, WOULD YOU LIKE TO SEE A MOVIE THAT ONE OF US WILL UNDOUBTEDLY HATE?
I ONLY LIKE MOVIES WITH SUPERHEROES, GEEKS OR ROBOTS. YOU PROBABLY ONLY LIKE MOVIES WITH TEARS, DISEASES AND WEDDINGS.
12-10-10 © 2010 Scott Adams, Inc./Dist. by Universal Uclick
DOES MY HONESTY TURN YOU ON?
I JUST STOPPED LIKING MAMMALS.

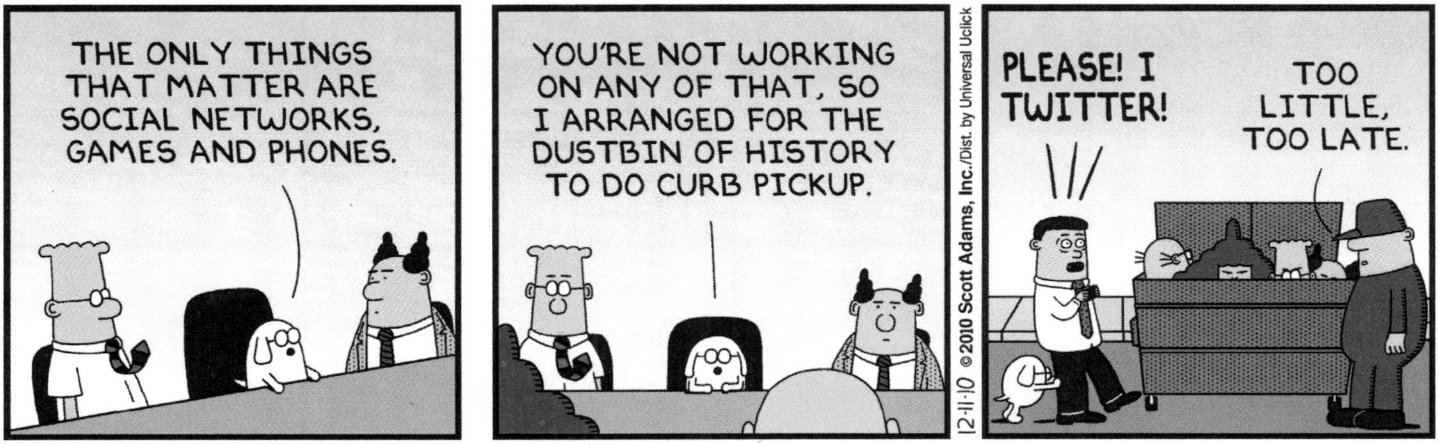
THE ONLY THINGS THAT MATTER ARE SOCIAL NETWORKS, GAMES AND PHONES.
YOU'RE NOT WORKING ON ANY OF THAT, SO I ARRANGED FOR THE DUSTBIN OF HISTORY TO DO CURB PICKUP.
12-11-10 © 2010 Scott Adams, Inc./Dist. by Universal Uclick
PLEASE! I TWITTER!
TOO LITTLE, TOO LATE.

WALLY, I NEED YOU TO TRAIN THE NEW MAILROOM GUY.
WHY ME?
BECAUSE HE'S UNIMPORTANT AND YOU'RE WORTHLESS.
OKAY. I WAS WORRIED THAT IT WAS THE OTHER WAY AROUND.
ALL IMPORTANT MESSAGES ARE SENT BY E-MAIL.
SO YOUR JOB IS TO SHOVEL ALL OF THE REGULAR MAIL INTO RECYCLING BINS.
WE WON'T BE PAYING YOU, BUT YOU CAN USE PACKAGES AND TAPE TO BUILD YOUR OWN IGLOO.
TWO WEEKS LATER
WHY IS MY DESK SO CLEAN?
YOU'RE WELCOME.
©2010 Scott Adams, Inc. /Dist. by Universal Uclick
12-12-10

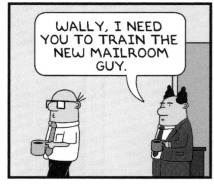

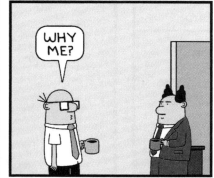

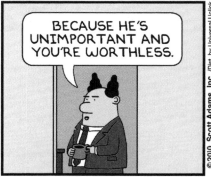

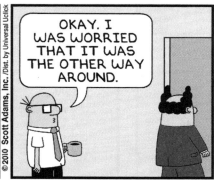

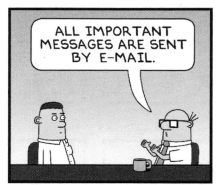

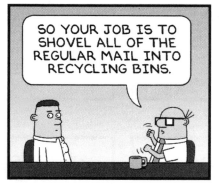

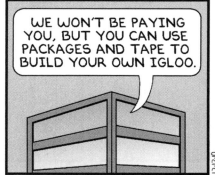

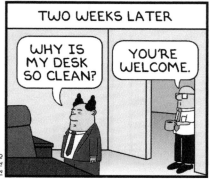

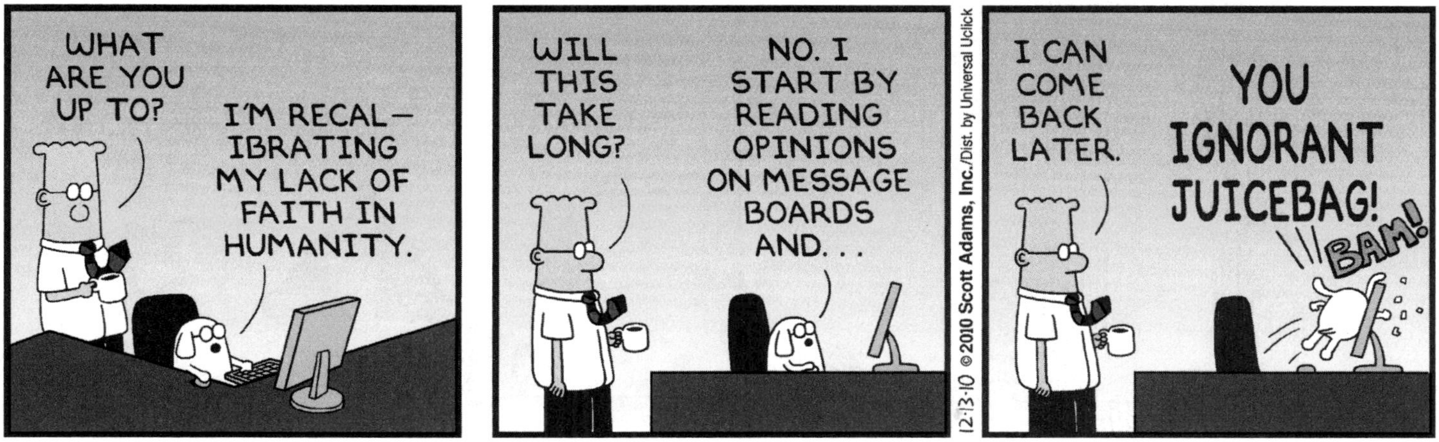
WHAT ARE YOU UP TO?
I'M RECAL-IBRATING MY LACK OF FAITH IN HUMANITY.
WILL THIS TAKE LONG?
NO. I START BY READING OPINIONS ON MESSAGE BOARDS AND. . .
I CAN COME BACK LATER.
YOU IGNORANT JUICEBAG!
BAM!
12-13-10 © 2010 Scott Adams, Inc./Dist. by Universal Uclick

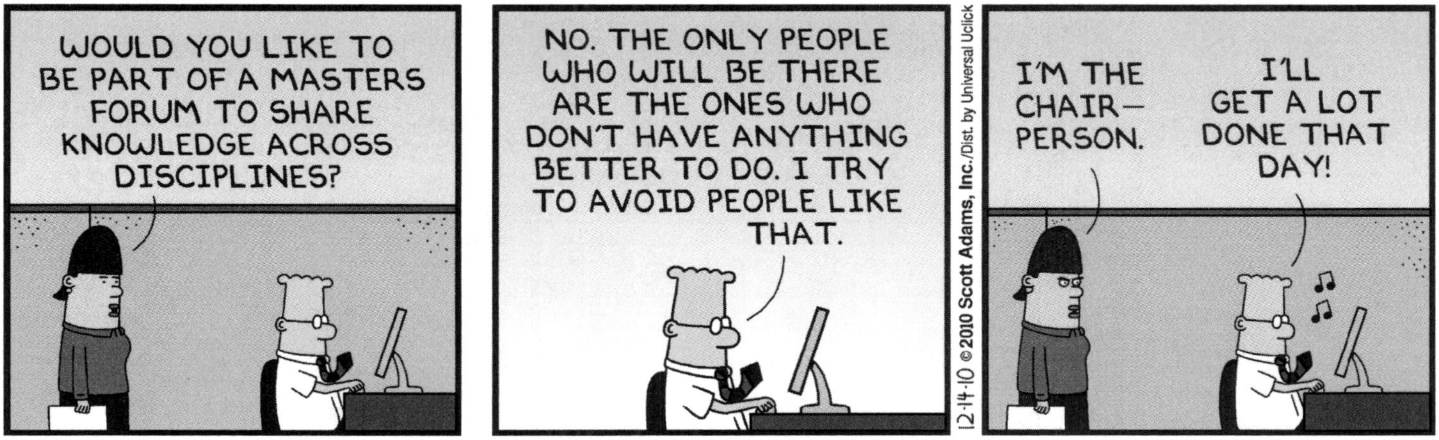
WOULD YOU LIKE TO BE PART OF A MASTERS FORUM TO SHARE KNOWLEDGE ACROSS DISCIPLINES?
NO. THE ONLY PEOPLE WHO WILL BE THERE ARE THE ONES WHO DON'T HAVE ANYTHING BETTER TO DO. I TRY TO AVOID PEOPLE LIKE THAT.
I'M THE CHAIR-PERSON.
I'LL GET A LOT DONE THAT DAY!
12-14-10 © 2010 Scott Adams, Inc./Dist. by Universal Uclick

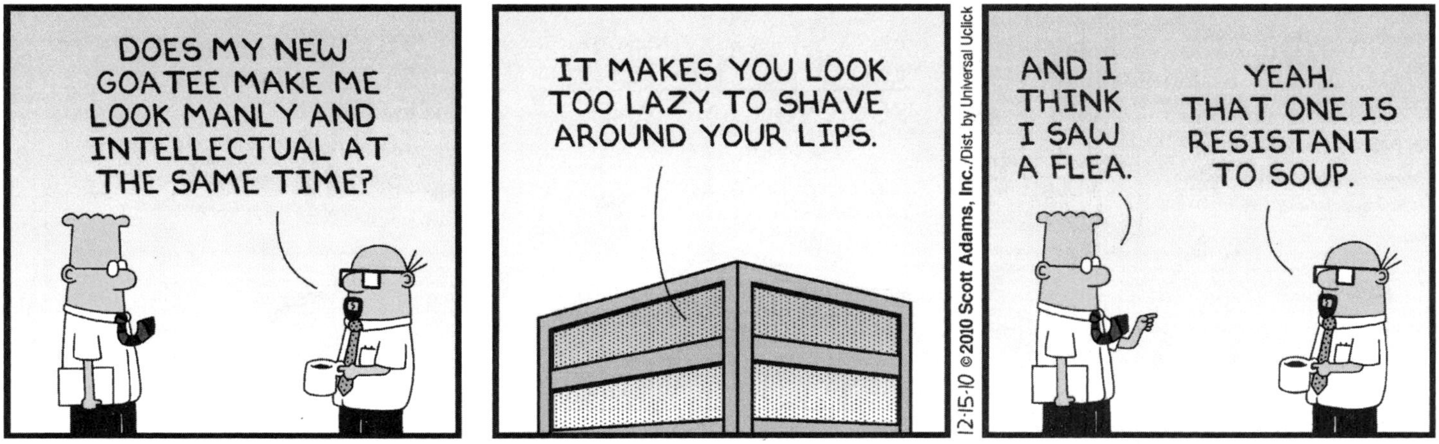
DOES MY NEW GOATEE MAKE ME LOOK MANLY AND INTELLECTUAL AT THE SAME TIME?
IT MAKES YOU LOOK TOO LAZY TO SHAVE AROUND YOUR LIPS.
AND I THINK I SAW A FLEA.
YEAH. THAT ONE IS RESISTANT TO SOUP.
12-15-10 © 2010 Scott Adams, Inc./Dist. by Universal Uclick

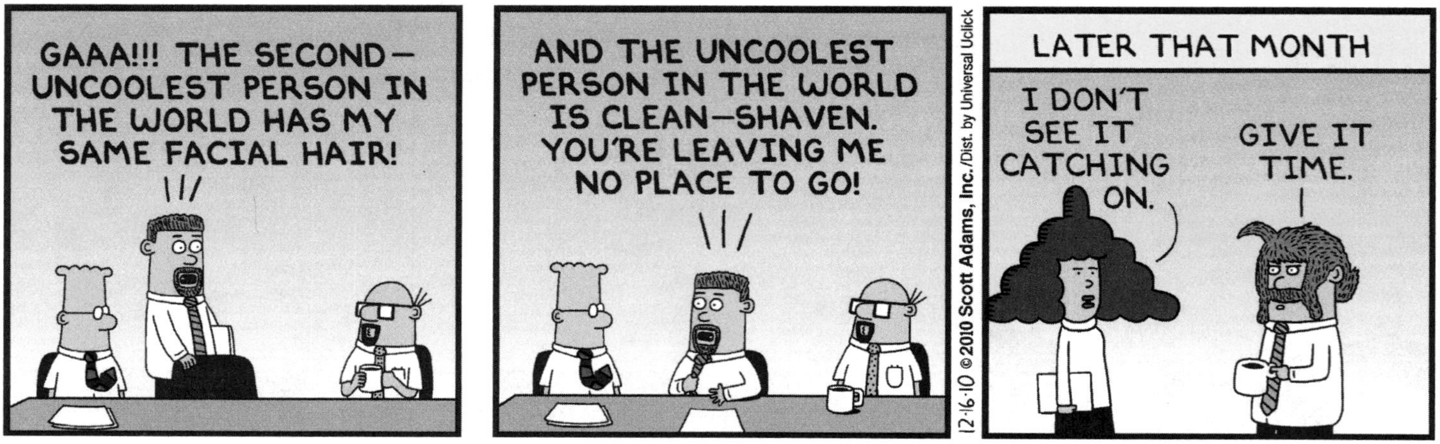
GAAA!!! THE SECOND-UNCOOLEST PERSON IN THE WORLD HAS MY SAME FACIAL HAIR!
AND THE UNCOOLEST PERSON IN THE WORLD IS CLEAN-SHAVEN. YOU'RE LEAVING ME NO PLACE TO GO!
12·16·10 © 2010 Scott Adams, Inc./Dist. by Universal Uclick
LATER THAT MONTH
I DON'T SEE IT CATCHING ON.
GIVE IT TIME.

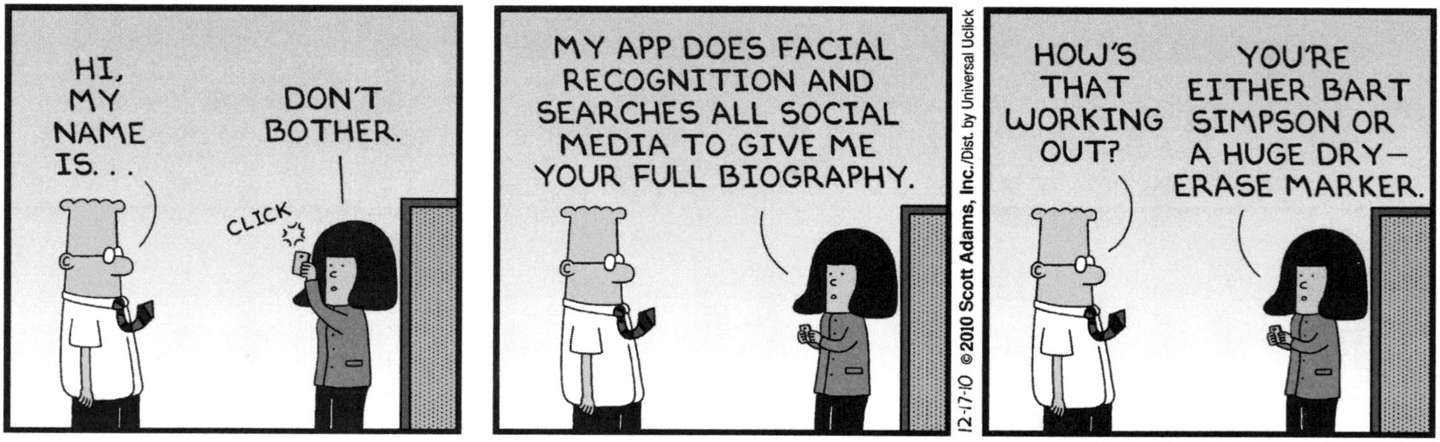
HI, MY NAME IS. . .
DON'T BOTHER.
CLICK
MY APP DOES FACIAL RECOGNITION AND SEARCHES ALL SOCIAL MEDIA TO GIVE ME YOUR FULL BIOGRAPHY.
12·17·10 © 2010 Scott Adams, Inc./Dist. by Universal Uclick
HOW'S THAT WORKING OUT?
YOU'RE EITHER BART SIMPSON OR A HUGE DRY-ERASE MARKER.

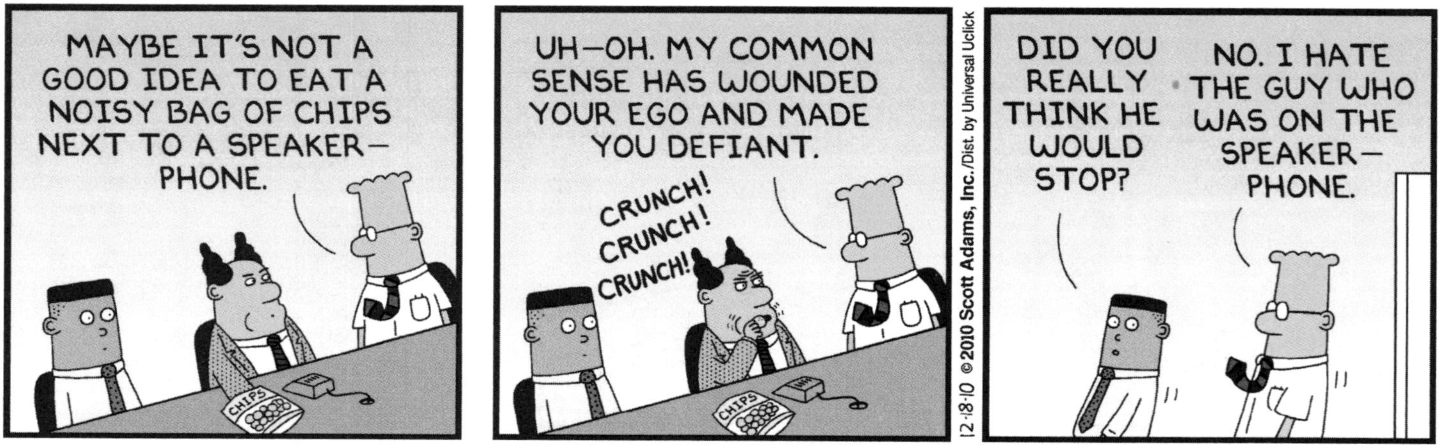
MAYBE IT'S NOT A GOOD IDEA TO EAT A NOISY BAG OF CHIPS NEXT TO A SPEAKER-PHONE.
CHIPS
UH-OH. MY COMMON SENSE HAS WOUNDED YOUR EGO AND MADE YOU DEFIANT.
CRUNCH! CRUNCH! CRUNCH!
CHIPS
12·18·10 © 2010 Scott Adams, Inc./Dist. by Universal Uclick
DID YOU REALLY THINK HE WOULD STOP?
NO. I HATE THE GUY WHO WAS ON THE SPEAKER-PHONE.

I WANT ALL OF YOU TO FEEL EMPOWERED ON THIS PROJECT.
YOU FORGOT TO GET OUR BUY—IN BEFORE YOU EMPOWERED US.
I'LL GET YOUR BUY—IN LATER.
IT'S FAR TOO LATE FOR THAT.
© 2010 Scott Adams, Inc. /Dist. by Universal Uclick
I'M GOING TO USE MY EMPOWERMENT TO DESTROY THIS POORLY CONCEIVED PROJECT FROM THE INSIDE!
DON'T DO THAT!
SO. . . NOW YOU'RE SAYING WE'RE **NOT** EMPOWERED TO DO WHAT WE THINK IS BEST?
CAN WE GO BACK TO OUR OLD SYSTEM WHERE WE'RE AFRAID TO MAKE DECISIONS AND YOU'RE NEVER AVAILABLE?
12-19-10
YOUR EYES SAY, "YES."

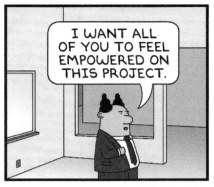

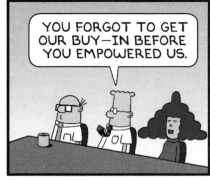

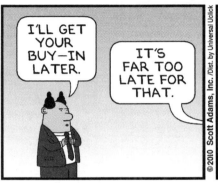

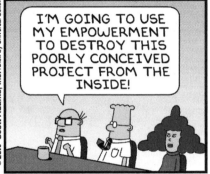

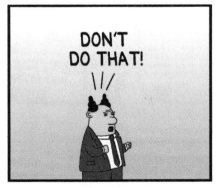

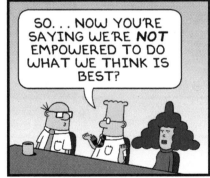

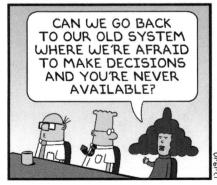

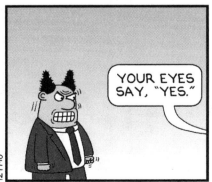

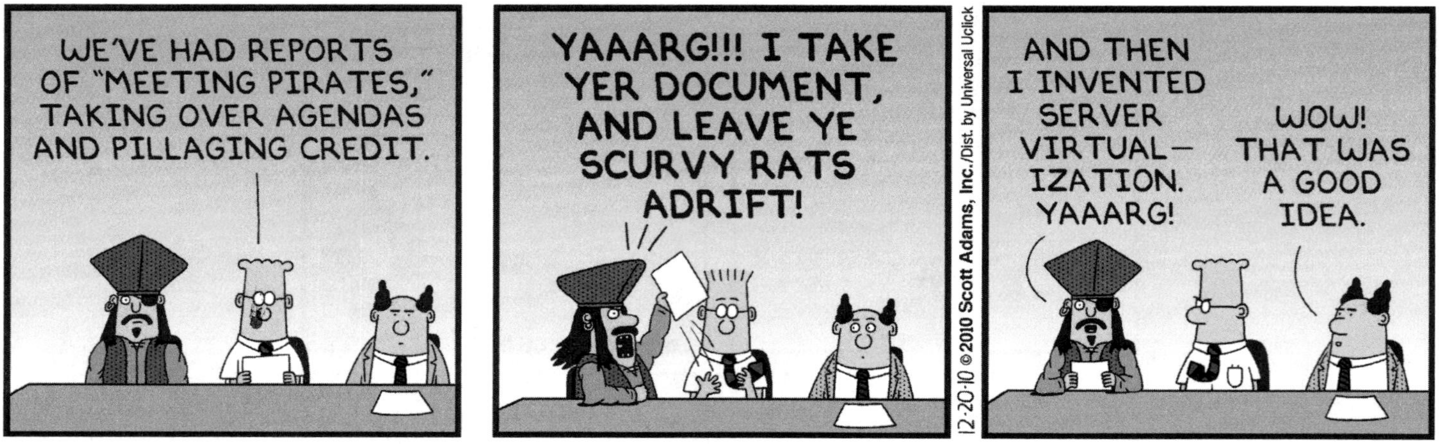
WE'VE HAD REPORTS OF "MEETING PIRATES," TAKING OVER AGENDAS AND PILLAGING CREDIT.
YAAARG!!! I TAKE YER DOCUMENT, AND LEAVE YE SCURVY RATS ADRIFT!
12-20-10 © 2010 Scott Adams, Inc./Dist. by Universal Uclick
AND THEN I INVENTED SERVER VIRTUAL-IZATION. YAAARG!
WOW! THAT WAS A GOOD IDEA.

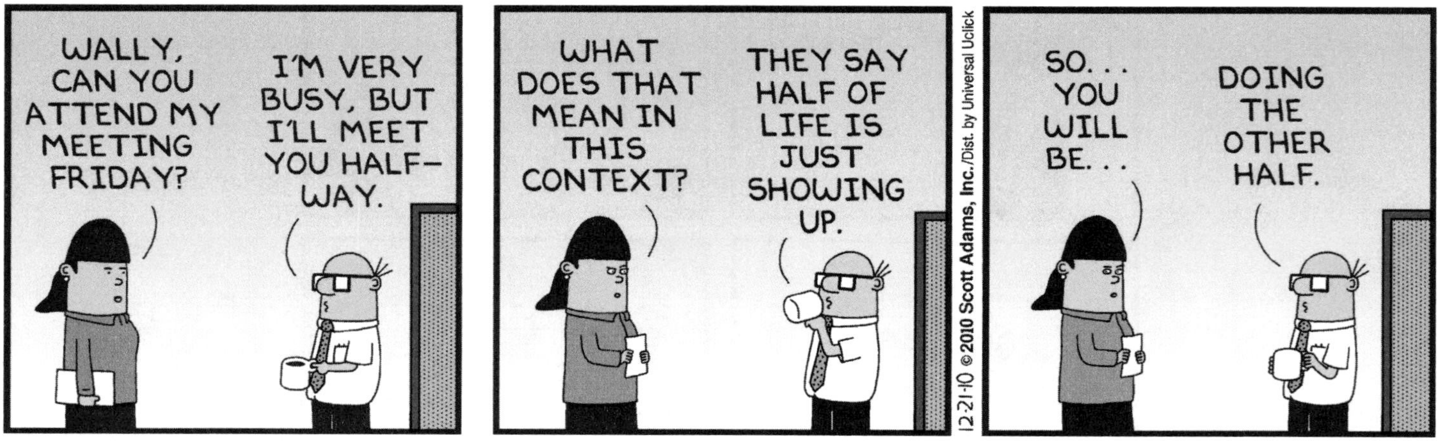
WALLY, CAN YOU ATTEND MY MEETING FRIDAY?
I'M VERY BUSY, BUT I'LL MEET YOU HALF-WAY.
WHAT DOES THAT MEAN IN THIS CONTEXT?
THEY SAY HALF OF LIFE IS JUST SHOWING UP.
12-21-10 © 2010 Scott Adams, Inc./Dist. by Universal Uclick
SO. . . YOU WILL BE. . .
DOING THE OTHER HALF.

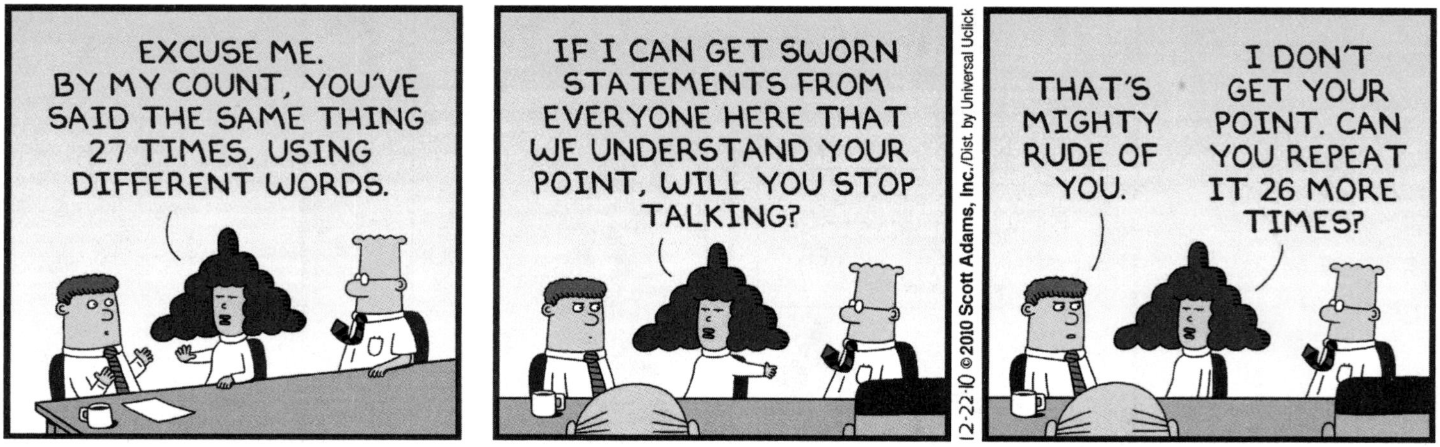
EXCUSE ME. BY MY COUNT, YOU'VE SAID THE SAME THING 27 TIMES, USING DIFFERENT WORDS.
IF I CAN GET SWORN STATEMENTS FROM EVERYONE HERE THAT WE UNDERSTAND YOUR POINT, WILL YOU STOP TALKING?
12-22-10 © 2010 Scott Adams, Inc./Dist. by Universal Uclick
THAT'S MIGHTY RUDE OF YOU.
I DON'T GET YOUR POINT. CAN YOU REPEAT IT 26 MORE TIMES?

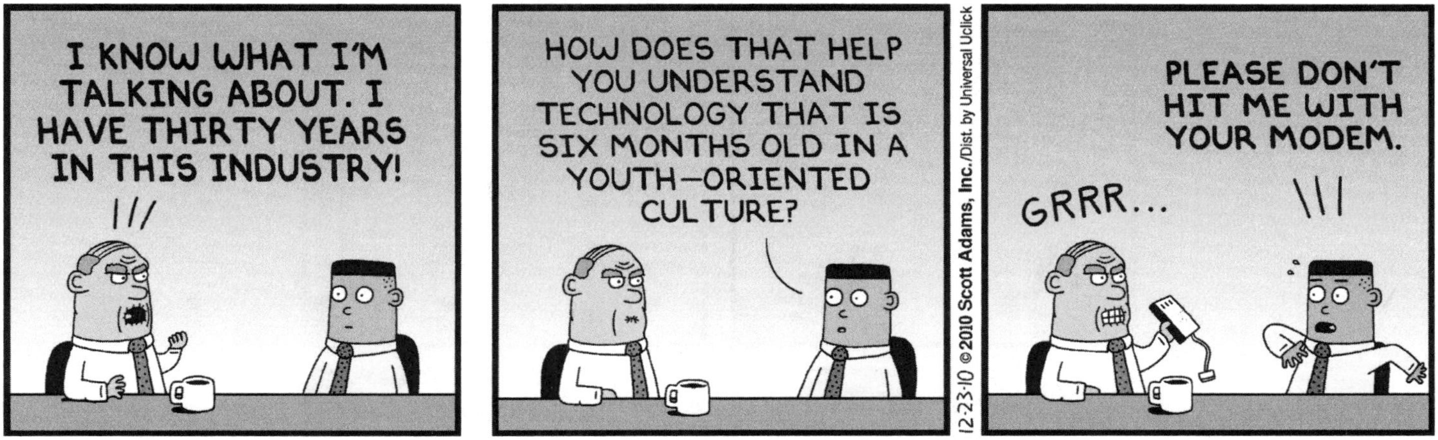
I KNOW WHAT I'M TALKING ABOUT. I HAVE THIRTY YEARS IN THIS INDUSTRY!
HOW DOES THAT HELP YOU UNDERSTAND TECHNOLOGY THAT IS SIX MONTHS OLD IN A YOUTH—ORIENTED CULTURE?
GRRR...
PLEASE DON'T HIT ME WITH YOUR MODEM.
12·23·10 © 2010 Scott Adams, Inc./Dist. by Universal Uclick

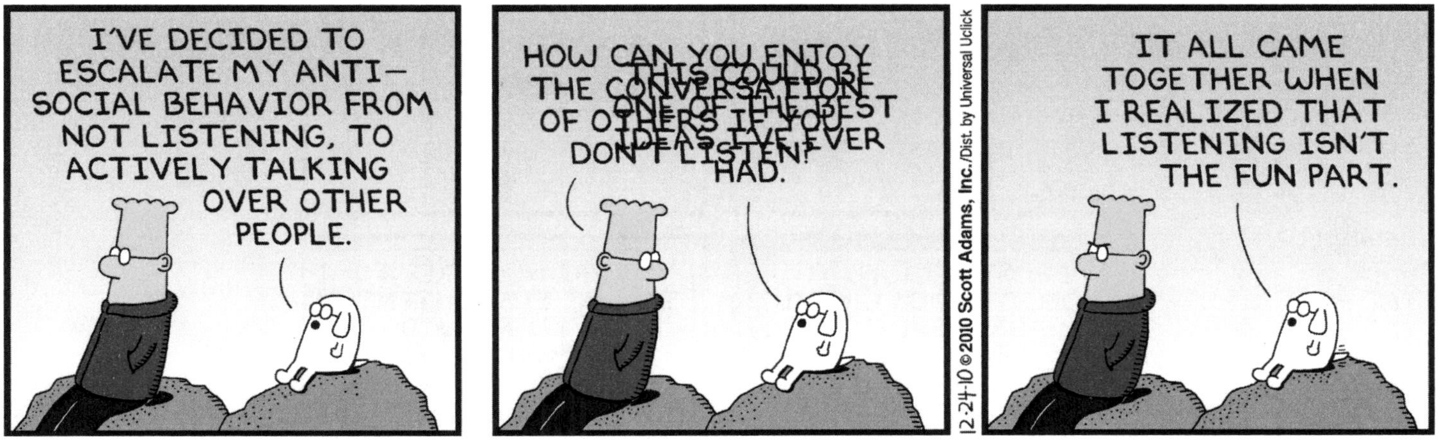
I'VE DECIDED TO ESCALATE MY ANTI-SOCIAL BEHAVIOR FROM NOT LISTENING, TO ACTIVELY TALKING OVER OTHER PEOPLE.
HOW CAN YOU ENJOY THE CONVERSATION OF OTHERS IF YOU DON'T LISTEN?
THIS COULD BE ONE OF THE BEST IDEAS I'VE EVER HAD.
IT ALL CAME TOGETHER WHEN I REALIZED THAT LISTENING ISN'T THE FUN PART.
12·24·10 © 2010 Scott Adams, Inc./Dist. by Universal Uclick

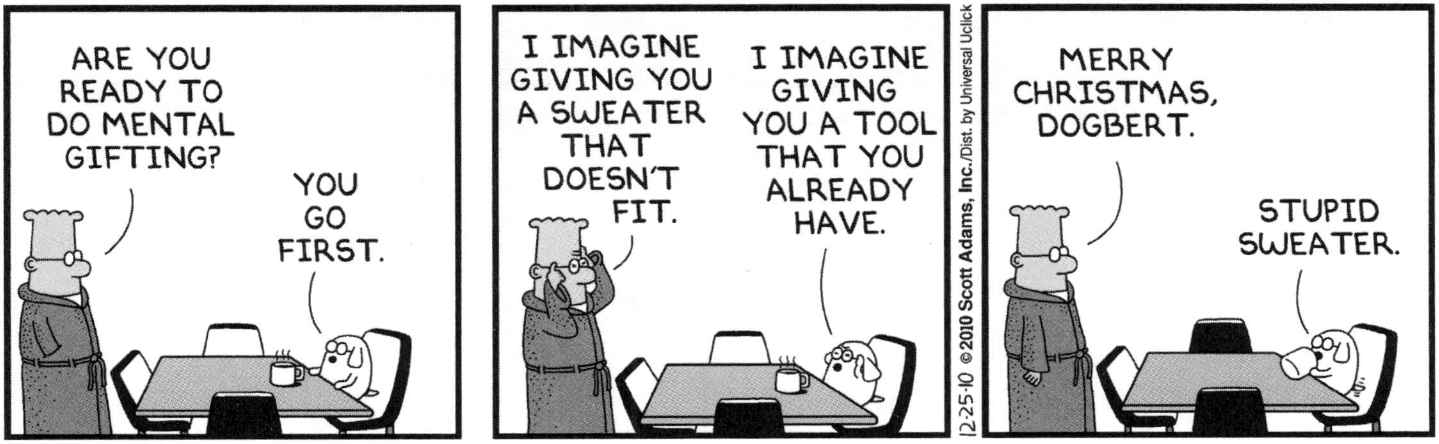
ARE YOU READY TO DO MENTAL GIFTING?
YOU GO FIRST.
I IMAGINE GIVING YOU A SWEATER THAT DOESN'T FIT.
I IMAGINE GIVING YOU A TOOL THAT YOU ALREADY HAVE.
MERRY CHRISTMAS, DOGBERT.
STUPID SWEATER.
12·25·10 © 2010 Scott Adams, Inc./Dist. by Universal Uclick

DID YOU READ MY LONG E-MAIL?
NOT YET. WHAT'S IT ABOUT?
I CAN'T SAY.
IF I TELL YOU WHAT I WROTE, THE EFFORT I PUT INTO WRITING THE E-MAIL WILL BE TRANSFORMED INTO A WASTE OF TIME.
I JUST DECIDED TO DELETE YOUR E-MAIL BEFORE READING IT. THEREFORE IT IS ALREADY WASTED.
YOU ARE NOW FREE TO TELL ME ITS CONTENTS WITHOUT REDUCING YOUR PRODUCTIVITY.
OH. OKAY.
IT WAS SOMETHING ABOUT IMPROVING COMMUNICATION, BUT I WORDED IT BETTER.
MAYBE YOU SHOULD READ IT.
MAYBE *YOU* SHOULD.
© 2010 Scott Adams, Inc./Dist. by Universal Uclick
12-26-10

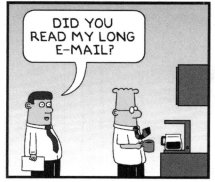

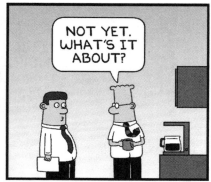

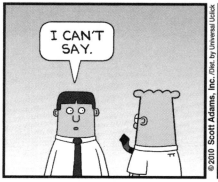

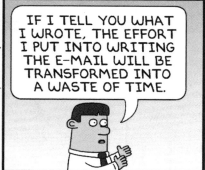

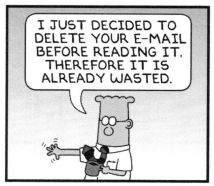

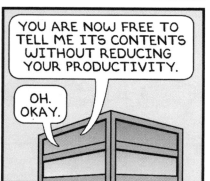

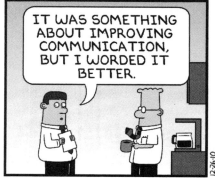

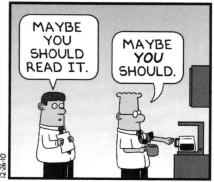

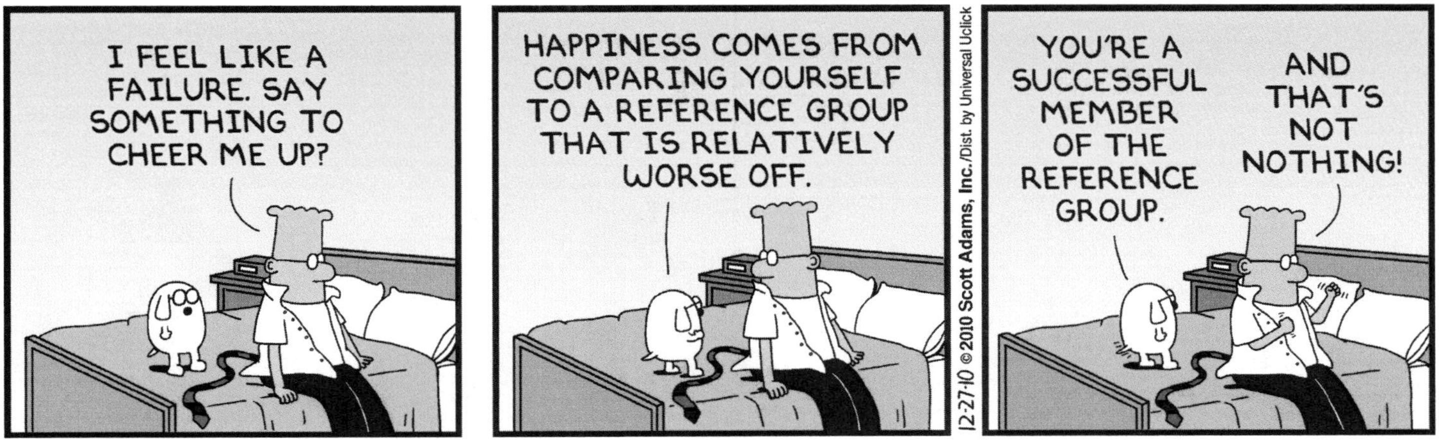
I FEEL LIKE A FAILURE. SAY SOMETHING TO CHEER ME UP?
HAPPINESS COMES FROM COMPARING YOURSELF TO A REFERENCE GROUP THAT IS RELATIVELY WORSE OFF.
12-27-10 © 2010 Scott Adams, Inc./Dist. by Universal Uclick
YOU'RE A SUCCESSFUL MEMBER OF THE REFERENCE GROUP.
AND THAT'S NOT NOTHING!

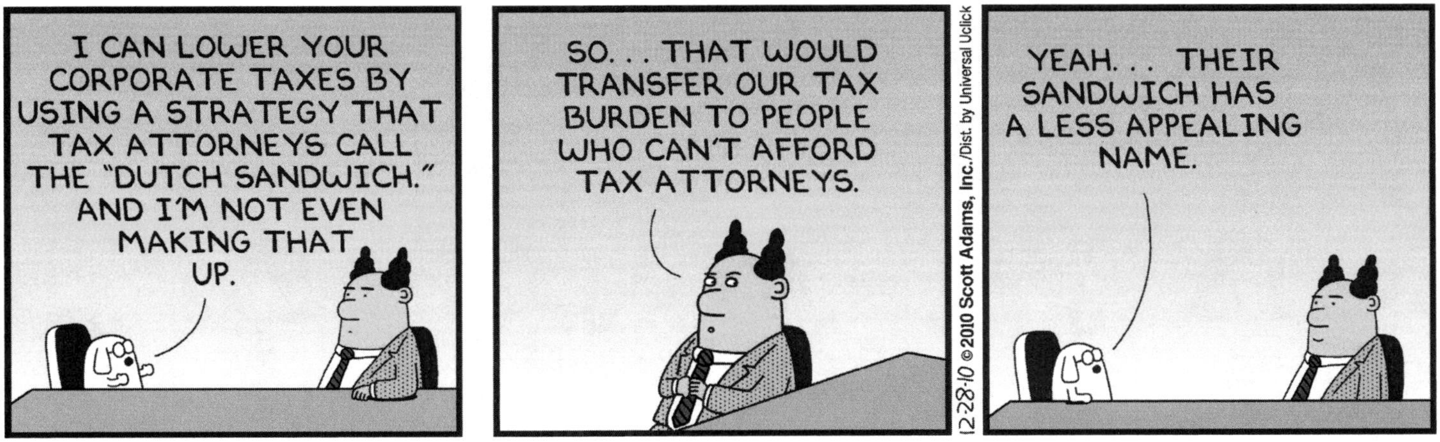
I CAN LOWER YOUR CORPORATE TAXES BY USING A STRATEGY THAT TAX ATTORNEYS CALL THE "DUTCH SANDWICH." AND I'M NOT EVEN MAKING THAT UP.
SO. . . THAT WOULD TRANSFER OUR TAX BURDEN TO PEOPLE WHO CAN'T AFFORD TAX ATTORNEYS.
12-28-10 © 2010 Scott Adams, Inc./Dist. by Universal Uclick
YEAH. . . THEIR SANDWICH HAS A LESS APPEALING NAME.

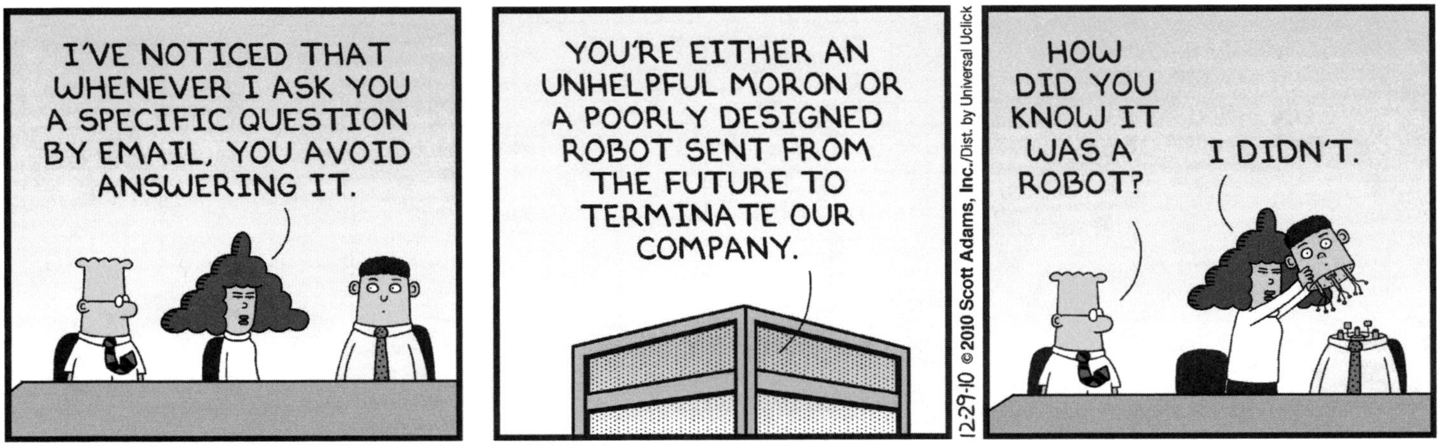
I'VE NOTICED THAT WHENEVER I ASK YOU A SPECIFIC QUESTION BY EMAIL, YOU AVOID ANSWERING IT.
YOU'RE EITHER AN UNHELPFUL MORON OR A POORLY DESIGNED ROBOT SENT FROM THE FUTURE TO TERMINATE OUR COMPANY.
12-29-10 © 2010 Scott Adams, Inc./Dist. by Universal Uclick
HOW DID YOU KNOW IT WAS A ROBOT?
I DIDN'T.

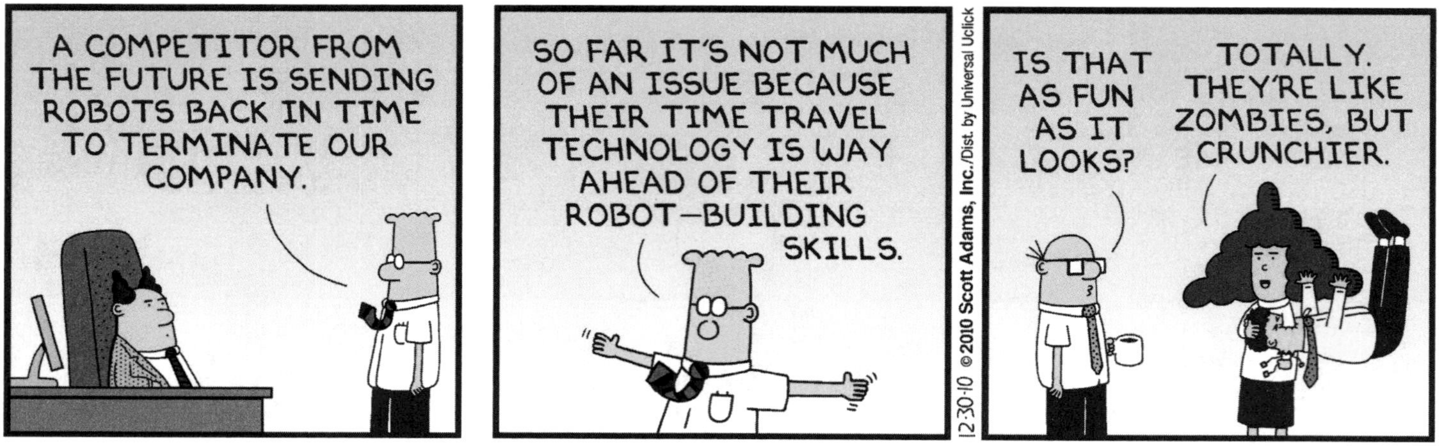
A COMPETITOR FROM THE FUTURE IS SENDING ROBOTS BACK IN TIME TO TERMINATE OUR COMPANY.
SO FAR IT'S NOT MUCH OF AN ISSUE BECAUSE THEIR TIME TRAVEL TECHNOLOGY IS WAY AHEAD OF THEIR ROBOT—BUILDING SKILLS.
IS THAT AS FUN AS IT LOOKS?
TOTALLY. THEY'RE LIKE ZOMBIES, BUT CRUNCHIER.
12·30·10 © 2010 Scott Adams, Inc./Dist. by Universal Uclick

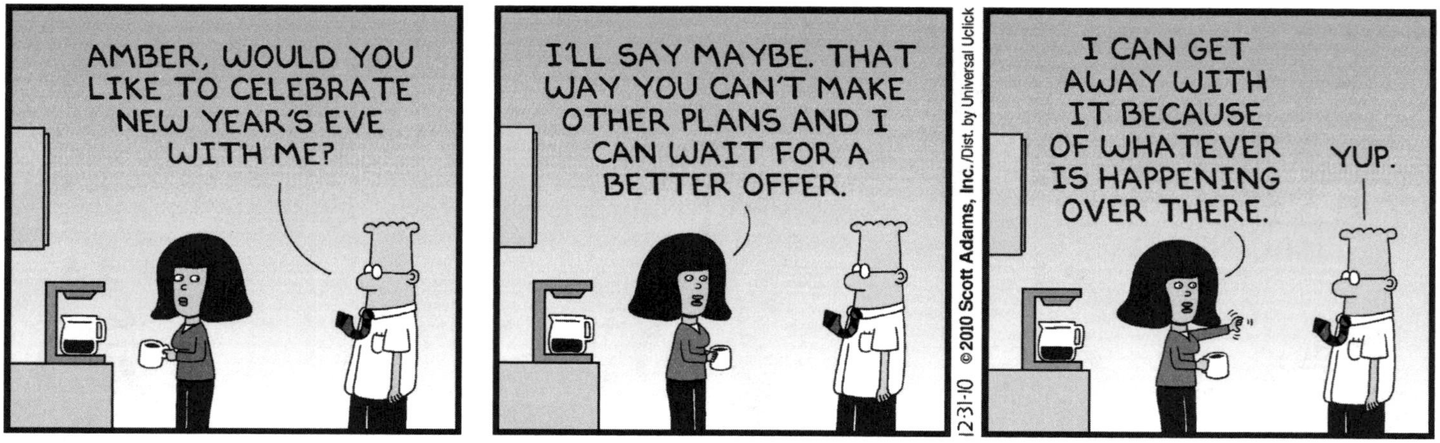
AMBER, WOULD YOU LIKE TO CELEBRATE NEW YEAR'S EVE WITH ME?
I'LL SAY MAYBE. THAT WAY YOU CAN'T MAKE OTHER PLANS AND I CAN WAIT FOR A BETTER OFFER.
I CAN GET AWAY WITH IT BECAUSE OF WHATEVER IS HAPPENING OVER THERE.
YUP.
12·31·10 © 2010 Scott Adams, Inc./Dist. by Universal Uclick

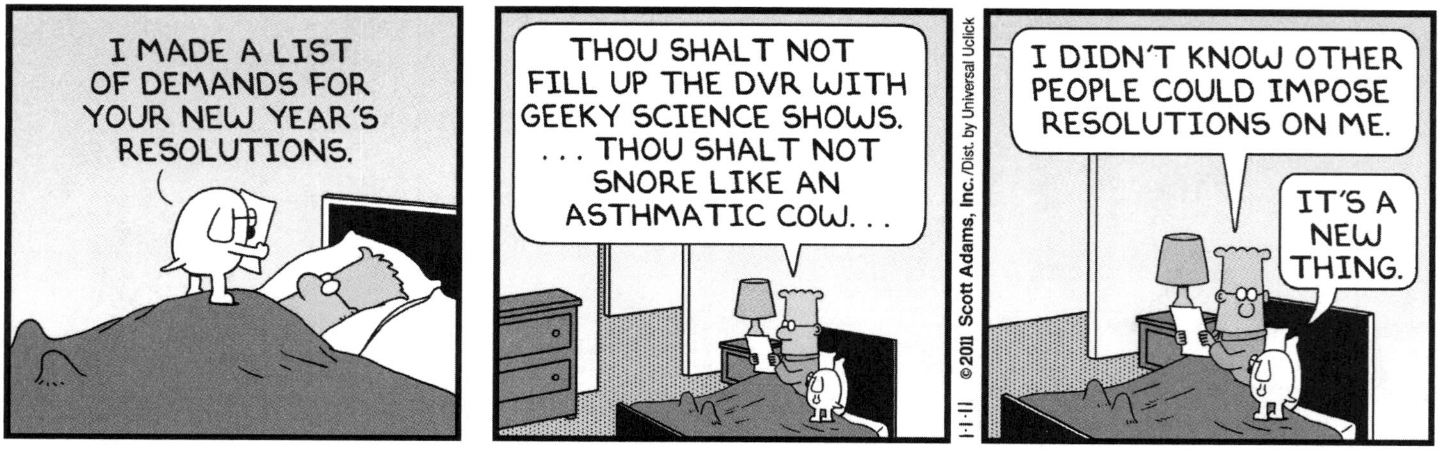
I MADE A LIST OF DEMANDS FOR YOUR NEW YEAR'S RESOLUTIONS.
THOU SHALT NOT FILL UP THE DVR WITH GEEKY SCIENCE SHOWS. . . . THOU SHALT NOT SNORE LIKE AN ASTHMATIC COW. . .
I DIDN'T KNOW OTHER PEOPLE COULD IMPOSE RESOLUTIONS ON ME.
IT'S A NEW THING.
1·1·11 © 2011 Scott Adams, Inc./Dist. by Universal Uclick

DILBERT, WOULD YOU LIKE TO JOIN US FOR LUNCH?
WHERE ARE YOU GOING?
WE HAVEN'T DECIDED.
IN THAT CASE, NO.
©2011 Scott Adams, Inc./Dist. by Universal Uclick
I CAN'T STAND WATCHING A SMALL GROUP OF PEOPLE TRYING TO MAKE A TRIVIAL DECISION.
IT MAKES ME LOSE ALL FAITH IN HUMANITY.
FOOD DOESN'T TASTE AS GOOD WHEN YOU HAVE NO HOPE.
I'LL JUST GET SOME-THING FROM THE VENDING MACHINE AND FANTASIZE THAT MY CO-WORKERS ARE COMPETENT.
LET'S SEE. . . WHAT GOES WELL WITH AN UNREALISTIC WORLDVIEW?

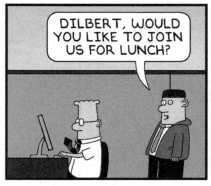

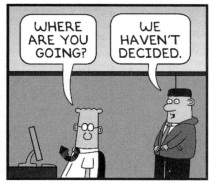

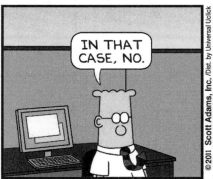

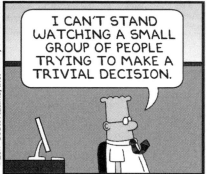

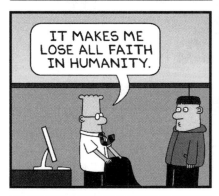

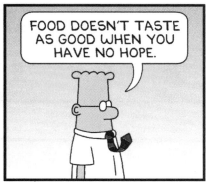

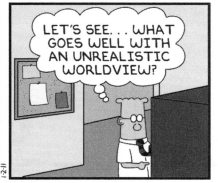

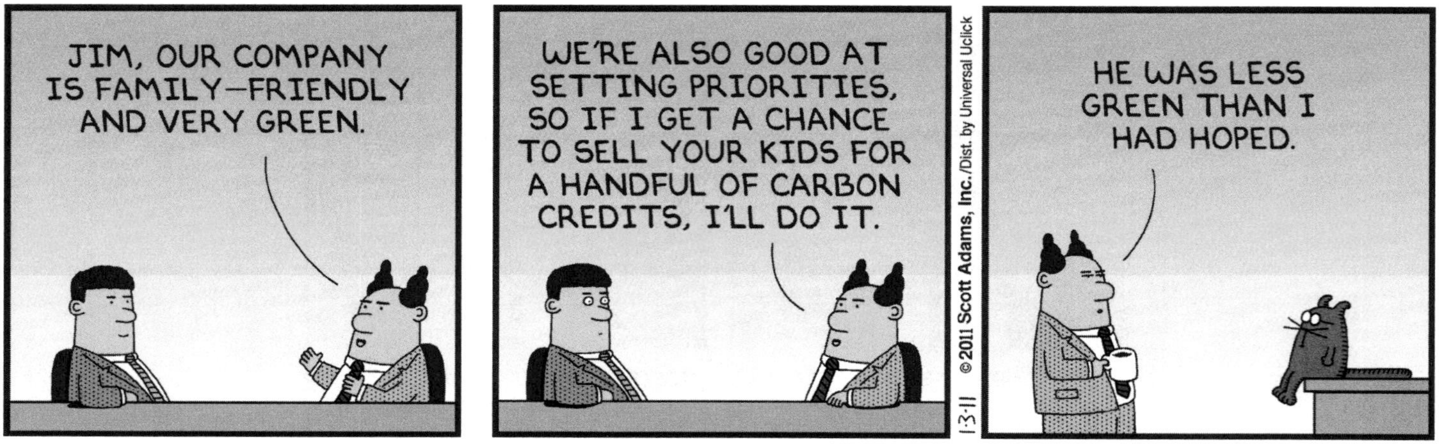
JIM, OUR COMPANY IS FAMILY—FRIENDLY AND VERY GREEN.
WE'RE ALSO GOOD AT SETTING PRIORITIES, SO IF I GET A CHANCE TO SELL YOUR KIDS FOR A HANDFUL OF CARBON CREDITS, I'LL DO IT.
1·3·11 © 2011 Scott Adams, Inc./Dist. by Universal Uclick
HE WAS LESS GREEN THAN I HAD HOPED.

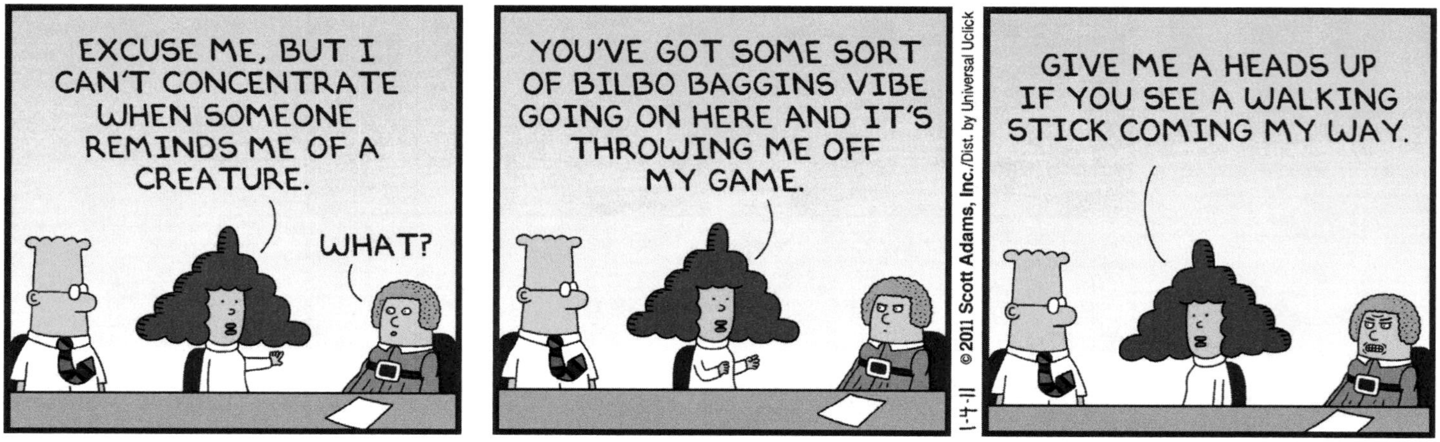
EXCUSE ME, BUT I CAN'T CONCENTRATE WHEN SOMEONE REMINDS ME OF A CREATURE.
WHAT?
YOU'VE GOT SOME SORT OF BILBO BAGGINS VIBE GOING ON HERE AND IT'S THROWING ME OFF MY GAME.
1·4·11 © 2011 Scott Adams, Inc./Dist. by Universal Uclick
GIVE ME A HEADS UP IF YOU SEE A WALKING STICK COMING MY WAY.

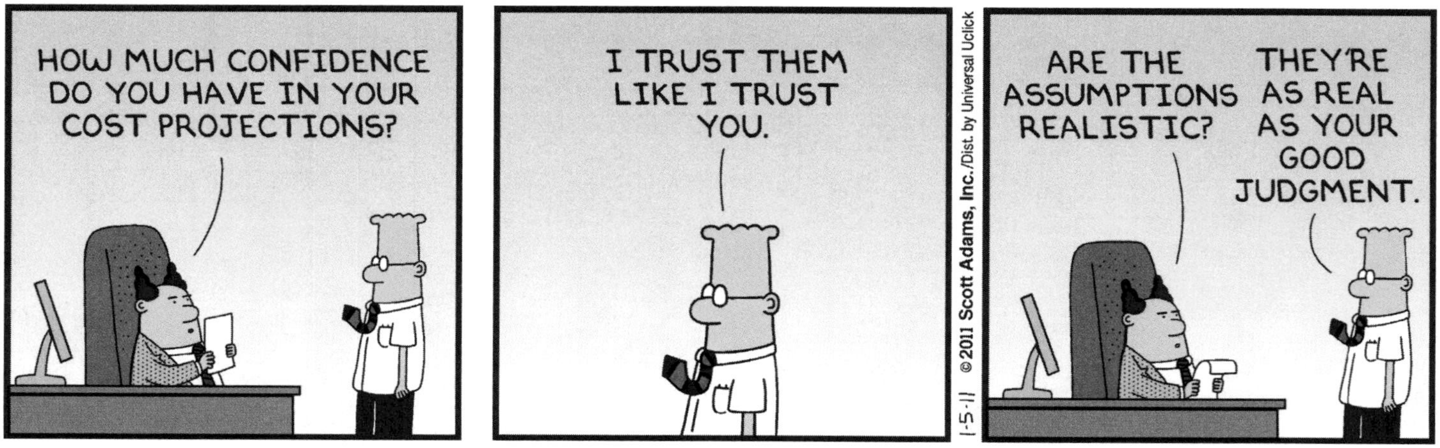
HOW MUCH CONFIDENCE DO YOU HAVE IN YOUR COST PROJECTIONS?
I TRUST THEM LIKE I TRUST YOU.
1·5·11 © 2011 Scott Adams, Inc./Dist. by Universal Uclick
ARE THE ASSUMPTIONS REALISTIC?
THEY'RE AS REAL AS YOUR GOOD JUDGMENT.

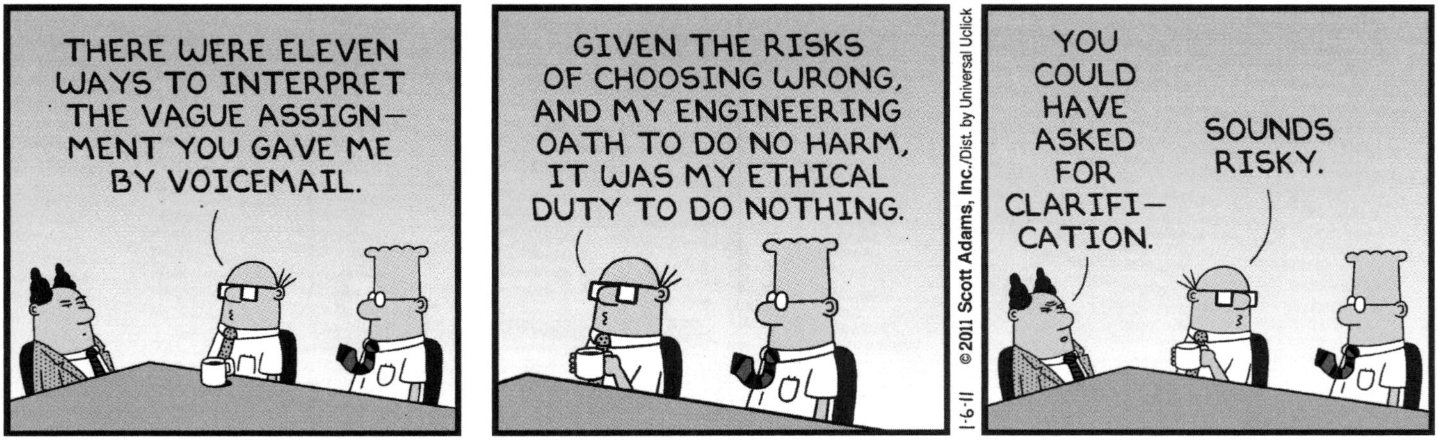
THERE WERE ELEVEN WAYS TO INTERPRET THE VAGUE ASSIGNMENT YOU GAVE ME BY VOICEMAIL.
GIVEN THE RISKS OF CHOOSING WRONG, AND MY ENGINEERING OATH TO DO NO HARM, IT WAS MY ETHICAL DUTY TO DO NOTHING.
1-6-11 © 2011 Scott Adams, Inc./Dist. by Universal Uclick
YOU COULD HAVE ASKED FOR CLARIFICATION.
SOUNDS RISKY.

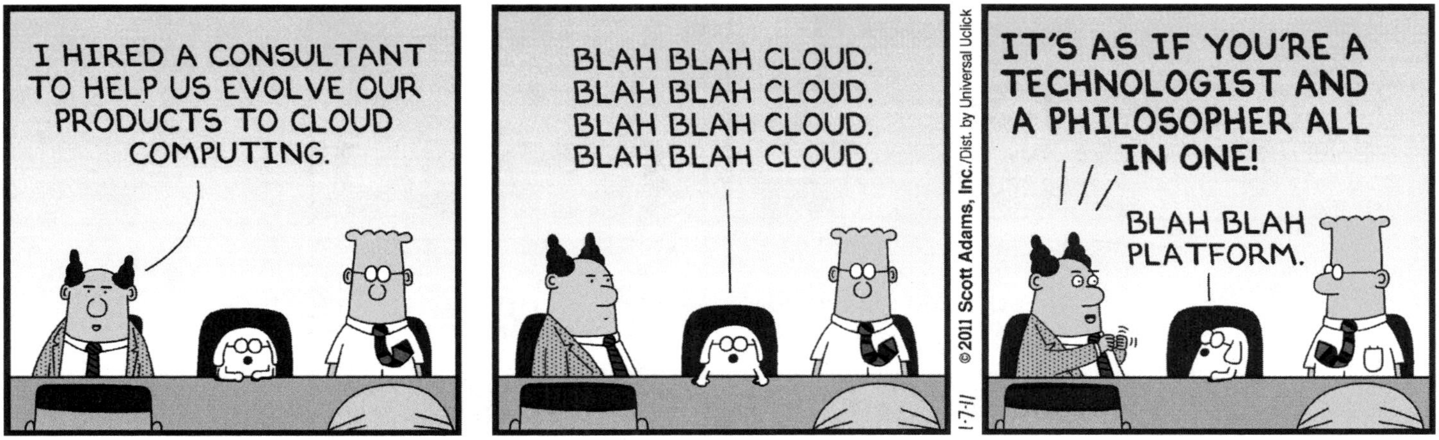
I HIRED A CONSULTANT TO HELP US EVOLVE OUR PRODUCTS TO CLOUD COMPUTING.
BLAH BLAH CLOUD. BLAH BLAH CLOUD. BLAH BLAH CLOUD. BLAH BLAH CLOUD.
1-7-11 © 2011 Scott Adams, Inc./Dist. by Universal Uclick
IT'S AS IF YOU'RE A TECHNOLOGIST AND A PHILOSOPHER ALL IN ONE!
BLAH BLAH PLATFORM.

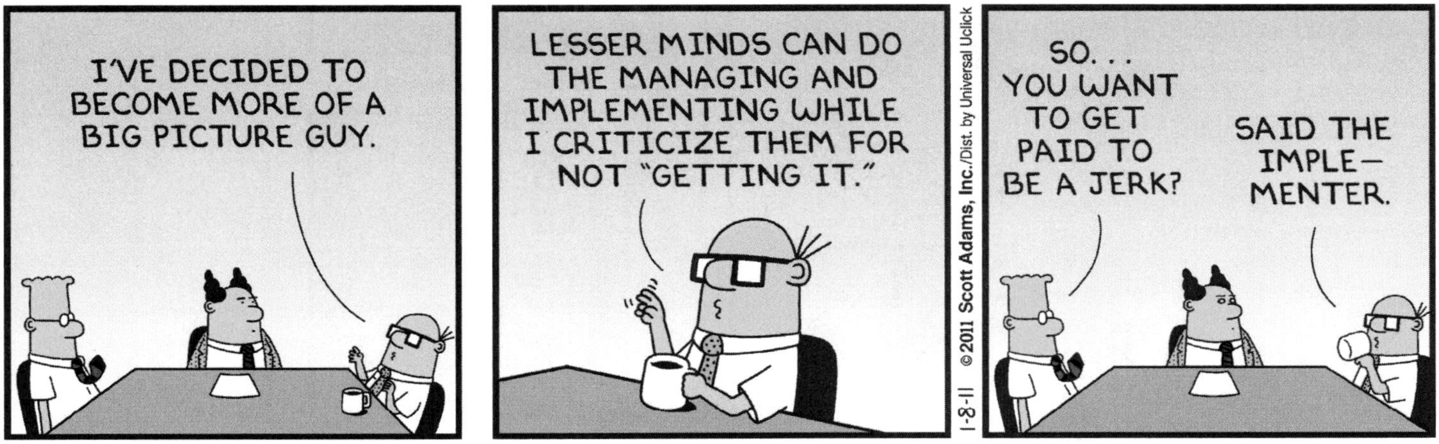
I'VE DECIDED TO BECOME MORE OF A BIG PICTURE GUY.
LESSER MINDS CAN DO THE MANAGING AND IMPLEMENTING WHILE I CRITICIZE THEM FOR NOT "GETTING IT."
1-8-11 © 2011 Scott Adams, Inc./Dist. by Universal Uclick
SO... YOU WANT TO GET PAID TO BE A JERK?
SAID THE IMPLEMENTER.

I HAVE TO DISAGREE WITH YOU, DILBERT.
ACTUALLY, YOU **DON'T** DISAGREE WITH ME.
I DON'T?
NO. YOU THINK YOU DISAGREE WITH ME, BUT YOU'RE MISTAKEN.
©2011 Scott Adams, Inc./Dist. by Universal Uclick
YOU'RE SIMPLY EXPERIENCING AN ILLUSION CAUSED BY THE LIMITS OF YOUR COMPREHENSION.
IF YOU WERE ABLE TO FULLY COMPREHEND BOTH THE PROBLEM AND MY RECOMMENDED SOLUTION, YOU WOULD AGREE WITH ME.
SO WHAT APPEARS TO BE A DIFFERENCE OF OPINION IS JUST YOU WRESTLING WITH YOUR OWN DEFECTIVE BRAIN.
THERE'S NO REASON TO GET THE REST OF US INVOLVED IN THAT MESS.
1-9-11
HAVE YOU EVER NOTICED THAT CLARITY MAKES PEOPLE ANGRY?

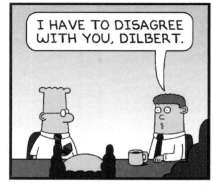

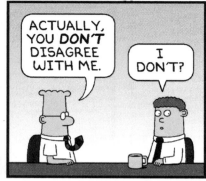

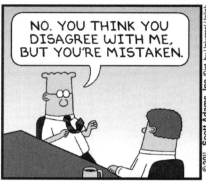

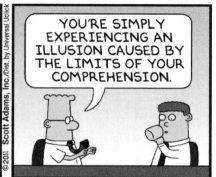

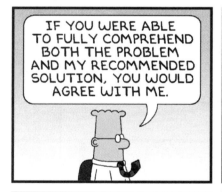

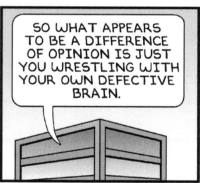

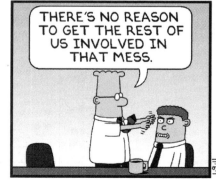

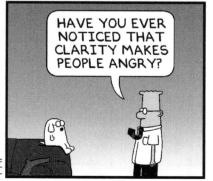

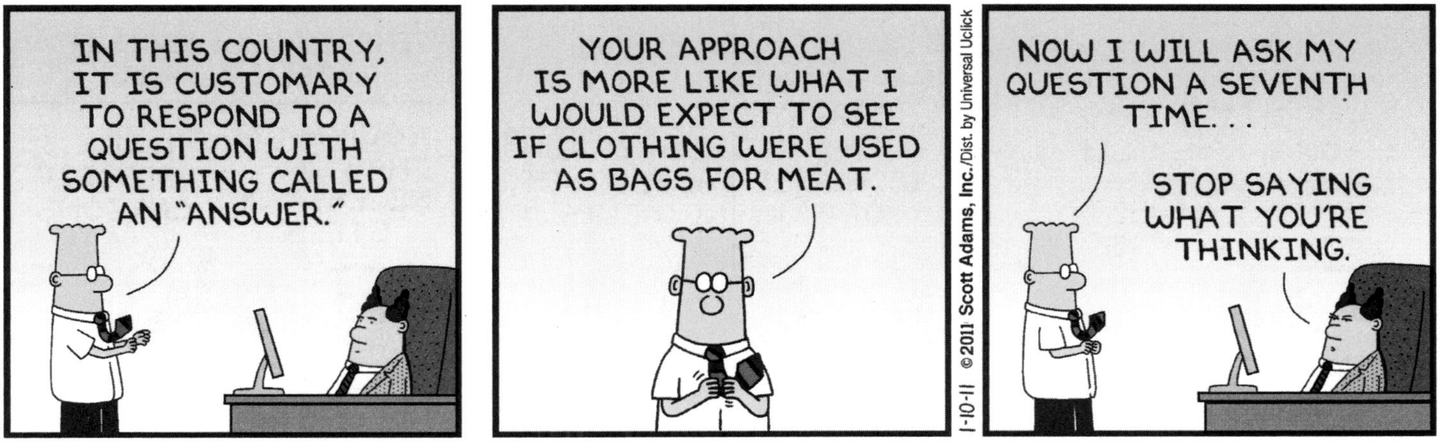
IN THIS COUNTRY, IT IS CUSTOMARY TO RESPOND TO A QUESTION WITH SOMETHING CALLED AN "ANSWER."
YOUR APPROACH IS MORE LIKE WHAT I WOULD EXPECT TO SEE IF CLOTHING WERE USED AS BAGS FOR MEAT.
1-10-11 © 2011 Scott Adams, Inc./Dist. by Universal Uclick
NOW I WILL ASK MY QUESTION A SEVENTH TIME. . .
STOP SAYING WHAT YOU'RE THINKING.

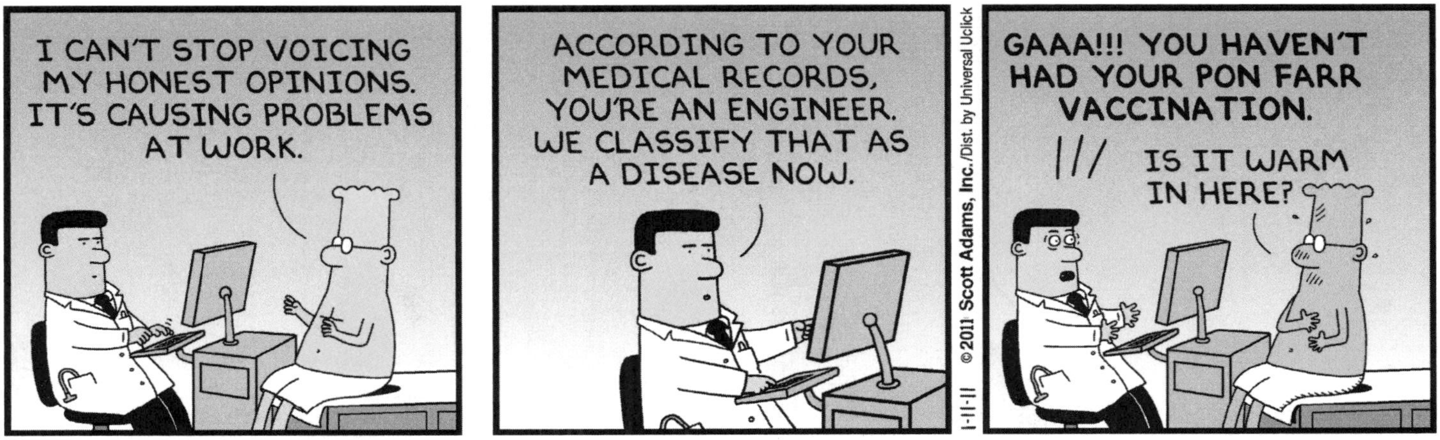
I CAN'T STOP VOICING MY HONEST OPINIONS. IT'S CAUSING PROBLEMS AT WORK.
ACCORDING TO YOUR MEDICAL RECORDS, YOU'RE AN ENGINEER. WE CLASSIFY THAT AS A DISEASE NOW.
1-11-11 © 2011 Scott Adams, Inc./Dist. by Universal Uclick
GAAA!!! YOU HAVEN'T HAD YOUR PON FARR VACCINATION.
IS IT WARM IN HERE?

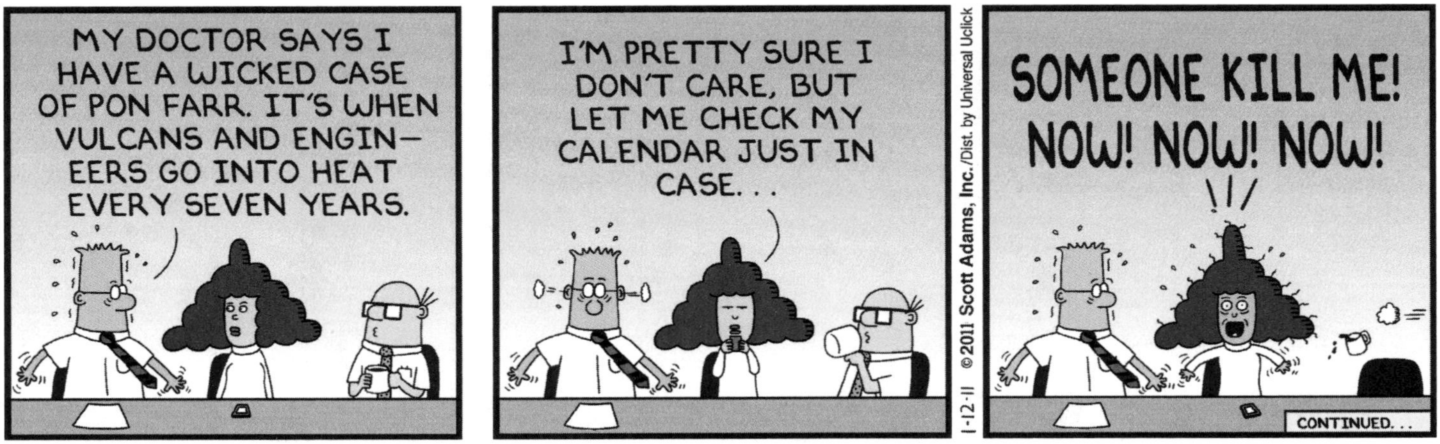
MY DOCTOR SAYS I HAVE A WICKED CASE OF PON FARR. IT'S WHEN VULCANS AND ENGIN– EERS GO INTO HEAT EVERY SEVEN YEARS.
I'M PRETTY SURE I DON'T CARE, BUT LET ME CHECK MY CALENDAR JUST IN CASE. . .
1-12-11 © 2011 Scott Adams, Inc./Dist. by Universal Uclick
SOMEONE KILL ME! NOW! NOW! NOW!
CONTINUED. . .

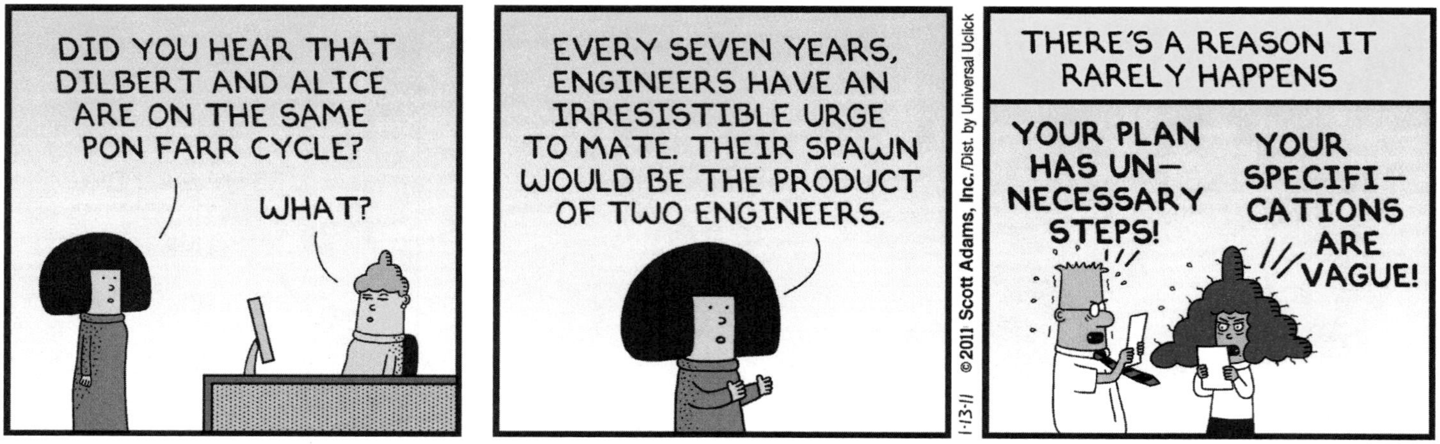
DID YOU HEAR THAT DILBERT AND ALICE ARE ON THE SAME PON FARR CYCLE?
WHAT?
EVERY SEVEN YEARS, ENGINEERS HAVE AN IRRESISTIBLE URGE TO MATE. THEIR SPAWN WOULD BE THE PRODUCT OF TWO ENGINEERS.
1·13·11 ©2011 Scott Adams, Inc./Dist. by Universal Uclick
THERE'S A REASON IT RARELY HAPPENS
YOUR PLAN HAS UN-NECESSARY STEPS!
YOUR SPECIFI-CATIONS ARE VAGUE!

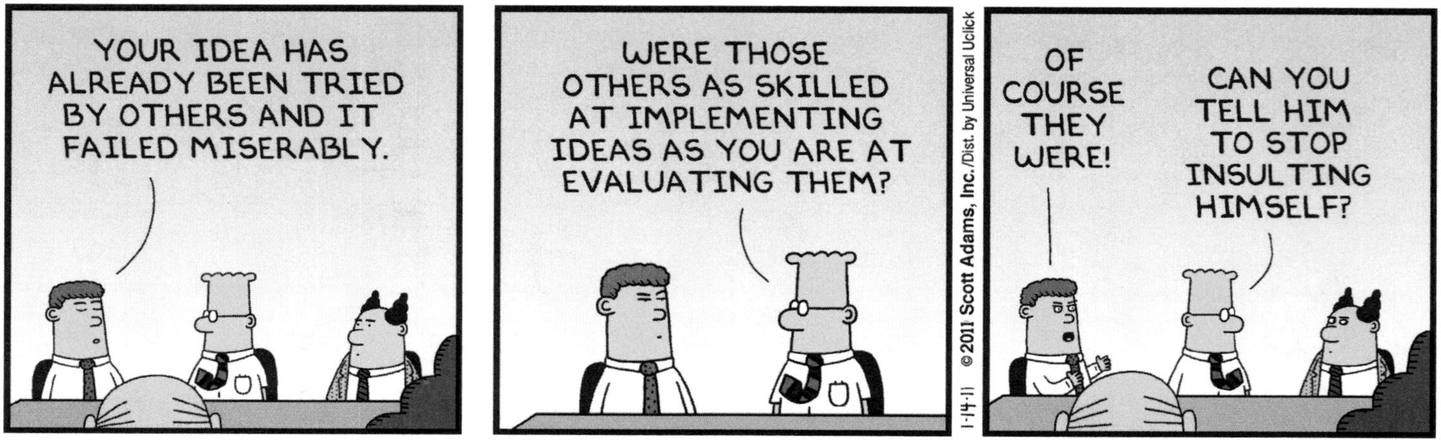
YOUR IDEA HAS ALREADY BEEN TRIED BY OTHERS AND IT FAILED MISERABLY.
WERE THOSE OTHERS AS SKILLED AT IMPLEMENTING IDEAS AS YOU ARE AT EVALUATING THEM?
1·14·11 ©2011 Scott Adams, Inc./Dist. by Universal Uclick
OF COURSE THEY WERE!
CAN YOU TELL HIM TO STOP INSULTING HIMSELF?

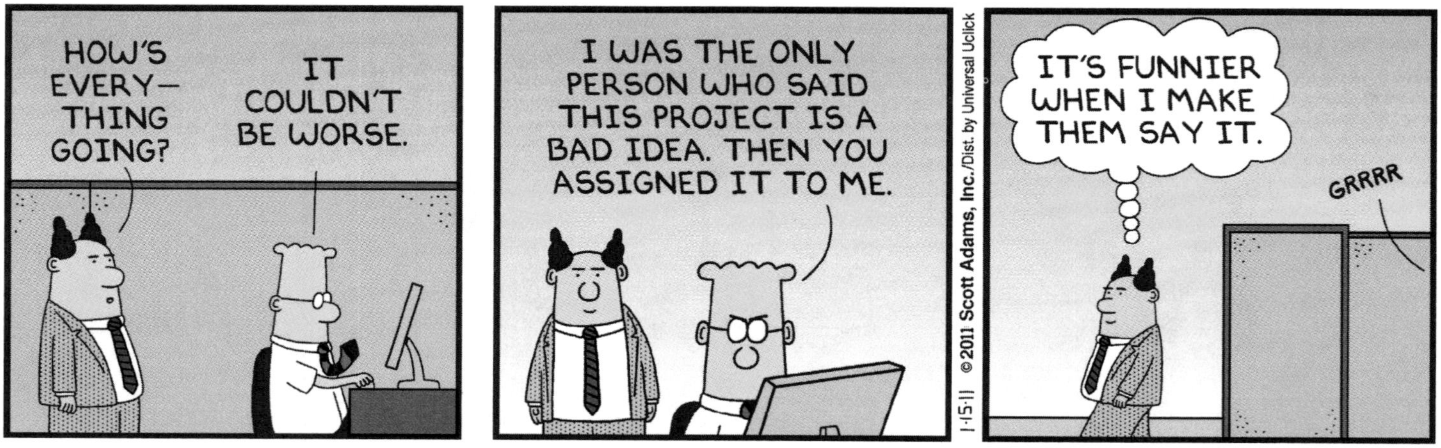
HOW'S EVERY-THING GOING?
IT COULDN'T BE WORSE.
I WAS THE ONLY PERSON WHO SAID THIS PROJECT IS A BAD IDEA. THEN YOU ASSIGNED IT TO ME.
1·15·11 ©2011 Scott Adams, Inc./Dist. by Universal Uclick
IT'S FUNNIER WHEN I MAKE THEM SAY IT.
GRRRR

OUR MEETING ROOM IS BEING USED BY A VICE PRESIDENT.
I NEED ALL OF YOU TO SEARCH FOR AN UNOCCUPIED ROOM. CALL MY CELL WHEN YOU FIND ONE.
I'LL STAY HERE IN CASE THEY FINISH SOON.
©2011 Scott Adams, Inc./Dist. by Universal Uclick
WHERE ARE YOU GOING TO LOOK?
I'M GOING TO TAKE A NAP IN MY CUBICLE AND HOPE THE PROBLEM TAKES CARE OF ITSELF.
GOOD IDEA. I'LL GO GET SOME WORK DONE.
PERFECT TIME TO RUN SOME ERRANDS.
1-16-11
OPTIMISM IS A LOT LIKE DISAPPOINTMENT.

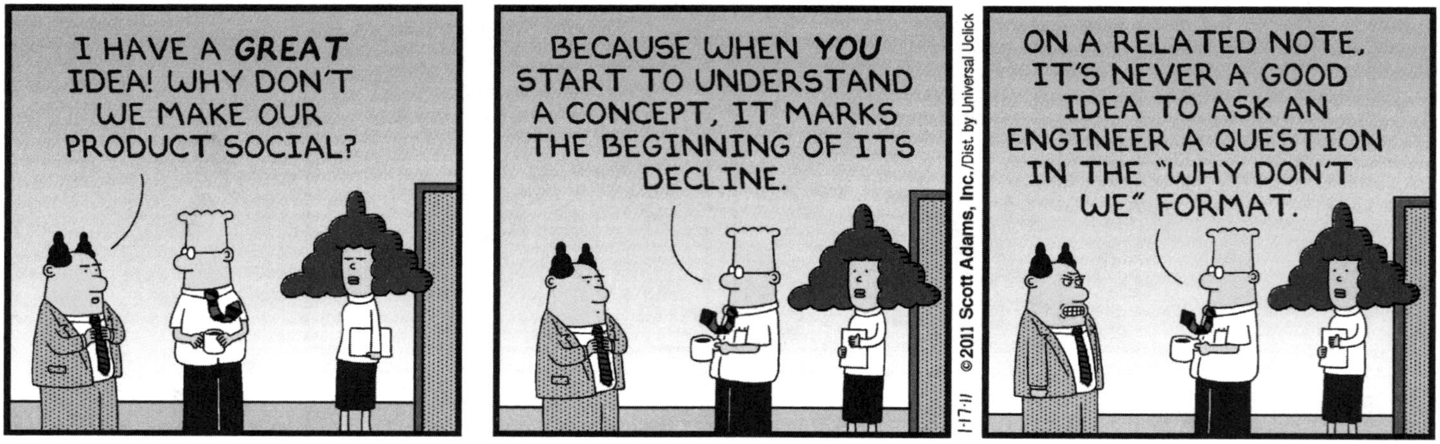
I HAVE A **GREAT** IDEA! WHY DON'T WE MAKE OUR PRODUCT SOCIAL?
BECAUSE WHEN **YOU** START TO UNDERSTAND A CONCEPT, IT MARKS THE BEGINNING OF ITS DECLINE.
ON A RELATED NOTE, IT'S NEVER A GOOD IDEA TO ASK AN ENGINEER A QUESTION IN THE "WHY DON'T WE" FORMAT.
1-17-11
©2011 Scott Adams, Inc./Dist. by Universal Uclick

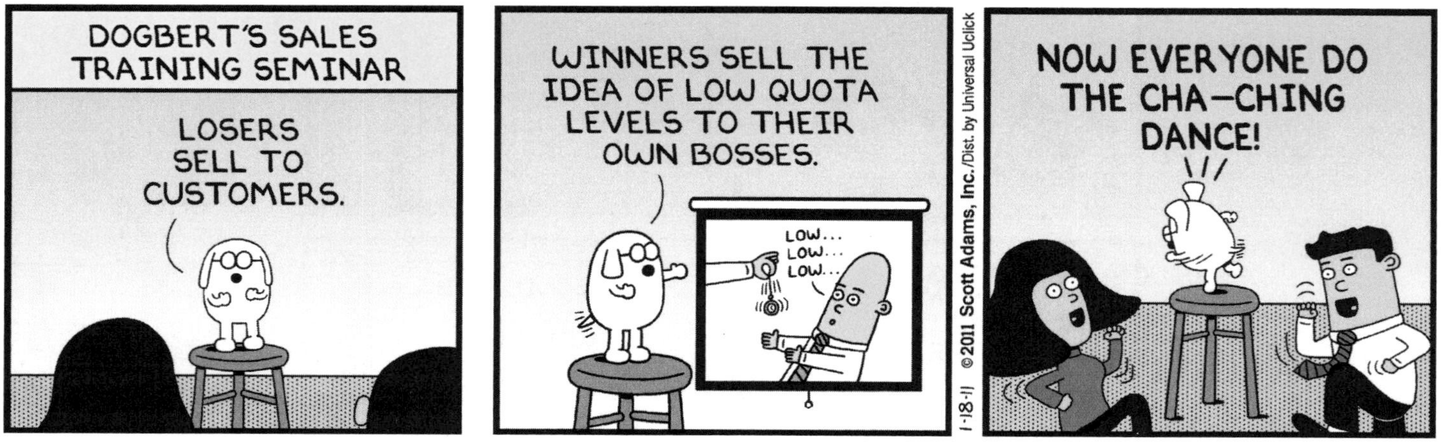
DOGBERT'S SALES TRAINING SEMINAR
LOSERS SELL TO CUSTOMERS.
WINNERS SELL THE IDEA OF LOW QUOTA LEVELS TO THEIR OWN BOSSES.
LOW... LOW... LOW...
NOW EVERYONE DO THE CHA-CHING DANCE!
1-18-11
©2011 Scott Adams, Inc./Dist. by Universal Uclick

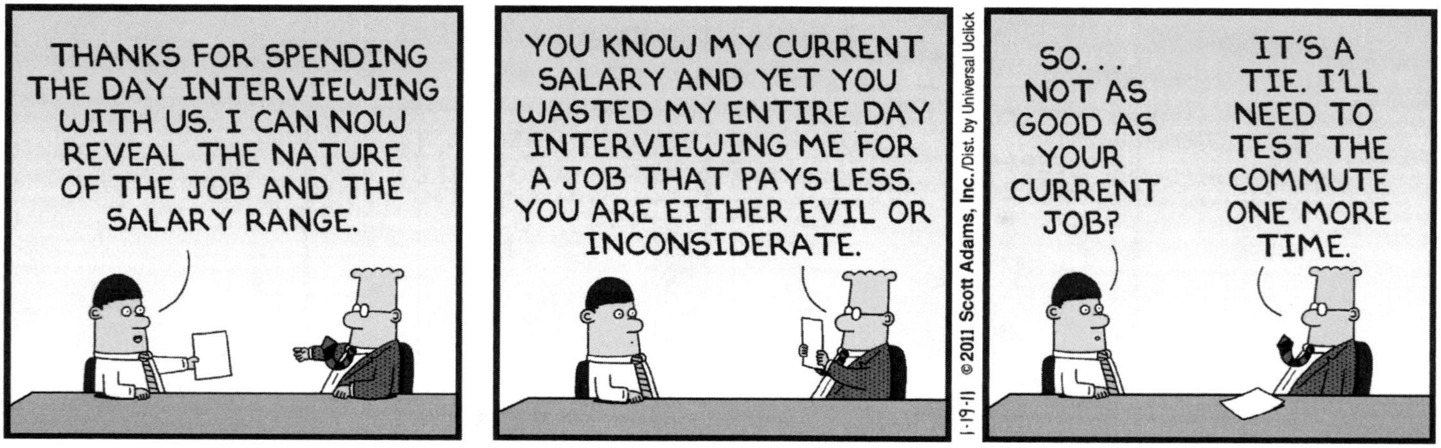
THANKS FOR SPENDING THE DAY INTERVIEWING WITH US. I CAN NOW REVEAL THE NATURE OF THE JOB AND THE SALARY RANGE.
YOU KNOW MY CURRENT SALARY AND YET YOU WASTED MY ENTIRE DAY INTERVIEWING ME FOR A JOB THAT PAYS LESS. YOU ARE EITHER EVIL OR INCONSIDERATE.
SO... NOT AS GOOD AS YOUR CURRENT JOB?
IT'S A TIE. I'LL NEED TO TEST THE COMMUTE ONE MORE TIME.
1-19-11
©2011 Scott Adams, Inc./Dist. by Universal Uclick

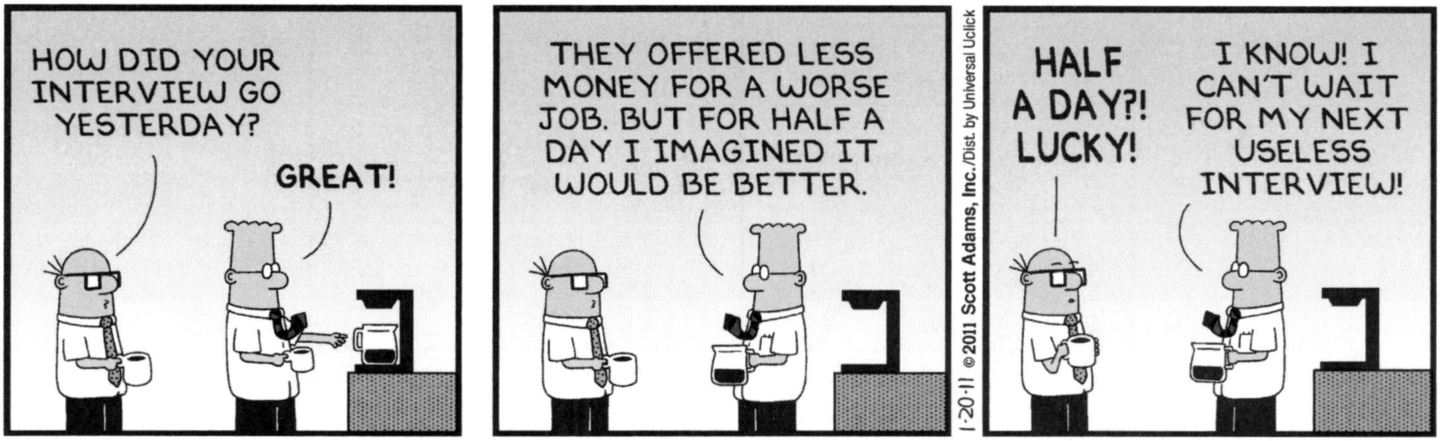
HOW DID YOUR INTERVIEW GO YESTERDAY?
GREAT!
THEY OFFERED LESS MONEY FOR A WORSE JOB. BUT FOR HALF A DAY I IMAGINED IT WOULD BE BETTER.
1-20-11 ©2011 Scott Adams, Inc./Dist. by Universal Uclick
HALF A DAY?! LUCKY!
I KNOW! I CAN'T WAIT FOR MY NEXT USELESS INTERVIEW!

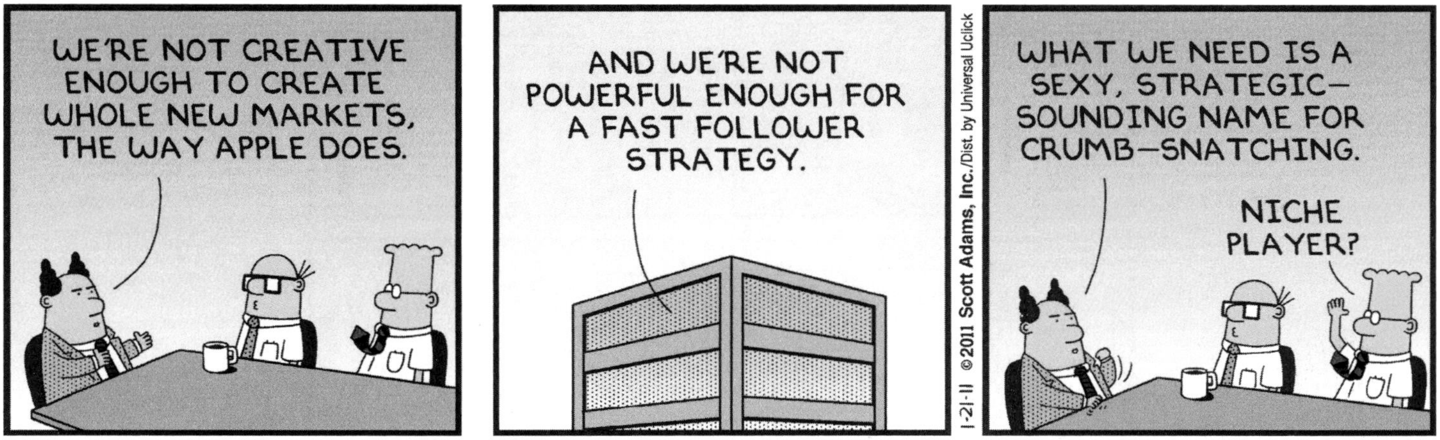
WE'RE NOT CREATIVE ENOUGH TO CREATE WHOLE NEW MARKETS, THE WAY APPLE DOES.
AND WE'RE NOT POWERFUL ENOUGH FOR A FAST FOLLOWER STRATEGY.
1-21-11 ©2011 Scott Adams, Inc./Dist. by Universal Uclick
WHAT WE NEED IS A SEXY, STRATEGIC–SOUNDING NAME FOR CRUMB–SNATCHING.
NICHE PLAYER?

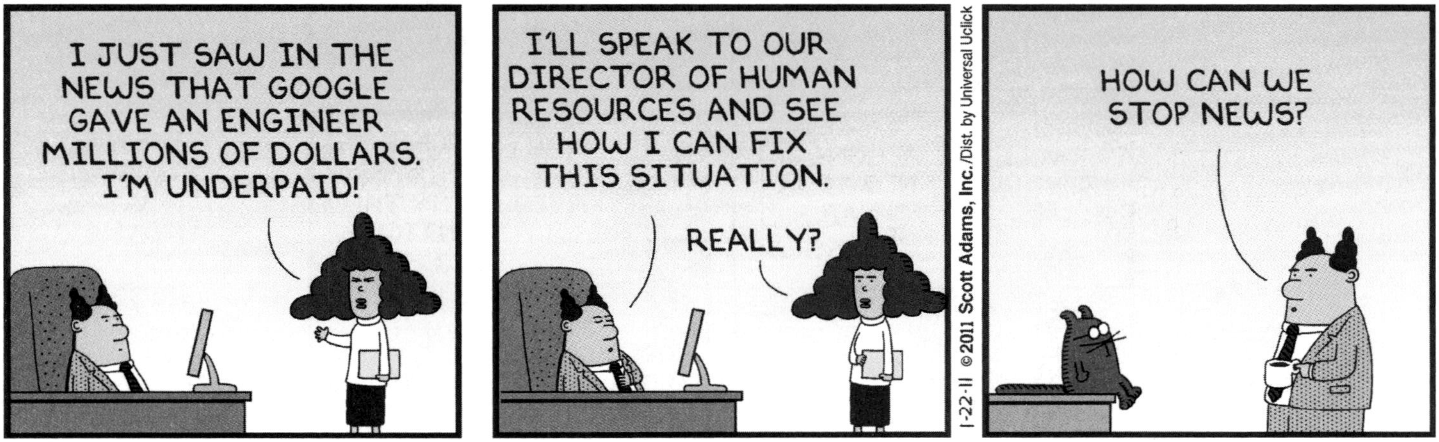
I JUST SAW IN THE NEWS THAT GOOGLE GAVE AN ENGINEER MILLIONS OF DOLLARS. I'M UNDERPAID!
I'LL SPEAK TO OUR DIRECTOR OF HUMAN RESOURCES AND SEE HOW I CAN FIX THIS SITUATION.
REALLY?
1-22-11 ©2011 Scott Adams, Inc./Dist. by Universal Uclick
HOW CAN WE STOP NEWS?

DILBERT, THIS IS ALAN. HE'S A FRENDOR.
HE'S NOT JUST A FRIEND, AND NOT JUST A VENDOR. HE'S SOMETHING IN BETWEEN.
HE'LL LAUGH AT YOUR JOKES AND INVITE YOU TO GOLF.
SOME PEOPLE ARE BOTHERED BY THIS CONDITIONAL TYPE OF "AFFECTION."
BUT IT'S BETTER THAN THE NOTHING YOU HAVE NOW.
THIS IS AWKWARD BECAUSE I ALREADY DECIDED TO BUY FROM HIS COMPETITION.
NOW YOU'VE DONE IT. YOU TURNED YOUR FRENDOR INTO A STALKOR.
I WONDER IF IT'S WRONG TO ENJOY THE ATTENTION.
© 2011 Scott Adams, Inc./Dist. by Universal Uclick
1-23-11

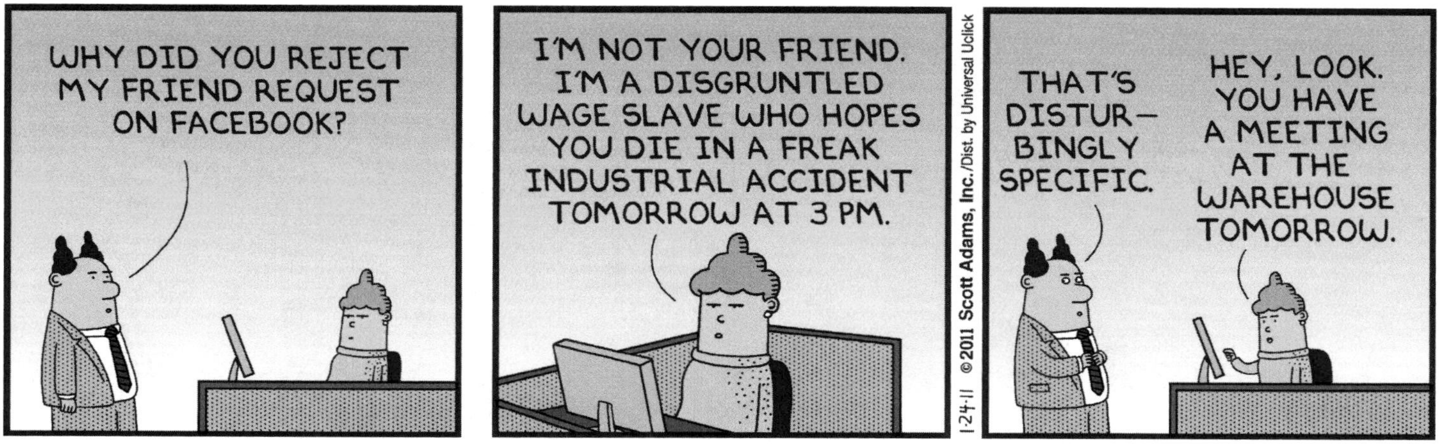
WHY DID YOU REJECT MY FRIEND REQUEST ON FACEBOOK?
I'M NOT YOUR FRIEND. I'M A DISGRUNTLED WAGE SLAVE WHO HOPES YOU DIE IN A FREAK INDUSTRIAL ACCIDENT TOMORROW AT 3 PM.
1-24-11 © 2011 Scott Adams, Inc./Dist. by Universal Uclick
THAT'S DISTUR– BINGLY SPECIFIC.
HEY, LOOK. YOU HAVE A MEETING AT THE WAREHOUSE TOMORROW.

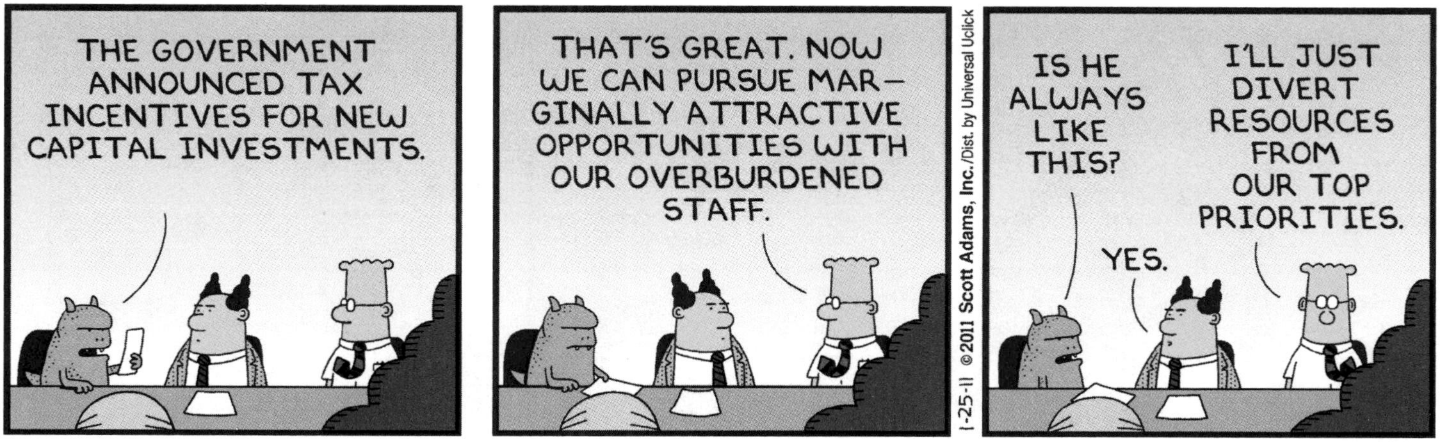
THE GOVERNMENT ANNOUNCED TAX INCENTIVES FOR NEW CAPITAL INVESTMENTS.
THAT'S GREAT. NOW WE CAN PURSUE MAR– GINALLY ATTRACTIVE OPPORTUNITIES WITH OUR OVERBURDENED STAFF.
1-25-11 © 2011 Scott Adams, Inc./Dist. by Universal Uclick
IS HE ALWAYS LIKE THIS?
YES.
I'LL JUST DIVERT RESOURCES FROM OUR TOP PRIORITIES.

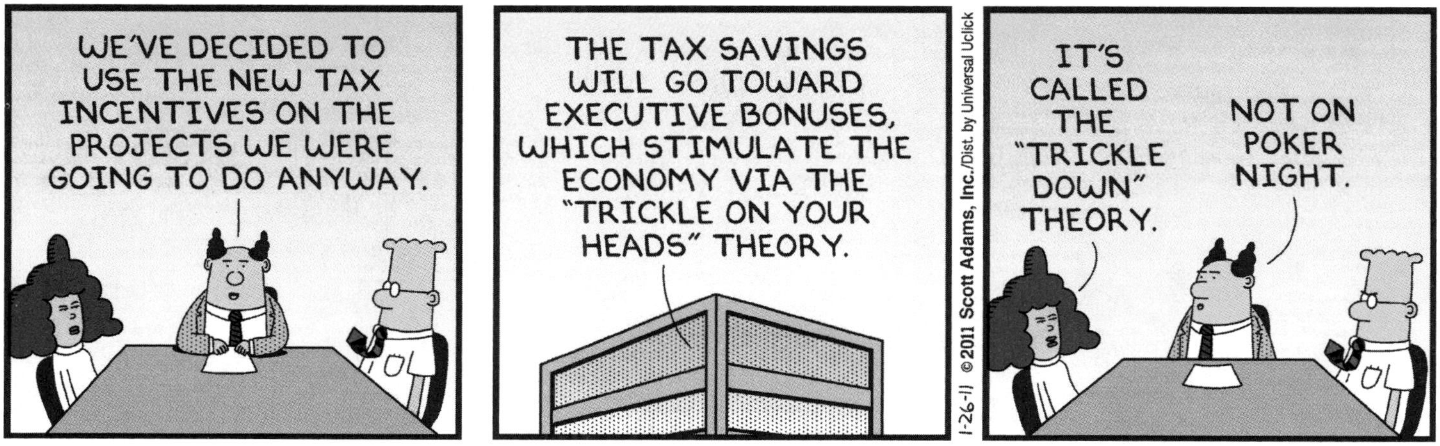
WE'VE DECIDED TO USE THE NEW TAX INCENTIVES ON THE PROJECTS WE WERE GOING TO DO ANYWAY.
THE TAX SAVINGS WILL GO TOWARD EXECUTIVE BONUSES, WHICH STIMULATE THE ECONOMY VIA THE "TRICKLE ON YOUR HEADS" THEORY.
1-26-11 © 2011 Scott Adams, Inc./Dist. by Universal Uclick
IT'S CALLED THE "TRICKLE DOWN" THEORY.
NOT ON POKER NIGHT.

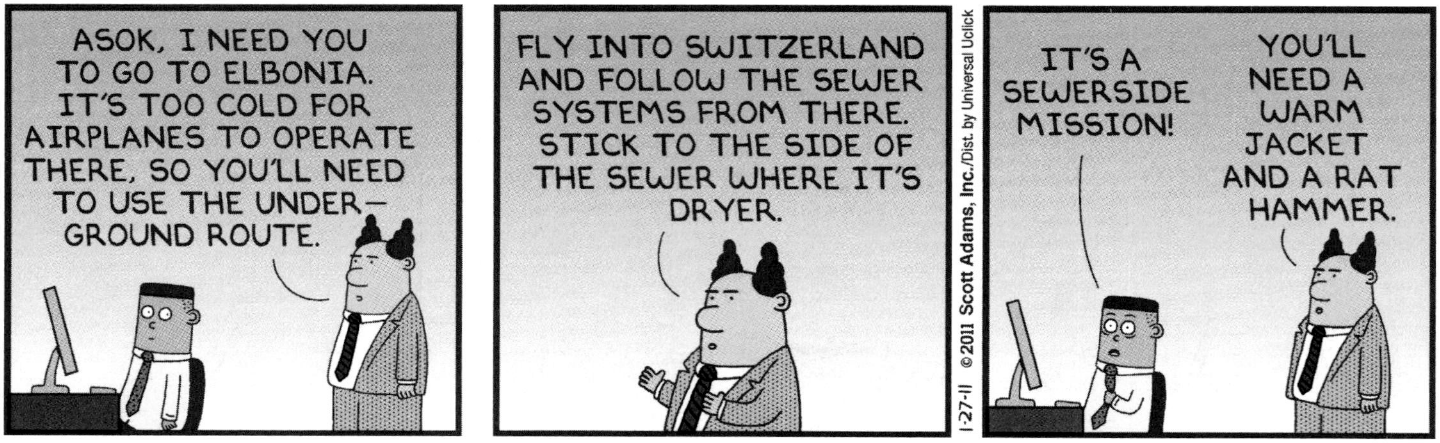
ASOK, I NEED YOU TO GO TO ELBONIA. IT'S TOO COLD FOR AIRPLANES TO OPERATE THERE, SO YOU'LL NEED TO USE THE UNDER-GROUND ROUTE.
FLY INTO SWITZERLAND AND FOLLOW THE SEWER SYSTEMS FROM THERE. STICK TO THE SIDE OF THE SEWER WHERE IT'S DRYER.
1-27-11 © 2011 Scott Adams, Inc./Dist. by Universal Uclick
IT'S A SEWERSIDE MISSION!
YOU'LL NEED A WARM JACKET AND A RAT HAMMER.

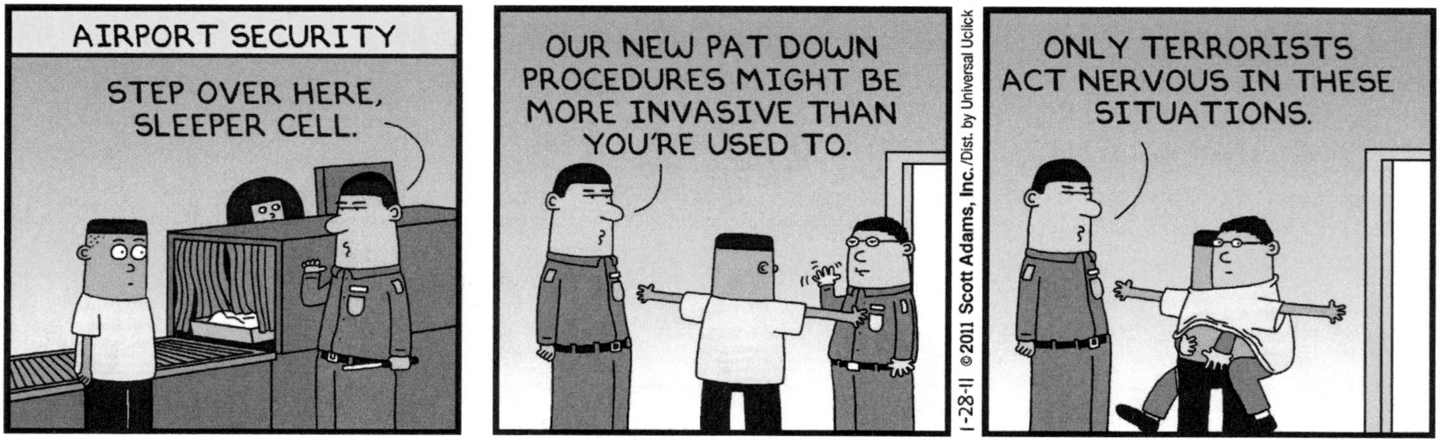
AIRPORT SECURITY
STEP OVER HERE, SLEEPER CELL.
OUR NEW PAT DOWN PROCEDURES MIGHT BE MORE INVASIVE THAN YOU'RE USED TO.
1-28-11 © 2011 Scott Adams, Inc./Dist. by Universal Uclick
ONLY TERRORISTS ACT NERVOUS IN THESE SITUATIONS.

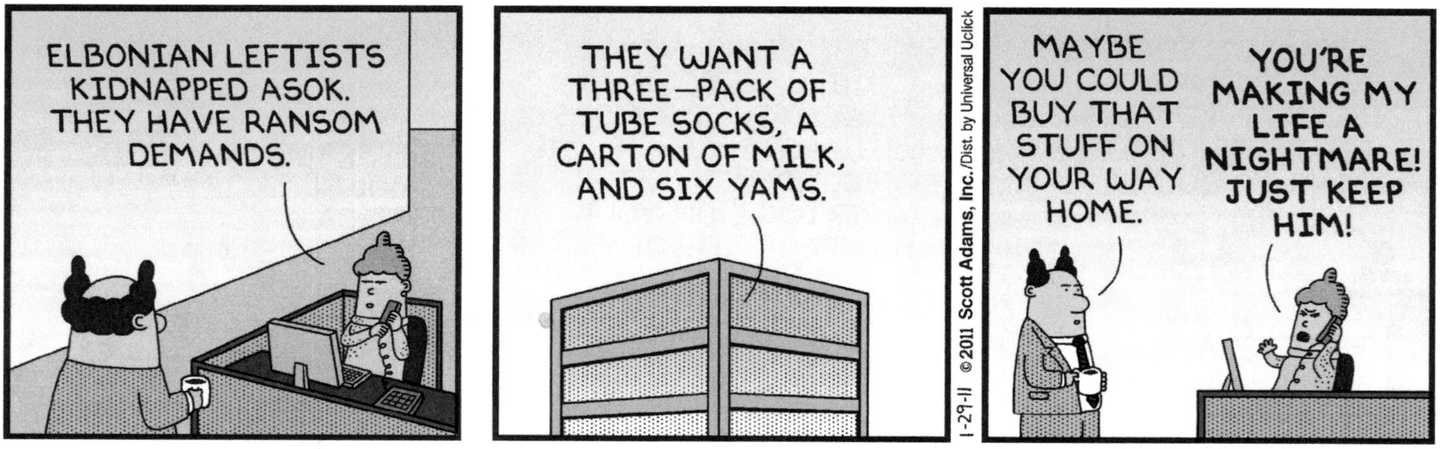
ELBONIAN LEFTISTS KIDNAPPED ASOK. THEY HAVE RANSOM DEMANDS.
THEY WANT A THREE-PACK OF TUBE SOCKS, A CARTON OF MILK, AND SIX YAMS.
1-29-11 © 2011 Scott Adams, Inc./Dist. by Universal Uclick
MAYBE YOU COULD BUY THAT STUFF ON YOUR WAY HOME.
YOU'RE MAKING MY LIFE A NIGHTMARE! JUST KEEP HIM!

DILBERT, YOUR BOSS ASKED ME TO GET YOUR INPUT ON THIS.
ABSO— LUTELY, RUTH.
WE HAVE TWO OPTIONS FOR WASTING OUR TIME HERE.
OPTION ONE: I COULD TELL YOU ALL OF THE THINGS YOU SHOULD CHANGE, AND YOU COULD IGNORE ME AS USUAL.
©2011 Scott Adams, Inc. /Dist. by Universal Uclick
OPTION TWO: I COULD LIE, AND TELL YOU THAT EVERYTHING IS PERFECT.
I PREFER THE LIE. THAT WAY I CAN PIN SOME BLAME ON YOU IF THINGS GO BAD.
EXCELLENT CHOICE. IT'S FASTER, AND I CAN LATER SAY I WAS MISINTERPRETED.
OKAY THEN, I DECLARE THAT YOUR DOCUMENT IS PERFECT, UNDER A CERTAIN SET OF ASSUMPTIONS THAT I WON'T LIST.
1-30-11
DID YOU HELP RUTH?
I'LL SAY YES, BUT IT'S SORT OF A GRAY AREA.

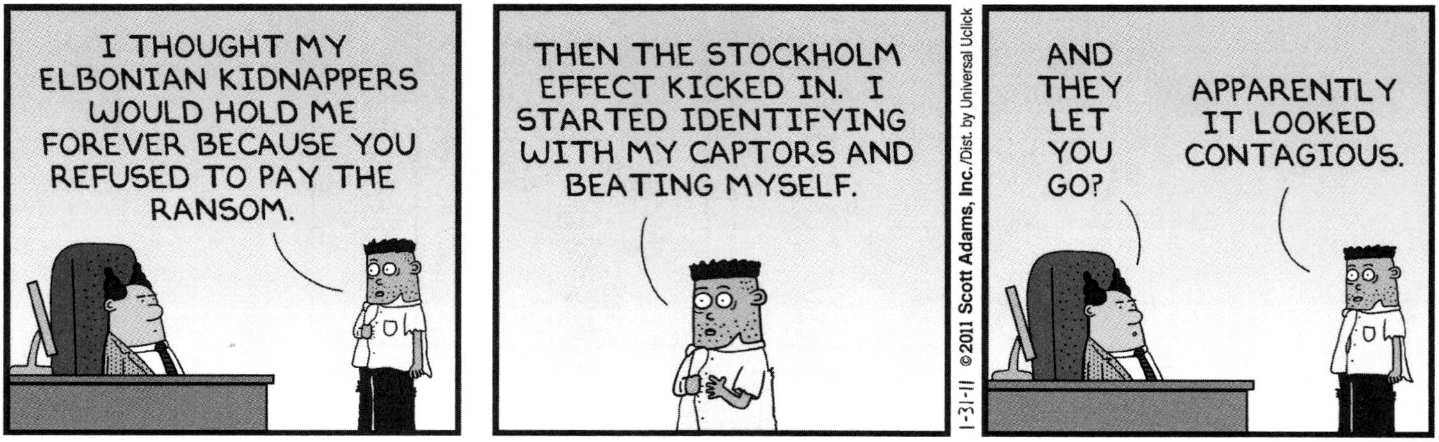
I THOUGHT MY ELBONIAN KIDNAPPERS WOULD HOLD ME FOREVER BECAUSE YOU REFUSED TO PAY THE RANSOM.
THEN THE STOCKHOLM EFFECT KICKED IN. I STARTED IDENTIFYING WITH MY CAPTORS AND BEATING MYSELF.
1-31-11 © 2011 Scott Adams, Inc./Dist. by Universal Uclick
AND THEY LET YOU GO?
APPARENTLY IT LOOKED CONTAGIOUS.

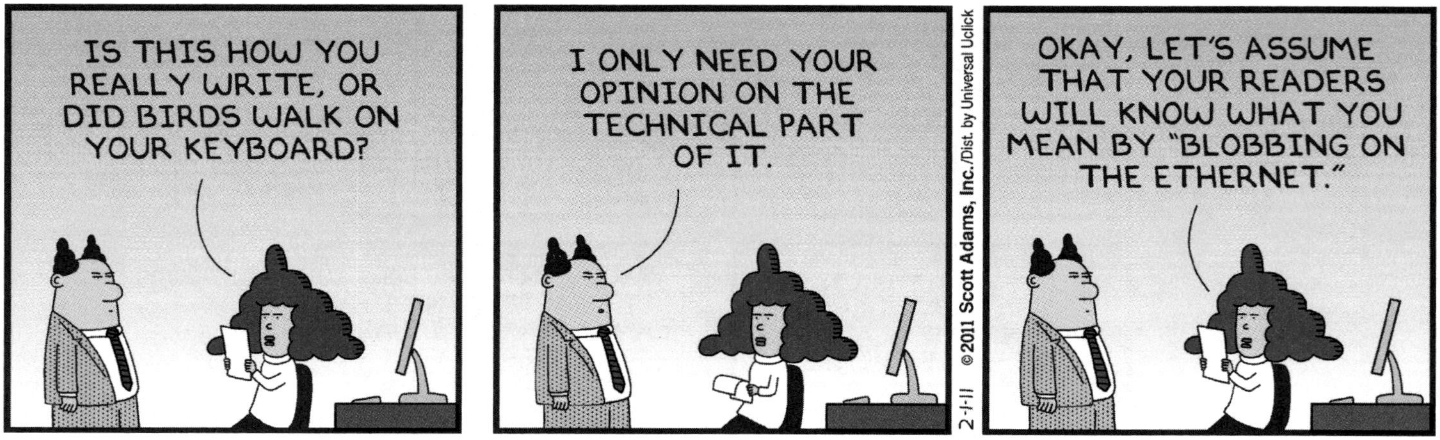
IS THIS HOW YOU REALLY WRITE, OR DID BIRDS WALK ON YOUR KEYBOARD?
I ONLY NEED YOUR OPINION ON THE TECHNICAL PART OF IT.
2-1-11 © 2011 Scott Adams, Inc./Dist. by Universal Uclick
OKAY, LET'S ASSUME THAT YOUR READERS WILL KNOW WHAT YOU MEAN BY "BLOBBING ON THE ETHERNET."

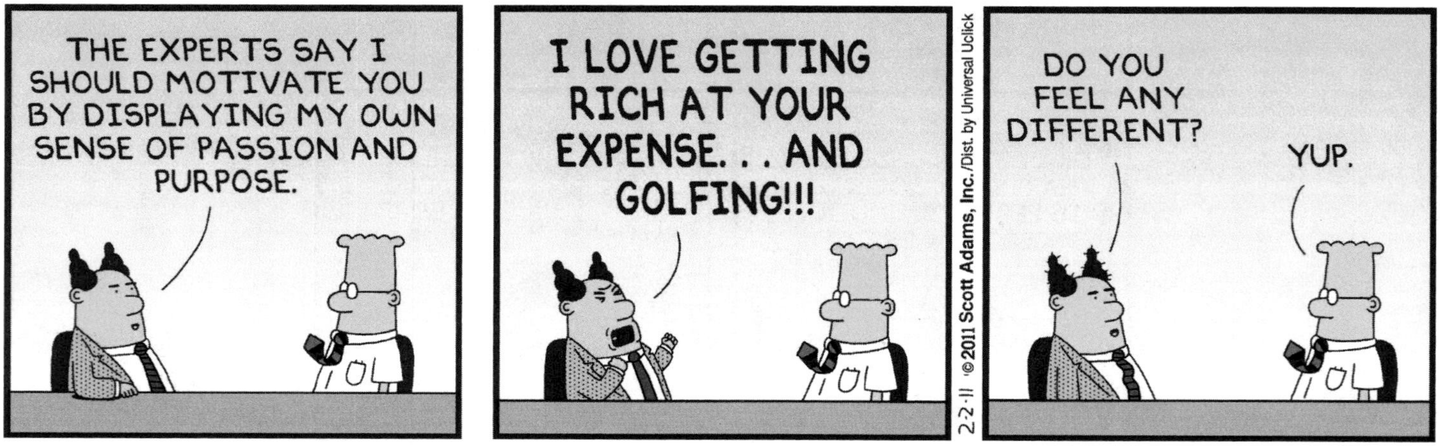
THE EXPERTS SAY I SHOULD MOTIVATE YOU BY DISPLAYING MY OWN SENSE OF PASSION AND PURPOSE.
I LOVE GETTING RICH AT YOUR EXPENSE. . . AND GOLFING!!!
2-2-11 © 2011 Scott Adams, Inc./Dist. by Universal Uclick
DO YOU FEEL ANY DIFFERENT?
YUP.

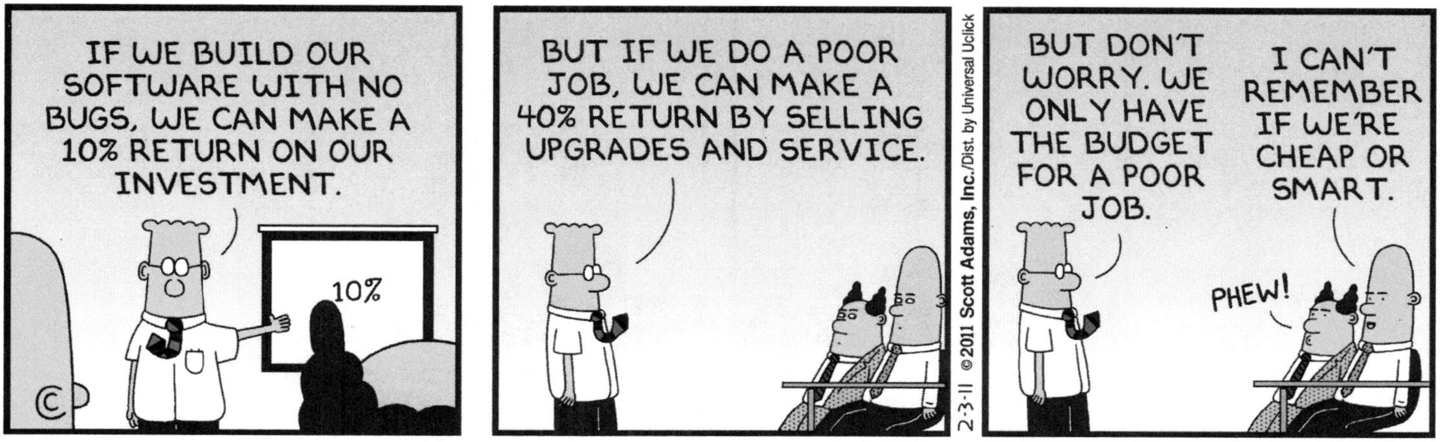
IF WE BUILD OUR SOFTWARE WITH NO BUGS, WE CAN MAKE A 10% RETURN ON OUR INVESTMENT.
10%
BUT IF WE DO A POOR JOB, WE CAN MAKE A 40% RETURN BY SELLING UPGRADES AND SERVICE.
2·3·11 © 2011 Scott Adams, Inc./Dist. by Universal Uclick
BUT DON'T WORRY. WE ONLY HAVE THE BUDGET FOR A POOR JOB.
PHEW!
I CAN'T REMEMBER IF WE'RE CHEAP OR SMART.

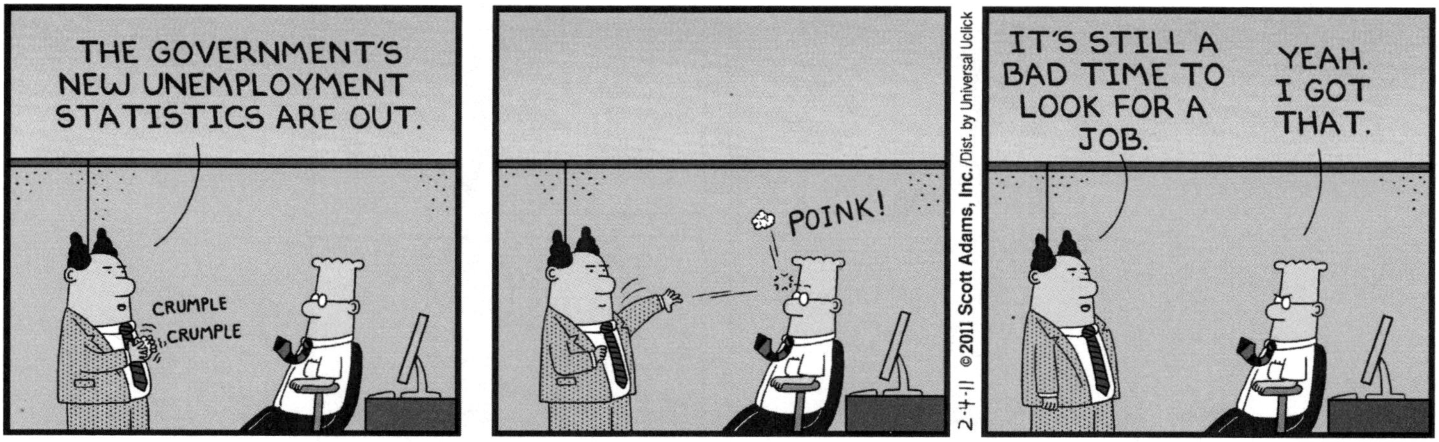
THE GOVERNMENT'S NEW UNEMPLOYMENT STATISTICS ARE OUT.
CRUMPLE
CRUMPLE
POINK!
2·4·11 © 2011 Scott Adams, Inc./Dist. by Universal Uclick
IT'S STILL A BAD TIME TO LOOK FOR A JOB.
YEAH. I GOT THAT.

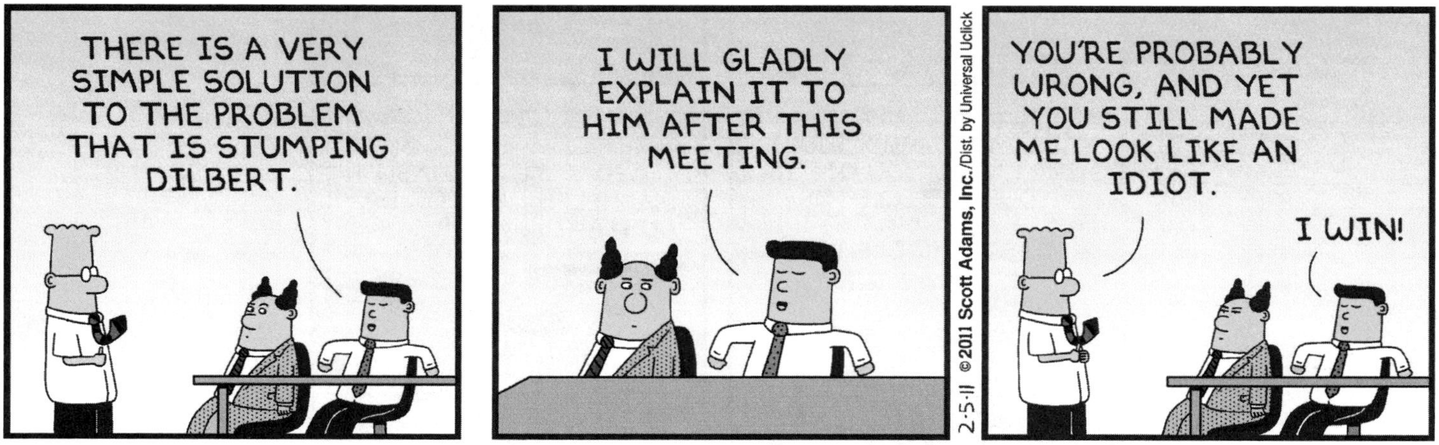
THERE IS A VERY SIMPLE SOLUTION TO THE PROBLEM THAT IS STUMPING DILBERT.
I WILL GLADLY EXPLAIN IT TO HIM AFTER THIS MEETING.
2·5·11 © 2011 Scott Adams, Inc./Dist. by Universal Uclick
YOU'RE PROBABLY WRONG, AND YET YOU STILL MADE ME LOOK LIKE AN IDIOT.
I WIN!

DILBERT, WORK WITH GUSTAV TO GET OUR NEW PRODUCT EXPLAINED ON OUR WEBSITE.
HERE'S WHAT I HAVE SO FAR.
IT'S AWFUL.
EXCUSE ME?
THERE'S NO INFORMA-TION. IT'S ALL IMAGES AND ANNOYING MUSIC.
© 2011 Scott Adams, Inc./Dist. by Universal Uclick
PEOPLE MAKE BUYING DECISIONS BASED ON WHAT THEY READ. THIS GIVES THEM NOTHING.
IF I CLUTTER THE DESIGN WITH USEFUL INFORMATION, IT WILL LOOK UGLY, AND I WON'T BE ABLE TO USE IT IN MY PORTFOLIO.
I NEED THAT PORTFOLIO TO GET A JOB AT A BETTER COMPANY. PLEASE HELP ME ESCAPE.
YOU'LL PROBABLY WORK HERE UNTIL YOU DIE IN YOUR CUBICLE NO MATTER WHAT THE WEBSITE LOOKS LIKE.
2-6-11
DID YOU HELP GUSTAV?
YES, BUT IT WASN'T A GOOD DAY FOR OUR STOCK-HOLDERS.